Futures for The Mediterranean Basin
The Blue Plan

This volume is published under the aegis of the United Nations Environment Programme within the framework of the Mediterranean Action Plan (MAP). This plan, adopted in 1975, is implemented collectively by all Mediterranean coastal states and the EEC, and they ensure its supervision and the main part of its financing. It comprises several components, and in particular:

1. a legal component, including the Barcelona Convention for the protection of the Mediterranean Sea against pollution, and its accompanying protocols on dumping from ships and aircraft, on combating pollution by oil, on protection against pollution from land-based sources, and on specially protected areas;
2. a scientific research and monitoring component concentrating on the state of the sea (MEDPOL);
3. an economic and social planning component concentrating on coastal regions and including the Blue Plan itself as prospective studies, and the Priority Actions Programme (PAP) focusing on environmental and natural-resource problems shared by Mediterranean countries.

The Blue Plan studies, which are the subject of the present volume, are carried out in Sophia Antipolis by the Mediterranean Blue Plan Regional Activity Centre (BP/RAC), an association under French law whose objective is to provide scientific and logistic support to these studies. The operation of BP/RAC is ensured for the main part thanks to the financial support of the French Ministry of the Environment.

MEDITERRANEAN ACTION PLAN CO-ORDINATING UNIT:
Vassileos Konstantinou 48
GR 11610
Athens
Greece

BLUE PLAN REGIONAL ACTIVITY CENTRE:
Place Sophie Laffitte
Sophia Antipolis
06560 Valbonne
France

Futures for the Mediterranean Basin

The Blue Plan

EDITED BY

Michel Grenon

AND

Michel Batisse

FOREWORD BY

Mostafa K. Tolba

OXFORD UNIVERSITY PRESS

1989

Oxford University Press, Walton Street, Oxford OX2 6DP

Oxford New York Toronto
Delhi Bombay Calcutta Madras Karachi
Petaling Jaya Singapore Hong Kong Tokyo
Nairobi Dar es Salaam Cape Town
Melbourne Auckland

and associated companies in
Berlin Ibadan

Oxford is a trade mark of Oxford University Press

Published in the United States
by Oxford University Press, New York

British Library Cataloguing in Publication Data

TD 186
F88
1989

Library of Congress Cataloging in Publication Data
Futures for the Mediterranean basin : The Blue Plan/edited by Michel
Grenon and Michel Batisse.
At head of title: United Nations Environment Programme,
Mediterranean Action Plan.
1. Pollution—Mediterranean Region.   2. Economic development—
Environmental aspects—Mediterranean Region.   I. Grenon, Michel.
II. Batisse, Michel.   III. United Nations Environment Programme.
Mediterranean Action Plan.
TD186.F88   1989   333.91'64'091638—dc20   89-25492
ISBN 0-19-8233124

Set by Oxford Text System
Printed and bound in
Great Britain
by Butler & Tanner Ltd
Frome & London

Foreword

MOTHER of civilizations and true centre of the world for thousands of years, the Mediterranean has seen its global importance overshadowed in the past centuries by the dynamism of development around the Atlantic and later the Pacific. Yet during the last two or three decades a new driving force has emerged based upon a combination of factors: the consolidation and southward expansion of the European Community; the recently acquired independence of the southern and eastern countries of the region and their rapid population growth; the fresh impetus provided by its oil and natural-gas resources; the unrivalled development of tourism along its shores. For these and other reasons the Mediterranean is regaining major world importance.

Even a quick look at simple facts shows that the Mediterranean basin is undergoing very rapid change in demographic, social, cultural, political, economic, and ecological terms. How is this happening? What does it imply? Where does it lead us? What should the people of the Mediterranean do about it? These questions are the subject of the present study.

For millennia those living in the Mediterranean region have enjoyed the blue of the sea, the harmony of the landscape, and the mildness of the climate which is so characteristic of the region. Yet these 'permanent' features are no longer permanent. Coastal waters are polluted and the sea level is rising, landscapes are spoilt by unplanned urbanization and ugly constructions, the climate itself is bound to change in the next decades. And, as elsewhere in the developing world, the countries south of the basin have to face formidable economic problems combined with continued demographic pressure and the legitimate aspiration for better living conditions.

What future lies ahead for the Mediterranean countries? How can they reconcile environmental quality with development needs? How should they organize themselves to face up to their mounting difficulties?

The Blue Plan was conceived as an attempt to answer these questions. Its aim is both orginal and ambitious: to explore the possible futures for the entire Mediterranean basin. As such, it constitutes a key component of the Mediterranean Action Plan adopted in Barcelona in 1975 on the instigation and under the auspices of the United Nations Environment Programme. Under this Action Plan, all the countries bordering the Mediterranean and the European Economic Community pledged not only to protect the sea from pollution but also to ensure environmentally sound development all along its coastal regions.

The idea of a prospective study of future interactions between the environment and development in the whole basin, geared to the harmonious management of its natural resources, emerged from the outset. It was the brain-child of Serge Antoine from the French Ministry of Environment. Once the Mediterranean countries had agreed on the concept, the procedures, finances, and methods were developed. It was then that the Egyptian economist Ismail Sabri Abdalla was given the delicate task of supervising the launching of the project during an exploratory phase which lasted from 1980 to 1984 and produced conprehensive reports on the problem of development and environment in the region.

The work presented in this volume follows from these early studies. It is based on the construction of scenarios of the future in which an attempt has been made to analyse the interactions between economic and environmental policies. From a patient examination and computation of available data, statistics, and documents concerning the economic sectors—agriculture, industry, energy, tourism, transport— and the social factors—demography, urbanization—as well as the natural-resource base—the soil, the forest, the inland waters, the coastal areas, the sea—it has been possible to highlight trends for the medium-term and long-term future according to consistent and credible hypotheses of the policies to be chosen jointly or individually by the countries of the region.

This is not just an academic exercise. Based upon reliable data and a proven methodology for constructing the scenarios, it also results in specific conclusions. It offers orientations for action to governments, international organizations, regional and local authorities, decision-makers, and agents of economic, social, and environmental activity. At the same time it provides a unique view of the dynamics of a vast and critically important region of the world which should be of lasting value to teachers and researchers in geography, history, economics, politics, sociology, the environment, and other specialized fields.

The significance of the report is, however, broader than the Mediterranean itself. Through the complexity of its geography and history, through the diversity of its people, of their cultures, religions, and social systems, through the tensions which divide it but also the inescapable unity which determines its fate, through the disparity between its industrialized countries to the north and its developing countries to the south, but also its demonstrated will for co-operation, the Mediterranean is a representative microcosm of the entire Earth.

The method used, the attempt to correlate quantitatively and qualitatively the activities of development with the evolution of the environment, the conclusions reached, the recommendations proposed concern not only the Mediterranean but also the world at large. Indeed, this work—pioneering and thus no doubt flawed in parts—should at some point be deepened and extended at the global level.

The Blue Plan exercise has been based on the continued support and co-operation of all Mediterranean governments, and in particular on the national scenarios which a number of them have developed. It has been able to use extensively the information and data from many United Nations bodies and scientific institutions. My appreciation goes to them all. It is a collective work to which many scientists from all over the Mediterranean have contributed and in which a number of them have taken a very important part. To all of them I would like to express my gratitude. Special thanks are due to the Study Group on Mediterranean Scenarios, which formulated the methodology and contents of the report. This innovative enterprise was a difficult and time-consuming one which required a broad grasp of a great variety of issues. My deep gratitude goes to Michel Batisse, President of the Blue Plan Regional Activity Centre, and to Michel Grenon, Scientific Director of the Blue Plan, who have been the two main actors in the work from 1985 to 1988 and without whom the task could not have been completed and the present volume produced.

MOSTAFA KAMAL TOLBA
Executive Director
United Nations Environment Programme

Nairobi
April 1989

Introduction

FOR the first time, all countries of a major region of the world have decided to explore together the evolving interactions between their economic and social development and their environment. Linked by a common sea which they have pledged to protect, the Mediterranean countries have realized that the degradation of the marine environment has resulted largely from their own acitivities on land—in both coastal areas and the hinterland—and that the protection of the sea depends upon the interplay of actions taken not only at the local level but also at the national and international levels. As a result, they have agreed, within the framework of their Mediterranean Action Plan, to conduct an exploration of possible futures for the basin as a whole—the subject of the Blue Plan. It is not a mere geographic overview of the economic, social, and environmental features which together characterize and dominate the region, but, first and foremost, a prospective study intended to analyse the likely evolution of the environment/development system, to highlight the linkage between events and actions, to illustrate tomorrow's consequences of decisions taken—or not taken—today, and to detect potential breaking-points in the medium or long term.

The objectives set forth by the coastal states for the Blue Plan were formulated as early as 1977 as follows: 'to make available to the authorities and planners of the various countries in the Mediterranean information which will enable them to formulate their own plans to ensure optimal socio-economic development without causing environmental degradation', and 'to help the governments of the states bordering the Mediterranean region to deepen their knowledge of the common problems facing them, both in the Mediterranean Sea and its coastal regions'. Clearly—and in spite of its name—the Blue Plan was never intended as a binding instrument for centralizing economic planning and resource management for the basin as a whole but rather as a tool to explore interactions between development policies and environmental situations, and to assist, in the decision-making process, all those concerned with the future of the region and its uncertainties.

The method chosen for this exercise was not an attempt to build some large-scale Mediterranean 'model', but rather to draw up, at the invitation of the coastal states themselves, a number of 'scenarios' providing possible images of the future for the horizons of 2000 and 2025. These Mediterranean scenarios were constructed by a small team of independent Mediterranean experts according to consistent sets of assumptions concerning the population, types of development and resulting economic growth, environmental policies, and the level of intra-Mediterranean co-operation. A large degree of freedom was given to the team in the choice of hypotheses and the formulation of the scenarios, and although the governments concerned constantly monitored the direction and progress of the work, they may not necessarily endorse all the conclusions that have been reached. Through the use of national scenarios wherever these were available, an effort was made to take into account as far as possible the strategies and policies of individual states. The contribution of a great variety of consultants and advisers from the developed and developing countries of the region helped to avoid the influence of specific viewpoints or particular economic or social theories.

A prospective study is neither a prediction nor a forecast of what the future holds. The long-term visualizations of the Blue Plan scenarios, described in the present volume, cannot attempt to predict what will happen or to furnish easy recipes for action. Their objective is to provide authorities, planners, and resource managers in the various countries with the opportunity of setting their national and regional development strategies within a context that assures, as far as possible, protection of the Mediterranean environment. They aim at offering a common frame of reference to underline the complex interactions of development and environment problems within and among the countries of the region and to highlight the areas in which the need or the opportunity for action exists.

By its very nature the Blue Plan had to consider the Mediterranean basin as a whole. On such a broad scale, development patterns and economic strategies can best be considered for the entire territory of coastal countries, and a macro-economic approach provides the necessary linkages within the region and with the rest of the world. At any rate, most economic statistics are available only at the national level. Conversely, environmental problems relating to pollution or to resource use are generally site-specific and environmental statistics are not available or have little meaning on a macro-scale. At the same time we do not know yet how to 'internalize' the degradation of environmental resources in economic computation. Whether considering non-renewable resources or so-called renewable resources which are not in fact actually renewed, confusion continues to occur between capital and income, and there is no generally accepted, still less generally utilized, method for creating such tools as 'satellite' accounts for environmental values in the conventional systems of national accounts. For these reasons, the results obtained from Mediterranean scenarios tend to be more quantitative for economic sectors—and also for population parameters—but more qualitative for environmental factors. Despite these difficulties, efforts have been made wherever possible to relate the scenarios to the Mediterranean regions themselves, considering the watershed or the coastal administrative unities of the various countries.

The broad scale and global nature of the Blue Plan scenarios may naturally conceal local trends stemming from specific circumstances and do not provide for an accurate description of what may happen in a given spot in the basin. Nor can they take into account unforeseeable events or sudden disruptions, such as ideological or political upheavals, major natural disasters, or catastrophic technological accidents. However, the approach provides the general context in which such local trends or events may occur, a context which in fact has a profound influence on them.

The whole exercise confirms an assumption on which it was largely based, namely, that the national strategies and development policies pursued by all the Mediterranean countries have a significant impact on the state of the environment in the region. It shows in particular that protection of the Mediterranean Sea, its shores and coastal regions, cannot be assured through action carried out on the sea alone, or its coastal regions alone, but depends largely on the overall development, environment, and physical planning policies followed by the Mediterranean countries at the national level. It also depends on economic and commercial interactions between these countries as a whole and the rest of the world in the agriculture, industry, energy, tourism, and transport sectors. In this respect, the scenarios confirm the validity of global analyses carried out in other studies, such as the report of the World Commission on Environment and Development or UNEP's 'Environmental Perspective to the Year 2000 and Beyond'.

Moving from the 1960s towards 2025, and taking 1985 as the reference year, the Blue Plan scenarios clearly show that the Mediterranean 'system' is a highly dynamic one with rapidly changing patterns for the economic sectors and the geographical milieux. A major fact emerges from this moving scene, namely, that over the periods under consideration most problems of development, natural-resources management, and environmental protection arise and are viewed in substantially different ways by the countries north of the basin and those to the south and east, for reasons stemming at the same time from differences in climatic and hydrological conditions, disparity in levels of economic development, and the very sharp contrast in population trends.

The various scenarios envisaged, whether they are based on the continuation, more or less enhanced, of current trends (the so-called 'trend' scenarios), or on a more goal-orientated strengthening of Mediterranean co-operation as regards both the environment and development (the so-called 'alternative' scenarios), lead to 'images' of the Mediterranean environment that do not radically differ at the horizon of the year 2000, and are very close to the present, for which the stage is already set. Whatever the scenario, up to this date the situation could in principle be kept more or less under control in most countries through contingency action, provided that declared policies and stipulated regulations are in fact implemented. However, the scenarios for 2025 (in less than forty years, the same span as from 1950 to 1988) indicate that the situation may change radically and that the state of the environment could deteriorate considerably. Considering the time-lag needed to obtain significant effects in the area of environmental protection, it is here and now that policies more vigorous than the current ones must be decided upon and implemented if the serious shortages and irreversible degradations threatening the future of the Mediterranean people are to be avoided or attenuated, particularly concerning soil, water, the forest, the coast, and urban environments.

More specifically, the Blue Plan exercise shows that, in any event—even in the most favourable scenarios—protection of the terrestrial and marine coastal strip will be very difficult in the long run because of growing human pressures and the vulnerability of its natural environment. This will generally be the case in the regions south and east of the basin, but also all along the urbanized coasts of the northern region. The coastal strip constitutes one of the greatest assets of all Mediterranean countries without exception, and its safeguard will require the continuous and unswerving determination of governments and public authorities, based on the active and lasting support of the populations concerned. The most favourable scenarios in fact imply a permanent mobilization on behalf of this coastal environment.

Rather than the open sea itself, the coastal strip, with its formidable problems of land-use planning, urban management, and pollution control, is where the future of the Mediterranean environment hangs in the balance. The urgent actions required in this respect are mostly local in character. Decision-making would benefit from the construction of 'coastal scenarios' on a sufficiently large scale, where environmental features and the role of local actors could be analysed in detail, utilizing modern geographical information systems. Coastal scenarios and ensuing local action would, however, have to take into consideration the broader regional, national, and international context, and in this respect the Mediterranean scenarios of the Blue Plan should provide substantial guidance and help.

During the coming decades considerable investment will be required to ensure an economic and social development compatible with the growing needs of the Mediterranean populations, especially in the south and east of the basin. Environmental protection should be incorporated in this investment from the outset, and should not be considered—as is still too often the case—as an additional cost, which can be dispensed with or postponed until later. In fact, environmental protection and the search for sustainable development may be a source of employment and wealth. The main fact that emerges from the scenarios, however, is that, in the case of the Mediterranean basin, development itself will only be achieved through protection of the environment: without it, the fragility of environments, particularly in coastal and mountainous areas, makes natural resources vulnerable; without it, landscapes and living conditions—the charm of the region—deteriorate to the cost of the populations and visitors alike.

In this respect, and in all the Blue Plan scenarios despite their fairly broad range, the magnitude and intricacy of problems stemming from socio-economic constraints affecting countries south and east of the basin show that efforts undertaken at the national and local level, however significant and relevant they may be, will not suffice. Greatly increased north–south solidarity and more determined south–south co-operation are fundamental for the protection of the sea and the region as a whole. Such solidarity and co-operation for environmental protection should not be confined to action focusing on this problem as such, but seem to imply, in addition, the harmonious growth of intra-Mediterranean trade (making it possible, in particular, to offset food shortages), the development of communication systems (in all forms), a mobilization geared to new technologies adapted to the conditions of the region, and a better understanding of the demands of the future on the part of each and every Mediterranean person.

The present volume contains the main report on the Mediterranean scenarios resulting from the Blue Plan prospective studies. It was submitted to the Mediterranean governments in 1988 in a provisional form and has already received a preliminary consideration within some international institutions such as UNEP or the World Bank. Although the work was conducted within an intergovernmental framework, an effort was made to present it as far as possible as a scientific volume which, it is hoped, should provide ideas and material for lively debate in the years to come. This volume does not constitute the only written product of the Blue Plan exercise. A number of thematic booklets corresponding to specific economic sectors (such as intensive agriculture, tourism, or fisheries) or geographical milieux (such as islands, forests, or protected areas) are being prepared in order to expand on their particular problems in the Mediterranean region and their prospective evolution in the light of the scenarios. In addition, a computerized demographic and economic data base and an environmental data base have been established for the region and are available to the countries.

The volume is presented in five parts:

Part I outlines the geographical context of the study. It recalls the distinctive characteristics of the Mediterranean basin, with respect to both physical and human geography, and identifies the main permanent features of the Mediterranean environment (climate, relief, ecosystems, etc.) to be considered as constants in the scenarios. It indicates the geographical boundaries which have been adopted for the work and the time-scales by which to assess trends.

Part II defines the five scenarios formulated for the horizons of 2000 and 2025. After recalling the interest in using this method of future-orientated study, it explains how the variable factors of the scenarios were chosen, whether environmental, economic, or demographic. This is followed by a description of the different kinds of scenario selected, their structure and outline, placing them in the context of economic and environmental policies. In particular, a selection is made of the hypotheses concerning population (demography, migrations, dependency ratio, etc.) on the one hand, and economic factors (growth-rates, trades, etc.) on the other. The scenarios are then depicted in detail for the horizons 2000 and 2025, according to the set of hypotheses chosen.

Part III presents the findings relating to economic activities and their impact on the environment for the five major sectors chosen (agriculture, industry, energy, tourism, and transport), as well as for urban systems and urbanization. In this part a presentation is made of the various sectoral scenarios which were established and of the consistency and interactions between the different sectors. Wherever possible the trends relating specifically to the coast and to the Mediterranean regions proper were indicated.

Part IV is devoted to an analysis of possible trends of the Mediterranean environment according to the different scenarios. For this analysis a number of environmental 'chains' or subsystems were explored with a view to quantitatively linking development activities with their impact on the five environmental variables chosen: the soil, the forest, water resources, the coastline, and the sea. Regarding the sea, however, subject of in-depth work under another component of the Mediterranean Action Plan, the MEDPOL programme, the Blue Plan has mainly attempted a prospective estimate of potential pollution from the main sectors of human activity.

Part V summarizes the main findings and major potential trends of change stemming from the scenarios, which helps to identify a number of suggestions for action at both the national and local level, and through intra-Mediterranean co-operation.

This report and the Blue Plan scenarios do not attempt to give optimistic or pessimistic views of the future, but simply to provide a basis for reflection and guidance for prompt action in each Mediterranean country and at the level of development assistance organizations and of the Mediterranean Action Plan itself. The scenarios show that the region's environment will be subject to increasingly strong pressures, but that ways exist to reduce considerably the effects of these pressures and to reverse the most adverse trends. Among the options, the most important ones seem to be:

- the search for new patterns of development in the region, based on stronger intra-Mediterranean co-operation and more resolute north–south solidarity;
- the systematic consideration of environmental factors in all sectors of development, in particular at the level of coastal regions, and especially in the coastal strip, together with the setting up or strengthening of appropriate institutions.
- the promotion of a better understanding of interactions between development and the environment in the Mediterranean, leading to the adoption of new kinds of behaviour among national or local decision-makers from both the public and private sectors, and among all Mediterranean peoples.

It is to be hoped that the publication and dissemination of the present volume will stimulate the choice of alternative paths in Mediterranean development policies and contribute to the preservation of the unique quality of this region and ensure for it a future commensurate with its past.

MICHEL BATISSE
President
Blue Plan Regional Activity Centre

Sophia-Antipolis
April 1989

Acknowledgements

THROUGHOUT the preparation of this report Messrs Michel Batisse and Michel Grenon have benefited from the advice of

Mr Ibrahim Helmi Abdel-Rahman, former Minister for Planning and former Executive Director of UNIDO;
Mr Serge Antoine, Head, Environment/Development Office of the French Ministry of Environment;
Mr Jacques Lesourne, Professor of Economics and former Director of the OECD project 'Interfutures';
Mr Aldo Manos, Co-ordinator of the Mediterranean Action Plan.

The central team working as from 1985 at Sophia Antipolis (France) under the direction of Michel Grenon included Mr A. Lahmidi (Morocco) for population studies, Mr L. Khaldoun (Algeria) for land-use planning, and Mr P. Komilis (Greece) for urbanization, with the assistance of Mrs E. Coudert for coastal studies, Mr J. P. Giraud for mathematical analysis, and Mrs C. Kuzucuoglu for ecology, and with Mr I. H. Abdel-Rahman (Egypt) acting as senior adviser.

The technical aspects of the work received advice regularly from an open 'Study Group on Mediterranean Scenarios' chaired by Mr Jacques Lesourne (France) and comprising Messrs M. Cherkaoui (Morocco), M. Benblidia (Algeria), K. Fourati (Tunisia), I. H. Abdel-Rahman (Egypt), A. Pruginin (Israel), J. Mourad and N. Haidar (Syria), C. Hamamci (Turkey), M. Papayannakis (Greece), F. Gasparovic, and I. Vekaric (Yugoslavia), Sacco Casamassima (Italy), S. Antoine, H. Aujac, J. Royer, and J. Theys (France), E. Fontela (Spain), E. Scicluna (Malta), and D. Milano (EEC). In addition, a number of experts took part in the preparation of sectoral studies, including Messrs M. Labonne for agriculture, J. Giri for industry, M. Figuerola and R. Lanquar for tourism, J. Margat and B. de Carmentrand for water, and H. Marchand for forests.

For the Blue Plan exercise, the Mediterranean countries set up a 'Steering Committee', which was placed from 1984 to 1987 under the chairmanship of Italy (Mr F. Ciarnelli), with Morocco, Spain, Syria, Turkey, and Yugoslavia as members for 1984–86 and Egypt, Greece, Israel, Malta, and EEC as members for 1986–87. From 1987 to 1988 the Steering Committee was chaired by Tunisia (Mrs H. Baccar), with Algeria, Cyprus, France, Lebanon, Libya, and Monaco as members.

As indicated in the Foreword, the Blue Plan scenarios were constructed on the basis of earlier studies in a first phase of the Blue Plan which took place from 1980 to 1984 under the leadership of Mr I. Sabri Abdalla (Egypt) as chairman of a small 'Group of Co-ordination and Synthesis' including Messrs M. H. Bennadji (Algeria), F. Gasparovic (Yugoslavia), P. Lagos (Greece), E. Makhlouf (Tunisia), J. M. Pliego (Spain), and M. Grenon (France). This initial work led to the preparation by twelve two-man teams of north and south experts of state-of-knowledge reports on the following subjects in the Mediterranean:

1. Land/marine systems and subsystems: A. Gharbo (Egypt) and J. P. Foret (France).
2. Water resources, competing uses, and human priorities: M. Ennabli (Tunisia) and Y. Emsellem (France).
3. Industrial growth, industrialization strategies, and subsoil resources: K. Maksoud (Egypt) and G. Luciani (Italy).
4. Old and new forms of energy: N. Berrah (Algeria) and R. Rigopoulos (Greece).
5. Health, population, and population movements: T. Nacef (Tunisia) and I. Baucic (Yugoslavia).
6. Land use, soil conservation, agriculture and rural development, urbanization, shore-line development, and town–country balance: L. Khaldoun (Algeria) and C. Muscara (Italy).
7. Tourism, tourist areas and the environment: A. Smaoui (Tunisia) and M. Baretje and J. M. Thurot (France).
8. Intra-Mediterranean economic relations: K. Abdel-Nour (Syria) and M. Papayannakis (Greece).
9. Transport and communications: M. Benchekroun (Morocco) and J. Cuena (Spain).
10. Cultural heritage and cross-cultural relations: Mrs K. Nestoros (Greece) and R. Habachi (Lebanon).

11. Awareness of the environment and value-systems: S. Ghabbour (Egypt) and F. González Bernáldez (Spain).

12. Impact of non-Mediterranean influences on the Mediterranean basin: A. Najib (Morocco) and V. Vukasovic (Yugoslavia).

The preparation of the manuscript of this volume by the secretariat of BP/RAC was supervised by Anne-Françoise Aoust.

The French-language original text was translated by Colette Kinnon.

The illustrations were designed and prepared by the Association Française pour le Développement de l'Expression Cartographique (AFDEC-Paris).

Contents

List of Figures

List of Tables

Abbreviations

BOD	biological oxygen demand
CAP	Common Agricultural Policy (of the EEC)
CFC	chlorofluorocarbon
COD	chemical oxygen demand
ECU	European Currency Unit
FAO	Food and Agriculture Organization (of the UN)
GDP	gross domestic product
GFCM	General Fisheries Council for the Mediterranean
GNP	gross national product
goe	grams oil equivalent
GRT	gross registered tonnes
IAEA	International Atomic Energy Agency
IBRD	International Bank for Reconstruction and Development (World Bank)
IIASA	International Institute for Applied System Analysis
IUCN	International Union for the Conservation of Nature and Natural Resources
koe	kilograms oil equivalent
kWh	kilowatt-hours
LNG	liquefied natural gas
LPG	liquefied petroleum gas
MAB	Man and Biosphere Programme (Unesco)
MAP	Mediterranean Action Plan
MARPOL	International Convention for the Prevention of Pollution from Ships (1973) and main Protocol (1978)
MEDPOL	Research and monitoring component of MAP
MWe	megawatts electric
N	nitrogen
n.a.	not available (or not known)
NOx	nitrogen oxides
NPK	Nitrogen-Phosphorus-Potassium
OECD	Organization for Economic Co-operation and Development
P	phosphorus
PAP	Priority Actions Programme (MAP)
ppm	parts per million
ROCC	Regional Oil Combating Centre of MAP
ro-ro	roll-on, roll-off (cargo ship)
SOx	sulphur oxides
SS	suspended solids
tce	tonnes coal equivalent
TDS	total dissolved salts
tdw	tonnes dead weight
toe	tonnes oil equivalent
TWh	terawatt-hours (10^{12})
UAL	utilized agricultural land
UNCTAD	United Nations Conference on Trade and Development
UNDP	United Nations Development Programme
UNEP	United Nations Environment Programme
Unesco	United Nations Educational, Scientific, and Cultural Organization
UNIDO	United Nations Industrial Development Organization
WHO	World Health Organization
WTO	World Tourist Organization
~	approximately

I The Geographical Context

1 Specific Characteristics and Permanent Features

Both its geography and history—one being closely related to the other—have made the Mediterranean basin an outstandingly original region. The sea itself (Mediterranean means 'in the midst of land'), the complex and tortured landscape that surrounds it, its unique climate, have all strongly influenced the extraordinary development of civilization along its shores. And this development, with its long evolution dating back to prehistory and its increasing intensity, has deeply marked and often irreversibly transformed a fragile environment with limited resources. Perhaps nowhere else has nature done so much for man, has man in turn so transformed nature. The geographical context in both its physical and human aspects predominates any study or prospective exercise on the Mediterranean.

It is not the intention here to provide a detailed picture of this Mediterranean geographical framework, frequently described elsewhere. It should be noted, however, that the Blue Plan prospective study requires the selection of a limited number of variable parameters for building scenarios, and this choice should not conceal other important parameters, which will be considered as 'constants'. These basic features of the Mediterranean environment, such as the marine system, relief, climate, fauna, and flora, and also urban sites and some socio-cultural elements, provide the setting for the Blue Plan scenarios, i.e. the framework for the study of possible futures. This does not mean that these features do not evolve within the basin's highly fragile system, but that their development is rather slow compared to the time-scales chosen.

1. The marine system

The Mediterranean Sea is the natural link and common wealth of all the coastal countries. Formed from the remnants of a huge ancient seaway—the Tethys geosyncline of pre-Tertiary time—which used to divide the Eurasian continent from the African, it is made up of two rather deep basins—western and eastern—separated by a threshold running between Sicily and Tunisia, no more than 400-metres deep. From Gibraltar to the Dardanelles it is broken up into a complex of smaller seas, each with individual features, different biocoenoses, and very deep trenches.

The Mediterranean is a virtually enclosed sea, subject to heavy evaporation which is not offset by inputs from rain and rivers and accounts for its relatively high salinity. Its level is maintained basically by an inflow from the Atlantic through the Straits of Gibraltar. Mediterranean waters are comparatively warm and governed by surface currents which change during the year. The complexity of these currents reflects that of the sea's structure. In addition, Mediterranean tides are weak, an extremely significant feature which facilitates shipping, but at the same time aggravates the problems of pollution along the coast and to some extent affects the way in which Mediterranean people view their relationship with the sea.

2. The Mediterranean relief

The growing artificiality of our world, the ever-increasing liberty taken to overcome obstacles presented by physical geography, the upheaval in transport and communication, cannot efface a basic fact: the Mediterranean basin is a region with a complex and fragmented relief. It lies at the centre of a very complicated patchwork formed by tectonic plates of the earth's crust sliding under one other, and is marked by the large Tertiary alpine fold, with occasionally some later alterations due to glaciers, volcanic phenomena, or erosion. The outcome is strong seismic and volcanic activity, whose repercussions on human life and society are a permanent feature of the region, but which cannot be taken into account directly in global scenarios because of its random nature.

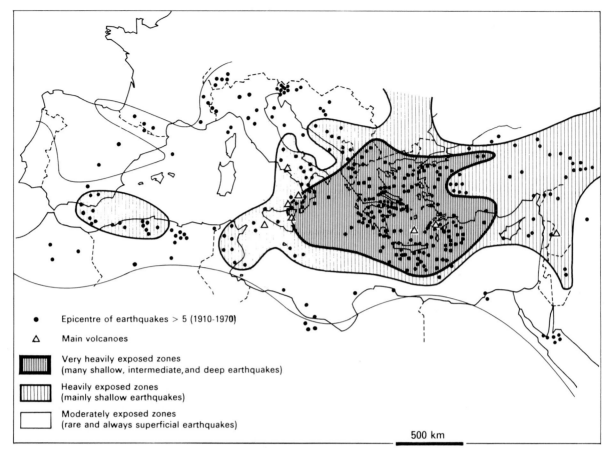

●   Epicentre of earthquakes > 5 (1910-1970)

△   Main volcanoes

▨   Very heavily exposed zones
     (many shallow, intermediate, and deep earthquakes)

▥   Heavily exposed zones
     (mainly shallow earthquakes)

☐   Moderately exposed zones
     (rare and always superficial earthquakes)

500 km

FIG. 1.1 Seismicity and volcanism. The north-eastern Mediterranean is a centre of intense seismic activity
Source: *Atlas of Seismicity and Volcanism* (1979).

The consequences of the young relief and the close contact between the sea and the mountains are important; for example, there are few large plains, little good agricultural land, few broad river basins, and ports and harbours are closely hemmed in between sea and rock.

Aside from the south-east—on some 3,000 kilometres along most of the Libyan and Egyptian coasts, where the Saharan platform directly meets the sea—mountains are omnipresent. The Mediterranean mountain regions, for centuries often self-sufficient units forced to diversify output even if the soil or climate were not particularly suitable, optimizing their modest resources through hard and endless work, have played a very important role in the past and will continue to do so. For the mountains receive the largest amount of rainfall, which replenishes the watercourses. In the mountains, the forest and vegetation must hold down the soil and stabilize the Mediterranean water-cycle, by nature very uneven. Traditionally, the mountains were a source of

manpower, exporting the labour they could not support, because mountain resources, although varied, are not plentiful and cannot bear over-exploitation. Already the terraces, so typical of the Mediterranean landscape, are being abandoned, unsuited as they are to modern tools. The population there find little reward for their efforts, resulting in degradation of the landscape, erosion, fires, and desertification.

Lying between the high mountains and the plains are the plateaux: the high Algerian plateaux, Emilia and Apulia in Italy, etc., and the hilly, but scarce, regions inhabited early by man in Languedoc, Provence, Tuscany, Sicily, Greece, and in the Maghreb, with the Algerian and Tunisian Sahel.

The plains, usually small, are very different. Those with a reduced surface area were easier to develop; the larger ones were harder to master, an event which was sometimes accomplished only recently, in areas such as the Mitidja near Algiers at the beginning of the century, the plain of Salonica

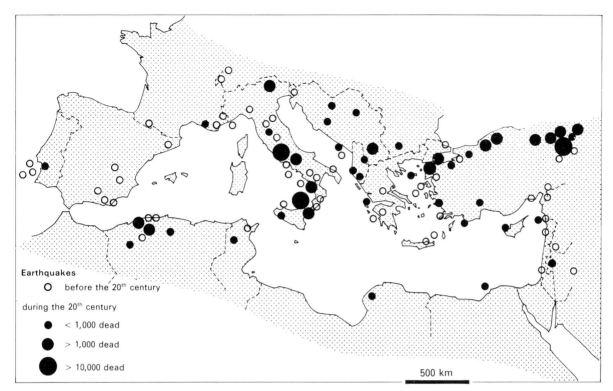

FIG. 1.2 Disastrous earthquakes. The number of victims of an earthquake depends not only on intensity or frequency, but also on the location of the epicentre with respect to ground surface, on its proximity to populated areas, or on related accidents or epidemics.

Source: adapted from C. Weber (1982).

around 1925, and the Ebro delta or the Pontine Marshes near Rome on the eve of the Second World War. Mastery of these few large plains required long and drawn-out efforts (often made by governments, always highly capitalistic), with repercussions on forms of ownership and water control.

The struggle to transform stagnant water into irrigation water and convert insalubrious (malarial) plains into high-yield land has been a very hard challenge for Mediterranean people, and one of the outstanding features of their rural history (comparable to northern Europe's mastery of its outer forest lands). These improvements, in which Arab civilization and techniques played an essential role, were often a response to the growing needs of nearby cities (Cairo, Rome, Tunis, Algiers, etc.). Nowadays, because of their all-consuming urbanization, these cities tend in turn to invade the same plains they had won to feed themselves, simultaneously appropriating the water traditionally used for agriculture.

There are many islands in the Mediterranean, sometimes grouped together in families or archipelagos. Their environment is fragile, their resources are never abundant, and water is often scarce. Unable to live off their own resources, they were obliged to open up to the outside world and look for economic or strategic 'niches'.

Apart from the coastal or delta plains, the Mediterranean coast, one of the main subjects in this report, is often very compartmentalized because of the relief. Its 46,000 km of shore are often broken up by the mountains falling abruptly to the sea (the Balearic coast, the creeks in Provence, or the Adriatic *canali*) and the virtually contiguous *rivieras* (Liguria, Provence, Catalonia, Valencia, and Andalusia), subject to the strongest human pressure. The traditional maritime provinces used to back on to wooded mountains, which in the past they stripped to a large extent for housing or naval construction.

Lastly, the four major river deltas (Rhone, Ebro, Po, and Nile) and the narrower deltas (Medjerda, Aliakmon, Calamas, Acheron, Ceyhan, Vardar, etc.) are unstable areas, which have changed greatly in the course of history. They are very sensitive to variations in the sea level, with rapidly alternating periods of erosion and sedimentation, reflected by advancing or retreating shore-lines.

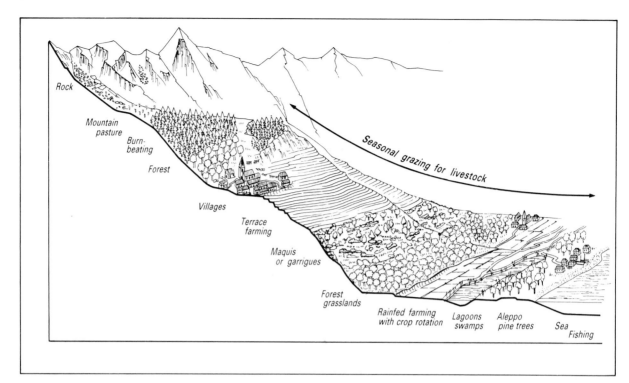

FIG. 1.3 (*a*) A traditional Mediterranean slope

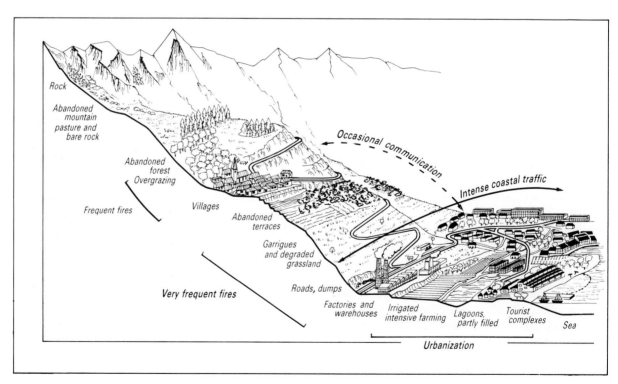

FIG. 1.3 (*b*) A Mediterranean slope today

Although in this study the relief is considered as a permanent feature, this naturally does not imply that it is impervious to change, either abrupt (from seismic movements, eruptions, or landslides) or from human activity. In fact, people have become particularly active geological agents in the Mediterranean. Buildings, works, and domestic animals all contribute highly to deforestation and subsequent soil erosion. People can construct virtually anywhere; the barrier to traffic long posed by the Mediterranean relief is now overcome. Motorways cross the mountain chains and coastal valleys through tunnels and bridges, as in the Genoa area. Soon, perhaps, Sicily will no longer be an island, and a project even exists to link Africa to Europe via Gibraltar.

3. The Mediterranean climate

The climate is another fairly permanent feature of the Mediterranean environment as regards the scenarios. It is so typical, with its associated plant life, that geographers made it a specific type, identifiable on other continents (in California, Chile, Australia, and South Africa). It is distinguished by hot, dry summers and mild, damp winters. In the Mediterranean basin this climate results from interactions with the desert zone in the south and the Atlantic Ocean in the west, i.e. from influences external to the Mediterranean.

Rainfall is distinctly irregular during the year and from one year to the next, especially in the south, where there is no assurance of rain-fed crops. It may be violent, likely to produce huge flash-floods in a few hours, which are often disastrous, tearing up and carrying away precious top soil. In 1981 in Larnaka (Cyprus), for example, 192 mm of rain fell in four hours, and the loss of soil from erosion was twenty-five times higher than during the whole of the previous year. Even if the Mediterranean climate is basically consistent, closer analysis reveals significant differences. The rainfall/temperature charts show the contrast between the north of the basin (autumn rain) and the south (winter rain). In summer, the concurrence of the highest tem-

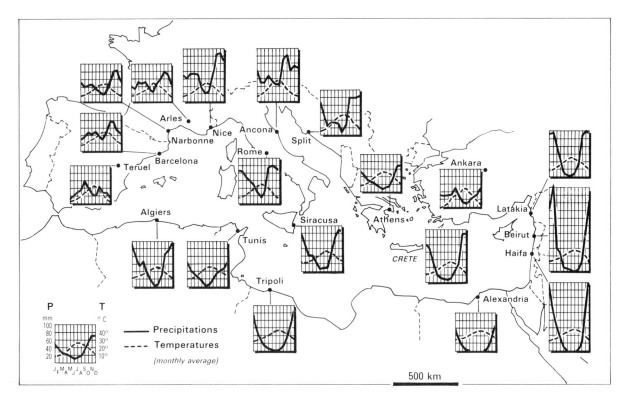

FIG. 1.4 Rainfall/temperature in the Mediterranean. These rainfall/temperature diagrams contain two curves, obtained by plotting horizontally the month and vertically both precipitation (mm) and mean temperature (°C) on a scale double that of precipitation. It is considered that the dry season corresponds to the period when precipitation is less than twice the temperature (area formed by the intersection of the two curves). In the Mediterranean the dry season corresponds with the hot season.

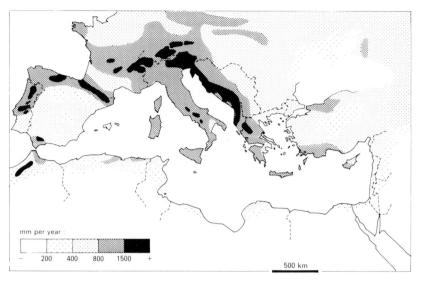

FIG. 1.5 Annual average precipitation

Source: *Climatic Atlas of Europe* (Unesco-WMO, 1970) and *World Water Balance* (Unesco, 1978).

peratures and the lowest rainfall causes strong evapotranspiration in plants.

Climate is not an absolute constant and evolves slowly over time. Between 10,000 and 12,000 years ago, the Sahara was covered with grassland; the Tassili paintings prove it. On the shorter scale of human experience, there have been less marked variations towards drier or wetter weather. A few years' drought can have a destabilizing effect on farming societies, their output and diet, especially in marginal areas such as the southern edge of the Mediterranean basin. In Africa, the Sahelian countries have been suffering a series of droughts for some fifteen years, and a random phenomenon of this kind cannot be excluded in the Mediterranean basin.

But most important of all, a prospective study has to mention the possible trend of the world climate towards heating up, due to the 'greenhouse effect' caused by the accumulation of carbon dioxide and other industrial gases such as freons (CFCs) and methane in the atmosphere. It will take several years of study before definite and accurate indications are available concerning the extent of the greenhouse effect and its consequences in the various regions of the world. It is generally admitted that the average temperature throughout the world could rise by 0.5 °C to 2 °C by 2030, and 3.5 °C by 2050, which is a considerable change compared to the historical past. Moreover, even if all carbon dioxide and CFC emissions were stopped today, inertia would cause a warming up of the planet in any event, because of the amounts already accumulated in the atmosphere.

This global trend will not fail to have considerable repercussions on the Mediterranean climate, which could occur rather rapidly during the coming decades, but it is scarcely possible at present to define their exact nature. It is fairly widely accepted that with an average increase of 1.5 °C in the temperature by 2025, the region will experience a shift of cyclonic systems towards the north, which will affect its central and western areas in winter. In these areas rainfall would continue to depend heavily on relief and would be higher in the north, but, conversely, areas of uncertain rainfall in the south could spread and evapotranspiration would rise everywhere. It goes without saying that a change of this kind would have serious consequences, notably for agriculture and the hydrological regime. Ensuing changes in the thermal structure of water bodies could also produce modifications in marine currents, which in turn would affect air currents in the region.

It is also admitted that the expected heating up of the climate will bring about a general rise in the sea-level. Historically speaking, Mediterranean shores have been unstable because of slow variations in the sea-level or localized tectonic movements, and there are records of submersions or emergences that occurred over past millennia. The general trend since the end of the glacial periods has been a rise in the sea-level. This has amounted to approximately 1.3 mm per year during the past century, and it is currently estimated that as a result of the greenhouse effect, which will cause the world's oceans to swell, an average increase in sea-level of between 15 and 40 cm is to be expected by 2025.

Whether these developments involve climatic variations such as drought or the permanent changes

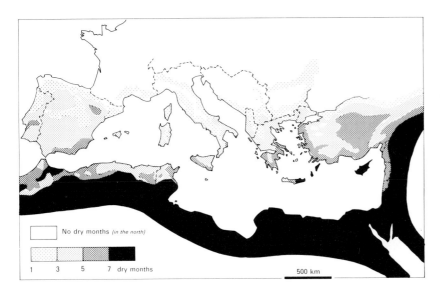

FIG. 1.6 Length of the dry season
Source: adapted from P. Birot and
J. Dresch (1953).

No dry months *(in the north)*

1   3   5   7 dry months

500 km

mentioned above, their course is still too uncertain for them to be usefully incorporated as such into the Blue Plan scenarios. Nevertheless, they remain present throughout the exercise in the form of 'hazards'.

In a different connection, the climate may be changed, in limited areas, by the appearance of micro-climates. Thus, urban climates may be modified by gas emissions (domestic heating, automobile transport, industry), which cause the climate to heat up locally and change the distribution of rainfall in time and space. The concentration of air-pollutants (NOx, SOx, CO, particulate matter, black smoke, etc.) in urban areas varies very widely, reflecting (at their highest level) specific meteorological conditions that cumulate at emission-points, related, for instance, to motor-vehicle traffic. Generally speaking, maximum values are recorded in the Mediterranean under conditions of thermal inversion which often occur in summer: a mass of warm air, which cannot rise because it is blocked by a mass of stable cold air, lies over the city, where the pollutants emitted then concentrate. The effects of a rise in concentration levels do not involve only urban centres: under the effect of daily cycles (air exchanges at the end of the day when temperatures drop), pollutants in the atmosphere spread over surrounding areas (surburbs), where they contaminate the night air. If the lack of rising air movement continues, the concentration of gases and particulate matter over the active city is such that all traffic has to be banned (Rome, 1986) as the health of the population may be at risk (combined with intense heat: Athens, 1987). Current knowledge about 'environmental meteorology' is still very

inadequate, and the Blue Plan can only stress the potential gravity of the occurrences according to the different scenarios.

4. The Mediterranean ecosystem

The Mediterranean ecosystem—in fact the body of ecosystems of this huge basin—is one of the characteristic and permanent features of the region, even if human activity has radically changed it over the centuries, bringing about its degradation or increasing artificiality. Plant life has had to adapt to a simultaneously hot and dry season—a basic characteristic of the Mediterranean climate—and this adaptation is made all the more difficult by the intensity of heat and dryness. Generally speaking, vegetation became drought-tolerant in order to survive. Forests are often open, and thus provide poor protection for the soil. Regeneration is difficult, which furthers degradation. Soil is often deeply scarred and it is not always possible to restore plant cover, even with heavy expenditure. Lastly, the Mediterranean region bears the brunt of history: it was subject very early on to careless exploitation. Its degradation dates from long ago.

These common features in no way imply uniformity, however. Mediterranean ecosystems are highly compartmentalized: the point of contact between land and sea is heavily indented, the relief is rugged, and the contrasting micro-climates clearly demonstrate the combined effects of terracing and exposure. Drought-resistant features of vegetation are clearly visible in semi-arid environments, where run-off and erosion reach disastrous levels because the environment is poorly protected by the plant cover and the soil has little resistance. In more humid environments, the climate stimulates the development of protective vegetation, which fulfils its role so long as it is not destroyed.

The original feature of Mediterranean soil derives from the fact that it escaped the Quaternary peri-glacial influences and underwent a more intense hydrolysis process than in temperate zones, which dissociated iron from silica. The weathering of rocks in the regions around the Mediterranean ceased at the stage of 'fersiallitization', characterized by a partial solubilization of base rock and silica, the preservation of clay inherited from previous climates, the formation of new clay, and the appearance of iron oxides (producing a red colour). This fersiallitic soil—known as 'terra rossa'—forms slowly on lime-stone massifs, but far faster on porous bedrock (schist, sandstone, etc.). There are varying degrees of fersiallitization, and 'terra rossa' in fact combines soils of very different ages. In most cases soil now evolves only sporadically, during damp years.

Other kinds of soil exist in the Mediterranean region which combine to varying degrees the fer-siallitization process and the accumulation of organic matter. Vertisols (black clay) develop in low-lying land with seasonal waterlogging. The migration of

calcium, which dissolves during damp periods and recrystallizes during dry ones, causes the formation of calcareous crusts. Azonal desert soil is present in the south of the basin. Lastly, 'rendzinas', dark humus-rich soils, are also found throughout the region on carbonated parent rock.

Given the characteristic climatic conditions pre-vailing throughout the entire basin, Mediterranean soil is unfortunately sensitive to physical and chem-ical degradation. From the outset its inherent fea-tures make it particularly fragile. As a resource, its development must be carefully monitored in the light of demands made on it, and drastic conservation measures must be taken.

The characteristic climate, the relief, and the soil make the Mediterranean basin one of the most original biogeographic regions in the world. Wild life and plant life have distinct features as regards both their composition and associations. Medi-terranean plant life, with a wealth of some 25,000 species, is all the more remarkable since more than half of these are endemic (i.e. specific to the region). A number of plant associations are relics, i.e. represent what remains of periods when ecological or climatic conditions were more favourable. En-demic or relict plant species are all the more sensitive to degradation because once they have disappeared

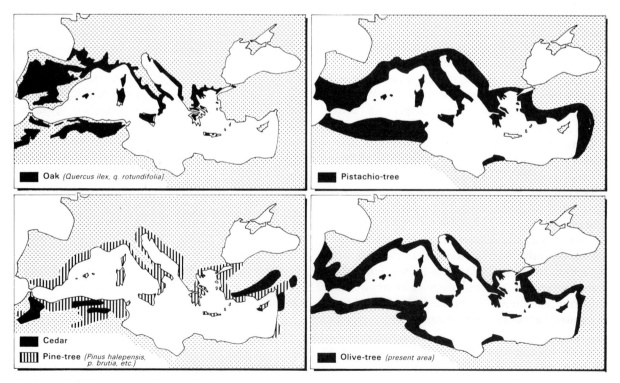

FIG. 1.7 Distribution area of some Mediterranean trees
Source: Blue Plan (from various authors).

BOX 1A. **Botanical conservatories for threatened plant species**

The aggressions of all kinds suffered by Mediterranean environments may have particularly serious consequences in the form of impoverishment of genetic material in the Mediterranean basin, since the combined action of biogeographical climatic factors in this region has contributed to the creation or survival of specific plant species and communities which exist nowhere else.

According to a recent survey carried out by the Porquerolles Botanical Conservatory on the French Mediterranean region, at least 526 taxons (species, subspecies, and varieties) are threatened to varying degrees. Among them:

- 83 have regressed slightly over their natural area as a whole, and should be monitored;
- 298 are at serious risk, as many populations have disappeared;
- 137 are on the verge of extinction;
- 8 have irrevocably disappeared from the French mainland Mediterranean region over the past twenty years. To this figure should be added some 30 species which have disappeared since the beginning of the century.

Furthermore, these many endangered species are also scattered. Too often their natural area is confined to three or four sites covering barely 10 m² or so. Conventional administrative protection measures for such areas are often inapplicable or not applied. Faced with virtual powerlessness to control the factors causing species to regress, botanists quite naturally settled on the idea of setting up establishments called 'gene-banks' or 'conservatories', which group together disappearing species and varieties. The development of such conservatories is to be encouraged.

However, considering the risk of genetic drift which can affect small populations, these establishments are only a contribution and cannot substitute for natural sites. The protection of natural sites is therefore vital and can only be envisaged with the support of all public or private bodies responsible for the management of natural areas.

they cannot easily regenerate in the present climatic and geographic context, which did not exist when they first appeared.

The Mediterranean forest, typified especially by evergreen trees such as the holm-oak (*Quercus ilex*) and cork-oak (*Quercus suber*) (considerably fire-resistant, which partly explains why they have spread), forms a transition belt. Towards temperate environments (in latitude, altitude, and inland location) deciduous trees mix with the holm-oak. Towards low latitudes, green oak is replaced by trees more resistant to drought (thuja) and to cold at altitude (conifers, including three species of cedar). This sclerophyllous forest, as well as the evergreen *maquis* or *garrigue*, does not exclude large pine-covered areas (*Pinus halepensis* or *Pinus nigra*).

Changes in plant life have derived mainly from interactions between environments and species on the one hand, and human activities and needs on the other, rather than from climatic evolution over millennia. Thus, during recent centuries many plants were introduced into the Mediterranean, an area suited by its climate to shrub crops. Some species are suited for human consumption (olive, fig, pomegranate, orange, tomato, aubergine, maize, etc.), others to industry (eucalyptus, acacia, etc.), others to landscaping (bougainvillaea, palm, etc.). These species, which originated in other parts of the world, have now become so well adapted to the region that it is easily forgotten that they were initially foreign to it.

In this way primary vegetation virtually everywhere has been replaced by regressive formations and secondary landscapes. The ecosystems of the region (both coastal and inland), which shelter animal populations and varied associated plant life whose survival depends on the stability of biotopes, are particularly threatened (drainage or introduction of fish in wetlands, destruction of the *maquis*, fires, or over-exploitation of the forest, effects of pesticides and fertilizers, etc.). A number of animal species have suffered from this development to the point of extinction or are in a critical situation: this is the case notably of certain anatidae, of large forest mammals such as the bear, lynx, or some antilopes, the monk seal, and large birds of prey (eagles, vultures). Excessive hunting has greatly contributed to the disappearance of bird life throughout the Mediterranean region. At the same time it is important to stress the very rich diversity of hardy varieties of cultivated plants and of races of domestic animals previously existing throughout the basin (bovine, ovine, and even porcine races, cereals, alfa, fruit-trees), at present very likely to disappear.

The Mediterranean marine fauna is very varied from the point of view of species (some 900 different species of fish), but it is not very plentiful. This is due to the fact that, on the one hand, Mediterranean

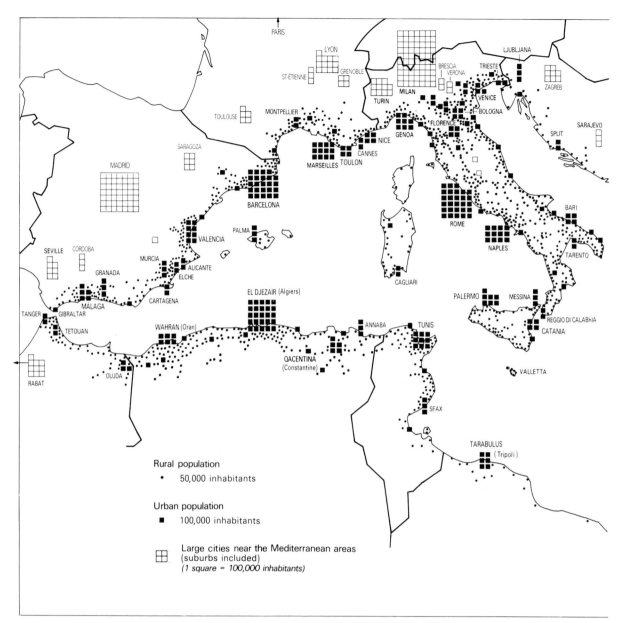

FIG. 1.8 Population distribution around the Mediterranean basin
Source: Blue Plan.

basin structures are very diverse (rocky or alluvial coasts, broad or very narrow continental shelf, compartmentalized basins, etc.), which changes the ecological conditions of production, and, on the other, the productivity of Mediterranean waters is poor (low level of organic matter, considerable average depth, limited surface area of continental shelves).

In the sea too, human pressures threaten some species such as the grouper or the swordfish, and endanger particularly the posidonia meadows and shallow coastal sea-bottoms. Finally, it should be recalled that the Mediterranean, and particularly its straits and narrow passages between the northern and southern shores, is a major migration route for land-bird life between Europe and Africa (Gilbraltar, Sardinia, Straits of Sicily, Crete, Cyprus, the Dardanelles).

Since human activities continue to increase, the fragility of the environments (the underlying factor in their degradation or disappearance) may in forty years' time lead to appreciable, even radical, changes, which should be taken into account when assessing the findings of the scenarios concerning

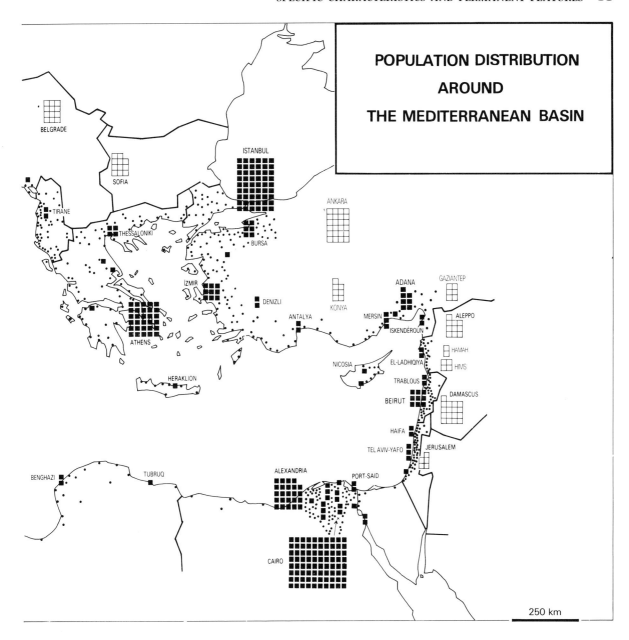

these activities. An attempt will be made in the scenarios, however, to evaluate possible trends in soil erosion and forest cover. But, on the scale of the next fifty years, it can generally be considered that the composition of Mediterranean wild life and plant life will evolve slowly even if there is an increase in the rate of disappearance of species or the introduction of new ones.

5. Socio-cultural features

Without attempting to define a 'Mediterranean identity', about which much has been written, certain socio-cultural features can be pin-pointed which are common to or largely shared by the populations of the coastal regions, despite significant differences deriving from their history, language, or religion. Thus, for thousands of years, from their origins to the contemporary period, Mediterranean civilizations have established themselves in a number of urban sites. A true network of towns and villages was formed very early on, and, as Fernand Braudel noted, the Mediterranean landscape developed around this network, and receives its animation and life from it. The current network, apart from a few exceptions, is the direct inheritance of 2,000 to 3,000 years ago, in particular the Roman empire. Mediterranean towns, all very old, bear the traces of successive civilizations, but the mark of history is still visible in their layout, sites, or stones.

The inheritance of each period is reflected in the urban landscape by layers of new constructions on top of older ones, or by an expansion which for some towns did not extend beyond medieval fortifications until the late eighteenth century. Towns grew through the increasing number of dwellings on the spot, reaching a huge residential density. Densities are higher in the Islamic towns south and east of the basin, and in the urban centres inherited directly from the Middle Ages. A relative slackening of the urban fabric, usually respecting a chequer-board layout, took place in the eighteenth century, but the creation of new urban areas, previously quite common, became infrequent. The old towns expanded but did not change site.

Human settlements in the Mediterranean, with their closely grouped houses, very concentrated and highly integrated, and their old districts gradually surrounded by modern areas, have specific features, despite the diversity of the civilizations they shelter. The problem of water supply continues to predominate. The town is often set in the countryside but rarely includes large green spaces. On the other hand, the traditional home is often planned around small irrigated gardens, forming microcosms in which are to be found the same attitudes as regards water, plants, outside dryness, and also the built environment. The surface area absorbed by new buildings had only a low propensity to grow with rising incomes until quite recently, when, unfortunately, there was a rapid spread, first in the north then increasingly in the south, of an American-style 'peri-urbanization', with horizontal buildings and commercial centres.

Detailed study of the dynamics of human settlements and habitat in the Mediterranean is vital, because inevitably fast urban development encounters very specific problems concerning human activities as a whole, affecting all other components of the environment. On a twenty- to forty-year time-scale, however, it is considered that urbanization will develop on the basis of the existing network of urban sites, which will be taken as the basic data for land use, even if the trend towards uninterrupted spread ('conurbation') is becoming increasingly strong, especially on the coast.

In addition, it should be recognized that some socio-cultural data, such as family relationships, social links, levels of education or health, will evolve within the scenarios as a function of economic development, and therefore cannot be considered as independent variables. Clearly the level of education is a fundamental vector—perhaps the most important one—for both development (adaptation to change, family-planning, responsibility for and mastery of technologies, spatial management, etc.) and the environment (teaching about daily life, living phenomena, functioning of systems, etc.). The same applies to the level of health, which will be taken into consideration especially because of its impact on population parameters, without being the subject of specialized prospective studies in the scenarios.

In the final analysis, in the Mediterranean as elsewhere, the evolution of interrelations between people and their environment will be largely conditioned by their perception of the environment, and by their behaviour towards it and towards the natural resources on which they depend.

Changes in attitudes and behaviour have necessarily been taken into account in the Blue Plan prospective study, but mainly at the level of the major types of hypotheses forming part of the construction of scenarios. However, these variations can scarcely be quantified. At the same time it can be considered that a 'common stock' of behaviour exists in the Mediterranean, with deep cultural or religious roots. These attitudes are usually related to certain realities and permanent features of the environment, and they underlie basic economic traditions. Thus, agriculture and farming practices have over the centuries made sparing use of land, soil, water, and the countryside. Land-tenure patterns differ from one country to another, but have common features. Food consumption depends on age-old traditions, always tinged with frugality. Attitudes concerning nature reflect the very old 'anthropization' of nature, which Mediterranean people over the centuries have been more inclined or more prompted to tame rather than to protect.

The contemporary cultural environment is destabilized by the massive intrusion of a rootless urban life-style and the arrival of the communication and consumer society, either through the influence of tourists or the viewing of foreign audio-visual productions. The media carry issues which have virtually no base in the local environment. They bombard local populations with references and models more related to the industrialized West than to the Mediterranean reality. A huge task of active instruction is required so that in the future adults and young people will understand the issues, risks, and also the renewal patterns which still provide the Mediterranean world with its values and individuality, even if new kinds of collective behaviour are added to the unchanging ones of the past.

Thus, the major factors of the physical and human geographical context described above were not considered as variables in the Blue Plan scenarios. They evolve slowly compared to the series of changes which the Mediterranean environment is undergoing, and which will be particularly highlighted. However, there can be no question of underestimating the importance of these special characteristics and permanent features. On the contrary, they are considerable constraints, which provide the framework for the various possible kinds of development. Among them, socio-cultural factors, attitudes, habits, and collective or individual behaviour are also levers and vectors which should enable Mediterranean populations to forge a future aimed at lasting development, attentive to the environment.

2 Time-Scales and Geographical Delimitations

1. Time scales and spans

A prospective study focuses on what could be the future in a given period. The choice of this period depends on the speed of the changes studied. Even if at present the rate of change everywhere tends to accelerate, that of economic, social, human, and environmental transformation varies greatly depending on the factors involved. The time-spans chosen as 'horizons' for the Blue Plan scenarios must be able to absorb the different lengths of change in a coherent fashion.

With regard to the environment, it takes a century to renew a forest, several decades to eliminate the most common forms of pollution from the soil or water, and only a few years to destroy a landscape with concrete. By 2025 the water of Mediterranean rivers would have been renewed one thousand times, that of lakes and shallow-ground water one to a few dozen times, whereas the water of deep aquifers and glaciers will remain virtually unchanged. The abrupt nature of some disastrous phenomena should not disguise the deep truth, that most environmental features, with their linkages and cumulative mechanisms, evolve slowly, often insidiously, and that action intended to counteract degradation requires a considerable amount of time.

Thus, soil erosion, which can be spectacular after a torrential storm, is more often a barely perceptible phenomenon: 2–3 mm a year. But in the twenty years between 1980 and 2000 this amounts to 5 cm of fertile soil lost, and by 2025 more than 10 cm. This is a substantial amount for thin soil layers and could, moreover, be multiplied by a factor of four in the case of soil on slopes. At the same time, any effort to protect or rehabilitate soil will require continuous work over a very long period.

The case is similar for development. The 'state' of the year 2000 is already determined by decisions adopted, investments allocated, and regulations enacted over the past few years. But the range of possibilities opens broadly for a more distant horizon,

and very divergent trends, fraught with consequence for many Mediterranean countries, can be envisaged for 2025. One example, among others, may be taken from the energy sector. It is likely that between 2000 and 2025 the oil-producing Mediterranean countries will have to stop their exports—a source of foreign currency and investment for development—or even become importers following the depletion of their reserves and the increase in their domestic consumption.

Technological evolution also requires time. The potential of production techniques and consumption structures for change—even transformation—is both considerable and unpredictable. The introduction of modern techniques for irrigation, for the selection of high-yield plant varieties, or for natural-gas liquefaction illustrates this time-dimension. What will happen in a few decades, with the use of biotechnology in agriculture, the spread of information technology, and the transformation of communication methods ? An excessively short-term view conceals these issues, and obscures the need to prepare now for the major choices to be made in the future.

Lastly, trends in the social and cultural domains follow hidden paths, influenced by both the 'long term' and passing fashion. Attitudes and habits hold back the necessary transformation of perceptions and behaviour. Education and the heightening of awareness require long-term action.

Thus, a relationship had to be established in the Blue Plan between, on the one hand, the time-span of environmental changes and the time needed to counteract them and, on the other, the length of time required for economic and social change, in an effort to examine a possible or desirable future. Incorporation of these time-scales into the study meant choosing reference horizons. The Mediterranean countries chose the year 2000 as the intermediate horizon and the year 2025 as the

BOX 2A. **Some time-scales**

'Renewal' of the Mediterranean Sea (c.90 years)

The water-flow in the Mediterranean is very complex, and in addition the structure of the sea-bed makes the basin a trap for sediment. It takes about 250 years for water to intermix vertically. Hence, the concept of 'renewal' scarcely corresponds to a physical reality, but helps to form an idea of the water-balance. The total volume of the sea is approximately 3,700,000 km³. Inputs from rivers (500 km³) and precipitation (900 km³), together with the inflow through the Dardanelles (400 km³), are low compared to the inflow through the Strait of Gibraltar (38,000 km³), which gives a 'renewal' time of about ninety years. Inflows are offset by losses from evaporation, and especially by the outflow through Gibraltar, which is almost as important as the inflow.

The forest (15–200 years)

In order the build up a stand or a successful plantation it takes:

- 15–25 years for poplar;
- 50–70 years for wild cherry or Douglas fir;
- 80 years for fir or walnut;
- up to 200 years for oak.

Coastal urbanization (25 years)

Twenty-five years were enough for the dense or sprawling—and often disorganized—urbanization of most of the Languedoc and Provençal coasts in France, of the Costa Brava or the Balearic Islands in Spain, or of Sicily in Italy, thus considerably changing the landscape, life-styles, and very nature of management problems. At the same time, 9 per cent of the French Mediterranean coast, i.e. 21,000 ha covering 148 km of coast, was bought by the state to protect part of the remaining natural areas ('Conservatoire du littoral').

Disappearance of the monk seal (15 years)

Formerly widespread in the Mediterranean between the Azores and the Black Sea, the monk seal (*Monachus Monachus*) would probably have disappeared by now without recent efforts not only to protect it but also to organize its survival. In 1987 there were only about 350 specimens left in the world, most of them near the coast of the Aegean Sea.

Waste-water treatment (40 years)

Sewage systems are a long-term problem. It will have taken ten years for the percentage of the coastal population connected to the system (including tourists) to rise from 20 per cent to 36 per cent in France, and it will not reach 60 per cent until 1995. In Israel it took twenty-five years for treatment rates for the resident population to rise from 26 per cent (1960) to 61 per cent (1985), the proportion of recycled waste growing from 6 per cent to 36 per cent over the same period. In Turkey investment programmes estimate forty years for 54 per cent of the urban population to be equipped by 2025.

long-term horizon, thus recognizing the significance of the quarter-century between 2000 and 2025.

Taking 1985 as the reference year, and on the basis of the recent past (going back usually to 1970), it is possible, with the horizon of 2000, to envisage the continuation of trends already under way and decisions that may be taken between now and 2000 with a reasonable margin of certainty. A range of possible futures opens up as from the end of the 1990s. With the horizon of 2025 it is possible to take into consideration the time-scales of ecological responses and of technological development and innovation. This horizon, however, is more uncertain as regards economic and social life and changes in attitudes. The period covered by the Blue Plan prospective study goes well beyond the scope of physical planning or national development plans and programmes. But because of the slowness of ecological, economic, technological, and societal responses, interactions must be clearly understood now, and a future compatibility sought between necessary development and an environment whose specific features and fragility have been stressed.

2. The variable contours of the Mediterranean area

From the inception of the Blue Plan it was agreed that the project 'should cover the entire Mediterranean basin, namely the Mediterranean Sea, as defined in the Barcelona Convention, and the adjacent coastal zone, where socio-economic activities are largely

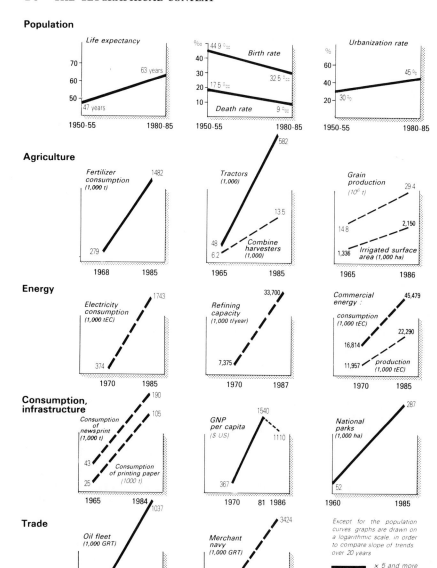

FIG. 2.1 Things may change radically in 20–30 years: The case of Turkey

governed by their relations with the seaboard. These coastal zones might vary in territorial depth from one area to another, depending on the problems to be considered and the nature of the disciplines involved.'

Since major socio-economic choices can only be made at the level of a whole country, and because continuous statistical series are usually available only at this level, the Blue Plan prospective exercise often takes into account the coastal countries of the Mediterranean basin as a whole, covering their entire national territory. This level is therefore broader than the 'eco-regional' component of 'Mediterranean regions' alone, or 'coastal zones' alone.

This level of study, determined by the national reality of economic situations, makes little difference to the analyses for most countries, especially those south and east of the basin, whose most densely populated and economically important regions are those bordering the Mediterranean. For some countries, however, chiefly Spain, France, Yugoslavia, Turkey, and Morocco, the relative importance of their Mediterranean regions, which in addition varies considerably depending on the activity considered, should be borne in mind in the analyses.

At the same time an effort was made to place the Blue Plan studies at the most appropriate geographic level with regard to the problems tackled, in ac-

Population

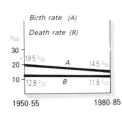

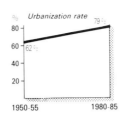

Agriculture

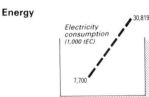

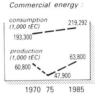

Energy

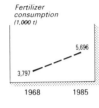

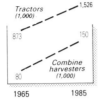

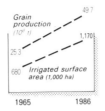

Consumption, infrastructure

Trade

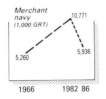

FIG. 2.2 The case of France

cordance with the wishes expressed at the outset. In this respect the global level, on the scale of entire countries, is very interesting even from the environmental viewpoint, strictly speaking. The regulation of and setting of standards concerning industrial pollution are necessarily carried out at the national level because of commerical competition between firms, or even at the level of several countries, as in the case—so important for the Mediterranean—of the European Community. Moreover, most environmental regulations which apply to Mediterranean regions are adopted at the national or international level.

However, the exercise comprises other geo-graphical levels. Thus, for all matters relating to fresh water—including land-based pollution from rivers—the most suitable level of study is that of the hydrological basin: the impact of the Rhone or Po waters, for instance, may originate in non-Mediterranean regions. So watersheds were selected as the geographical context for the prospective study of water requirements and resources, a vital factor in relationships between the environment and development for the entire region. Nevertheless, those areas of the watersheds in countries which do not border the Mediterranean, especially with regard to the Rhone and the Nile, were considered 'external'.

In fact, the concept of a 'Mediterranean region'

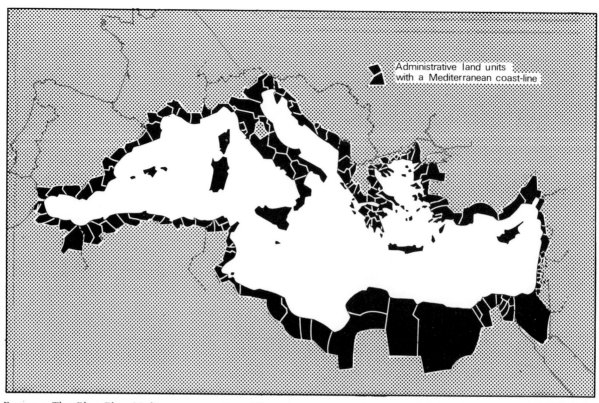

Administrative land units
with a Mediterranean coast-line

FIG. 2.3 The Blue Plan Mediterranean regions. There is no commonly accepted delineation of the Mediterranean region. For most purposes, particularly population, urbanization, tourism, and coastal activities, the Blue Plan regional prospective studies had to be based on a suitable administrative definition, namely the territorial units located on the coast and for which statistical data are available. For some countries like Italy and Greece these cover a very large portion of the country. For others, including Morocco or Syria, only a small part of the country is thus covered. For certain subjects a broader geographical basis was used, namely the hydrographic boundaries of the watershed.

has for many years been the subject of debate among geographers, botanists, climatologists, economists, and sociologists, and although many definitions exist, and are equally valid for a given topic, none of them can be used for all purposes. As to the idea of a 'coastal zone' it depends greatly on local topography, and its depth on the nature of the subject studied.

These conditions led to the choice of an operational definition to meet the practical needs of the Blue Plan scenarios. In each country all the administrative territorial units located on the coast were chosen as Mediterranean regions. These units form decentralized components of the executive authority (provinces, departments, governorates, etc.), for which statistical data are available, notably regarding population growth. Aside from the islands which were taken as a whole, the Mediterranean region thus considered forms a continuous coastal strip, whose depth varies but does not usually exceed 100 km. This division is clearly a practical one, but

it does not diverge too much from a frequently used biogeographical delimination, that of the area in which the olive-tree grows.

Whatever the borders chosen for the study of different problems, the Blue Plan usually considers the Mediterranean basin as a whole and does not subdivide it into smaller geographical units. Contrasting economic conditions, however, often make it necessary to distinguish what is happening on the southern and eastern shores from the situation on the northern shore. In this respect, use of the terms 'northern countries' and 'southern and eastern countries' clearly does not imply a uniform situation in each of these two groups, but stresses the importance of contrasts. Turkey is often in an intermediate position, forming a 'hinge' between the two groups. Depending on the matter under review, it will be included either with the northern group (for certain economic sectors in particular) or with the southern and eastern group (notably for population growth and urbanization).

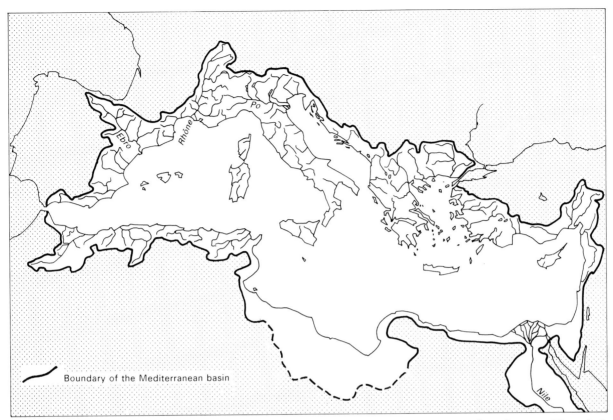

FIG. 2.4 The Mediterranean watershed. For the sake of clarity small rivers are not indicated on this map. Watershed boundaries in very arid areas are approximate.

Source: adapted from J. Margat (1988).

Lastly, a study at the overall level of the basin clearly cannot 'go down' to the geographical levels of individual countries' coastal zones. For regions of very special importance, more detailed local or national prospective studies would doubtless be very valuable, particularly with a view to physical planning. These could use to advantage the methods followed and the general findings obtained at the level of the basin as a whole.

II The Scenarios: Choice of Hypotheses

3 Why Use Scenarios?

Since the main object of the Blue Plan is to study the relationships between certain kinds of development and the Mediterranean environment, the starting-point had to be the choice of the elements of the 'Mediterranean system', and more specifically:

- the main 'components' of the environment;
- the main 'sectors' of economic activity.

The determining factor when making this choice was the importance of interactions between these elements: the impact of economic activity on the environmental component and feedback effects on development due to changes in these components (growing scarcity of resources, degradation of certain media, etc.). In addition, the most appropriate tool had to be identified to obtain the desired results by simulating a number of potential trends in the Mediterranean system. The 'scenario method' seemed to be the most suitable.

1. The relevance of exploring the future

During the long period of relative economic stability in the world from 1950 to 1970, assumptions about future developments could be based on trends which seemed to be well established. This was the period, to some extent a good one, of forecasting. In the last fifteen years, however, the world, including, among other regions, the Mediterranean basin, has embarked on a period of unrest and uncertainty. It would be even more useful to forecast the future, but this needs a sound basis—or, in more technical terms, 'smooth statistical variations'—which is no longer available to decision-makers or officials. Should one then be resigned to inaction, shutting out creative imagination and just reacting to events as they occur? Not necessarily, because there is still one certainty: that *something* will happen.

By combining certain assumptions in a coherent way, a series of gradual 'changes' can be defined which make it possible to explore the outcome of the hypotheses (termed an 'if ... then ...' sequence).

To construct an initial change sequence, a cautious starting-point would be several well-identified 'major trends' whose potential repercussions can be anticipated. But this is not enough: the exercise has to be pursued further, as precisely the last fifteen years have shown that these trends have often had to be revised. Hence the need to deviate from them in order to broaden the exploration as far as possible, without excluding events that are not easy to foresee (if only in terms of predicting the date on which they may occur) but not unlikely: hazards or 'surprises' to which systems are usually all the more vulnerable because the event had been considered less likely, impossible, or even unthinkable. The established hypotheses can be qualitatively very realistic but quantitatively arbitrary, without losing their relevance or the validity of the conclusions.

2. What is a scenario?

One of the main features of a scenario is the establishment of a link—a pathway—between the present and the future. This link or pathway is not haphazard; it is constrained by two factors—the initial hypotheses and the rules of the game. A scenario rests basically on a set of hypotheses, or assumptions. Whether these hypotheses are 'upstream' and general (focusing on international economic trends, population growth, or technological advances), or 'downstream', more practically oriented or sectoral (concerning the choice of export crop or the trends in types of tourist, for instance), they must always be clearly explained and justified. These fundamental hypotheses which make it possible to construct scenarios must respect a number of rules, and must be:

- clear, in order to be understood by all;
- probable, which does not exclude hazards;
- consistent, both internally among themselves, and at all levels;
- relevant, in terms of the desired objectives; and lastly
- adequate, i.e. sufficiently large in number to cover a wide range of possible futures, but not

so many as to be redundant, or produce more combinations than can be handled.

Choosing these hypotheses is the first of the major difficulties in any exercise in formulating a scenario. Once chosen, even if they are not recalled at every moment, they must always be kept in mind.

On the basis of a clearly defined initial image, these main hypotheses make it possible to stage certain events (hence the term 'scenario') according to a sequence subject to the rules of the game, an internal logic. The basic difference between a scenario and a mere image of the future stems from this staging of events, in other words, the 'pathway' mentioned above. This is built up in 'stages', e.g. five- or ten-year periods, which must be:

- inherently possible (barring disasters—usually excluded from normal scenarios—trends must show a certain continuity);
- consistent (a finding obtained in one area must not be incompatible with another elsewhere).

Establishing a pathway of this kind also makes it possible to calculate the cost of the resources to be mobilized, the length of time they will be needed, and the deadlines by which decisions must be taken, bearing in mind the period of implementation.

The consistency fundamental in the choice of hypotheses must be maintained all along the pathway. Maintaining consistency throughout a scenario is therefore the second major difficulty in the exercise: consistency between sectors, between activities within a given sector, between activities and available resources, between activities and the supporting capacity of the environment, etc. Hence the paramount importance of the 'feedback loops': discontinuities, the 'warning lights' in the scenarios, are essentially breaks in consistency. Where should the path stop? Where should images be 'frozen' in the scenario? Clearly at the selected horizons: in the case of the Blue Plan, the years 2000 and 2025 (the necessarily arbitrary nature of these dates is admitted).

In brief, a scenario must necessarily comprise four components: an initial or starting image, a choice of hypotheses, a pathway, and an image of the final situation (with possible intermediate images), the whole linked by an internal logic, i.e. the rules of the game. The 'images' are simplified pictures of reality or of the future. Some features of the final (or intermediate) images obtained by induction or the consistent extension of quantified findings are given for didactic purposes, or to facilitate comparison with the starting image.

3. How to use scenarios?

The figures obtained from the scenarios should not be given undue importance, nor should they be erroneously considered accurate. The interest of the scenarios lies far more in their ability to highlight trend mechanisms, in the effect of their interactions (some effects may prove to be counter-intuitive, even perverse), and especially in the comparison that can be made of the outcome of different trend hypotheses. As with all tools, however, they have their limitations and it is important to know how to use them to provide a coherent framework for reflecting on the future, making it possible to understand the interactions between various issues. Moreover, the way to use the scenarios varies according to whether they concern:

- events which may happen, but over which influence can barely—or not at all—be exerted, within the context of both major trends and unexpected events. Scenarios therefore help in preparing to react for the best, avoiding 'surprises';
- events on which influence can be exerted. The scenarios make it possible to examine several alternatives and compare their outcome (the choice of specific development or environment policies, for instance).

Finally, when assessing scenarios a posteriori, it is important to distinguish between those which proved incorrect because they were completely unrealistic (in this case the choice of hypothesis is usually at fault, and possibly the rules of the game) and those which proved incorrect because . . . they were correct. The energy sector offers a good example. Because most of the scenarios in the 1970s led to images of shortages, development failures, and economic bankruptcy, many governments and economic agents had to and did take drastic measures to save energy and thus avoid the very pessimistic future that the scenarios had depicted. Were they then useless or unfruitful?

When a number of scenarios are available, the first step is to assume a 'position' within them. This position has to be regularly reviewed, as one may move gradually from one scenario to another. A set of scenarios has to be regarded as a permanent tool, which must be managed on a regular basis and kept up to date.

4 Choice of the Environmental Components

In order to define the 'Mediterranean system'—subject of the scenarios—its various elements have first to be selected: the components of the environment, then the sectors of development activity. If the features of the Mediterranean region mentioned in Part I are considered as relatively stable, environmental 'components', on the contrary, evolve faster, especially under the effect of economic and social development. They may be considered as 'variables' in work focused on the horizons 2000 and 2025. Within the Blue Plan perspective, it is important to choose the most significant and relevant environmental components as compared to the development activities which will affect them, in order to define and understand the dynamics of the system of relationships between the environment and development.

Five main subsystems or 'components' of the overall Mediterranean environment system, related to its distinctive features, were selected:

- the soil;
- inland water;
- forests;
- the coast;
- the sea.

The geographical extension of these environments plays a special role by enabling them to provide a medium for various human activities.

1. Soil

The soil, depending on its features, fulfils two essential functions, the basis of many activities:

- *Use in economic production.* In this case, the chemical composition, structure, and evolutive dynamics of the soil play a crucial role. This production could be:
  - agricultural, in broad terms (agriculture strictly speaking, stock-breeding, and forests), and involving essentially the surface layer;
  - industrial, involving both the surface layer

(stone, clay, peat, etc.), and the subsoil (extraction or storage activities), in which the soil itself plays only a transitory role.

In terms of surface area, agricultural production is by far the most important (Figs. 4.1, 4.2).

- *Use as a support for man and his activities,* starting with homes and urbanization, infrastructure (roads, airports, dams, etc.), industrial installations, etc. Although they cover a smaller surface area, these activities too often invade some of the most fertile land and make it sterile (e.g. the expansion of Cairo into the Nile valley and delta).

Much Mediterranean land was almost entirely wooded until the current historical period. The conquest of agriculture led to the disappearance of plant cover, though it also ensured, at least in the beginning, the protection or conservation of the soil. Then major deforestation took place, the work of institutions or systems outside the rural sector whose objectives were other than agricultural (building of merchant and military fleets, construction of towns, or production of energy for blast-furnaces at the beginning of the industrial era and for crafts). There were many cases of over-exploitation, with dramatic consequences during past centuries. Thucydides and Plato already regretted what was happening in Greece!

Each population increase led to the cultivation of marginal land, including the slopes. As long as the feeding requirement—for men and beasts—was not too heavy, and farmers had the time and energy to look after their fields and soil (by bringing soil back up the slope when it had been carried down by run-off, or by building terraces), soil remained on the mountains. Local over-population, parcelling out, clearing for various purposes, and over-grazing, both on grassland and in forests, are at the origin of the degradation or disappearance of protective plant cover and the development of erosion from run-off on the farmed or grazed slopes, especially on the loose and crumbly soil in some Mediterranean regions (Italy, Morocco, etc.).

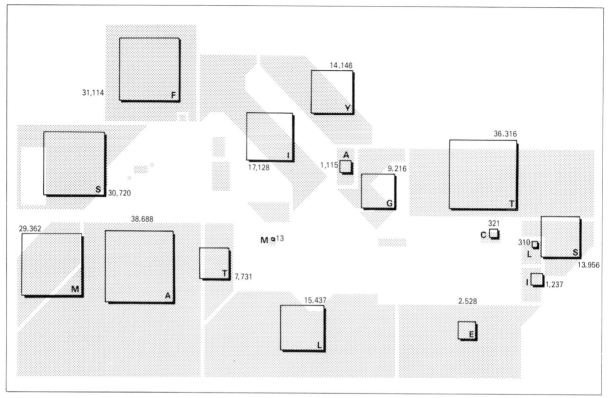

FIG. 4.1 Utilized agricultural land in the Mediterranean countries, 1986 (1,000 ha)
Source: *Production Yearbook* (FAO, 1987).

BOX 4A. **Soil, water, erosion**

A few examples of the sediment load of Mediterranean watercourses are given below.

Tunisia. The Medjerda, at 75 km from its mouth, has an average annual solid load of 21.5m. t of sediment; the average concentration of particles is 30 g/l, which means that the level of erosion in the drainage basin is 1,020 t km²/year.

Yugoslavia. In Yugoslavia the direct damage caused by erosion has been estimated at more than 1.3 per cent of the country's annual GNP. This is only part of the total loss.

Analyses made at the mouth of the Velika Morava show that in 24 hours the river carries 1,312m. m³ of mud, containing 850 t of nitrogen, 33 t of phosphorous, and 85 t of potassium, equal to a 20-cm layer of fertile soil over an area of 500 ha.

Water erosion can also be assessed in the form of:

- loss of potentially productive topsoil (loss of solid organic and mineral matter can also be considered as a loss of nutrients);
- accumulation of sediment, depending on particle size, in low-lying areas (including dam reservoirs and port zones);
- the instability of watercourse banks, associated with stronger and muddier floods;
- inflow of suspended solid matter into the sea, one of the principal ways of introducing pollutants (organic, inorganic, heavy metals, particles, chemicals, etc.).

Water erosion is not the only threat to Mediterranean soil. Two other agents can contribute to it:

- the wind, on the southern borders of the basin, but also to the east and in Spain, in flat areas or on gentle slopes;

- salinization, developing on irrigated land: it is an underlying threat, which recurs sooner or later in the case of poor management of irrigation and drainage networks.

The recent increase in populations to be fed, partly concentrated on the coast, led to an intensification

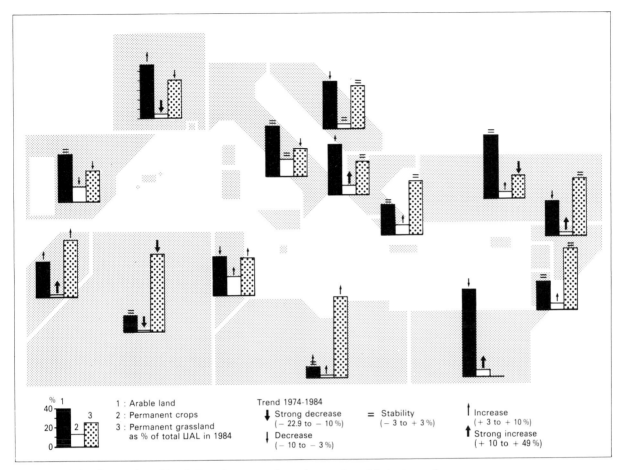

FIG. 4.2 Utilized agricultural land: Distribution and trends, 1976–1986, by type of use
Source: Production Yearbook (FAO, 1987).

of soil exploitation. The mechanization of ploughing (giving a deeper furrow), the reduction of fallow land, the gaining of new land at the expense of grazing land (to the detriment of stock-breeding, i.e. with a reduction in organic inputs), the subsequent deterioration of soil structure, and changes in the soil's water balance also serve to increase the vulnerability of soil to degrading agents. In the Mediterranean basin, however, pedogenesis is virtually blocked (barring a few areas of damp woodland), so that soil lost is virtually gone for ever.

Mediterranean land with its soil, long exploited and essential for the survival of the population, is a scarce and non-renewable resource. It has been chosen as the first 'environmental component'.

2. Inland water

Inland water fulfils many functions:

• *A biological function.* Precipitation, vital for plant life and agriculture, is a natural factor of production. Water is also a habitat for aquatic life.

• *A production function, as of raw material,* essential for various purposes and exploited for:

• direct human consumption: drinking water is consumed in a minimal amount compared to other uses, but required quality is currently at risk in many Mediterranean countries;

• domestic use for households (mostly met by drinking water);

• agricultural production, through irrigation, the basic method of intensifying and regulating agriculture in the Mediterranean basin;

• industrial production, either as an intermediate product (for example as a solvent in manufacturing processes), or as a cooling agent (for most processes, notably for power stations);

• energy production, through hydroelectricity (without deterioration in quality).

• *Transport and leisure functions:*

• as a medium for river transport;

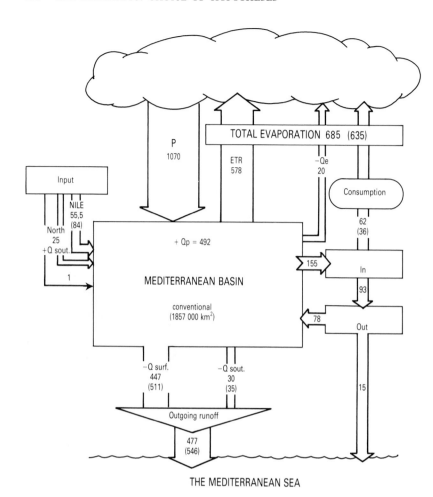

FIG. 4.3 Water balance in the Mediterranean basin. The chart gives the current mean flow: figures in brackets correspond to previous flow-rates.

Source: Blue Plan (J. Margat).

Unit : billion m³/annum
P : Rainfall.
ETR : Real evapotranspiration
+Qp : Runoff potential (=effective rainfall)
−Qe : Runoff loss via evaporation
+Q sout : Underground input
−Q surf : Outgoing surface runoff → sea
−Q sout : Outgoing underground runoff → sea

• as a recreational environment;
• as a carrying agent for evacuating waste water (this irreplaceable function is supplemented by a self-cleaning function, nowadays quite inadequate).

Fig. 4.3 summarizes the overall water balance in the Mediterranean basin.

At the regional level, water is a scarce resource and poorly distributed. The increase in functions and uses implies the possibility of conflict, both between the various human uses (such as production and *in situ* use) and between these and the natural functions. Table 4.1 summarizes the situation of

water supply and demand (on the basis of uses) in the Mediterranean catchment area in the middle of the 1980s. The first stage consists of quantifying physical water resources (columns 2 and 3). These concern available resources, i.e. excluding rainwater but including spontaneous outflows from neighbouring countries. These resources are renewable. Resources deriving from the exploitation of reserves such as fossil water, considerable for most African countries, are therefore not included, neither are various non-conventional resources, such as the production of fresh water from the desalinization of sea water, etc. (The total excludes duplications due

Table 4.1 Water supply and demand in the Mediterranean catchment area

Catchment area	Estimated population (m.)	Supply (resources) (Gm³/yr)		Demand (Gm³/yr)		Exploitation index ratios	
		Total water resources	Stable or stabilized resources	Water distributed (draw-offs)	Net consumption	Supply: (4) in relation to (2)	Demand: (4) in relation to (3)
	(1)	(2)	(3)	(4)	(5)	(6)	(7)
Spain	~ 16.00	31.10	7.500	13.800	11.700	38	184
France, Monaco	12.40	74.00	35.200	15.750	~ 2.370	21	45
Italy	57.20	187.00	30.500	46.350	~ 15.000	25	152
Malta	0.33	~ 0.03	0.023	0.023	0.020	~ 77	100
Yugoslavia	~ 2.40	77.50	11.500	1.500	0.280	2	13
Albania	2.20	21.30	6.500	~ 0.200	0.036	1	3
Greece	9.44	58.60	7.700	7.000	3.650	12	91
Turkey	11.90	~ 67.00	15.600	6.700	3.270	10	43
Cyprus	0.66	0.90	0.270	0.540	~ 0.400	60	200
Syria	~ 1.70	4.00	2.300	0.880	0.510	22	38
Lebanon	3.16	~ 4.00	~ 2.800	0.600	0.380	15	21
Israel	4.34	~ 1.30	0.280	~ 1.500	~ 0.950	115	536
Egypt	46.70	57.30	55.800	55.900	~ 39.000	98	100
Libya	~ 2.30	~ 0.70	0.200	1.600	1.250	229	800
Tunisia	5.50	3.10	~ 1.500	~ 2.000	1.450	65	133
Algeria	15.00	10.90	2.500	1.700	~ 1.000	16	68
Morocco	2.20	3.80	0.900	1.100	0.570	29	122
TOTAL	193.	602.	. .	157.	82.	. .	. .

Source: Blue Plan (J. Margat, 1988).

to spontaneous exchanges between neighbouring countries in the basin, in the order of 28,000m. m³/year). Not all of these resources are necessarily accessible. The most available are the naturally stable flows of watercourses and ground water, or flood-flows regulated by existing installations (reservoirs) (column 3, which has not been totalled as there is some uncertainty about these installations). Gross draw-offs for all uses combined, which mobilize stable, regulated and also unstable flows of water, are equal to the volume of water allocated (column 4). Part of this draw-off is not returned to the waters of the natural environment. Calculated according to general coefficients, this part represents the net volume of water consumed (column 5). Two ratios make it possible to compare supply and demand:

- the ratio of draw-offs to the total resources— (4) over (2);
- the ratio of draw-offs to the stable flows—(4) over (3).

It is worth noting that for the Mediterranean basin:

- the construction of dams has increased natural regular resources by at least 55 per cent (20 per cent from the Nile development alone);

- of the 154,000m. m³ drawn off per year, about 72 per cent (110,000m. m³) are used for irrigated agriculture, 10 per cent for the production of drinking water supplied to urban agglomerations (mainly for domestic use), and 16 per cent for industries not linked to the water supply, including power-stations;
- a large part of the water discharged into the Mediterranean (balance of theoretical resources minus net volumes consumed—column (2)—column (5), i.e. 486,000m. m³/year) carries sewage, which greatly reduces its value as an available resource from the qualitative standpoint. High exploitation rates in most countries imply low levels of future availability (20 per cent for Egypt, for instance), even nil in extreme cases (Israel, Libya, and Malta, for example, where exploitation rates already exceed 100 per cent).

The volume of polluted water discharged into the sea on the one hand, and potential conflicts linked to growing demand to meet the needs of agricultural intensification and of urbanization (drinking water) on the other, have led to the choice of inland water as the second 'environmental component'.

3. Forests

The functions of the Mediterranean forest have evolved over the centuries. They are currently as follows:

● *Ecological function.* This includes the protection of soil on slopes, stabilization of water-flows, and conservation of plant and animal genetic resources by the protection of increasingly threatened habitats and ecological niches. This function is crucial in the Mediterranean region.

● *Economic production function.* If appropriately managed, the forest is a renewable resource. It benefits from the prudent withdrawal of its growth for human requirements, a practice which can maintain its other functions while ensuring its continuation. In the Mediterranean wood production, compared to that of the temperate northern or tropical forest, is poor in quantity and quality, even if the often relict vegetation is of remarkable genetic variety and wealth. Nevertheless, the introduction of certain species, such as the eucalyptus from Australia or pines from America, furthered the development of industrial plantations (especially for paper pulp). The noble species supply high-quality wood for various crafted goods. The forest also provides local populations with other products (cork, resin, honey, seeds, etc.).

Aside from these products, the forest has two other uses which take advantage of its natural productivity in wood, grass, and leaves:

● supplying fuel (from gathering, and also often poorly controlled felling) for domestic needs such as cooking and heating and for the needs of local crafts;

● providing grazing land, as the forest can, without detriment, feed a certain number of animals (under conditions of access controlled to ensure the reproduction of grass, leaves, and wood).

Over-exploitation for fuel or grazing, however, leads to the degradation or even disappearance of woodland, because the regeneration of over-exploited species can no longer take place.

● *Social function.* By this is meant use of the forest for recreation, leisure, and the landscape, a function that is not always well understood. In the north of the basin, the surface area of woodland is increasing in the Mediterranean regions because of abandon-

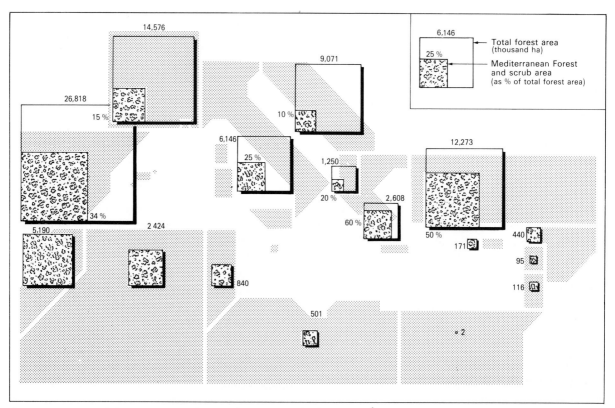

FIG. 4.4 Types of forest in the Mediterranean, 1980s. This map illustrates the proportion of Mediterranean bioclimatic-type forest compared to the total forested area of each country.
Source: Blue Plan (H. Marchand, 1988)/FAO.

ment of land previously under cultivation. Neglect of the forest encourages increasingly widespread fires (an average of 200,000 ha of forest are destroyed each year by fires started maliciously or through negligence).

Damage to the forest threatens its ecological function in particular. The serious turn taken by trends, though not involving all coastal states in the same way, was the reason for choosing the forest as the third 'environmental component'.

4. The coast

The coast is a natural area where land, river, and sea influences meet and interact, with many transitions and gradations stemming from the variety of geological media, soil, humidity, and salinity conditions, geomorphologic processes, microclimates, etc. As regards the Mediterranean basin, coastal environments are fragile and of great morphological, biological, and geographical diversity.

Used without undue damage since ancient times, the coast has in a few decades become the most desirable area for the more or less haphazard location of many activities. Hence a double set of growing conflicts: conflicts between competing activities on the one hand, and between the activities and the environment on the other. These involve:

● *Conflicts between competing activities.* Examples are:

- urbanization, either dense or sprawling, concentrated on the coast (encroachment by secondary residences);
- agriculture (traditional crops, market gardening, horticulture);
- fishing and aquaculture;
- quarrying (sand, gravel, salt, etc.);
- industry, because of easy access to imported raw materials and outlets on domestic and/or foreign markets;
- energy (loading and unloading ports, refineries, thermal power-stations);
- industry–port complexes;
- commercial and fishing ports;
- airports;
- tourism, the most recent activity but currently developing very strongly, and a big user of coastal areas (hotels, sports grounds, camp sites, marinas, etc.).

Most of these activities are mutually exclusive, or have not yet found good solutions for coexistence.

● *conflicts among these activities and the environment.* All these activities exert considerable qualitative and quantitative pressure on resources and the environment, especially on land, inland water, and nearby forests, as well as the coastline and coastal seabed, with sometimes irreversible consequences:

- from the decreasing permeability of soil to the definitive loss of agricultural land;
- from the salinization of ground water to the discharge of waste water and chemicals;
- from deforestation to the stripping of age-old landscapes;
- from the disturbance to the physical destruction of habitats, through variations in turbidity due to industrial waste or in temperature because of discharges by thermal power-stations into the sea, or through the disappearance of posidonia meadows (spawning grounds or nurseries, whose destruction could upset all or part of a biological or food-chain);
- from the disturbance of geomorphological processes (the disappearance of beaches, for instance) to the mechanical destruction of organisms through over-fishing or crushing in cooling-circuit turbines, etc.

With regard to the coastline strictly speaking (Fig. 4.5 and Table 4.2), accretion coasts (beaches, dunes, marshes, lagoons, estuaries, deltas) depend on the

Table 4.2 Distribution of coasts according to type

	Type of coast			
	Rocky		Accretion	
	km	%	km	%
Spain[a]	80	3	2,370	92
France	1,090	64	613	36
Italy	3,181	40	4,772	60
Malta	180	100	0	0
Yugoslavia	4,893	80	1,223	20
Albania	125	30	293	70
Greece	10,500	70	4,500	30
Turkey	3,115	60	2,076	40
Cyprus	391	50	391	50
Syria	119	65	64	35
Lebanon	146	65	79	35
Israel	10	5	190	95
Egypt	50	5	900	95
Libya	90	5	4,680	95
Tunisia	260	20	1,040	80
Algeria	600	50	600	50
Morocco	256	50	256	50
TOTAL	25,086	54	21,047	46

Note: Figures may vary slightly depending on statistical source.

[a] More than 5% non-natural coast.

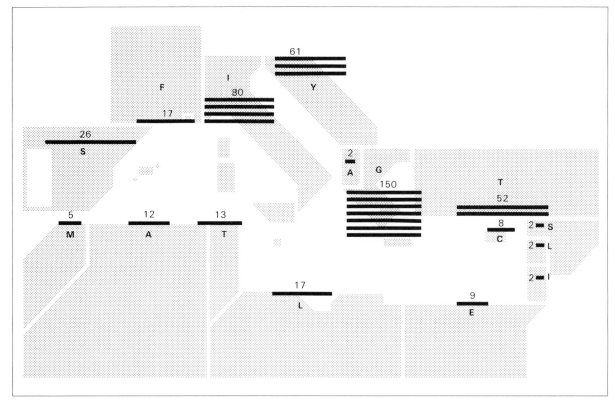

Fig. 4.5 Length of Mediterranean coast, by country (100 km)
Source: Blue Plan.

inputs of land and sea sediment resulting from the effect of natural erosion in watersheds and rocky coasts, and on marine dynamics (waves and swell, currents). These sedimentary coasts are therefore very sensitive to any change in the system of interactions between these elements:

- dams and reservoirs, even far upstream, trap sediment and alter the flow of watercourses;
- changes in plant cover in catchment areas have an effect on sediment loads, which increase and silt up the coast;
- sea-control works block or alter coastal erosion, but also disturb coastal currents and thus accretion zones;
- extraction of materials may reduce the volume of sediment, etc.

This leads, among other things, to a destabilization of deltas and the erosion of beaches, together with silting up in other areas. This last phenomenon is a good example of a 'feedback loop' in which economic activities may considerably degrade the environment (beaches), degradation that in the long term constrains or excludes these activities (seaside tourism). A very different aspect of fears about the Mediterranean coastline is related naturally to the possibility of a long-term rise in the sea-level as a result of the greenhouse effect.

The coast, likely to become an increasingly serious concern for the coastal countries, is an essential 'environmental component' for the Blue Plan prospective study; it could even be considered a 'system' by itself on account of its complexity.

5. The sea

The bonds between the Mediterranean Sea and the economic and social life of the coastal countries are both old and close. The Mediterranean, an area for navigation, contact, and occasionally conflict, has gradually developed other functions:

- *an economic production function*: the sea is a source of food and mineral raw materials;
- *a social function*: it is a preferred area for holidays and recreation;
- *a waste-reception function*, based on its waste-assimilative capacity, which should not be considered as infinite.

The high seas are virtually only used by navies and yachts, the number of which is steadily rising.

Marine transport-lines criss-cross the seas, together with numerous sea-links between the islands. The continental shelf is an area of recent activities such as oil prospection, or more traditional ones, such as fishing, especially on the narrow coastal fringe, where fish stocks are concentrated, since the water is enriched by nearby land-based sources, and conditions are suited to reproduction.

The first two protocols to the Barcelona Convention (Protocol for the Prevention of Pollution of the Mediterranean Sea by Dumping from Ships and Aircraft, 1978, and the Protocol concerning Co-operation in Combating Pollution of the Mediterranean Sea by Oil and other Harmful Substances in Cases of Emergency, 1978) are intended to reduce pollution and its consequences for the whole marine system, and are the first steps in Mediterranean co-operation. A new protocol in preparation, concerning offshore mining, aims in particular at the hazards which could stem from activities on the continental shelf.

The worst pollution, however, is land-based, related to everything that happens, and especially that will happen, around the Mediterranean. This kind of pollution, subject of the protocol on the Protection of the Mediterranean Sea against Pollution from Land-Based Sources, which came into effect in 1983, is to some extent at the beginning and end of the Blue Plan studies. It should be recalled that some of this pollution is atmospheric—roughly 50 per cent for some heavy metals, for example—but the mechanisms by which it spreads are rather poorly known ('aerial catchment areas').

The sea, with regard to human activity, is the fifth 'environmental component' in the Blue Plan studies. Although both an 'input variable' and an 'output variable', it has not been the subject of special study since, as regards pollution at least, this is the responsibility of another part of the Mediterranean Action Plan, the MEDPOL programme.

5 Choice of the Economic Sectors

The chief development sectors were selected to complete the 'Mediterranean system'. After due consideration it was decided to concentrate on five main sectors of activity, all important in their own way and components of what could be called the development 'subsystem'. They are:

- agriculture (or, more specifically, food production);
- industry;
- energy;
- tourism;
- transport.

1. Agriculture

The importance of agriculture in the Mediterranean basin is greater than its share of the GDP—usually lower than 20 per cent—implies. On the one hand, it still provides employment for nearly half the labour force in the countries in the south and east of the basin. On the other, it uses 80–85 per cent of developed water resources and a very large area of land, uses which will grow considerably in the countries south and east of the basin, sometimes in fierce competition with both urbanization and environmental conservation. As a whole, Mediterranean agriculture is unlikely to generate surplus income. Its growth-rates are usually lower than those of overall economic growth, and lower still than those of industrial growth; the gap is widening between these two kinds of economic activity. On both sides of the basin (confining considerations on the northern side to the Mediterranean regions only) agriculture therefore seems to be a basic component of conflict and imbalance, hitherto heightened, rather than reduced, by the economic environment.

Since population growth has been faster than progress in food production, many Mediterranean countries are no longer able to feed themselves, notably in the Maghreb and Egypt, whereas a few decades ago these countries balanced their trade with the sale of agricultural products (Morocco, for example, was a cereal exporter up to the beginning of the 1970s). More or less extensive dry farming has probably reached maximal growth. Small farmers using traditional methods produce yields often under 10 quintals per hectare and marginal crops speed up soil degradation. Potential irrigation areas are few and rudimentary techniques (though occasionally ingenious) use water inefficiently, with significant losses from run-off or evaporation. The density of the rural population is an obstacle to modernization because of the splitting up of farms upon division of an inheritance, with no possibility of increasing the size of plots.

Necessary intensification is beset by other problems. Yields remain low despite modern production techniques, between 10 and 20 quintals per hectare or even less (cereal crops in northern Morocco, Anatolia, or the Syrian Djezireh, for instance), with the risk of pollution from fertilizers and pesticides, and the speeding up of desertification linked to the use of mechanical tools. For irrigation works (such as those in Syria, Turkey, and Morocco) to be efficient and profitable they must be supplemented with work on plots, which does not always happen; in addition, the erosion of upstream soil, often related to deforestation, threatens to silt up the dams in the medium or long term.

Finally, on the northern side most of the markets for 'Mediterranean' produce, such as durum wheat, wine, fruit and vegetables, and olive oil, are faced with an increasingly expensive crisis (substantial increase in payments from the EEC Agricultural Guidance and Guarantees Fund since 1981) and pose a problem in some regions.

How will Mediterranean agriculture respond to the formidable challenges of the coming decades? What systems could meet a demand growing by 4–5 per cent per year? What will be the impact on fragile soils and on water resources already much in demand? What will be the possible long-term contribution of new biotechnologies? How will all this affect development in the rural world? These are all questions to be tackled in the scenarios.

2. Industry

For many years development meant industrial development (does this thinking not still prevail?), which was a necessary stage in it. In the Mediterranean basin, as elsewhere, the industrial sector, unlike the agricultural sector, has usually been given priority—to varying degrees depending on the country and strategy—not only regarding investment, but also with research and development programmes, the promotion of new technologies, assistance in innovation, regional development policies, restructuring, rationalization, and modernization efforts, training expenditure, etc.

Since the end of the Second World War, industrial development in Mediterranean countries has on average been faster than in the world as a whole, and even spectacular in some cases (such as Spain, Yugoslavia, Turkey, Egypt, etc.), usually heavily dominated by public authorities, which radically transformed low-productivity agricultural economies, with rudimentary industrial development, within the span of a few decades. Although industrial development in the countries to the south and east of the Mediterranean basin speeded up after 1970, whereas growth in the northern countries gradually slowed down and stagnated, even with recession in some sectors, major imbalances still exist between north and south: Spain, France, and Italy still concentrate about 85 per cent of the basin's manufacturing industry (taking the whole country into account: 70 per cent considering their Mediterranean regions alone).

Except for oil, natural gas, and phosphates, the mining industry has not developed much in the Mediterranean basin, and is scarcely in a position to stimulate, or elicit, a true industrialization process. The manufacturing industries of the countries in the south and east of the basin, closely related to the spatial distribution of the population, are located in or around the major cities, where it is easier for them to mobilize the necessary labour and find outlets for their production. However, Mediterranean countries have not generally been able to identify competitive market niches (as some newly industrialized countries have done), of a kind likely to ensure a world outlet for a number of manufactured products and enabling them to base their development on the increased growth of exports.

Industrial development in the Mediterranean is heavily concentrated in a few coastal areas : the regions of Barcelona, Valence and Fos-Marseilles, Taranto and Venice, Croatia, the Bay of İzmir, the Alexandrian coast, the coast of the Maghreb, with Tunis, Algiers, etc. This coastal concentration of industry, a source of conflict with other economic activities, is particularly noticeable as regards refining and the major petrochemical complexes (in Sicily and Sardinia, near Marseilles, in Taragona, Porto Marghera, on the Libyan coast at Ras Lanuf, etc).

Industrial pollution has tended to follow the trends in siting (strong growth of basic industries in the south and east) and in structure (more sophisticated industries in the north with greater risk of accidental pollution).

Bearing these factors in mind, what role will industry continue to play in the development of countries to the south and east of the basin, faced with considerable need for manufactured goods, and with changing values and consumption models? Will major installations continue to be located preferably on the coast (considering, among other things, limited water resources in the interior), thus exacerbating the problem of waste water and related pollution hazards? To what degree will existing technology be used to protect the environment? How will the northern countries face up to the greater risk of accidental pollution linked to increasingly sophisticated industries? What will be the importance of north–south or south–south co-operation? All these questions are vital for the future of the Mediterranean countries and will be explored in the scenarios.

3. Energy

Energy, the prerequisite for all activities, the basic—and for many years inexpensive—ingredient of growth, has become one of the key items of economic balances since the beginning of the 1970s.

● It is often a major source of financing the exporting countries' development programmes (for instance, approximately 95 per cent of exports, in terms of value, for a country like Algeria, and 30 per cent of its 1983 budget at the time of the highest prices on the oil market).

● Conversely, it can be a heavy constraint, cause of indebtedness, and even a curb on the development of countries obliged to import it, with market fluctuations further complicating any medium-term planning in both cases.

In fact Mediterranean basin countries can be divided into two categories:

● importing countries on the northern side, together with Turkey, Cyprus, Lebanon, Israel, and Morocco, one of the least-endowed countries with respect to conventional energy resources and whose fuel imports account for some 30 per cent of the total value of imports (and 50 per cent of the value of exports);

- exporting countries, either comparatively small exporters like Syria or Tunisia, medium-sized, like Egypt, or large, like Algeria (oil and especially natural gas, of which it is one of the biggest exporters in the world) and Libya (one of the major oil producers, considering its reserves and resources).

The most industrialized countries in the Mediterranean basin usually resort to every source of energy: coal (domestic or imported), oil, natural gas (especially for the past two decades or so), and hydraulic, geothermal, and nuclear energy (a recent development). The countries south and east of the basin developed their consumption of oil products in particular, which may produce up to 90–95 per cent of their total energy consumption. This trend has only recently been affected by the breakthrough of natural gas, or by coal imports for electricity production, since most of these countries are virtually without any coal resources. Some countries which are currently oil exporters are likely to become importers during the coming decade, following the depletion of their deposits, a development with a tremendous social and economic impact.

Concerning electricity production, a similar variety of sources exists in the north, along with the predominance of oil in the southern and eastern countries (with the exception of natural gas in Algeria). In north-western countries (France and Spain in particular) nuclear energy developed rapidly, then recently slowed down; in other countries the use of coal is increasingly considered. In the medium term the pattern of electricity production is likely to change substantially in most countries.

The considerable growth of the population in Mediterranean cities during the last decades raises huge problems of power distribution and supply—electricity, fuel, motor-fuel, etc.—especially as most other services depend in turn on the availability of energy. Urban energy consumption produces serious problems of air pollution (Rome, Athens, Cairo, Algiers, etc.), not to mention the socio-economic problems related to increasing traffic congestion. On the other hand, in the countryside population pressure is often exerted on increasingly scarce fuel-wood resources for basic domestic needs such as cooking and heating, and local crafts. Fuel-wood

resources are increasingly likely to disappear altogether, contributing to desertification, soil erosion, etc.

From the environmental viewpoint, in addition to the problem of depletion of resources, energy has many aspects in common with industry, often sharing the same kind of chain from source to consumer: production, initial transformation and/or transport, possibly conversion, then distribution. Three aspects should be stressed with regard to the Mediterranean basin:

- heavy reliance on hydrocarbons, likely to continue in many countries;
- importance of the sea for the transport of these hydrocarbons, not only to meet the needs of coastal countries, but also those of non-coastal countries (in northern Europe, for instance), for which the Mediterranean is basically an international route;
- the siting on the coast of a large number of often large-scale power-plants, the source of various kinds of air or water pollution: oil or natural-gas loading or unloading terminals, and soon those for coal; refineries (petrochemical complexes were mentioned along with industry); and thermal power-stations: these installations often act as poles of development for other industrial activities, which also set up on the coast and may lead to the establishment of true 'power-industry–port' complexes.

How will the developing Mediterranean economies be able to face up to their transformation from exporter to importer of hydrocarbons? What will be the role of new energy technologies, which have made considerable progress over the past couple of decades? What will be the exact share of new sources of energy? Can decentralized solar energy contribute to both solving the fuel-wood crisis and meeting the energy needs of rural populations? On what sources could the inevitable increase of electrical capacity be based, and where will they be located? Will natural gas become the main energy resource in the Mediterranean and a pivot for trade between the northern and southern sides? These are some of the questions which will be tackled in the scenarios.

4. Tourism

With more than 100 million international tourists, the countries of the Mediterranean basin as a whole are the most important tourist destination in the world (it receives about one international tourist in three). Tourism is an activity which concerns all these countries, and all count on its continued expansion, both international and domestic. International tourism accounted for approximately 7 per cent of the Mediterranean countries' GDP on average, fluctuating from less than 1 per cent (Libya) to approximately 10 per cent for countries such as Italy and Spain, and in the order of 12–15 per cent for Malta, Cyprus, and Israel. It covers between 10 and 20 per cent of imports for nearly half the countries. It also provides a large number of jobs, though often seasonal. Seasonality also raises problems as to the timeliness and profitability of investments.

Modern tourism originated on the French and Italian coasts. It gradually spread to all the basin countries, and one of its basic and most dynamic components has been mass tourism in seaside resorts, naturally located on the coast, whose population may swell as much as tenfold in the high season. Sometimes described as an industry, tourism could in fact be more appropriately compared to agriculture with respect to its impact (positive and negative) on the environment, and its features, including an identical risk of over-exploitation of its main resources (starting with its historical sites like Venice, the Acropolis, or Luxor). The water consumption of tourists has an even greater impact because it reaches its peak during the dry season when it is most scarce; it then competes with the water needs of other users. The problem is particularly acute on the islands (the Yugoslavian coast, the Aegean Sea, the Balearic Islands, Djerba, etc.).

The surface area covered by tourist installations seems considerable because of their location (though in fact their importance is more qualitative than quantitative) and the infrastructure required. Forests are threatened by fire, largely because of too many visitors. Wild life and plant life can also become victims of tourist development: underwater fauna because of the growing popularity of skin-diving, and near-shore marine flora because of the expansion of marinas or the increased number of open berths (the Mediterranean basin is the second most important area for nautical tourism in the world, after the Caribbean).

From the socio-cultural viewpoint, some of the largest markets of origin lie outside the Mediterranean basin. However, they are very important in the basin because of their holiday style and cultural influence. It is not always easy to achieve a balance between these two aspects of the tourist industry in terms of relationships between populations: there is the chance of mixing and mutual enrichment of cultures on the one hand, or the likelihood of destabilization or modification of the cultural identity on the other. The sometimes 'synergetic' combination of these effects has, moreover, led experts to introduce the concept of 'saturation' or 'load-limit' for some very popular tourist areas. In fact the impact on fragile environments could be reduced by foresighted integrated planning and sound management practices.

Will world tourism continue to develop at the same rate as in recent decades, and will the Mediterranean still remain the principal destination of international tourism? With the growing concentration on the coast, what lines will Mediterranean countries follow when organizing their tourist areas: either *laissez-faire* (as was usually the case for the 'rivieras') or goal-orientated (concerted and planned development, as in the case of the Languedoc-Roussillon, where the environment was incorporated into plans from the outset)? Will the quality of the environment become one of the chief tourist resources, and how will conflict over use of sites be solved?

5. Transport

The transport sector is sometimes described as 'derivative' to the extent that it reflects the level of activity of the other economic sectors, but both on land and at sea it has a direct link with the environment. In the Mediterranean basin land transport has long been hampered by the compartmentalization caused by the relief, and only recently have roads (with often expensive infrastructure on account of the relief) made it possible to open up the region. Conversely, conditions have long been particularly conducive to the development of maritime transport and the establishment of a dense port network, whose fate depended on economic trends over the centuries. With the opening of the Suez Canal, then the growing importance of oil, the Mediterranean became a transit area used by ships of more than twenty nations. Finally, air transport furthered the development of international tourism in the region and the conclusion of major infrastructure work.

As regards its relationship with the environment, which naturally depends on the kind of transport considered, the transport sector resembles industry to some extent because of the use of machinery and energy consumption, although site coverage is larger, due to its widespread infrastructure. Historical towns and, worse still, many new cities have been unable to adapt to modern transport, and to the virtually unchecked advance of the motor car. Many Mediterranean cities, whose expansion is sometimes blocked by the surrounding mountains or hills (Genoa, Algiers, etc.), are particularly affected by traffic congestion, with its serious economic consequences and, above all, air pollution, which occasionally exceeds the critical level, especially in areas with temperature inversion.

Road transport, often preferred because of its door-to-door facilities—further encouraged in the Mediterranean by 'roll-on, roll-offs'—is a major source of air pollution (nitrogen oxide, lead, poorly burnt hydrocarbons) and water pollution (spills, used oil, chemicals carried by run-off on waterproofed surfaces). Transport infrastructure, organized into more or less dense networks, covers a large surface area, roughly equal to that of a département in France, for instance. In the Mediterranean regions the motorway network is often developed at the expense of good agricultural land in the valleys, with large-scale civil engineering works which cause soil erosion or destroy the landscape. Finally, while roads have undeniably brought men closer together by considerably reducing distances, they have also caused a number of disruptions, between people (two neighbouring villages separated by a motorway are no longer in touch), but especially among animals, by forming an impassable barrier, to the extent of breaking some ecological chains.

The transport of hydrocarbons by sea has a dual impact on the environment: pollution directly related to tankers, and pollution related to the specialized installations located on the coast—not many, but very large in scale. The evolution of these impacts is closely linked to the future of hydrocarbons in the Mediterranean basin and throughout the world, and also to technological progress, such as the replacement of methane tankers by gas pipelines (e.g. the trans-Mediterranean line between Algeria and Italy via Tunisia and Sicily).

How will the various means of transport evolve? Will the Mediterranean air-transport networks extricate themselves from the predominance of major cities? Will a thousand-seater aircraft be developed one day to offload crowds of tourists at airports specially built for their sole needs? Will high-speed trains find their niche between the motor car and the aeroplane? Will urban motor vehicles soon be electric, to solve the problem of air pollution? Is there room for new transport technologies? These are many hypotheses for a limited number of scenarios.

6. Interactions

These economic sectors are not independent. Industry supplies inputs for agriculture, such as fertilizers or machinery; and agriculture provides industry with its raw materials. Energy production requires transport, but there would be no transport without energy. Tourism has an impact at the same time on agriculture, industry, energy and transport, and so on. Nor are the five main components of the environment independent of each other. Soil, water, and the forest form a schematic ecological system: the forest, for example, fixes the soil and retains water. If one of the components is degraded the other two are at risk. This ecological subsystem is itself related to what happens on the coast and in the sea. All the components of the environment are

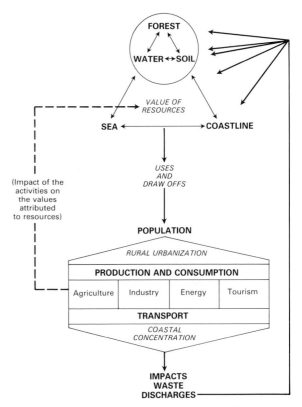

FIG. 5.1 Interactions between environmental components and development activities

thus subject to dynamic interactions, which change with time under the effect of natural evolution, but now increasingly under the effect of human activity related to economic, social, and cultural development. Nothing illustrates this system better than the increasing artificiality of the coast, which affects all the environments and the many relationships between them and man.

However, the complex relationships between the socio-economic parameters of development (growth, employment, infrastructure, etc.) and the environmental components must be explained in order to specify and interpret all meaningful interactions. The various components form ecological systems ('milieux'). By attributing a value to all or part of these environments—currently an economic value in particular, but it could also be a religious, cultural, or social value—man has transformed them into resources. By the use he makes of them, i.e. by his development activities, he modifies environments and resources through direct impact (draw-offs, for example) or through waste, discharges, and so forth. In reality, the large number of milieux, resources, and human activities to be taken into consideration, bearing in mind that each activity can draw off or put back in several different environments, quickly leads to a very complex pattern. For the Blue Plan, however, it had to be simplified, the main point being to highlight and understand the relationship mechanisms of the most important 'chains' or 'feedback loops' for the environment, leading to a better understanding of the dynamics of the whole system.

Fig. 5.1 is an overall diagram of the main components of the environment–development system which will be enlivened in the scenarios.

6 Choice of the 'Dimensions' and Types of Scenarios

Having specified what is meant by a scenario and defined the components chosen to represent the Mediterranean system, we must now proceed:

- to identify the subjects on which the scenario hypotheses will focus;
- to produce a possible ranking of these hypotheses so that they contribute as effectively as possible to overall consistency.

The areas or topics on which the general hypotheses will focus, and which will act as variables, in broad terms, in the scenarios, are called 'dimensions'. The dimensions chosen must be both the most meaningful for the evolution of the Mediterranean system and sufficiently open to lead to contrasting avenues for the future.

One or several values, or rather 'positions' (a term which reflects more accurately the potential complexity of the hypotheses), have been attached to each dimension. These positions may be:

- quantitative, such as population or economic growth-rates; a position may be defined by a single rate, but more often by several (e.g. marriage, birth, mortality rates) or by a composite 'indicator';
- qualitative, such as strategic choices (giving priority to either agriculture or heavy industry, making it possible to distinguish two positions), or likely attitudes with respect to environment (latitudinarian or *laissez-faire*, mindful of the environment but with limited resources, or clearly orientated towards environmental protection and conservation, making it possible to distinguish three positions), etc.; or
- combining both aspects (e.g. an economic growth-rate linked to a country's degree of openness to international trade).

1. Choice of the main dimensions

Since the main objective of Blue Plan scenario formulation is to assess the effects of various de-velopment strategies on the Mediterranean environment, the first 'dimension' chosen is the way in which this environment is taken into account by the various agents, governments, (central or local) public authorities, businesses, local populations, etc.

The impact of human activity on the environment is closely linked to the way in which these activities are distributed throughout the land and to how this land is allocated among the various agents. The second 'dimension' chosen is therefore spatial management.

Taking the environment and spatial management into account in fact covers only two important aspects of national development strategies, which also aim at the organization of the various sectors of activity in terms of socio-economic and cultural objectives. Thus, consideration of the environment and spatial management has to be positioned within the broader context of national development strategies, which are therefore the third 'dimension'.

Definition of the socio-economic and cultural objectives of development is itself influenced by demographic trends and the major population movements associated with migration and tourism. The starting-point must therefore be hypotheses on demography, the level and structure of populations, and their movements (the fourth 'dimension'), in order to define a range of development strategies.

The Mediterranean countries are not isolated from one another, however, or from the rest of the world, and they cannot formulate their national development strategies without taking into account the international economic context, which provides the last 'dimension'.

To summarize, five main dimensions were chosen in order to formulate the scenarios:

- the international economic context;
- the Mediterranean populations and their movements;
- national development strategies;
- spatial management;
- consideration of the environment.

BOX 6A. **Methodology: dimensions, hypotheses, and scenarios**

The number of scenarios, i.e. of possible combinations, grows very quickly with the number of dimensions. With five dimensions, two positions (or clarification of the hypotheses) for each dimension gives 32 combinations; three positions give 243; and so on. Most of these combinations are uninteresting or even unrealistic. A sufficiently broad range of representative situations can be covered by limiting the exercise to a small number of well-chosen combinations.

In the case of the Blue Plan scenarios, several hypotheses, or positions representing them—not necessarily independent of each other—were linked to the five dimensions, which helps to ensure the consistency of the combinations. The number of positions varied according to the dimension, from two up to occasionally five, in order to achieve subtle shades of difference between the scenarios.

Lastly, in addition to consistency, the choice of scenarios leant towards diversity and contrast when, among other factors, the logic behind the combination of two hypotheses was not clearly evident. In other words, the most pessimistic hypotheses (no doubt 'blackening' reality), or conversely the most optimistic ones, were often combined in order to arrive at the most contrasting situations.

Thus, the art of using the scenarios ultimately consists of judiciously blending elements from different scenarios in order to formulate composite and probably more likely scenarios, but with a less clear-cut impact. Readers are invited to use their judgement in this respect in the light of the situation they are considering.

Various contrasting hypotheses, which seemed the most meaningful, were defined on the basis of these dimensions and reflected by a number of 'positions'. Each of the five scenarios chosen was characterized by a certain combination of these main hypotheses. Moreover, the most important aspect in this first stage of 'focusing' was not so much the quantification of positions conveying the hypotheses as their formulation into a coherent and general set, able in turn to generate other downstream hypotheses, notably for the various sectors of activity.

(a) The international economic context

The Mediterranean countries, being very accessible to the rest of the world, are subject to many influences. While the importance of the political context is recognized, the influences chosen are primarily economic, backed up, naturally, by technological ones. These influences are exerted by a few major agents, such as the United States, the Soviet Union, Japan, etc.

In the Mediterranean basin the major industrialized countries exert a special influence on, among other things:

- relationships among all the countries of the basin, which may lie either in a multilateral context (to the point of 'collegiate' management) or a bilateral context (in which the economic or financial balance of power weighs more);
- commercial relations, permeated by either a free-trade or protectionist bias, depending on the country or the circumstances, and often influenced by transnational corporations;

- the growth-rate of the countries as a whole, on account of the major industrialized countries' role of economic 'locomotive'. The influence of the international economic context on the Mediterranean countries will be even greater if or when intra-Mediterranean economic relations are at a comparatively lower level. Anticipated growth-rates for the Mediterranean countries will partly depend on this international context, including many factors such as the price of oil and the possible trend of the energy market, the price of cereals and the movements of the agricultural market (these two markets affecting the Mediterranean producer and consumer countries in opposite ways) the commercial policies of the major industrialized or newly industrial countries, etc.

Some recent major trends should be borne in mind concerning the international context and relationships between industrialized and less developed countries, although, strictly speaking, they are not hypotheses which provide a basis for defining contrasting positions, used to distinguish between the scenarios:

- Raw materials play a less important role in the world economy. The diminishing amount of material required for a given manufactured product, technological progress, the stabilizing effect of prices on substitution between products, and plentiful resources (contrary to the fears expressed in the first Club of Rome report in 1972) have all contributed to a comparative slackening of world demand and the slow erosion of prices (in 1986 raw material prices dropped to their lowest level ever compared to manufactured products; the price of lead and copper, for example, were lower than in 1932);

● The industrialized countries are obliged to undertake a thorough restructuring of their industry as will be seen later; whole sectors, such as steel which seemed to be the very symbol of industry, have suffered long-term regression, while the service sector is experiencing strong growth. This has been reflected by weaker growth rates, the trend towards protectionism and structural problems of employment;

● Since trade is increasingly based on the transport of lighter weight, very diversified products, dynamic dispersal centres are appearing within the context of combined carriage. These centres are fairly distant from industrial production sites; on the other hand, they are closely linked to decision-making poles in the tertiary sector, among which (in the Mediterranean too) port complexes continue to be a determining factor. Concentration around ports persists, to the advantage of a few large units likely to meet the requirements of complex management and distribution technologies;

● Lastly, capital movements have been a major factor in the world economy. In 1986 for example, flows of floating capital stood at 170 thousand million dollars per day, i.e. twenty times higher than those of trade.

The underlying influence of this 'international economic' dimension is considerable in all the scenarios.

(b) Mediterranean populations and their movements

The importance of the population issue in the Mediterranean basin kept recurring during preparation of the scenarios, at the level of both the hypotheses (the population 'dimension') and the findings (spatial distribution, impact, etc.).

The dynamism of Mediterranean populations, characterized in the south and east by strong growth, means that in this region relationships between the population, development factors, and the environment will be consistently changing both quantitatively and qualitatively. Starting from a still fairly modest basis, consumption as a whole will experience strong growth: consumption of food, water, energy, housing, transport, manufactured goods, etc. Waste water and solid domestic waste will grow in line with consumption, and so should purification and conditioning facilities. Lack or inadequacy of these facilities could lead to the pollution

of aquifers used for the water supply, the proliferation of parasites, even the spread of epidemics or deficiency diseases, all negative factors or curbs on development.

The hypotheses for the scenarios (see Chapter 7) focused in the first place on the levels and age structure of Mediterranean populations, stemming from the interplay of birth and death factors, influenced in turn first by social underpinnings and behaviour, secondly, for some countries, by national population policies. Considering the slowness of demographic phenomena, the differences arising from the hypotheses are naturally a lot sharper for the further horizon of 2025 than for the year 2000, especially because many countries south and east of the basin will not yet have completed their demographic transition and will continue their population growth.

The second aspect of the population dimension on which hypotheses were based concerns the major phenomenon of urbanization (rates already over 50 per cent in most Mediterranean countries, in which the rural exodus is a dynamic factor): trends in urbanization rates at the national and regional level, and also kinds of urbanization, starting with the distribution of urban population among different-sized cities (the problem of the megalopolis or counter-magnets, the optimal size of cities, etc.). Both a cause and effect, urbanization permeates all development and aggravates relationships between development and the environment, as mentioned above (interactions with water resources, among other things), as well as raising problems of land appropriation and degradation, encroachment on agricultural land or forest around cities, deterioration of the landscape, not to mention social aspects, which naturally go beyond the context of this report. (The importance of urbanization should not, however, overshadow the fact that rural overpopulation also has serious effects on the environment.) Coastal concentration ('littoralization') has similar effects, since it includes heavy urbanization, as well as industrial infrastructure (access to the sea and cooling methods), transport infrastructure (ports, railways, airports), and tourist activities (seasonal movements of the population).

The increasing mobility of populations, between countries and between cities and the countryside or recreational areas, implies the systematic organization of urban and interurban transport, suited to comparatively contrasting hypotheses. On the other hand, the phenomena of worker migration and employment are mostly perceived as results of various development options or strategies (migration phenomena are nevertheless the subject of hypotheses concerning emigration and immigration policies).

(c) National development

National development strategies are partly restricted by the international context through economic and technological relations, and, depending on the country, by interdependence ties (import or export of foodstuffs, energy, raw materials, manufactured goods, etc.). Within these constraints, the strategies correspond to a more or less goal-orientated reaction on the part of national, regional, or local communities to the challenge of social needs and objectives. This 'dimension' is no doubt the one which lends itself best to a variety of hypotheses, at either the national or the sectoral level, and to the diverse interplay of numerous agents. A number of hypotheses were chosen for the scenarios, as not all could be kept:

- type of development, i.e. the choice of 'model';
- the main sectoral options, and in particular:
  1. agricultural strategies and the place of agriculture in development plans;
  2. types of industrialization, including the distribution in the economy of large companies (transnationals in particular) and small- and medium-sized firms in the formal or informal sector;
  3. energy choices, with the distribution among various possible sources of supply, and the role of electricity;
  4. strategies for developing tourism, including their economic effects;
  5. choices for the organization and possible co-ordination of the transport of goods and individuals;
- the intensity of intra-Mediterranean, north–south or south–south co-operation.

(d) Spatial management

Management of Mediterranean areas is set within the context of the management of the national territories of the coastal countries, with a set of physical planning regulations, including the delimitation of protected natural areas, the formulation of construction or land-use regulations, and so forth. Among the main hypotheses concerning spatial management which help to characterize the scenarios, a distinction should be made between:

- the extent to which space-planning policies are goal-orientated (intentions and implementation);
- the nature of the desired objectives, such as controlling urban expansion, keeping up agricultural zones (especially around cities), desertification control, or achieving a better balance between:
  1. the 'north' and 'south' in some countries (even if the dividing-line is not as horizontal as in the case of Italy);
  2. urban and rural areas;
  3. the hinterland and the coast;
- the kind of resources deployed.

These may include the planned construction of new towns, the development of medium-sized towns, the designation of areas to be developed as a priority, the prohibition of sprawling growth, large-scale reforestation. Land-tenure policies should also be mentioned, on which types of urban expansion, farming, industrial installations, tourist development policies, transport infrastructure, and so forth all depend.

(e) Taking the environment into account

The last dimension concerns the greater or lesser degree of attention given by decision-makers to environmental protection, and in particular to the prevention of pollution and to the degradation of natural resources. Consideration is given at various levels:

- *The international community.* This involves the gradual outlining of a 'universal or world discipline': protection of the ozone layer is a good example (Montreal Protocol, 1987). People no longer feel concerned solely about their 'close' environment, but also about collective hazards and issues.
- *The European Economic Community.* There is now enhanced co-operation among states: some seventy directives adopted in Brussels over the past fifteen years or so, and the review of the Treaty of Rome in 1987 (decisions no longer taken unanimously, but on a majority vote, and recognition of the environment as a subject of community legislation).
- *Mediterranean co-operation.* This has led to joint commitments concerning the environment (the Barcelona Convention and its protocols). The hypotheses concerning the effective application of these proto-

cols, especially the Protocol for Protection of the Mediterranean Sea against Pollution from Land-Based Sources, provide opportunities for distinguishing between the scenarios.

● *Particular states* which, especially in the Mediterranean basin, enacted laws for the protection and conservation of the natural and cultural environment. In some cases this has been continuing since the beginning of the century, and in virtually all countries since 1960, strengthened since 1975 by special acts for coastal protection and the increasingly frequent obligation to undertake impact studies (in Greece and France since 1977, Israel since 1981, Algeria since 1983, etc.).

● *Regional or local authorities*. These have gained importance over the past twenty years (in different ways depending on the country) and now, directly involved, are increasingly and directly responsible.

Environmental policies are implemented by various means: the setting of standards and regulations, economic incentives, the establishment of specialized bodies (coastal conservancies, river-basin agencies, forestry commissions, etc.), the construction of facilities (sewage or ballast-water reception plants), technological innovation (clean technologies), and resource-management methods (e.g. recycling). Thus, spatial management and consideration of the environment are two of the five dimensions for all the scenarios: consequently they are not regarded as the mere outcome of the economic hypotheses. The policies associated with them are even true factors of development, particularly in the alternative scenarios.

2. Kinds of scenarios

The choice of hypotheses focusing on the 'dimensions' and their coherent combination around a few main themes, such as strong economic growth, with some consideration given to environmental protection, or economic growth based on international co-operation with a concern for resource conservation, led to the identification of two kinds of scenario:

● trend scenarios;
● alternative scenarios.

Trend scenarios describe evolutionary processes that do not diverge radically from trends observed hitherto.* Alternative scenarios, on the other hand,

*This is less a matter of statistically established trends—although the scenarios indirectly depend on them—than of policies or strategies, atmosphere of co-operation, etc.

describe evolutionary processes which deviate from the trends observed up to now and are characterized by a more goal-orientated approach on the part of Mediterranean governments at both the domestic and the international level.

These scenarios, logically developed throughout the period under review (forty years), clearly underestimate the capacity of the socio-economic system for adaptation. In reality, the likelihood of an impasse here or there would lead from one scenario to another, although experience shows that trends are only modified after being identified, i.e. when it is already too late. By exploring the scenarios up to the end of the period, without changing the initial trends, it may be possible to assess the reaction capacity of the system and to identify the kinds of options that facilitate adaptation, in other words to delimit the 'range of possibilities'.

(a) Trend scenarios

The economic engine of the trend scenarios is the expansion of an international market still characterized by American–Japanese economic and technological predominance. The dynamism of the American economy would enable the United States, among other things, to maintain a long-lasting lead over Europe in high technology. In this context, whether from a political, economic, cultural, or other viewpoint, Europe does not manage to assert itself as much as it would like. Similarly, in the Mediterranean individual countries of both the north and the south adapt more or less successfully to the joint United States–East Asia predominance.

In these circumstances it seemed that three trend scenarios should be identified, their differences depending on how far the above pattern was developed. The reference trend scenario T1, the continuation of current trends, lies between two diverging scenarios. In the worst trend scenario T2 international economic growth remains weak, especially because the dominant partners in the world economy are unable to co-ordinate their politital, financial, and macro-economic policies. Consequently, the problem of Third World debt remains acute. Conversely, in the moderate trend scenario T3 a better co-ordination of economic policies between the European Community, the United States, and Japan makes it possible to achieve comparatively stable economic growth.

As regards the environment, the three trend scenarios lead to an adjustment of government efforts depending on economic possibilities, greater in the moderate trend scenario T3 than in the worst trend scenario T2. In all cases, it should be considered that the strongest economic and technological partners may also press for the adoption of certain environmental standards, a handicap for various national economies.

Only the two extreme scenarios—the worst trend T2 and the moderate trend T3—were considered for some aspects of the exercise, the reference trend scenario T1 then being an intermediate or average situation between the two.

(b) The alternative scenarios

The main feature of the two alternative scenarios is the greater influence of the Mediterranean countries, facilitated by the existence of a multipolar world structure in which Western Europe, the United States, Japan, and perhaps one or two other countries or groups of countries assert themselves. In particular, political Europe is more visible, although playing a different role in each scenario.

The two alternative scenarios differ essentially in the kind of relations established among the countries of the Mediterranean basin:

● Reference alternative scenario A1 involves the choice of an overall 'Mediterranean' concept of relations among coastal countries, in which the countries of the European Community and other Mediterranean countries, whether heavily industrialized or industrializing, strive together to forge a region of harmonious development with the optimal opening up of exchanges, and agreement on migratory flows. In this scenario Mediterranean exchanges flow mostly from north to south, since the European Community has a certain overspill role.

● The 'integration' alternative scenario A2 involves the choice of a more 'regional' concept of these relations, with economic co-operation preferably involving groups of countries, e.g. the countries of the enlarged European Community, the Maghreb countries, the Arab East, etc., with maximal opening up of exchanges and migration within these groups, while maintaining certain barriers between them, as countries wish to protect themselves to some extent from international influences. In this scenario the role of the European Community is less dominant, and coastal countries that are not members

of the European Community manage to establish comparatively well-integrated subgroups.

A certain degree of Mediterranean autonomy exists in both cases, weaker in the integration alternative scenario A2, but perhaps more effective initially in terms of growth in the reference alternative scenario A1 because of the economic and technological importance of Europe.

Development strategies in the alternative scenarios may be termed 'self-reliant', understood here as the search for complementarity between the development of a 'modern' sector, patterned on that of the advanced industrialized nations, and the development of small- and medium-sized businesses in the formal and informal sector within urban societies. This is perhaps easier in the integration alternative scenario A2 (since integration allows for better planning and larger markets) than in the reference alternative scenario A1. However, the concept of self-reliance also implies reduced dependence (food or otherwise), including the gradual adaptation of behaviour and life-styles, whether at the level of individual or of collective consumption. The two alternative scenarios therefore assume a greater mobilization of Mediterranean resources, within the context of a more goal-orientated 'production geography' and a more determined struggle against waste or degradation of resources—areas in which innovation has a major role to play—and the long-term growth in intra-Mediterranean exchanges.

In the alternative scenarios physical planning and environment policies are better incorporated into decision-making processes and development plans. For example, preference is given systematically to low-pollution manufacturing processes, biological processes, water-saving irrigation methods, or solutions that are more 'systemic' than mechanical.

Before describing these scenarios in more detail, the population and economic hypotheses—both further upstream and more general than the others—will be examined more thoroughly. These two dimensions have been the subject of numerous national and international studies, due no doubt to their importance and their decisive influence on all the other sectors, but also to the fact that they lend themselves better than the others to quantification and even modelling.

7 Population Hypotheses

Population growth is the major trend in the Mediterranean basin, and it is important to set it within the context of world population trends. This has been done on the basis of United Nations data and projections, which are the most complete in this sphere. Moreover, the projections have presented stable conclusions for a good number of years.

1. The Mediterranean countries in the world population

During the past decades the world population has experienced unprecedented growth-rates. This demographic upsurge stemmed basically from natural population movements in the less developed regions. In the second half of the 1960s, for example (the maximal growth period, except for Africa), these regions had an annual growth-rate of 2–3 per cent, whereas the most developed regions had a rate of less than 1 per cent, falling continuously since the post-war baby boom of the 1950s. The graphs in Figure 7.1 illustrate recent trends of various population indicators and their projections up to 2025 for the world and for the Mediterranean countries, according to the average variant of the latest United Nations population projections.

Declining fertility often goes along with the appearance of new generations with a better education and higher standard of living. Technical and sanitary progress has, in addition, contributed significantly to prolonging the life-span. It took more than a century and a half for average life expectancy to rise from 30 to 60 years in Europe and less than half a century in the less developed countries.

Demographic transition—the change from a traditional pattern of demographic balance, with high death and fertility rates, to a modern pattern of demographic balance, with low death and fertility rates—has generally ended in the most developed regions and has slowly been taking place in the less developed regions over recent decades. Thus, in many cases the less developed countries will reach their highest growth-rates in the second half of the twentieth century, whereas the most developed regions will experience a decline, sometimes even severe, in fertility during the same period. Table 7.1 helps to place the Mediterranean countries in this context. It gives population figures in 1950, 1980, and 1985, forecasts for 2000 and 2025 (United Nations mean variant), and growth-rates during the corresponding periods for the whole world, the most developed countries, the less developed countries, and the Mediterranean countries as a whole. Dependency ratios are also given for the five different years under review (proportion of the population from 0 to 14 years old and over 65 as compared to the population of working age, between 15 and 64). Finally, it should be recalled that with the United Nations mean variant, world population as a whole would only reach the 'stationary' stage of about 12,000m. in the second half of the next century, and would then fluctuate around this level.

2. Population of the Mediterranean countries

The previous remarks apply to the countries of the Mediterranean basin. However, rather than following strictly the United Nations distinction between developed and developing countries, study of the demographic features of the eighteen coastal countries led to the identification of three 'demographic' groupings which are useful in presenting the findings of the evaluations and population projections, namely:
- Region A: Spain, France, Greece, Italy, Yugoslavia;
- Region B: Algeria, Egypt, Libya, Morocco, Syria, Tunisia, Turkey;
- Region C: Albania, Cyprus, Israel, Lebanon, Malta, Monaco.

The population of these three groups are given in Table 7.2 for 1950, 1980, 1985, 2000, and 2025 (projections were based on the United Nations mean variant for 1984 estimates and projections).

As a whole, the population of the Mediterranean

Gross birth rate (%)

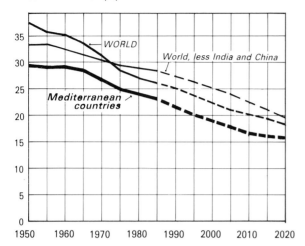

Total fertility rate

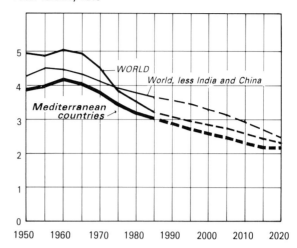

Gross death rate (%)

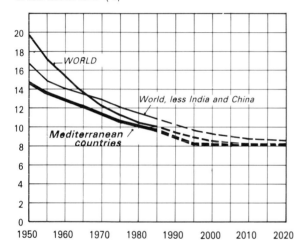

Rate of natural increase (%)

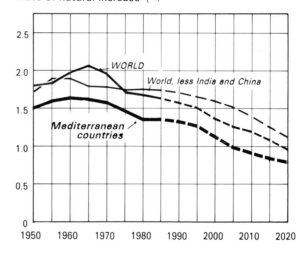

FIG. 7.1 World population indicators
Source: UN/Blue Plan.

basin increased by 68 per cent in the thirty-five years from 1950 to 1985, an annual average growth rate of 1.5 per cent. The real rate peaked towards the end of the 1960s. It has slowly declined since, and is lower than that for the world as a whole (1.9 per cent, but should remain comparatively high (in the region of 1.3 per cent) between 1985 and 2000, and around 0.9 per cent between 2000 and 2025).

This trend varies in the three regions. The countries in Region A have had distinctly lower growth-rates than those in Regions B and C: 0.8 per cent compared to 2.5 per cent and 2.3 per cent respectively between 1950 and 1985. In 2025 Region A will have no more than 36 per cent of

the total population of the basin, compared to 66 per cent in 1950 and 52 per cent in 1985. Conversely, in 2025 Region B alone will comprise nearly 60 per cent of the entire population of the Mediterranean basin—twice its current number, and nearly five times more than in 1950.

(a) Fertility and mortality trends

Current fertility and mortality levels and trends are very different in countries to the north of the Mediterranean basin from those to the south and east. During the period 1960–85, fertility plummeted in Region A (Fig. 7.3), a trend which started for most of these countries from the mid-1960s,

Table 7.1 World and Mediterranean population trends

	Population (000s)					Annual average growth rate (%)				Dependency ratio: (0–14 yrs + over 65 yrs)/15–64 yrs				
	1950	1980	1985	2000	2025	1950–80	1980–85	1985–2000	2000–25	1950	1980	1985	2000	2025
Whole world	2,515,652	4,449,568	4,836,646	6,121,813	8,205,764	1.92	1.68	1.58	1.18	0.66	0.70	0.65	0.59	0.53
More developed regions	831,857	1,136,668	1,173,811	1,276,647	1,396,476	1.05	0.65	0.56	0.36	0.55	0.53	0.50	0.52	0.59
Less developed regions	1,683,796	3,312,899	3,662,835	4,845,166	6,809,289	2.28	2.03	1.88	1.37	0.72	0.77	0.70	0.61	0.51
Mediterranean countries	211,943	332,659	355,591	433,484	547,097	1.51	1.34	1.33	0.94	0.60	0.67	0.63	0.59	0.51
Share of Mediterranean countries in world pop. (%)	8.4	7.5	7.4	7.1	6.7	—	—	—	—	—	—	—	—	—

Source: United Nations, Blue Plan

Table 7.2 Population trends in the countries of the Mediterranean basin

Mediterranean countries	Population (m.)					Growth factor[a]		
	1950	1980	1985	2000	2025	1985	2000[b]	2025[b]
Region A	140	180	185	194	199	1.03	1.08	1.11
Region B	67	142	161	226	329	1.13	1.59	2.32
Region C	5	10	11	14	19	1.10	1.40	1.90
TOTAL	212	333	356	433	547	1.07	1.30	1.64

[a] 1980 = 1.
[b] United Nations mean variant for 1984 estimates and projections. This has been used for the T3 scenario.

Source: United Nations, Blue Plan.

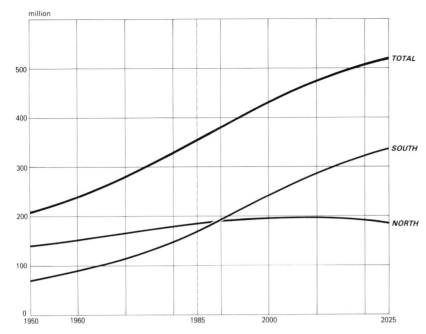

FIG. 7.2 Population in the Mediterranean countries: Trends 1950–1985 and average scenario 1985–2025. The rate of population growth in the Mediterranean countries as a whole tends to level off as from around 2000. The population of the southern and eastern countries exceeds that of the northern countries as from 1990.

Source: UN/Blue Plan.

stemming on the one hand from the decline in the marriage index and, on the other, from the voluntary reduction in the number of children per family. During the period 1974–85 the fertility rate in France, Italy and Spain continued to fall (with variations according to the country), finally to reach levels below the replacement threshold (2.1 children per woman of child-bearing age). The same situation as in Italy, where the estimated fertility indicator fell very early on, reaching the extremely low level of 1.42 children per woman in 1985, is now observed in Spain (1.71 in 1983), both countries having started with comparatively high rates of 2.4—2.9 children per woman. Greece, which long had a surprisingly stable fertility rate (2.1–2.3), has now reached a level insufficient for long-term replacement. Lastly, Yugoslavia has joined the other industrialized countries. In France, however, a very slight recovery has been observed recently compared to the lowest ever recorded in 1983 (1.79).

In Region B the decline in fertility is more or less general and affects all the countries, even those where signs of stabilization were observed (Algeria, Libya, Morocco, and Syria). The extent of the decrease varies from one country to another, but it seems that for some of these countries the downturn in the estimated fertility indicator has accelerated since the 1970s. In Morocco, for example, the indicator fell from 7.2 children per woman to 5.7 in twenty years (the crude birth-rate dropping from 4.61 per cent to 3.86 per cent). The countries in Region B have three points in common:

- they have all entered into a phase of declining fertility;
- their estimated fertility indicator remains very high, usually more than five children per woman;
- there remains a major difference between fertility in urban and in rural areas.

In Egypt, for example, the estimated fertility indicator in 1976 was calculated at 5.52 for the country as a whole, but at 3.89 for Cairo and Alexandria.

In Region C decline in fertility has been uneven and irregular. Cyprus has a fertility rate similar to that of Greece, whereas Malta's has been falling since the 1950s. In Israel the drop is noticeable but the rate remains high (3.85 in 1960, 3.14 in 1980).

There was a general drop in mortality throughout the Mediterranean countries between 1950 and 1980. An increase of 7–12 years in average life expectancy has been recorded in the countries to the north of the basin, and of 9–18 years in the other countries. Major regional discrepancies exist, however, between general mortality and that of infants and children, as well as between sexes and between urban and rural areas. Urban concentration, with possibly substandard living and hygiene conditions, may sometimes lead to higher mortality, despite a larger number of doctors and hospitals. The down-swing in mortality means the increasing coexistence of several generations, with many consequences for economic and social planning.

Gross birth rate (‰)

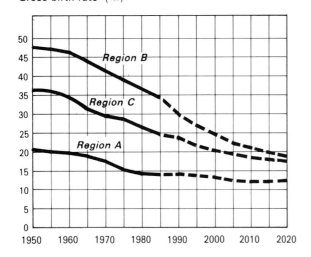

Total fertility rate

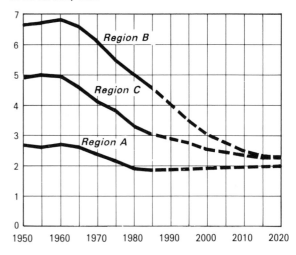

Gross death rate (‰)

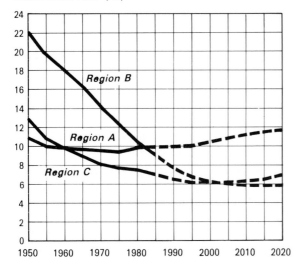

Rate of natural increase (%).

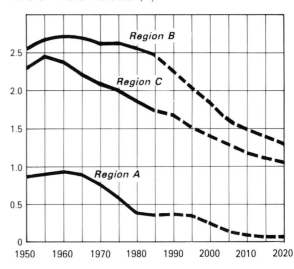

FIG. 7.3 Population indicators by Mediterranean regional grouping.
Region A: Spain, France, Italy, Yugoslavia, Greece
Region B: Turkey, Syria, Egypt, Libya, Tunisia, Algeria, Morocco
Region C: Monaco, Malta, Albania, Cyprus, Lebanon, Israel
Source: UN/Blue Plan.

(*b*) International migration

International migration is the third element, after fertility and mortality, for assessing population prospects of the Mediterranean basin countries. The subject is so complex that it has to be confined to a few considerations, sufficient to identify the elements needed to construct the scenarios. Since the 1960s a considerable proportion of the poorly skilled manual workers in the countries of northwest Europe have been immigrants from other areas of the Mediterranean region. In these areas agriculture was the main source of income and employment; most industrial activities were still incipient. Thus, a little over half the foreign population in the EEC states is currently of Mediterranean origin.

Changes in economic structures have brought about a reversal of the migration situation in some of the southern European countries (Spain, Italy, and Greece), which are now receiving immigrants, especially nationals from the countries on the southern side of the basin. In addition, trends in socio-economic differences between the north and south,

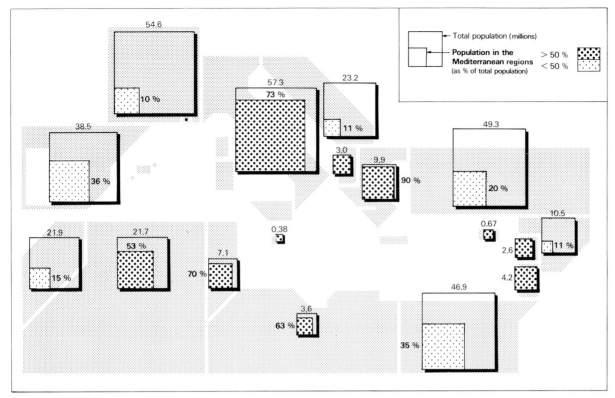

FIG. 7.4 Population in the Mediterranean regions of each country, 1985
Source: Blue Plan/UN.

and the fresh dynamism of small- and medium-sized businesses brought about by the enlargement of the European Community, make one feel that recourse to clandestine workers will continue. This involves a skilled labour force whose educational level is constantly improving, rather than manual workers. On the other hand, the part played by the oil-producing Gulf countries and Libya up to 1986 in receiving foreign labour has been threatened by cyclical variations in oil prices.

Migration flows are now subject to controls, on the part of both the country of origin and the host country. New regulations concerning international migration are being organized through bilateral agreements. But the interests of the countries of origin and the host countries no longer coincide with migrants' wishes. Immigration and the employment of labour follow more the laws of the market rather than administrative regulations, and the persistence of clandestine migration indicates the limitations of these measures.

Migration is therefore a very complex dynamic process. Recent experience of immigration in Europe or that of the Arabian–Persian Gulf and Libya does not seem to provide models on which an assessment

of future prospects could be based. Neither the current economic and socio-cultural situation nor the existing geopolitical context helps to predict migration flows in the coming decades. It seems in fact that a new phase has begun in the history of migration, one which will be characterized by the possible social integration of the majority of foreign populations; this does not exclude the fact that economic needs or the attitudes of some social groups may generate new south–north or south–south migrations.

3. Choice of population hypotheses for the scenarios

The United Nations population forecasts used to establish the population hypotheses of the Mediterranean basin for the scenarios are based on:

- a single mortality hypothesis, called the trend hypothesis: an increase of 2.5 years in life expectancy every five years up to 62.5 years, then a sliding scale of increases until a more or less stable level of 79 years (75 years for men and 82.5 years for women);

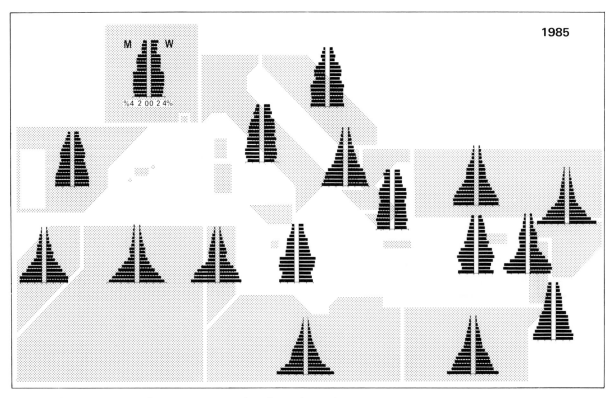

FIG. 7.5 Age structure, 1985, as percentage of total population (5-year age-groups)

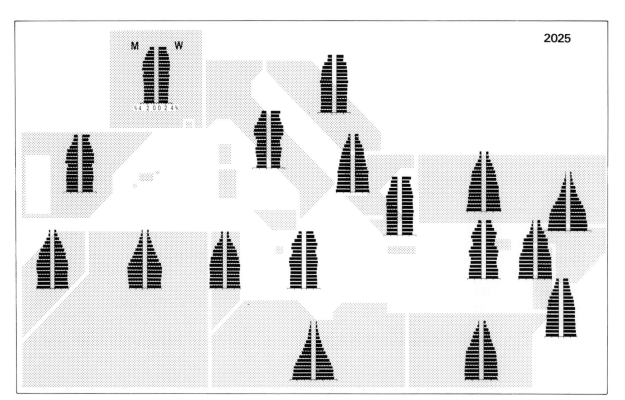

FIG. 7.6 Age structure, 2025, as percentage of total population (5-year age-groups). In 2025 the age structure in the southern countries will tend to resemble that of the northern countries.

● three fertility hypotheses, termed respectively average, high, and low: fertility would fall fairly fast in the less developed countries, and would end by rising sooner or later in the most developed countries, until it fluctuates around 'replacement' levels, i.e. a crude reproduction rate equal to 1.

The United Nations forecast discounts the possibility of unexpected eventualities such as war, famine, epidemics, etc.; however, prior events leave their mark on the population pyramids.

The consistency of these population hypotheses

Table 7.3 Fertility hypotheses of the United Nations population division, as chosen for the five Mediterranean scenarios

Region	Scenarios				
	T1	T2	T3	A1	A2
A[a]	L	L	A	A	H
C					
Monaco	A	A	A	A	A
Malta	A	A	A	A	A
Albania	A	A	A	A	H
Cyprus	A	A	A	A	A
Lebanon	A	A	A	A	H
Israel	A	A	A	A	H
B[b]		A	H	A	L	L

Key: A = average; H = high; L = low.

[a] Spain, France, Italy, Greece, Yugoslavia.
[b] Turkey, Syria, Egypt, Libya, Tunisia, Algeria, Morocco.

with the conceptual framework of the Blue Plan scenarios was checked, and the fertility variants are given in Table 7.3. This overall pattern reflects, among other things, the assumed relationships between demographic reactions and the economic conditions or development strategies of the various Mediterranean societies for each scenario.

In the worst trend scenario T2, for example, persistence of the fertility decline in the countries to the north of the basin, and the slow-down of this decline in the countries to the south and east, were linked to slow economic growth. Conversely, in the integration alternative scenario A2 a recovery of fertility was assumed in the north, together with an acceleration of the fertility decline in the south and east through the combined effects of education, mobility, and modernization, with a long-term convergence of all the Mediterranean countries towards the replacement threshold. It seemed interesting— though admittedly somewhat arbitrary—to explore in at least one scenario the hypothesis of a slight recovery of fertility in the north (the possibility of other reversals was not considered).

The Mediterranean population figures chosen for the five scenarios in 1980 (base year), 1985, 2000, and 2025 are given in Table 7.4. For the Mediterranean basin as a whole, the difference between the two extreme population hypotheses was 50m. people in 2025 (with a maximum deviation of 34m. for group A and 64m. for group B). If the United Nations projection used had been combined (non-weighted) with socio-economic conditions (by

---

BOX 7A. **Population outlook for 2000 in Algeria**

The assumptions for 2000 imply:

● an annual average population growth-rate of 3.19 per cent;
● a total population of 34,500,000.

Population growth could, however, differ according to the major geographic regions, depending on national planning and regional development objectives, even if their outcome is not entirely up to expectations.

Aside from the northern area, outside the capital, where the final demographic growth-rate (reached between 2000 and 2025) is the same as that of the total population, population growth will be higher than that of the total population in the high plateaux and the south on account of a return and/or a decline of population living in the north.

The priority location of productive investment and major infrastructure in the high plateaux and the south should bring about the definitive redeployment of a population of about 1,500,000 to these areas.

Consequently, the total population would reach 57.5 million in 2025, and the national urbanization rate would be 80.6 per cent.

Urban population growth, although declining along with the overall population trend, would maintain different rates in the various regions, in accordance with the objectives of achieving regional balance and rational distribution throughout the country. The urban population in the south and the high plateaux would grow at a rate of 2.3 per cent compared with 1.73 per cent in the northern wilayats, representing a complete reversal of current population trends in the country: this is the desired objective.

Source: Algerian national scenarios for the Blue Plan.

Table 7.4 Population in the five Mediterranean scenarios (000s)

	1980	1985	Scenarios T1 2000	T1 2025	T2 2000	T2 2025	T3 2000	T3 2025	A1 2000	A1 2025	A2 2000	A2 2025
Region A[a]												
Spain	37,400	38,500	41,900	44,900	41,900	44,900	42,200	46,000	42,200	46,000	43,900	51,800
France	53,700	54,600	55,200	52,600	55,200	52,600	57,200	58,400	57,200	58,400	58,300	63,500
Italy	57,100	57,300	57,800	53,600	57,800	53,600	58,600	57,200	58,600	57,200	60,500	63,300
Greece	9,640	9,880	10,100	9,560	10,100	9,560	10,400	10,800	10,400	10,800	10,800	12,100
Yugoslavia	22,300	23,200	24,700	25,000	24,700	25,000	25,200	26,800	25,200	26,800	25,800	29,000
TOTAL	180,000	183,000	190,000	186,000	190,000	186,000	194,000	199,000	194,000	199,000	199,000	220,000
Region C[a]												
Monaco	26	27	30	36	30	36	30	36	30	36	30	36
Malta	369	383	418	459	418	459	418	459	418	459	418	459
Albania	2,730	3,050	4,100	5,780	4,100	5,780	4,100	5,780	4,100	5,770	4,260	6,500
Cyprus	629	669	762	902	762	902	762	902	762	902	762	902
Lebanon	2,670	2,670	3,620	5,220	3,620	5,220	3,620	5,220	3,620	5,220	3,830	5,950
Israel	3,880	4,250	5,300	6,870	5,300	6,870	5,300	6,870	5,300	6,870	5,720	8,120
TOTAL	10,300	11,000	14,200	19,300	14,200	19,300	14,200	19,300	14,200	19,300	15,000	22,000
Region B[a]												
Turkey	44,500	49,300	65,400	91,900	68,600	105,000	65,400	91,900	62,300	81,700	62,300	81,700
Syria	8,800	10,500	17,000	31,800	18,300	15,500	17,000	31,800	17,000	28,100	17,000	28,100
Egypt	41,500	46,900	63,900	90,400	65,700	97,300	63,900	90,400	62,200	85,000	62,200	85,000
Libya	2,970	3,610	6,080	11,100	6,240	12,500	6,080	11,100	5,920	9,910	5,920	9,910
Tunisia	6,390	7,080	9,430	12,900	9,830	14,000	9,430	12,900	9,060	12,100	9,060	12,100
Algeria	18,700	21,700	33,400	50,600	34,700	56,500	33,400	50,600	32,200	46,500	32,200	46,400
Morocco	19,400	21,900	29,500	40,100	31,400	45,000	29,500	40,100	28,900	39,100	28,900	39,100
TOTAL	142,000	161,000	226,000	329,000	235,000	366,000	226,000	329,000	218,000	302,000	218,000	302,000
TOTAL MEDITERRANEAN COUNTRIES[a]	333,000	356,000	430,000	533,000	439,000	571,000	433,000	547,000	426,000	521,000	432,000	544,000

[a] Additions based on non-rounded figures (3 significant figures).

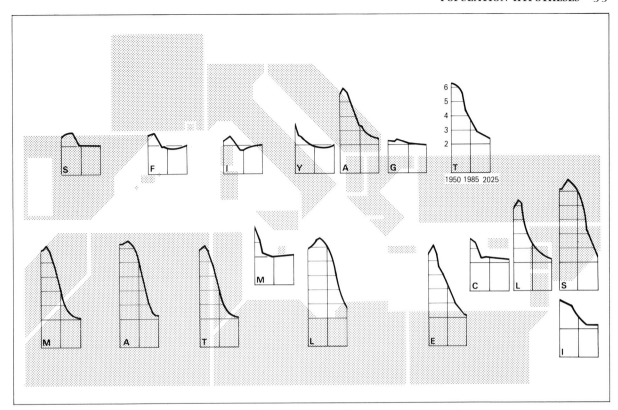

FIG. 7.7 Number of children per woman: Trends 1950–1985 and average scenario 1985–2025
Source: Blue Plan.

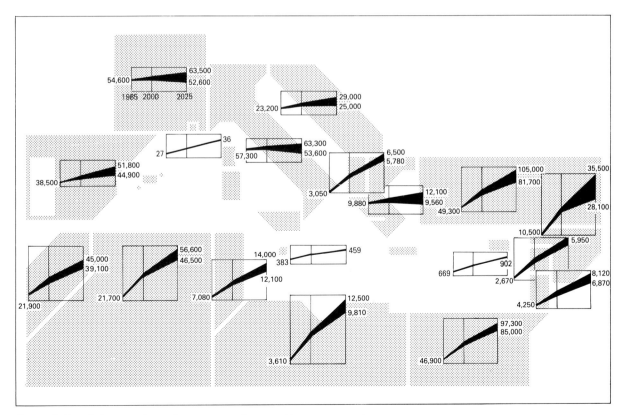

FIG. 7.8 Population trends, 1985, 2000, and 2025: Extreme scenarios
Source: Blue Plan.

amalgamating either all the weakest forecasts or all the strongest ones), the gap in 2025 would have been double that obtained. This gap of 50m. or so in 2025 is virtually equivalent to the current population of Egypt, or all three Maghreb countries.

The population pyramids associated with these estimates (Fig. 7.4) indicate significant discrepancies from one group of countries to another. Thus, in the north of the Mediterranean the age-group 0–14 years drops from 21.9 per cent in 1985 to 18.2 per cent in 2025, whereas it rises from 28.2 per cent to 46.1 per cent for the subgroup Syria, Algeria, and Libya, where fertility is virtually the highest in the basin. The situation will be the reverse for the respective adult populations, and the average age will remain higher in the northern countries than in the southern and eastern ones. Socio-economic problems will therefore be very different depending on the country and the scenarios.

4. Entries into and withdrawals from the labour market

The Blue Plan studies did not concentrate on the labour market or on employment. At this stage it will simply be stressed that the composition of the population by age clearly plays a vital role in the labour markets, although real activity rates are a lot more uncertain than foreseeable population trends to the horizons 2000 and 2025. The potential intake (age-group 15–24 years) and withdrawals (age-group 55–64 years) differ from one country to another, and from one region to another, as illustrated in the Table 7.5 and Fig. 7.10 for the moderate trend scenario T3.

Throughout the period 1985–2025 growth of the labour force would continue to slow down and workers would be increasingly older in Region A,

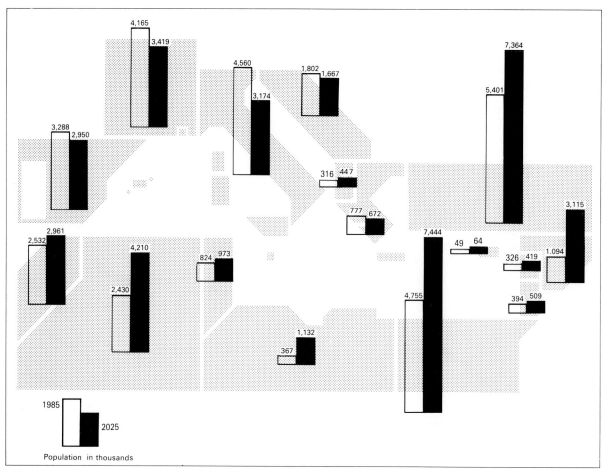

FIG. 7.9 Population aged 15–19 in 1985 and 2025 (000s): Average scenario. Analysis of the 15–19 age-groups helps to assess some of the problems of employment dynamics and related socio-economic aspects.
Source: Blue Plan.

Table 7.5 Trend of potential entries into (15–24) and withdrawals from (55–64) the labour market in the Mediterrranean countries, by region and according to the T3 scenario for 1985–2025

	Nos. (m.)				
	1950	1980	1985	2000	2025
Region A					
15–24 years	17.33	15.71	15.89	13.38	12.12
55–64 years	8.55	9.12	10.92	10.48	13.46
ratio	2.04	1.72	1.46	1.28	0.90
Region B					
15–24 years	19.56	20.11	20.19	19.69	16.42
55–64 years	9.89	6.66	6.69	5.93	9.03
ratio	1.98	3.02	3.02	3.32	1.82
Region C					
15–24 years	18.30	19.05	19.10	17.51	15.05
55–64 years	6.12	6.17	6.45	6.57	10.04
ratio	2.99	3.09	2.96	2.67	1.50

Note: To facilitate comparison between the three groups of countries, potential entries into working life have been assimilated into the 15–24 age-group, and potential withdrawals into the 55–64 age-group. The average age of entry into or withdrawal from working life varies from one country to another. This difference is explained on the one hand by the lengthening of studies and, on the other, by the postponement or advancement of definitive withdrawals from working life.

the countries in the north of the basin, where fertility is low. At the beginning of next century the number of workers would even start to dwindle in France and Italy, reflecting a significant shortage of young adults on the labour market. However, the entry of women into the labour force should continue and could partly offset the shortfall. In the countries in the south and east of the basin, with comparatively high fertility, potential intake would expand faster than withdrawals and the gap would continue to widen until it peaks towards 2000. In other words, pressure of demand is likely to exacerbate

SPAIN, FRANCE, ITALY, GREECE, YUGOSLAVIA

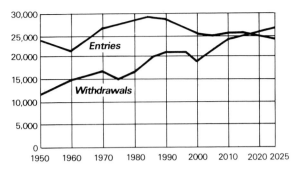

TURKEY, SYRIA, EGYPT, LIBYA, TUNISIA, ALGERIA, MOROCCO

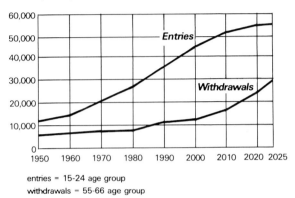

entries = 15-24 age group
withdrawals = 55-66 age group

FIG. 7.10 Entries into and withdrawals from the labour market (000s): Trends 1950–1985 and average scenario 1985–2025
Source: Blue Plan.

employment problems and influence the direction of socio-economic development strategies; nevertheless, various strategies to cope with the situation seem feasible.

These changes, linked to demographic structures, would clearly be more adverse in the worst trend scenario T2 than in the alternative scenarios.

8 Economic Hypotheses

The general hypotheses concerning growth and trade define the international context of the scenarios and fix the trends of production structures.

1. Context and constraints of growth

Disregarding short- and medium-term fluctuations, work was based on an annual average growth-rate of 2.5 per cent for the United States of America, sustained over the forty-year period from 1985 to 2025, which reflects long-standing trends. The growth-rate for Japan would be 3.75 per cent per year for the fifteen-year period from 1985 to 2000, and 3.3 per cent after 2000. These hypotheses are valid for all the scenarios, justified in an exercise whose application is strictly confined to the Mediterranean area. The choice of several growth-rates for the United States and Japan would have increased the number of scenarios and in the end obfuscated the exercise.

On the other hand, the growth-rate for the European Community, important for all the Mediterranean countries, varies according to the scenario from 2.1 per cent to 2.8 per cent per year from now to 2000, and from 3 per cent to 3.4 per cent per year beyond that date (see Table 8.1). This growth assumes a general recovery of international economic activity during the 1990s (justified further on), without, however, counting on Japan or the European Community returning to their growth-levels of the 1960s. The European Community may in fact experience two opposing trends. It can be imagined on the one hand that the nature of

growth will be different and rates lower because the economies are mature—reflected, for instance, in shorter working hours and more free time for leisure. The trend towards smaller numbers of workers arriving on the labour market, even a decline of the population, heads in the same direction and production structures would mirror this new state of growth, characterized by low rates. On the other hand, however, the Single European Act and the huge internal market in 1992 would provide a fresh stimulus to growth. Even if the economic and technological predominance of the United States and Japan persists, it can be assumed that the European Community will experience higher rates (particularly in the alternative scenarios) at the beginning of the next century, especially as economic growth may make up for the sluggishness of the period 1970–85. Table 8.1 reflects these considerations.

The effect of these hypotheses on the growth of Mediterranean countries depends heavily on trade conditions. Major trends since 1970 in fact correlate the economic activity of the Mediterranean countries with the international economic situation, and three factors in particular: the oil situation, the trend towards participation in the world market, and the debt burden.

The price of oil is determined by the balance of supply and demand on the world market, strongly influenced by United States demand. The oil-price rises during the 1970s had a strong impact on growth in producer countries, and, conversely, the slack demand which has lowered prices over the past few years has considerably curtailed investment projects. The influence of the oil market is felt indirectly in other countries south and east of the Mediterranean basin, notably Egypt, Lebanon, and

Table 8.1 Growth-rates selected for the main industrialized countries (% p.a.)

	Scenarios (1985–2000)					Scenarios (2000–2025)				
	T1	T2	T3	A1	A2	T1	T2	T3	A1	A2
USA	2.50	2.50	2.50	2.50	2.50	2.50	2.50	2.50	2.50	2.50
Japan	3.75	3.75	3.75	3.75	3.75	3.30	3.30	3.30	3.30	3.30
EEC	2.30	2.10	2.70	2.80	2.80	3.00	3.00	3.30	3.40	3.30

Syria, through financial flows: public transfers and private remittances (of migrant workers), and revenue from oil pipelines.

In the oil-importing countries north of the basin the impact of oil prices on their economies has dwindled due to falling prices and energy-saving efforts. The oil bill of the importing countries in the south and east has also been lower, although they benefited less from the drop in prices because their exports include other primary products whose prices tailed off either before or at the same time as those of oil (the case of phosphates in Morocco).

In countries south and east of the basin the trend towards participation in the world market first appeared during the period of expansion in the 1970s. The policy followed at that time focused not only on diversification of commodity exports, but also on promotion of industrial projects geared to processing them for the world market (aluminium, iron, and steel). With the weak economic situation in the 1980s this policy received increased support from international financial institutions in the context of the adjustment in trade-deficit policies required of debtor countries.

Indebtedness itself, often associated with strong growth in the 1970s, contributed to the trend towards participation in the world market. The two phenomena are in fact related: thanks to world prices for raw materials, some exporting countries benefited from growth over and above world rates and sought to maintain it during the price reversal by borrowing from banks; as from 1981, however, money was more scarce and interest rates soared on the money market. So from then on indebtedness must be considered as one of the international market's chief 'drive-belts' for the debtor countries' economies (see Table 8.2).

At the end of 1985 the outstanding debt of the Mediterranean countries amounted to $156,000m., approximately 16 per cent of the total debt of developing countries. The debt-servicing burden (amortization and interest) in 1984, a fairly good year for exports, exceeded 30 per cent of export revenue for Turkey and Yugoslavia in the north and for Morocco, Algeria, and Egypt in the south, and approached this amount for Greece and Tunisia. Debt this high is likely to shackle the growth of countries in the south and east of the basin, whose exports are more vulnerable to commodity price fluctuations than are those of the countries in the north, some of which benefit in addition from the backing of the powerful financial centres of the European Community.

2. Growth in Mediterranean countries

Once the growth-rates of the major industrialized regions were fixed, a study was made of past links between national growth-rates and those of the

Table 8.2 Debt of some Mediterranean countries, 1985

	Oustanding medium-term debt		Debt service (% of exports)
	$1,000m.[a]	% GDP	
Southern Europe			
Greece	18.5	36.5	28.8
Malta	0.1	11.8	1.6
Turkey	22.0	42.8	32.1
Yugoslavia	20.0	46.0	34.3
Southern and eastern Mediterranean			
Algeria	19.7	32.9	35.5
Egypt	30.9	67.9	47.6
Israel	21.9	82.5	21.7
Lebanon	0.5[b]	..	10.0
Morocco	13.7	88.0	41.8
Tunisia	5.7	58.7	29.6
Syria	2.6[b]	16.1[b]	14.3
TOTAL	155.6		

[a] Nominal dollars.
[b] End 1984.

Source: UNCTAD Statistics, 1986 supplement.

Table 8.3 GDP in 2000 ($1000m. at 1975 value) and growth-rates 1985–2000

	1980		1985		T1		T2		T3		A1		A2	
	GDP	Growth-rate (%)[a]	GDP	Growth-rate (%)[b]	GDP	Growth-rate (%)	GDP	Growth-rate (%)[c]	GDP	Growth-rate (%)	GDP	Growth-rate (%)[c]	GDP	Growth-rate (%)[c]
Spain	110.20	5.7	117.97	1.4	199.00	3.5	180.60	2.9	217.20	4.1	222.25	4.3	222.25	4.3
France	398.80	4.6	421.67	1.1	640.80	2.8	622.30	2.6	696.90	3.4	709.20	3.5	709.20	3.5
Italy	230.20	4.1	241.03	0.9	342.10	2.4	332.10	2.2	364.20	2.8	387.60	3.2	387.60	3.2
Yugoslavia	37.28	5.8	38.33	0.7	59.67	3.0	56.83	2.6	63.64	3.4	68.65	3.9	68.65	3.9
Greece	22.94	6.3	24.49	1.3	42.41	3.7	38.18	3.0	45.82	4.3	49.02	4.7	49.02	4.7
Turkey	41.76	5.3	52.75	4.8	82.30	3.0	73.54	2.2	82.61	3.0	90.45	3.7	90.45	3.7
Syria	7.38	7.7	8.76	3.5	12.57	2.4	12.09	2.1	13.59	2.9	14.07	3.2	14.38	3.3
Lebanon	2.42	5.6	2.42	0.0	4.02	3.4	4.02	3.4	4.02	3.4	4.02	3.4	4.02	3.4
Israel	13.06	6.9	13.06	0.0	27.10	5.0	27.10	5.0	28.62	5.4	30.90	5.9	30.90	5.9
Egypt	20.31	6.4	29.08	7.4	36.82	1.6	35.63	1.4	40.10	2.2	44.25	2.8	49.45	3.6
Libya	18.37	17.9	14.12	−5.1	28.95	4.9	27.84	4.6	52.59	9.2	56.84	9.7	56.84	9.7
Tunisia	5.04	6.4	6.15	4.1	9.01	2.6	8.67	2.3	9.93	3.2	11.39	4.2	12.89	4.8
Algeria	13.87	3.7	17.42	4.7	22.82	1.8	20.61	1.1	24.76	2.4	27.60	3.1	36.80	5.1
Morocco	12.97	6.8	14.72	2.6	22.75	2.9	20.24	2.1	24.30	3.4	25.86	3.8	26.77	4.1

[a] Ratio for the years 1980/1960.
[b] Ratio for the years 1985/1980.
[c] Ratio for the years 2000/1985.

Table 8.4 GDP in 2025 ($1000m. at 1975 value) and growth-rates 2000–2025

	T1		T2		T3		A1		A2	
	GDP	Growth-rate (%)	GDP	Growth-rate (%)	GDP	Growth-rate (%)	GDP	Growth-rate (%)	GDP	Growth-rate (%)
Spain	500.70	3.8	414.60	3.4	598.80	4.1	631.80	4.3	613.00	4.1
France	1,464.00	3.4	1,422.00	3.4	1,728.00	3.7	1,809.00	3.8	1,760.00	3.7
Italy	798.80	3.4	775.40	3.4	925.30	3.8	1,014.00	3.9	985.80	3.8
Yugoslavia	153.80	3.9	146.50	3.9	179.70	4.2	220.10	4.8	213.40	4.6
Greece	114.20	4.0	93.33	3.6	136.10	4.4	150.30	4.6	145.50	4.4
Turkey	215.20	3.9	161.60	3.2	237.80	4.3	294.90	4.8	311.80	5.1
Syria	35.02	4.2	33.68	4.2	42.86	4.7	49.02	5.1	60.25	5.9
Lebanon	12.18	4.5	12.18	4.5	13.58	5.0	14.08	5.1	17.33	6.0
Israel	70.42	3.9	64.10	3.5	78.15	4.1	112.90	5.3	135.50	6.1
Egypt	91.04	3.7	88.10	3.7	107.80	4.0	135.00	4.6	180.50	5.3
Libya	69.40	3.6	57.57	2.9	203.40	5.6	215.00	5.2	215.00	5.5
Tunisia	25.51	4.2	23.14	4.0	29.02	4.4	37.93	4.9	55.19	6.2
Algeria[a]	58.49	3.8	49.90	3.6	70.64	4.3	82.90	4.5	101.36	4.1
Morocco	59.45	3.9	48.05	3.5	69.80	4.3	85.46	4.9	105.30	5.6

Note: All growth-rates are for the years 2025/2000.
[a] GDP at factor cost.

European Community through 'coupled elasticities' (or the ratio between the growth-rate of a given country and that of the EEC) and in order to choose the growth-rates for each Mediterranean country. As these elasticities are comparatively stable, growth-rates for each country were chosen on the basis of observed elasticities and weighted by a country analysis. The figures given in Tables 8.3 and 8.4 may therefore be considered as fairly consistent sets.

(a). Countries south and east of the basin

Because of the circumstances mentioned above, southern and eastern coastal countries cannot experience strong growth from 1985 to 2000 in the trend scenarios. This stems directly from their linkage with an international economy which itself lacks dynamism. For these countries as a whole, annual growth-rates are around 3.1 per cent in the reference trend scenario T1, a little lower in the worst trend scenario T2, and rise to 4.3 per cent in the moderate trend scenario T3. Average per capita GDP growth varies between 0 per cent and 2.1 per cent per annum for these scenarios, to the extent that in some countries the per capita GDP would be lower in 2000 than it was in 1985 in adverse circumstances. Conversely, the very fact of accepting a certain 'decoupling' from the international economy in the alternative scenarios provides the opportunity of introducing higher rates, with annual average per capita GDP growth in the order of 3 per cent (2.9 per cent and 3.4 per cent respectively).

From 2000 to 2025 all rates rise, reaching an average level of 3.8 per cent per annum in the reference trend scenario and 5 per cent or more in the alternative scenarios over the period. These rates (Tables 8.3 and 8.4) may seem low compared to growth in the period 1960–80 (7 per cent per annum), but they stem from ECC-coupled elasticities (according to the method described above) of 1.4–1.9, flanking the figure of 1.5 observed from 1960 to 1980. In correlation, per capita GDP growth-rates remain low; in this case population constraints add to those of the economy. They would be in the region of 2.2 per cent per annum on average in the reference trend scenario T1, and about 3 per cent in the alternative scenarios.

(b) Countries north of the basin

In the north a distinction is made for France and Italy, too closely integrated to the European Community to have a growth-rate noticeably diverging from that assumed for the Community as a whole (the growth-rate for Italy may in fact be underestimated because insufficient allowance may have been made for the so-called 'underground economy').

Spain, Yugoslavia, Greece, and Turkey (considered here as part of the north) make a rather heterogeneous group, in which standards of living varied from 1 to 3 in 1980. However, they all experienced much higher growth-rates than those of the European Community from 1960 to 1980, and some of them suffered from the recession of 1980–6. Their development over the period 1985–2000 will therefore follow rather closely the hypotheses made concerning Community growth and cohesion, whether they are members or not. The growth elasticity for these countries as a group should therefore rise from the worst trend scenario T2 (1.3) to the moderate trend scenario T3 (1.5). No difference was introduced for this period in the two alternative scenarios.

Beyond 2000 the countries to the north of the basin benefit from a larger market and slightly faster European Community growth (3.4 per cent compared to 3.3 per cent) in reference alternative scenario A1. These features make the A1 scenario the most propitious for the northern coastal countries.

(c) Comments on growth-rates

It is interesting to compare the assumed growth-rates of Mediterranean countries from 1980 to 2025. It can be observed that the GDP of the countries in the south and east of the basin would grow nearly fourfold during the period 1980–2025 in the reference trend scenario T1 and the worst trend scenario T2, sevenfold in the moderate trend scenario T3, and eight- or ninefold in the two alternative scenarios. This can be compared to the multipliers obtained for the countries in the north of the basin over the same period, which never exceed 5.

On the other hand, comparisons between multipliers of per capita GDPs reflect the very different patterns of population growth in the two groups of countries, as shown by Table 8.5.

Considering that per capita standards of living vary according to productivity levels, growth of production would be obtained in very different ways in the two groups, with productivity rising on average more slowly in the south and east, but with a faster-growing labour force (which corresponds to the economic laws of resource allocation).

To conclude on a word of caution, it should be stressed that the figures for individual countries are given only as an indication and had to be defined fairly early on in the exercise. They are naturally less reliable than collective averages, on which the above observations have been made. Nevertheless, they proved useful for sectoral analyses, despite their somewhat arbitrary nature, and made it possible to cover a fairly wide range of possibilities in the field of economic growth.

3. Monetary and financial constraints

In order to compare growth hypotheses with economic policies, the balance of trade was taken as an indicator. This balance is in turn one of the key components of the broader balance of payments, which also includes:

● the balance of services, important for countries like Morocco, Tunisia, and Egypt because of income from tourism and due to some extent to the 'adjustment policies' adopted;

● the balance of the capital account, adversely affected by payments of interest on debt and of dividends on foreign investment. It is negative for all the indebted countries in the Mediterranean basin, and deteriorates each year for most of them;

● the balance of private transfers, which includes

Table 8.5 Per capita GDP multipliers according to the scenarios, 1980–2025

	T1	T2	T3	A1	A2
Spain	3.8	3.1	4.4	4.7	4.0
France	3.8	3.6	4.0	4.2	3.7
Italy	3.7	3.6	4.0	4.4	3.9
Yugoslavia	3.7	3.5	4.0	4.9	4.4
Greece	5.0	4.1	5.3	5.9	5.0
Turkey	2.5	1.6	2.8	3.8	4.0
Syria	1.3	1.1	1.6	2.1	2.6
Lebanon	2.6	2.6	2.9	3.0	3.2
Israel	3.0	2.8	3.4	4.9	5.0
Egypt	2.1	1.9	2.4	3.3	4.3
Libya	1.0	0.7	3.0	3.5	3.5
Tunisia	2.5	2.1	2.9	4.0	5.8
Algeria	1.6	1.2	1.9	2.4	2.9
Morocco	2.2	1.6	2.6	3.3	4.0

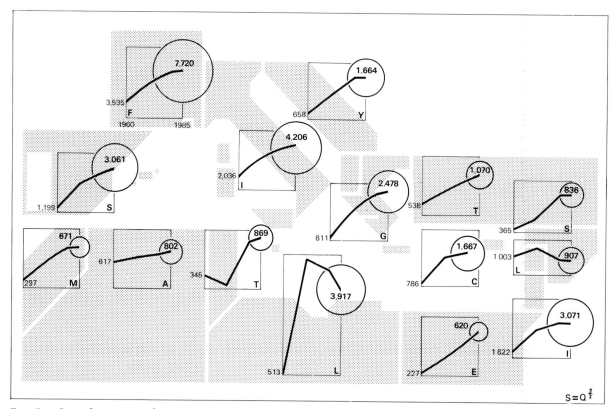

FIG. 8.1 Gross domestic product per capita: Trends 1960–1985 (1975 $US)
Source: UN statistics.

amounts deposited by immigrants or remitted by emigrants, very important recently for Egypt.

At the beginning of the decade balances of payments were virtually all negative for the countries in the south and east of the Mediterranean basin, even taking into account official development assistance. With respect to the industrialized countries on the northern side, the balance of services is positive for all countries (except for Yugoslavia), because of major contracts for capital goods and income from banking services and telecommunications, which boost the positive balance derived from tourism. Conversely, capital-account balances are negative for all countries, either because of their indebtedness (France, Yugoslavia, and Turkey) or because the outflow of dividends from foreign firms in Europe exceeds the inflow of dividends from national firms established abroad. A low dollar stimulates European investment in North America, but Japanese investment in Europe could take up the slack and keep the balance negative.

What can be deduced from this short analysis of medium-term development prospects, especially in the trend scenarios? The world-wide expansion of services could be considered a challenge similar to that of technology for the industrialized countries, which will have to be as efficient in the services as in the high-technology industries if they wish to keep a positive trade balance.

What is the situation in the countries in the east and south of the Mediterranean, this time including Turkey? The difficulties of the major oil-exporting countries (Mediterranean and Arabian–Persian Gulf) stemming from falling prices and the weak dollar should be stressed first of all. The deterioration of their trade balance obliges them to reverse policies fairly abruptly, with an impact on other items of the national budget: cancellation of major civil works already under way, in order to relieve the service account, repatriation of immigrant workers, reduction of assistance granted to other countries, and lowering of the GDP growth-rate.

The misfortunes of the major oil exporters will have a serious impact on the balance of payments of other countries in the south and east of the Mediterranean basin, especially because of the repatriation of their emigrant workers (private transfers, not to mention the social problems caused by the return and integration of these workers, as in Egypt or Tunisia, for instance).

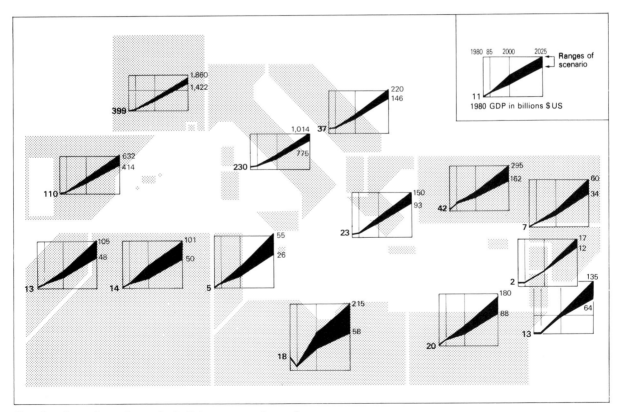

FIG. 8.2 Gross domestic product: Extreme scenarios 1980–2025
Source: Blue Plan.

BOX 8A. **Spain in Europe and the Mediterranean**

The integration of Spain into Europe raises the problem of the future role of Spain in the European productive system, and also the broader issue of relationships between Europe and the Mediterranean. In this context, the role of Spain could develop in very different ways: it could become a pole of traditional industry, recovering the kinds of production in which the north European countries would have lost the struggle for competitivity, especially as regards the Third World. On the other hand, it could become host to advanced industrial activities no longer responding to the technical and economic criteria of location which, in the past, justified the concentration of new industrial developments in the north of Europe.

In the first extreme hypothesis, Spain would be a 'developing country' among advanced industrialized countries, a situation which has characterized the Italian Mezzogiorno during the past twenty years without any identifiable progress being observed in attempts to reduce the gap in per capita income. In the second extreme hypothesis, Spain would be a new 'pole of innovation' among the advanced industrialized countries, similar to California in the United States. Clearly the most likely future is somewhere between these two extreme situations, and 'two Spains' could even emerge, host to both of the industrialization models envisaged.

In fact, many sociological and economic studies have reached the conclusion that there *are* two Spains: an urbanized and industrial Spain, turned towards Europe, with a high standard of living (Catalonia, the Basque country, Madrid, and other north-eastern regions); and an agricultural, Mediterranean, and considerably poorer Spain. Major internal migration flows have been recorded, especially in the post-war period. In 1955 33.5 per cent of the population lived in Madrid, Catalonia, Valencia, and the Basque country; in 1975 the figure was 44.6 per cent. In terms of value added, the activities of these regions represented 48.5 per cent in 1955 and 56 per cent in 1975. Among these richest regions there is also the greatest desire for autonomy, strengthened by clearly different languages and cultures (Basque and Catalan).

Source: Spanish national scenarios for the Blue Plan.

Faced with these trends (the severest being those depicted in worst trend scenario T2), the scenarios implicitly assume that countries will resort to economic recovery policies such as:

- improvement of the balance of tourism through investment in this sector (with the risk of a more or less haphazard development in the hands of national or international investors and inadequate protection of coastal areas);
- procurement from the industrialized countries of increased official development assistance or, along similar lines, of debt relief, involving a slow orientation of the international community towards rescheduling of long-term debts (to stay consistent with the trend scenario hypotheses, however, it was assumed that the debt burden would remain comparatively heavy, depending on the scenarios, and offical assistance moderate up to 2000);
- all-out efforts to restore the trade balance, while sacrificing a minimum of growth.

However, to understand better the interplay between economic, social, and environmental constraints, a distinction should be made between opportunities in the industrial and in the agricultural sectors:

- *Industrial potential and constraints.* Considering the necessarily reduced and selective contribution of foreign investors (the case of the trend scenarios), two assumptions are made about the financing of industrial promotion. The first is the possibility of releasing considerable resources from domestic savings—hence austerity measures in both rural and urban sectors; the second is the ability to set up industries that are competitive on the world market, necessitating a quick mastery of industrial processes. If possible, efforts should also be made to ensure a domestic market for their output. Clearly this option does not leave much margin, but it is not impractical if the social structure can bear the rigorous constraints, as illustrated by the efforts of various Mediterranean countries (and some East Asian countries with high levels of growth and domestic savings, although they benefited from an opening of the American market).

- *Agricultural potential and constraints.* The difficulty for agriculture in the countries in the south and east of the Mediterranean basin (Turkey excluded) is to reconcile the internationalization of trade with a policy of employment and the long-term management of scarce resources. In fact, this trade pattern would lead to the persistence of an international division of labour involving the export of fruit and vegetables and the import of food staples (cereals, meat, milk products, oil-seed products, and sugar). In 1980, for instance, the cereal shortfall in the southern Mediterranean countries was equal to between 90 per cent and 100 per cent of agricultural trade, and that of foodstuffs between 56 per cent and 100 per cent. For non-food agricultural products the shortfall exceeded 75 per cent in the Maghreb (including Libya), but was virtually nil for Egypt because of substantial cotton exports. Aside from this, agriculture and food deficits are in fact considerable.

Massive imports of cereals and other food staples, dumped on international markets as a result of competition between industrialized countries to offload their food surpluses, would dramatically undermine traditional agriculture in the countries to the south of the basin in a very short time. It would stimulate the exodus of migrants from the country, who would be unable to find jobs quickly enough in the cities. In these circumstances the proliferation of shanty towns can be expected around major urban centres and coastal cities, with their social and environmental consequences, whose impact has been simulated in the trend scenarios.

There seems, moreover, to be a paradox in the fact that the southern countries export market-garden produce (early fruit and vegetables, citrus fruit, grapes, etc.), taking advantage of the seasonal or climatic complementarity with the countries in the north of the basin. In the final analysis, is this not the export, in the form of fruit and vegetables, of *water*, a scarce resource which, largely subsidized, is thus not sold at its real cost?

4. Production structures

The mechanisms governing the structures of the economy are very different in the industrialized countries and in the developing countries. In the countries north of the basin, although growth has a considerable impact, technological change alters the business environment just as radically, introducing new complexity and increased mobility into what will henceforth be world-wide markets. In the developing countries, the changes in the domestic market plays a part, notably the improvement of food consumption. Aside from trade, however, income distribution is also an important factor, which justifies its inclusion in the alternative scenarios.

(b) Countries north of the basin

Any long-term projection is based on a view of the economy. The basic phenomenon since the mid-1970s has been the down-swing of the developed economies, including those on the northern side of the Mediterranean. Is this a lasting phenomenon? If so, for how long and for what reason? Many people see it as the outcome of a series of events which shook the world economy, starting with the breakdown of the Bretton Woods monetary system, followed by the oil shocks, exaggerated fluctuations on the money and financial markets, and the waves of inflation and deflation throughout the world. Certainly these disruptions had an impact on growth, in the same way as the current disequilibria in the North American economy will affect growth in the coming years. But this is not a complete explanation. The crux of the matter lies in the interrelated imbalances stemming from a demand which is saturated in some major sectors and dynamic in others, combined with technological change and social rigidities, especially in the European economies:

- saturation, as indicated by the regression of some sectors (steel and coal, for instance) and the sluggish growth of other markets, especially the motor car—offset, however, by strong demand in service sectors, such as health, tourism, and communications;
- technological change, centring on the electronic revolution, with its many elements—informatics, robotics, telematics, mass-audience television, etc.;
- social rigidities, starting with the institutions and economic agents whose behaviour determines the supply of and demand for products, which evolve more slowly, strictly speaking, than technology: the adaptation of institutions and behaviour, both of businesses and of consumers, is constantly lagging behind technological developments.

Thus, the situation is one of 'structural disequilibria' because former fast-growth sectors, such as electromechanics, are too big compared to demand, whereas potential growth sectors such as information technology are not large enough. Even if these sectors take off, their relative insignificance in production prevents them from pulling the economy as a whole. International upheavals, whether or not related to these structural disequilibria, hamper adjustment, particularly by slowing down investment, hence technological change. The solution to the crisis, aside from the reabsorption of distortions in the international economy, must therefore await the slow, reciprocal adaptation of the structures of demand and supply. This is a major process because it depends not only, as mentioned above, on technological development in general, but also on the institutions and behaviour governing supply and demand. For the scenarios it was assumed that these radical social changes would be producing results during the 1990s.

The countries on the northern side of the basin, led by France and Italy, are involved in these problems, which affect trends in their production structures. Overall, the most important hypothesis is the stagnation of agricultural production, in terms of volume, throughout the period up to 2025. As regards industry, multipliers around four times the 1980 level are advanced, with major differences depending on the sector. In the case of the services, growth in terms of volume is meaningless, but even taking into account the blurred border between products and services, the latter have advanced considerably in terms of value, as this sector will, in the long run, represent between 70 per cent and 80 per cent of the GDP.

An indication of the distortion of structures within the manufacturing sector, with reference to manufacturing value added and employment in France and Italy, is given in Table 8.6. The main trend lies in the continued expansion of the capital goods industry ('machinery' in Table 8.6) to the detriment of other branches: at the end of the period over half the manufacturing jobs would be in this branch of industry. Still in terms of employment, the agricultural and food industries would lose 2 percentage points, primary transformation industries ('heavy industry' in the table) would lose twice as much, and light industry three times as much, this progression reflecting implicit priorities.

Althouth these observations are very general, they are interesting in that they adumbrate an international division of labour in which industrialized countries like France and Italy would export technology in the form of capital goods in exchange for imports of products from other branches. It is precisely this kind of specialization that is supposed to take place, not on the world market as in the trend scenarios, but between the northern and southern sides of the Mediterranean in one of the alternative scenarios (A1). If Spain and Greece are

Table 8.6 Manufacturing structures 1980, 2000, and 2025

Branch of industry	1980		2000			2025		
	MVA	EMP	Mult	MVA	EMP	Mult	MVA	EMP
(a) France and Italy (T1 scenario)								
Agro-food	15.1	10.2	1.5	13.2	9.4	3.1	11.4	7.9
Heavy	28.5	22.2	1.5	26.1	20.0	3.3	23.4	18.4
Light	21.1	30.3	1.6	20.3	27.3	3.5	18.3	23.1
Machinery	35.3	37.3	1.9	40.4	43.3	5.4	46.9	50.6
SECTOR TOTAL	100.0	100.0	1.7	100.0	100.0	4.1	100.0	100.0
(b) Turkey (A1 scenario)								
Agro-food	25.4	21.1	1.6	14.6	9.5	5.9	12.8	8.7
Heavy	44.4	31.6	2.3	37.1	25.7	9.0	33.9	23.8
Light	18.4	32.2	3.7	30.0	40.8	16.1	25.3	32.4
Machinery	11.8	15.1	4.3	18.3	24.0	27.9	28.0	35.1
SECTOR TOTAL	100.0	100.0	2.8	100.0	100.0	11.7	100.0	100.0
(c) Egypt and the Maghreb (A2 scenario)								
Egypt								
Agro-food	18.1	16.9	2.5	17.6	16.8	11.6	15.1	15.8
Heavy	31.5	32.0	2.5	30.8	31.4	16.0	36.6	38.4
Light	33.8	42.8	2.4	31.5	41.8	9.8	24.1	33.4
Machinery	16.6	8.3	3.1	20.0	10.0	20.1	24.2	12.3
SECTOR TOTAL	100.0	100.0	2.6	100.0	100.0	13.9	100.0	100.0
Maghreb								
Agro-food	28.1	18.6	1.9	19.6	13.1	12.2	21.3	16.8
Heavy	31.3	25.9	2.5	29.4	18.7	16.8	32.7	19.3
Light	30.0	45.8	3.6	40.8	57.9	16.2	30.3	48.1
Machinery	10.6	9.7	2.6	10.2	10.3	23.7	15.7	15.8
SECTOR TOTAL	100.0	100.0	2.7	100.0	100.0	16.1	100.0	100.0

Key: Mult = volume multiplier in relation to 1980 (1980 = 1);
MVA = % manufacturing value added (1975$);
EMP = employment as % of total employment in manufacturing branch.

added to France and Italy, the average for the Mediterranean countries of the European Community changes little as these two countries are gradually reaching the same kind of structure.

This structure can be compared to that obtained for Turkey (Table 8.6b). In terms of major sectors, trends seem fairly positive for Turkish agriculture, whose domestic market is far from saturation point. Output in volume would increase by 2.6 in 2025 compared to 1980, admittedly a multiplier lower than that of the GDP anticipated in the A1 scenario, a fortiori also lower than that of the electricity and gas infrastructure (10.8), and of manufacturing industry (11.7). In 1980 the agriculture and food industries, and initial processing of raw materials ('heavy industry' in the table) represented more than 70 per cent of the manufacturing value added and provided over half the jobs, a typical structure for developing countries. Assuming a rather high growth-rate and economic integration into the European Community (scenario A1), these industries would lose their dominance by 2025, to the benefit of light and capital goods industries, the former growing faster up to 2000, the latter after that date. Turkey in 2025 would resemble Spain in 2000, not only in production volume but also in its manufacturing structure.

(b) Countries south and east of the Basin

The case of southern and eastern countries is illustrated by two examples, the Maghreb (Algeria, Morocco and Tunisia) and Egypt (Table 8.6c). A comparison of the initial structures of the two in 1980 highlights the relative importance of Egyptian agriculture (22 per cent of GDP compared to 15 per cent in the Maghreb) and of its industry (20 per cent of GDP compared to 17 per cent in the Maghreb), offset by the construction and service sectors. These differences would persist for agriculture in the projections to 2000 and 2025, and would diminish or even be reversed—depending on the scenario—for industry, which would reach 27–29 per cent of GDP in both cases (except in the worst trend scenario).

It is interesting to make a comparison with Turkey. In all cases infrastructure for electricty and gas would grow faster than GDP, but on the southern side primary transformation industries ('heavy industry' in the table) would remain important, at least in terms of volume, which can be ascribed to their wealth of natural resources (petrochemical industries). As regards employment, light industry would predominate, providing a third of jobs in Egypt and nearly half in the Maghreb (reflecting the international division of labour simulated here). Capital goods industries would experience strong growth, with a twentyfold increase in production in 2025 (in volume) compared to that of 1980, although still distinctly lower than in the Turkish projection.

5. Comparison of the determinants of growth

To conclude this analysis of the hypotheses for economic growth and production structures, the breakdown of industrial growth can be examined in the light of two factors, employment and productivity, for the countries or group of countries under reference (Table 8.7). In fact the annual growth-rates of employment and productivity per worker can be added together to give the growth-rate of industrial production. According to these projections, productivity per worker would increase at the rate of 2–3 per cent per annum for France and Italy between 1980 and 2025 (corresponding figures per hours worked would be higher). Growth of industrial employment would be slower, but nevertheless positive, between 1.2 per cent and 1.4 per cent per annum. Moreover, the phenomena of the underground economy have not been taken into account: these tend to increase the growth of employment considerably in the south of Europe. In all, the scenario projections show employment in

Table 8.7 Industrial growth determinants, 1980–2025

	Scenario T2			Scenario A[a]		
	Production	Productivity	Employment	Production	Productivity	Employment
France and Italy	3.2	2.0	1.2	3.7	2.3	1.4
Turkey	3.6	0.7	2.9	5.8	1.6	4.1
Maghreb	3.9	0.7	3.2	6.4	2.2	4.1
Egypt	3.3	1.2	2.1	6.0	2.5	4.4

[a] A1 for France and Italy, and for Turkey; A2 for the other countries.

industry and the services as being complementary.

For Turkey, Egypt, and the Maghreb it can be noted that contrary to trends in the industrialized countries, industrial employment should grow faster than productivity, which corresponds to factor endowments. In the worst case (worst trend scenario T2) employment should grow at the rate of 2–3 per cent per annum, and in the best case (scenario A2), more than 4 per cent per annum. These rates depend on at least three variables: the general growth-rate, structure by branch (notably, an increase in high-productivity heavy industry tends to reduce the growth of employment), and lastly the distribution within the production structure of large-, medium-, and small-sized businesses, the latter tending to generate more employment. Application of a policy promoting this last group, and more generally low-productivity sectors, is in fact assumed in the A2 scenario, in which employment growth would reach its maximum.

9 Presentation of the Scenarios

1. The trend scenarios

The framework of the trend scenarios can be presented on the basis of the five dimensions chosen earlier. The starting-point is the international economic context (first dimension), in which it is assumed that the Mediterranean protagonists will be eclipsed to some extent, and decision-making centres outside the Mediterranean, chiefly the United States and Japan, will predominate. National development strategies (third dimension) accordingly hinge as a priority on policies of participation in the world market. Another strong hypothesis is a certain passivity as regards management of coastal areas (fourth dimension) and consideration of the environment (fifth dimension): in the best of cases a short-term ecological view is advanced, closely tied to the demands of competition characterizing the international economic context; in the worst case negligence prevails. If in addition it is assumed that a *laissez-faire* policy is adopted on population growth, notably with respect to urbanization phenomena (second dimension: population movements), this all gives a very undesirable picture, which emphasizes the features of the major trends observed.

The framework thus built up seems to be fairly consistent. In an economic environment in which competition is harsh, the weak are vulnerable, and long-term economic needs are not recognized, participation in the world market seems to be an inevitable priority, almost regardless of the social or environmental impact. It should be stressed, however, that these trends are not necessarily compatible with each other beyond the short or medium term. In the long term—horizon 2025 of the Blue Plan—the priority given to macro-economic success may indeed produce positive results as regards growth, modernization of the economy, foreign trade, and the balance of payments, although the countries are not all on the same footing in this struggle. Nevertheless, even in the case of good economic results, short-sightedness concerning environmental management, notably through the wastage of scarce resources such as water or coastal areas, could be counter-productive, to the point of jeopardizing both the economic and social aspects of development. These contradictions will later be pinpointed, and the importance of better-balanced policies shown in the alternative scenarios.

(a) The international economic context

The parameters to be considered are first the growth of the world economy, then trade, and lastly regulations concerning finance and debt. Growth would remain weak until 2000, then subsequently recover, slowly in the worst trend scenario T2, more robustly in the moderate trend scenario T3 (the T1 scenario lies between the two).

Regarding trade, the main hypothesis is that it will take place within the context of a policy of participation in the world market. For some countries this trend merely extends the effect of the forces pulling away from intra-Mediterranean trade. For others, chiefly the Mediterranean countries belonging to the European Community, it is a matter of suspending their integration policy. These aspects are worth considering, by reviewing trends over the past fifteen years.

The yardstick adopted for measuring the degree of integration between either two countries or groups of countries is the so-called 'economic tie' between two partners. This indicator compares the market share of country A's exports in the imports of country B with the world-market share of country A. If this ratio is equal to or higher than one, there is a 'special economic tie' for A's exports to B.* The interest of these indicators is their long-term stability, so they are rather useful for measuring a 'trade structure'. These indicators will be used to analyse briefly intra-Mediterranean 'ties', then to define the

* So for each pair of partners there are two measurements of their ties, depending on whether trade from A to B or from B to A is considered.

Table 9.1 Special economic ties in intra-Mediterranean trade, 1980

	Morocco	Algeria	Tunisia	Libya	Egypt	Lebanon[a]	Syria[b]	Israel	Spain	France	Italy	Greece	Malta	Yugoslavia	Cyprus	Turkey	Whole Mediterranean
Morocco	··	5.0	··	1.2		2.2	2.4		3.7	3.9	1.2	2.4		1.3		1.8	2.5
Algeria	3.9	··							2.2	2.1	1.3	1.3		1.0		3.1	1.4
Tunisia	··		··	1.8					3.1								3.3
Libya			1.8	··					3.1		4.1	7.0				8.7	2.1
Egypt	1.6			30.0	··	2.9	2.6	16.0	1.0		6.3	6.2		3.0	1.8		2.6
Lebanon[a]	0.8				4.4	··	20.2					0.8	1.8	1.9		6.3	1.3
Syria[b]					7.7	2.5	··				4.5	10.7		7.7		1.0	2.0
Israel								··		0.8	1.1	1.1		0.9	9.5	1.9	0.9
Spain	8.7	4.6	3.4	3.8		2.0	2.7	1.8	··	2.5	1.7	1.2	2.0	0.7	2.2	1.3	2.1
France	5.2	4.9	4.8	1.3		2.2	1.8		2.5	··	2.7	2.3		0.9	1.0	1.3	1.5
Italy	1.5	3.5	3.9	7.3		2.3	2.6		2.3		··	3.3	6.3	2.3	3.1	1.5	1.7
Greece		2.4	7.4	7.2		6.6	8.5			1.1	2.1	··	3.7	2.7	28.8	1.1	1.9
Malta				17.4		1.8					1.3		··	1.8			1.0
Yugoslavia	1.2	1.5		4.1	3.7	1.0	0.8				2.0	3.8	1.3	··	1.2	2.0	1.2
Cyprus				18.2	3.5	7.2	45.3					5.4	3.6	1.3	··		0.9
Turkey	2.6		2.6	4.6	1.5	29.2	10.1	0.7		0.9	1.6	0.7		1.3	2.0	··	1.2
Whole Mediterranean	3.2	3.4	3.5	3.3	2.0	2.4	2.1	0.8	1.5	1.1	1.9	3.1	2.3	1.4	2.3	1.9	1.6

Note: Definition of an economic tie between exporter i and importer j:

$$\Delta_{ij} = \frac{\text{market share of } i \text{ in total exports of } j}{\text{share of total world exports of } i}.$$

The tie between i and j is said to be 'special' when the coefficient Δ_{ij} is greater than 1. The table refers only to values over 0.7. The groups of countries whose special ties seem particularly important have been boxed, as well as the final row and column, which indicate a given country's tie with the Mediterranean as a whole.

[a] Figures are for 1970.
[b] Figures are for 1975.

Source: UNCTAD.

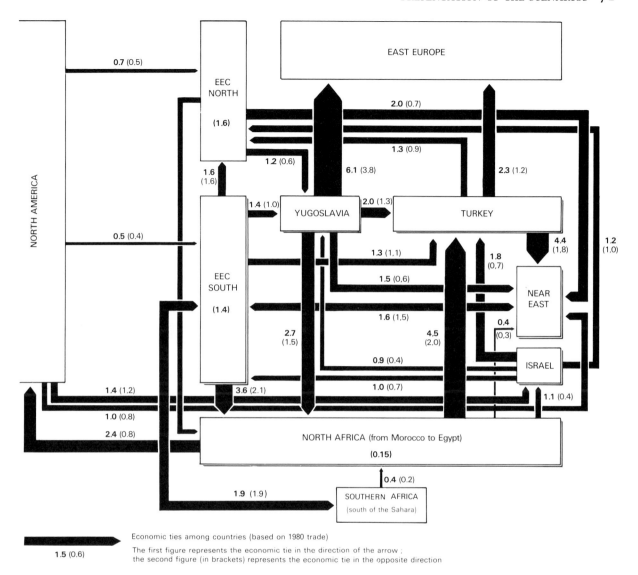

Economic ties among countries (based on 1980 trade)

1.5 (0.6) The first figure represents the economic tie in the direction of the arrow ;
the second figure (in brackets) represents the economic tie in the opposite direction

FIG. 9.1 Economic ties of Mediterranean countries, 1980
Source: UNCTAD/Blue Plan.

major trends to be taken into account in the scenarios.

Concerning intra-Mediterranean ties, an examination of the two ties of each country with the Mediterranean basin as a whole, e.g. for 1980 (Table 9.1 and Fig. 9.1), produces an initial, very significant conclusion: some degree of economic integration clearly exists among the Mediterranean countries—because of their proximity due to the sea or else on account of the influence of the past. Out of thirty-two indicators (two per country, since both directions are taken into account), thirty are greater than 1, thus reflecting 'special ties'.

The trend of the countries' ties with the basin as a whole can easily be traced before 1980 but with

less detail after this date because calculations are very complex. Taking the most complete indicator possible for this intra-Mediterranean tie (comprising the ties of all the basin countries with all other basin countries), it can be observed that it was 1.7 in 1970, fell to 1.4 in 1975 (perhaps a result of the first 'oil shock'), and climbed again in 1980 to 1.6, just below the 1970 value. The down-swing in fact stemmed from diverging trends between some ties which contracted sharply and others which expanded. The Maghreb countries, Yugoslavia, and Turkey reduced their exports to the Mediterranean, and Algeria, France, and Yugoslavia reduced their imports from the basin, whereas Egypt and Spain expanded their Mediterranean exports and Libya,

Greece, and Turkey increased their imports from the Mediterranean countries.

It can be confirmed, for example, that the exploitation of natural resources (phosphate and oil) in the three Maghreb countries and Libya systematically led to an expansion of the economy within the world context during the 1970s. The use of trade surpluses for imports, especially in the case of Algeria, led to attempts to diversify suppliers, prompted by their growing competition on the world market. These orientations, in which manufactured products play an important part, seem therefore to form a major trend, very likely to persist in the absence of interventionist policies (such as those assumed in the alternative scenarios). Libya, an exception, illustrates the importance of this large import market for the other Mediterranean countries after 1973. The contraction observed for France reflects the diversification of energy supplies: France's ties with all the other countries of the Mediterranean basin as regards energy products fell from 2.5 in 1970 to 0.7 in 1980.

Conversely, it is possible to observe an exceptional redeployment of Spanish exports towards the Maghreb, the other Mediterranean countries of the European Community, and Turkey. Lastly, analysis of imports shows that Greece and Turkey actively diversified their suppliers, especially in the west of the basin (Maghreb, southern Europe), more so than outside the Mediterranean.

How can this kind of analysis be used for the trend scenarios? To do so, countries or groups of countries outside the basin also have to be taken into account. Then the strength of the ties (first for exports, then for imports) of the EEC Mediterranean countries with the whole of North Africa (2.1 and 3.6 respectively), the Near East (1.6 and 1.5) and even sub-Saharan Africa (1.9 and 1.9) becomes apparent, as well as the comparative weakness of their ties with North America. The only countries with a strong exporting tie with North America are those of North Africa (2.4), chiefly because of hydrocarbons. The analysis also confirmed the weakness of inter-Arab trade or 'ties', which plunged in the 1970s—both within North Africa (0.15) and between North Africa and the Near East (approx. 0.3). This weakness contrasts with the strength of ties forged among the four Mediterranean countries of the European Community (1.4), and between these four countries and the rest of the European Community.

Examination of the evolution of some of these ties between 1970 and 1985 (Table 9.2) indeed confirms the continued strengthening of integration within the European Community. On this point the trend scenarios in fact diverge from the trend by assuming that the world market could go as far as disrupting intra-Community ties. This hypothesis is based on the fierceness of some current trade disputes (the issue of American maize exports to Spain, the market for long-distance aeroplanes, or the commercial offensives of Japan and East Asia), and assumes a

Table 9.2 Trends in some economic ties, 1970–1985

	Export			Import		
	1970	1980	1985	1970	1980	1985
EEC 12: *with*						
EEC 12	1.4	1.50	1.7	1.4	1.5	1.7
North America	0.6	0.40	0.6	0.7	0.6	0.5
Japan	0.2	0.15	0.1	0.3	0.4	0.4
Yugoslavia: *with*						
EEC 12	1.1	0.70	1.0	1.5	1.2	0.8
Eastern Europe	3.5	6.10	6.2	2.1	3.8	3.6
Turkey:[a] *with*						
EEC 12	1.4	1.20	1.2	1.5	1.1	0.9
North America	0.6	1.20	0.3	0.3	0.5	0.6
Japan	0.7	0.20	0.1	0.3	0.4	0.4
Near East	6.1	4.40	6.1	2.0	1.8	4.5
North Africa:[b] *with*						
EEC 12	2.0	1.30	1.9	1.7	1.9	1.7
North America	0.1	2.40	1.1	0.6	0.8	0.7
Japan	0.2	0.30	0.3	0.4	0.8	0.7

[a] Latest figures are for 1983.
[b] Latest figures are for 1984 and 1985.

Source: UNCTAD.

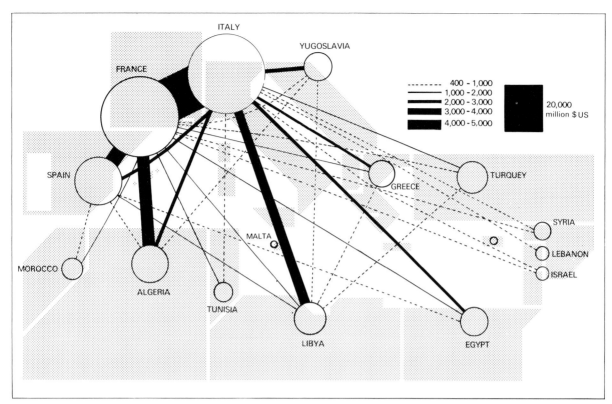

FIG. 9.2 Intra-Mediterranean trade, 1980 (imports and exports in $m.)
Source: UNCTAD/Blue Plan.

certain slackening of Europe's political cohesion. These hypotheses are naturally much clearer in the worst scenario T2 than in the moderate scenario T3.

The analysis also reveals the so-called 'ratchet effect' with regard to imports by Mediterranean countries' (the EEC countries, also Turkey and North Africa) from non-Mediterranean countries (Japan in the lead, and the United States): growth of imports during the expansion of world trade, then consolidation (or at most slight decline) despite the reversal of trends, whereas the inverse ties (exports towards these non-Mediterranean countries) continue to contract. These exports were naturally affected by the value of the dollar, high during the first half of the 1980s.

Finally, Yugoslavia's export and import ties with Eastern Europe tightened throughout the period under review, which may be related to its weakening position with respect to market economies and to payment difficulties.

In conclusion, it seems that the trend scenarios must take into account both incipient economic integration among Mediterranean countries, the Community apparently gaining strength as a focal point on the northern side, and two factors that may on the contrary weaken these Mediterranean ties. The first is the internationalization of the hydrocarbon and raw-material markets, with its radiating effects. The second is the 'ratchet effect' with regard to imports from non-Mediterranean countries (which has spread to include other countries in the Pacific region, and may continue its expansion), linked to the increasing internationalization of trade within a neo-liberal context, whose initial impact was detected in the 1970s. The trend scenarios assumed that this major orientation would continue to develop, and in the worst case, T2, include the strong hypothesis that it could even affect the cohesion of the European Community.

(b) National context of the trend scenarios

The population hypotheses (Chapter 7) concerning the trend scenarios make the search for full employment difficult for the disadvantaged masses of the population in the countries south and east of the basin. They would tend to widen even further the per capita income gap between north and south, especially in the worst trend scenario T2, in which population growth-rates are maximal in the south and minimal in the north.

These scenarios postulate poorly controlled urbanization in the south, and even in the north. But two phenomena complicate the hypotheses. In absolute terms, the rural exodus is swollen by the size of the population and rural poverty (the situation in the worst scenario T2), although poverty could represent a curb on mobility. Relatively speaking, economic growth could speed up the rural exodus (the situation in the moderate scenario T3), particularly towards the largest cities (the case during the 1970s, contrary to planners' intentions). These scenarios cannot exclude the fact that social tensions in the less industrialized countries south and east of the basin may provoke political confrontation with the more industrialized countries in the north. Thus, by taking the hypotheses to the extreme, it is suggested that the policies simulated in the trend scenarios, once incorporated into an overall perspective, could tip the balance in the Mediterranean basin and so threaten the long-term interests of the more industrialized countries too. Approaches that pay particularly close attention to the future are simulated in the alternative scenarios.

Concerning management of scarce resources, such as water and land, the difference between the two extreme trend scenarios, and between the worst trend T2 and the moderate trend T3, should be stressed. The sluggish growth postulated in the first scenario in a way minimizes pressure on resources. However, even if the growth of demand slows down, a breach between the supply and demand of urban water could occur because of inadequacy of investment (particularly in dams), to the extent that the comparative passivity postulated with respect to the environment could be equated with lack of foresight. In the moderate scenario T3 the risk will be heightened by strong pressure exerted by both the supply of large urban centres and agricultural requirements (including those for exports).

In the same way, cities and their infrastructure exert considerable pressure on coastal areas in the moderate scenario T3. Coastal management would be faced with the conflicting needs of industry, urbanization, and more or less disorganized tourism. The efficiency of institutions responsible for physical planning will be sorely tested, since economic policies would tend towards a concentration of modern industry around a few urban poles, with the virtually uncontrollable expansion of cities.

With regard to pollution, risk also seems lower in the slow-growth scenarios than in the case of fast growth; but this may be a mistaken impression to the extent that the shortage of public services could lead to the supply of poor-quality water and the inadequacy of waste-water networks. In the strongest-growth scenario, air pollution in cities and epidemiological hazards in rural areas linked to the extension of irrigation are additional problems.

In all, the trend scenarios are likely a priori to be harmful to the environment. Formulation of the scenarios should make it possible to check or confirm this assumption. The moderate scenario T3 in particular should help to test the effect of prolonged uncontrolled growth on the environment, which was the case when there was less concern about ecology, or even none at all. A reaction to environmental degradation is very likely to occur—in other words a back-lash on the economy at the end of the period.

2. The alternative scenarios

For the countries north of the basin the alternative scenarios are based on the pursuit of European integration with its repercussions, together with a growing concern for spatial management and environmental protection. For the countries in the south and east of the basin they are based on the adoption of goal-orientated development policies focusing on domestic objectives, which in no way excludes a realistic appreciation of external or environmental constraints.

(a) General presentation and international context

European integration is reflected by the simultaneous advance of political and monetary institutions, in which the ECU plays an international role. In the world context the importance of Europe is sufficient to give a multipolar structure to the international institutions governing trade, money, and financial transactions, which implies a disruption of current balances based on the strengthening of the economic and political role of the Pacific region. Europe's self-assertion provides many countries with a broader margin for action than in the past, and the north–south dialogue benefits, becoming more active and diversified.

In the first alternative scenario, A1, (the reference scenario), Europe draws on an ideal of north–south solidarity to provide exemplary development assistance in the Mediterranean basin, endorsing a true 'Pax Mediterranea' in an atmosphere of cultural exchange. A huge coherent region is formed on both sides of the Mediterranean. The institutional aspects of this co-operation, comprising both sides of the basin, are necessarily varied, from possible adhesion to the European Community for some countries to more flexible contractual commitments for others, all structures of dialogue being designed in a long-term perspective.

The second alternative scenario, A2, retains the principle of a multipolar world system, with a strong Europe open to north–south solidarity. Unlike the first scenario, however, the links between the northern and southern side of the Mediterranean are not institutionalized as such, but are formed within world institutions. This in particular is the level at which solutions to Third World debt are found, and the rules of trade and of technology transfer between industrialized and less industrialized countries are applied. The second premiss of this scenario is the development of subregional solidarity within the Mediterranean basin (even including some nearby countries). Aside from the European Community, 'groups' are formed which are not described in detail here—but, to outline a few examples, the greater Maghreb would be strengthened, Egypt would play a pivotal role between the Mediterranean, sub-Saharan Africa, and the Near East, Turkey would link the eastern Mediterranean with western Asia, and Yugoslavia would act as a liaison between the European Community, the Mediterranean, and Eastern Europe. The hypotheses specific to each of the two alternative scenarios are described below.

(b) Reference alternative scenario A1

Once the international context has been defined by strong links between the European Community and the other Mediterranean countries within the framework of long-standing *ad hoc* institutions, the terms of development strategies can be specified. On the side of the European Community, a proportion of savings are invested in Mediterranean development. In exchange, the Community benefits in the long run from a larger agricultural and industrial market. Growth is therefore stronger than in the moderate trend scenario T3 (as shown above in Table 8.1).

For the countries south and east of the Mediterranean basin, this scenario is no doubt the one in which the modern sector grows fastest, fostered by numerous cultural, technological, commercial, financial, and even monetary links with the Euro-

pean Community. With credit and support from the Community's financial centres, a satisfactory solution is found for the debt problem, so that long-term domestic savings, supplemented by foreign assistance, can be invested in development.

This growth in the countries south and east of the Mediterranean basin is based on industry, which can develop with a guaranteed market in the north in conditions similar to those experienced by east and south-east Asia with respect to the United States and Japan: the north–south division of labour provides outlets first for the food industry, light industry, and primary transformation industries, followed by the capital goods industry. Transfer of technology is facilitated by direct investment from Europe, which enables her—as is currently the case of Japan through its industries located abroad—to keep a share in the world market for products in which the southern and eastern countries of the Mediterranean basin are more competitive.

With regard to agriculture, the coastal countries on the northern side (from Spain to Turkey) and on the southern and eastern sides manage to reach a compromise which attenuates competition. For the southern and eastern countries, access to modern irrigated agriculture on the one hand reduces pressure on scarce resources such as water and land (and reduces the use of fertilizer) and, on the other, enables them to gain market shares. This reproduces to some extent the Ricardian division of agricultural labour analysed in the trend scenarios—fruit and vegetable from coastal regions in exchange for food staples from the temperate climates (from cereals to animal products). The impact of this trade on the south and east of the Mediterranean should be assessed.

The appearance of a middle class with growing economic and political influence has a stabilizing effect on institutions. But there is also an undeniable negative impact on employment in traditional agriculture, in direct competition with less expensive imports from the north. Three factors may nevertheless offset this effect as compared to the trend scenarios:

● The growth of modern agricultural and industrial sectors is stronger and therefore generates employment.

● The governments of the southern and eastern countries of the Mediterranean basin may obtain assistance for traditional agriculture from the European Community, similar to the regional assistance granted to member states to ease transitions.

● Regulations concerning the admission of migrant workers into Europe are more liberal, which somewhat relieves the effects of a growth in the labour force. Although the population hypotheses for the north are the same as in the moderate trend scenario T3, they are more favourable for the south and east as population growth is slower, corresponding to higher standards of living.

In addition to agricultural and industrial products, north–south trade includes natural gas, to the advantage of industry on both sides of the Mediterranean. As regards the tourist trade, flows are important both from northern Europe towards the Mediterranean shores and within the coastal countries themselves, since the rise of the middle class is conducive to the growth of domestic tourism. Conflict over the use of coastal areas remains acute, as in the trend scenarios, since more restrained urban development is offset by high levels of irrigated agricultural production and industrialization.

The trend towards increased polluting emissions due to the higher level of economic activity is offset by a more rigorous position on the part of governments concerning the quality of life and by real north–south solidarity aimed at conserving the Mediterranean. Hence a common concern to resort to less polluting technologies in all sectors, the adoption of common standards, and the setting up of effective networks for monitoring pollution levels or environmental degradation, starting with the sea itself and the coast. This solidarity leads to a fair sharing of rehabilitation costs.

(c) Integration alternative scenario A2

Compared with A1, this subregional co-operation scenario is characterized by better control of the internal structures of the economy in the south and east of the Mediterranean, accompanied admittedly by greater external risks, and by a lesser economic and financial commitment towards Mediterranean development in the north, related to slower growth.

The northern economy is tied more to the world market and less to the Mediterranean market than previously, and the European Community is the focal point for a number of countries with which it has special relations (in keeping with the Lomé agreement). In order to vary the hypotheses, the population trends of the European countries recover in this scenario, unlike the other scenarios, in which replacement level is not reached in a growing number of countries (it is admitted that this hypothesis, which combines rather well with that of a strong Europe, is somewhat arbitrary). European

industry is little affected by this variation, but its agriculture has greater difficulty in finding foreign outlets, which further restricts its production capacity.

In the south and east of the basin industry diversifies its outlets, which implies a difficult breakthrough on to the world market. On the other hand, the subregional solidarity postulated in this scenario, materializing in the form of initiatives like the Maghreb Union, enables industry to rely on an enlarged 'domestic market', whose size corresponds to each regional group. Technological advance is an essential parameter, which excludes any hope of self-reliant development. It is assumed that the world system is conducive to direct investment in the context of the guarantees furnished by international codes.

Governments and modern industrial circles attempt to foster the productivity of those informal activities—usually urban—whose structures are the most advanced, by encouraging subcontracting between these two sectors with different levels of productivity through fiscal policy, training incentives, credit, price structures, salary legislation, etc.

Unlike industry, agriculture can be largely dissociated from world influences, the dual aims being to ensure a high level of self-sufficiency in food and to maximize rural employment as long as other sectors are unable to provide a sufficient number of jobs. These objectives involve efforts to maximize the productivity of both traditional farms and those in irrigated plains, or to organize rural industrial or service activities for farming families. This growth of agricultural productivity is achieved through radical reforms, including an appropriate price structure, the suitable orientation of research, and agricultural extension work, the organization of rural credit, etc. These efforts are geared not only to reducing the gap between urban and rural incomes but also to economizing scarce resources, in particular water and agricultural land.

In this optimal social-policy scenario, the lower population growth-rate provides the best conditions for reducing both urban unemployment and underemployment in rural and urban areas. To achieve this, however, considerable levels of savings are required to finance not only productive activities but also all the public budget items needed to attain the levels of education, training, and public health without which these objectives could not be realized.

With regard to trade, Europe tends to diversify further its sources of raw materials and energy, to the point of changing the hierarchy of its energy sources. Tourist flows and styles of tourism are more varied, with greater importance inside subregional groups. These groups also contribute to a better mastery of physical planning, aimed at improving the balance between, on the one hand, rural and urban areas and, on the other, coastal and hinterland areas. Management of coastal areas stems not only from an expressed goal, but also from all the mechanisms governing the economy. Pressure on natural resources (forest, soil, water) is not necessarily reduced because of this: irrigation techniques aim at saving water, but water is required over larger surface areas, and crop areas are larger than those in the other scenarios.

Governments do not gain as much as in the previous scenario from anti-pollution measures resulting from European Community assistance, and so do not adopt European standards. However, the state of pollution in cities is less alarming because of the better balance between rural and urban areas and between large- and medium-sized agglomerations. The comparatively large number of low-productivity activities also helps, at an equal level of production.

Lastly, two general observations can be made. The first is that these scenarios do not lack plausible components. The second is that variations between the two scenarios aim at revealing different avenues for protection of the Mediterranean environment, bearing in mind development constraints. Even if reality is very unlikely to resemble either of the hypothetical situations described here, the aim of these very diverging scenarios is to assist decision-makers to enhance their perception of the nature and repercussions of their choices, in the absence of any miraculous solution which optimizes at the same time growth, employment, and the environment, just to mention the major issues.

III The Economic Activities and their Impact on the Environment

Introduction

Development activities naturally form a coherent set, but to facilitate their study they have been divided, as already mentioned, into a number of sectors: food and agriculture, industry, energy, tourism, and transport. Similarly, a development scenario, with its impact on the environment, has to be multisectoral. In effect, the use of 'sectoral scenarios', agro-food, industry, tourism, etc. in the following chapters is an over-simplification. A few simple models were developed for the sectoral scenarios, occasionally even for certain subsectors (e.g. road transport), the findings being transferred from one model to another although there is no automatic linkage between models.

The major lines of the past and current development of each of these activities have been described, followed by an attempt to identify possible trends up to 2000 and 2025, as deduced from the 'sectoral scenarios'. Since these activities have very different features, methods of analysis and identification of trends are not entirely uniform, a trait which tends, moreover, to become more pronounced over a longer period.

An additional difficulty is linked to technological forecasting: even though laboratory findings make it possible to imagine accurately the impact of a certain breakthrough or new development (bio-technology, nuclear fusion, photovoltaic cells, etc.), opinions diverge concerning the point at which these innovations will effectively have en economic impact. The time-span will depend not only on the extent of the research-and-development efforts undertaken or envisaged, but also on the ability of the institutions to mobilize the necessary resources and/or marketing and industrial structures. This uncertainty as to the moment when technology will actually penetrate the market contrasts with an accurate definition of the 'pathway', essential for distinguishing a scenario from a mere image of the future. All the activities to be reviewed have a fairly siignificant impact on Mediterranean areas, natural resources, and the environment in the broadest sense. These specific impacts on the most important environmental components will be presented for each of the activities in turn, regardless of eventual aggregation or synergy, as this aspect will be dealt with in Part IV of the report.

10 Agro-Food Prospects

Section 1 of this chapter outlines the issues concerning food and agriculture in the Mediterranean by identifying the specific features of the Mediterranean countries and trends in the demand for agro-food. There is certainly room for progress in agricultural production, but this potential can only be exploited when a number of constraints have been better understood and overcome.

On this basis, section 2 tackles the prospective study for food and agricultural production in the Mediterranean. The general hypotheses of the economic scenarios are specified as regards their content and meaning for food and agriculture, leading to a modelling of the sector in order to explore the future. The term 'explore' refers to major lines, and is well chosen, for there can be no question of making projections of agricultural output product by product, since it is too dependent on price policies, subsidies, taxation, marketing, or physical limitations. The possible shape of changes to come is then outlined.

It should be recalled that the aim of the exercise was not to define agro-food policies, but to assess the consequences of certain options on natural resources and the environment in the Mediterranean. This goal guided the choice of factors and of their interrelationships. Agriculture and environment interact in many ways. The essential points described in section 3 start with the necessary upstream and downstream industrialization and its impact on the environment, including the specific features of 'soil-less' agriculture, which is highly polluting. In addition to land under cultivation, attention has been paid to the effects of variations in plant cover or uncultivated soil either through soil impoverishment (problems which will be dealt with in Chapter 18) or through a reduction in grazing land. Special consideration has also been given to fertilizers and pesticides, essential inputs for agricultural intensification. The matter has been tackled through the environmental 'chain' method, linking development activities and impacts on the environment in order to obtain data on the possible discharge of nitrogen and phosphorus of agricultural origin into inland or sea water.

Section 4 briefly considers possible trends of the Mediterranean fishery sector within the context of the scenarios, and finally section 5 summarizes conclusions and raises some related queries.

1. Agro-food issues in the Mediterranean

(a) Some features of agriculture in the Mediterranean countries

The study of food and agriculture issues in the Mediterranean is influenced by two ever-present factors: the limitations and fragility of natural resources, and food dependency.

Regarding natural factors, it should be recalled that there are few alluvial plains (Rhone, Po, Nile), and that agricultural areas are compartmentalized. A large part of the land can be used only for extensive stock-farming (or for forests). Adaptation to climatic constraints has taken the form of dry farming and traditional rain-fed shrub and tree crops (grapes, olives, almonds, pistachios). Greater intensification of agriculture necessarily requires the introduction of artificial elements into the environment—basically irrigation—with the mobilization of investment in capital and labour. All this, combined with the limited size of holdings or available land, explains to a large extent the comparative inertia of Mediterranean agriculture. Industrialization of the production process is likewise hampered, and so spreads rather slowly, especially because some operations are difficult to mechanize.

In the Mediterranean countries the area of land under annual or perennial crops is always less than 50 per cent of the total surface area, and even less than 10 per cent in some cases (Algeria, Libya, Egypt, comprising mostly desert). For a total surface area of approximately 850m. ha, 125m. are under annual or perennial crops, and several hundred million hectares are devoted to ranges and grazing land—extensive stock-farming areas poorly suited to furnishing the basis for increased productivity

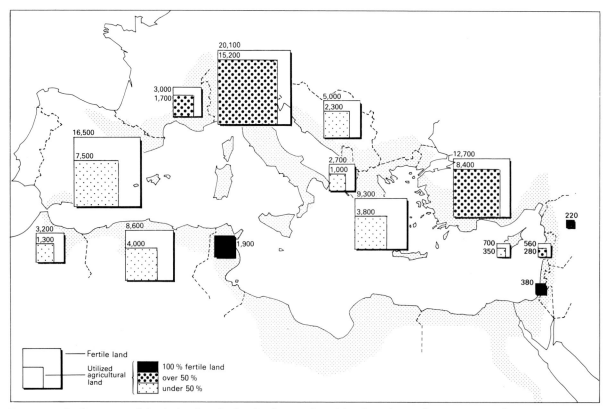

FIG. 10.1 Surface area of fertile land and of utilized agricultural land in the Mediterranean catchment area (1,000 ha). The larger squares indicate the surface area of fertile land—i.e. soil without major factors limiting fertility—in the Mediterranean catchment area of each country. The smaller squares indicate the utilized agricultural land in these areas (as derived from national reports). The shading of smaller squares suggests the intensity of pressure on fertile land and the more or less accentuated tendency to utilize marginal lands in the Mediterranean regions.

Source: Blue Plan, from FAO and national reports.

(which does not exclude the possibility of improved management). Even if the surface area under cultivation remains fairly stable for the Mediterranean as a whole, there are countries in which it is contracting (France and Italy).

Concerning the use of water resources, six countries irrigate more than a quarter of their cultivated land, the others around 10 per cent or less. (The case of Egypt, where agriculture is entirely irrigated, is an exception.) More than 60m. ha are currently under irrigation; in the past fifteen years the area has increased by 3m. ha, and the growth-rate seems to have stabilized at around 200,000 ha per annum. This assumes the availability of an additional capacity of some 2,000m. m³ of water per annum for agriculture alone, which poses a difficult choice between agricultural and urban needs when allocating water resources. The recovery and recycling of both urban and agricultural waste-water may become necessary in a number of countries, with the possiblity, for example, of creating green belts, market gardens, and orchards around cities.

A large part of agriculture in the Mediterranean countries has been modernized and intensified since 1970. For example, global fertilizer consumption has increased by nearly 50 per cent, and the number of tractors in service has increased by more than 40 per cent. But this increase in the means of production is very unevenly distributed: the richest countries have benefited most from intensification (with France, Italy, Israel, and Yugoslavia in the lead). Considering its intensive labour-based production system, Egypt is second among fertilizer consumers (248 kg/ha), but its level of motorization, although it increased at the average rate (40 per cent), remains very low (fewer than fifteen tractors per thousand hectares). Yields are therefore extremely variable, ranging, in the case of cereals, from less than 10 q/ha in the Maghreb to 40 in Egypt and well over 50 in the countries north of the basin (taken as a whole). In addition, there are shortcomings in crop protection, which also contributes to low cereal yields. Lastly, progress resulting from the improvement of varieties is slow,

BOX 10A. **Algerian agriculture**

The main features of Algerian agriculture are still:

- a limited agricultural area;
- inadequate production compared to the needs of the population and the prevailing consumption model in the country;
- low yields per hectare.

A limited agricultural area

The land used for agriculture covers 39.7m. ha, i.e. 16.6 per cent of the total surface area of the country, unproductive land covering 79.6 per cent of the surface area. Out of the land used for agriculture, 7.5m. ha correspond to farmland—barely 3 per cent of the national territory.

Studies undertaken by the BNEDER (National Office for Rural Development Studies) indicate that total agricultural farm land could scarcely exceed 10m. ha. It is easy to understand that efforts to increase agricultural production necessarily imply 'the intensification of production, the increase of yields per hectare, the reduction of fallow land, the combination of stock-farming and cropping, the protection of soil against all hazards (erosion, salinity, alkalinization, etc.), extension work in agricultural techniques suited to the nature of the soil in the country, and the mastery of mechanization and its profitability'.

Trends in agricultural production

1. *Crop production*. Even if the production of cereals and dry pulses has stagnated to some extent (despite the 30m. quintals produced in 1985), market-garden and industrial crops developed considerably between 1966 and 1984.

Cereal production varied between 14.8m. and 26.8m. q from 1966 to 1975, whereas it varied between 11.4m. and 24m. q from 1976 to 1984. The production of dry pulses fell continuously between 1974 and 1984, from 754,570 to 449,340 q.

Market-garden production increased by a factor of 3 between 1966 and 1984 (from 5.7m. to 15.4m. q). Industrial crop production rose from 638,980 to 1,320,819 q.

Conversely, production of traditional crops (citrus fruit, olives, dates, figs) has dropped continuously.

2. *Meat production*. Over the last ten years the numbers of bovine, ovine, and caprine herds have increased by about 50 per cent, although a considerable drop was recorded in 1983–84. Inspected slaughterings of cattle increased up to 1979, at which time slaughtering fell again to the 1977 level (in tonnes). Slaughtering of sheep and goats has remained on the increase, reaching 31,000 t for sheep in 1984.

3. *Agricultural yields*. Trends have been similar to that of production, confirming the dependence of agricultural production on climatic hazards, and are shown in the accompanying table. Output remains comparatively low despite major efforts made for several years with respect to both the organization of agriculture and its supply of equipment and tools, even though the petrochemical industry provides various kinds of fertilizers (phosphates and nitrogen).

Variations in agricultural yields 1976/7–1983/4 (q/ha)

	1976/7	1977/8	1979	1980	1981	1981/2	1982/3	1983/4
Cereals	4.11	5.86	5.61	7.60	6.46	5.93	5.63	5.45
Dried pulses	6.90	6.10	4.50	4.10	4.40	3.30	3.00	2.87
Market-garden crops	56.90	57.90	60.20	64.10	56.40	65.75	57.12	76.53
Industrial crops	86.50	43.80	72.00	46.50	92.20	41.97	89.35	61.12
Artificial fodder	18.20	20.00	20.40	21.20	20.20	17.00	16.00	15.90
Natural fodder	11.40	11.60	12.00	10.70	15.40	13.21	11.23	13.12
Citrus fruit	113.50	99.60	102.60	98.90	86.10	37.04	30.18	63.60
Olives	10.00	7.00	12.00	7.80	16.20	8.09	7.34	6.33
Dates	20.00	31.00	33.30	32.60	31.40	29.03	25.56	25.67
Figs	19.00	18.00	20.70	16.80	18.60	7.32	11.00	9.93
Other fruit	22.60	18.80	18.90	19.30	22.50	8.28	9.28	18.40

The main trend for agriculture is towards stagnation of production and output, leading to a broadening of the gap between food needs and the possibilities of meeting them, which hampers the goal of self-sufficiency in food and calls for special efforts in the coming decades.

Source: Algerian national scenarios.

either because innovations are few, or because the dissemination of new strains takes a long time.

The diversity of situations is particularly striking when examining the use of technical factors, the less wealthy countries having a less intensified agriculture, although the possibility of doubling yields for most of their crops seems quite conceivable. The traditional sector is very small in the most developed areas of some less industrialized countries, but obsolescence can affect certain areas which were considered modern only a short time ago. The traditional sector often includes extensive forms of resource exploitation (pastoralism, rain-fed cereal and tree crops). This is often linked to a high population growth-rate, which requires the cultivation of virtually infertile land. Far from being a hindrance, however, the traditional sector can act as a complement, if not as competitor, to the modern sector, and its usefulness can be demonstrated by the dynamics of the agro-food system. Activities deriving from the traditional craft sector may be innovative and result in significant productivity increases (small-scale mechanization, inputs, transformation, marketing).

But a country's agro-food situation also depends on the international environment. As a result of the natural and socio-economic conditions of the Mediterranean countries, their specialization in 'Mediterranean products' (fruit and vegetables, seeds, etc.) will intensify as trade prospects expand. The corollary to this is food dependency, although the countries south and east of the basin would be likely to have a food deficit in any event. With respect to trade, the Mediterranean is at the crossroads of different influences: the EEC, other non-Mediterranean Arab countries, then the United States and the Eastern European countries (CMEA). The latter have significant economic relations with the Mediterranean countries which moderate the influence of the EEC.

(b) Trends in demand for food and agriculture

Mediterranean agricultural production is basically intended to meet food demand; the most important non-food industrial crops are tobacco and cotton (although the latter provides oil from its seed), which, considering the unattractive prospects on the international market, are geared more to quality (special tobaccos, long-fibre cotton) than to large output.

Trends in food demand depend basically on four factors, whose individual influence is difficult to grasp in practice:

● Population growth is the most obvious, reliable, and easily predictable factor in the growth of food demand. It is the principal factor in the dynamics of food demand in the countries east and south of the basin.

● Per capita income has an impact through income elasticity. This is low and less than 1 for consumer staples (cereals in particular), higher and even greater than 1 for animal products.

● Varying price levels can be attributed to differences in purchasing power, which have the same effect as an income variation (excluding specific changes, with possible product substitution when the price of only some products varies).

● There is an often neglected trend effect which influences and modifies individual consumption—regardless of prices and incomes—through advertising, novelty, fashion, upbringing, availability, etc. This effect increases as on-farm consumption drops and new life-styles appear: urbanization plays a significant role in changing habits, including eating habits.

The traditional Mediterranean consumption pattern is based on cereals. Two other features are found in virtually all countries: the comparatively high level of fruit and vegetable consumption and the large proportion of vegetable oil in fat intake. However, these features are more or less pronounced depending on the standard of living, particularly with respect to the direct consumption of cereals, which may vary by a factor of two. (Patterns may differ considerably between the Mediterranean and non-Mediterranean regions of the same country.)

On the whole, up to 2000, trends will most probably reflect a certain inertia, with possibly a slight increase in the consumption of animal products if price ratios do not change (increase of per capita income in the less industrialized countries may be curbed by population growth). The demographic variable will therefore be a determinant in the variation of net global demand for food products: low or zero in the north, rising fast in the south and east, possibly heading for an increasing shortfall in the main food products.

In 1983, out of seven countries south and east of the basin (Morocco, Algeria, Libya, Tunisia, Egypt, Syria, and Turkey) all, save Turkey, had a significant shortfall in the main food products except meat, for which the deficit was small but with very low consumption levels.* In 2000, according to the FAO average trend scenario, all these countries, except Turkey for sugar and meat, would experience a shortfall, particularly in cereals, for which the increased demand deriving from stock-farming could not be met from domestic sources. Levels of self-sufficiency would drop between 1983 and 2000, despite significant growth-rates for various kinds of produce. According to the same FAO scenario, the estimated shortfall in 2000 for these southern and eastern countries would be in the region of 30m. t of cereals, 3.5m. t of sugar, 2.5m. t of vegetable oil, and, for the southern countries alone, 600,000 t of meat. In addition to financial difficulties, this would pose problems related to transport, warehousing, and processing, which would be carried out mostly near port zones, i.e. on the Mediterranean coast, increasing environmental stress through acquisition of land, water consumption, discharge of effluents, and a growing population attracted by new jobs.

(c) Scope for progress in agricultural production

The future agro-food situation in the countries of the Mediterranean basin depends on natural potential and existing techniques, and on the ability of societies to exploit them. On the basis of the current situation, it is a matter, on the one hand, of identifying the scope for possible progress in agricultural production and, on the other, of comparing it to the various constraints which impede practical applications. Despite several basic common features, Mediterranean agriculture is very heterogeneous, and an initial distinction could be made between less industrialized and industrialized countries.

In the less industrialized countries, generally speaking, technical performance in the agricultural sector is rather weak and advances little; increase in the surface area devoted to wheat takes place at the expense of fallow and rough grazing, and on increasingly marginal land. Techniques remain extensive and yields have scarcely changed in twenty years or so. The technological level remains very low in general, as demonstrated by the limited use of industrial inputs: motorization remains below one tractor per 100 ha and, aside from Egypt, fertilizer consumption does not exceed an average of 40 k/ha. Increased use of inputs during the past decade has not produced a really significant leap in the

modernization of agriculture (Fig. 10.2). The incorporation of agriculture in general economic activity is delayed. The labour force is both plentiful and mostly unskilled compared to what is required by modern agricultural practices, and is therefore poorly remunerated and has difficulty in acceding to physical factors of intensification and their efficient use. Domestic production is increasingly unable to meet food demand, which rises along with the population.

The situation is different in the industrialized countries. Climatic conditions are less dry (except for Israel). The countries' general economic development means that agriculture employs a smaller labour force and that production is located in more suitable places, such as the coastal plains for the Mediterranean regions. Marginal areas or those difficult to exploit, such as the mountains, play only a secondary role in production. The existence of large fluvial plains (Ebro, Rhone, Po) makes it possible to produce major crops; and, on the coastal plains, the specialized and highly intensive cultivation of 'Mediterranean produce' has been introduced, with high value added and gross income, and fast productivity gains. In these countries, or in the economic groups to which they are linked (EEC), Mediterranean zones of modernized agriculture facilitate this kind of complementary specialization, while the general standard of living ensures remunerative outlets.

This kind of agriculture needs very strong linkages with upstream activities, because production requires numerous and varied industrial inputs (fertilizers, pesticides, appropriate machinery, irrigation or crop-covering equipment). The often fragile crops must then have access to packaging and processing infrastructure, fast transport, and efficient marketing networks to be able to meet the demand of exigent consumers. All this is made possible by the availability of capital at all levels of the agro-food system, in the form of direct transfers (establishment of infrastructure, subsidies) or indirect transfers (cheap credit). In this case market management is the principal driving force of agriculture.

This comparison between the agricultural situation in the industrialized and other countries shows that the resources used to implement agro-food policy are very different in the north and in the south or east of the basin. The starting-points are also very different, since the southern and eastern countries have not yet reached a level of intensification comparable to that of the northern countries. In the years 2000 and 2025—the scen-

* Blue Plan analysis and FAO studies.

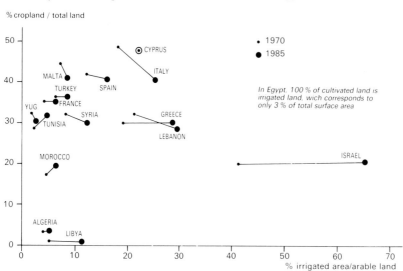

Total cropland and irrigated areas   Trends 1970-1985

FIG. 10.2 Some recent trends for agriculture

Source: Blue Plan (M. Labonne and J. Royer).

In Egypt, 100 % of cultivated land is irrigated land, wich corresponds to only 3 % of total surface area

Industrial inputs in agriculture   Trends 1970-1985

arios' horizons—agro-food systems in the less industrialized countries could be improved by tightening up current linkages with upstream and downstream activities, if only to apply well-known technologies used on a large scale in the northern countries. But this access to and application of modern techniques will depend on general economic growth and on the content and dynamics of international relations.

Production levels over the past twenty to thirty years for virtually all products in all countries have

tended to rise fairly steadily, naturally in an irregular fashion for rain-fed crops which depend on the vagaries of rainfall. Over this long period yield growth-rates in the region of 3–5 per cent per annum were fairly frequent in the countries of the Mediterranean basin.

The intensification needed by some countries will be reflected technically by a bigger direct or indirect use of energy (fossil fuels in particular) and economically by the use of more capitalistic forms of production. (It should be noted that the option between labour-based or capital-based intensification is out of place in the Mediterranean: capital, land, and labour will be combined in varying proportions, although efficient intensification will nevertheless be the one incorporating the most capital.) Increasing yields will depend on the more or less widespread use of industrial inputs, linked to the introduction of more productive plant and animal strains. These more or less hardy varieties require good control of the environment and the reduction of natural climatic hazards in particular. The development of irrigation is a response to this need for production control.

In the north, the area of land under irrigation has increased significantly (Fig. 10.2), whereas the area of land under tillage or permanent crops has shrunk. In the southern and eastern countries irrigation could be the basis of a fundamental qualitative leap towards food security (and the saving of foreign currency), beyond the goal of increasing agricultural income. Linked to intensification, this control of production will be an important condition for establishing a profitable processing industry, ensured of a more or less regular supply. Agricultural intensification therefore means development of upstream and downstream industries. According to the scenarios, this progress could be furthered to a greater or lesser extent by the transfer of technology and capital from the north to the south and east, together with an opening of market outlets for processed products.

(d) Produce with intensification potential

Despite progress achieved between 1960 and 1980, average yields are still low in the same countries where they had already been poor twenty years earlier. Results attained in experimental stations indicate the margins for improvement and suggest, at the technical level, the possibility of doubling yields for most plant production by 2000. A tripling or quadrupling of yields by 2025 is not to be discounted in a number of countries, as shown by some examples, since this gain would depend on the generalized and efficient application of techniques already well known today.

(i) Cereals

In dry farming systems current yields for wheat and barley are low in the south and east of the Mediterranean basin when varieties are cultivated with traditional techniques. Depending on rainfall, yields vary, for example, between 3 and 8 q/ha in Algeria and between 7 and 15 q/ha in Tunisia, and are in the region of 10 q/ha in Syria. In the Fretissa experimental farm in Tunisia, yields of 50 q/ha have been obtained, still with dry farming. Taking possible yields of 30–40 q/ha as a basis, productivity could increase by a factor of about 3–4 in Morocco and Tunisia, 2–3 in Syria, and 4.5–6 in Algeria for rain-fed wheat, and between 4 and 6 for rain-fed barley in these countries. Productivity gains for maize would be even higher.

(ii) Industrial crops

In dry farming systems yields are currently limited to 300 q/ha for sugar-beet (400–500 q/ha in irrigated systems). Rain-fed Israeli yields give an idea of what can be achieved: 500–550 q/ha with improved strains and good nitrogenous fertilizer. These levels would make it possible to increase yields by a factor of 2–2.5 in Algeria and Syria, by 1.5–2.5 in Turkey, and by 1.5 in Tunisia and Morocco.

(iii) Fruit and vegetables

Many Mediterranean countries are improving tomato-growing techniques, notably by developing covered crops (plastic tunnels) with yields in the region of 800 q/ha (in the Ferhat estate in Algeria, for instance). Taking as a reference base 600 q/ha under cover and plastic tunnels, 800 q/ha in heated greenhouses, and 2,000 q/ha with hydroponic farming methods (which require sound mastery of fertilization techniques and trickle-drip irrigation), the following productivity margins are obtained for Morocco, Tunisia, Syria, and Egypt: a potential threefold increase in yields with the spread of covered farming, a fivefold increase with heated greenhouses, and eight- to tenfold increase with hydroponic farming. For Algeria and Yugoslavia the increases are six-, eight-, and twentyfold respectively.

The yields of Mediterranean citrus groves vary in a ratio of 1 to 4. The highest yields are obtained in the Moroccan royal estates, with 400 q/ha. Yields of this level can be considered attainable elsewhere to the extent that irrigation, fertilization, and the upkeep of groves are correctly carried out, and if the grove is undamaged by virosis (on the other hand, some low yields are a result of the poor soil quality of many groves established in marginal areas). Taking 400 q/ha as a reference base, yields of most of the other producer countries in the Mediterranean basin, currently in the 100–200 q/ha bracket, could be doubled or quadrupled.

(iv) Animal products

In irrigated areas intensive cow-milk production, using European stock, with techniques of fodder and concentrate feeding, can be incorporated fairly easily into irrigated production systems, since these require large amounts of fertilizer. This kind of system can produce at least 4,000 litres of milk per lactation, yields depending heavily on efficient follow-up in the herd. Taking 300–400 litres per lactation with local breeds as a reference-base for current milk yields in the traditional sector, yields could be increased approximately tenfold with a change of breeds and intensive herd management. In non-irrigated areas, and taking as reference current productivity of local southern Mediterranean breeds of 80–100 kg weight increase per cow and progeny, and of 200–300 litres of milk per cow and progeny, a doubling of meat and milk yields could be expected (assuming that a solution is found for problems related to reproduction and breeding within the herd carried out by the stock-farmer).

In the same way, goat-breeding yields in irrigated areas could be increased by a factor of 1.5–2 for meat production, and 4–8 for milk production. On the other hand, the countries south and east of the Mediterranean basin are developing their poultry breeding along similar lines to the practice in the north and are obtaining comparable yields.

In conclusion, currently known improved farming techniques and high-yield varieties make it possible in principle to increase output considerably for most of the crops reviewed. It is possible at least to double yields as from now for all crops and for meat and milk production, but in some cases this is the limit of productivity gains, given the current state of

agronomic knowledge (maize in Italy and Greece, sugar-beet in Greece, sunflower and legumes in Egypt, Italy, and France, where yields are already high). In most other cases yields could be increased by a factor of 3–4, even up to 7 or 8 for some crops, by using improved techniques now known for over a decade.

Table 10.1 recapitulates the estimated productivity margins, expressed through multipliers, for all the Mediterranean countries and for the different crops. These encouraging figures do not take into account, however, either the socio-economic problems related to the application of improved farming techniques, nor those concerning their dissemination among agricultural populations. Nor should they on any count be interpreted as a forecast of Mediterranean agricultural yields to the horizons of 2000 and 2025. They simply help to identify the productivity margins in agriculture. In fact, many constraints exist and add to the technical limitations of farming.

(e) Constraints on agricultural growth

Important work, notably that carried out by FAO, such as its study on the carrying capacity of soil in developing countries, or 'Agriculture 2000', provides a rough estimate of the differences in agricultural growth which could result from a slackening, to a greater or lesser extent, of a number of constraints in the less industrialized countries. So only the major existing constraints will be recalled here, stressing their specific characteristics according to the country.

With respect to land, surface areas under cultivation are contracting in the more developed

Table 10.1 Theoretically possible multipliers for various crops (productivity margins)

	Dry farmed wheat	Dry farmed barley	Irri-gated wheat	Maize (grains)	Sugar-beet	Sunflower	Tomato	Citrus fruit	Soya	Broad bean	Chick-pea
Algeria	4.5–6	6	2–3	4–5	2–2.7	2–3	6–20	2–4		4.5	4.4
Egypt			2–3	2–3	—	1.6–2	3–8	2–4	2	1.5	1
France			2–3	2–3	2.2	1.3–1.7	1.3–4.5	2–4	2.5		
Greece			2–3	2	1.7	2–2.6	1.3–4.5			2.2	1.5
Israel		5	2–3	2–3	2.2		1.3–4.5	1		1.5	1.5
Italy			2–3	2	2.2	1.6–2	1.7–5.7		2	2.2	1.5
Morocco	3–4	4	2–3	7–8	1.4–1.6	2	3–8	2–4		4.5	2.5–3
Spain			1.5–2	2–3	1.4–1.6		1.7–5.7		2.5	3	2.5–3
Syria	2–3	4	2–3	2–2.5	2–2.7	1.8–2.5	3–8			1.5	2.5–3
Tunisia	3–4	6	2–3	—	1.4–1.6	1.5–2.5	3–8			4.5	2.5–3
Turkey			1.5–2	2–2.5	1.6–1.9	2–2.6	1.7–5.7		5	1.5	1.5
Yugoslavia			1.5–2	2–3	2.6	2–2.8	6–20		2.5		1.5

Source: Blue Plan (M. Labonne).

countries north of the basin, and economically marginal areas are being returned to fallow. In the southern and eastern countries only 10m.–11m. ha (out of 600m.) are highly suited or reasonably suited to bear crops, according to FAO; 4m. are marginally suited, and the surface areas actually under cultivation (including fallow land) amount to 20m.–21m. ha. This means that submarginal land has been opened up and that this trend has not yet been halted. This is the point at which a physical limitation is reached.

Output control around the Mediterranean requires irrigation. Very high annual increases in the demand for water, a resource whose limitations have already been mentioned, imply competition with industry or human consumption, especially in cities. It is clear that the problem of water will be crucial during the period from 2000 to 2025. Surface areas under irrigation will reach a ceiling that can only be exceeded by the use of water-saving irrigation methods, with an increase in farming intensity during the periods of lower evapotranspiration. In the scenarios this ceiling for irrigated crops has been estimated in the traditional way, i.e. with an input of water per plot in the order of 10,000 m³/ha (in accordance with FAO's various prospective studies).

Another kind of constraint is the fact that agriculture in the less industrialized countries—contrary to that in the Mediterranean regions of industrialized countries—must stay fairly mixed in order to ensure a certain degree of food security for the population. The scenarios took this into account, including the use of limited natural resources.

Regarding constraints related to animal and plant genetic material, a modification of the genetic heritage is visible all round the Mediterranean. In the case of animal resources it is linked to the introduction and dissemination of several improved breeds, whereas the hardy local ones tend to remain static, if not dwindle. A good example of this is the virtual disappearance of Guelma cattle in Algeria. New breeds require environmental control and the introduction of artificial elements, which implies a capitalistic style of agriculture centred around improved stock-farming methods. The part played by feed-lot poultry breeding in the meat supply is another example of this change. But the resources available to improve high-yield breeds or create new ones differ greatly from one country to another, and the possibility of reaching performance ceilings in animal production still seems remote. The same situation and the same differences prevail for plant production.

Generally speaking, there arises the question of research-and-development capacity, which is lower in the southern and eastern countries. Whereas in these countries there is a vast margin for intensification, in the north the qualitative aspect of the use of inputs prevails over the quantitative aspects (mechanization of certain areas, fertilization techniques, resistance of different varieties, etc.).

Depending on the countries, still other constraints are linked to availability of capital and access to financial resources (transfer policy), including farmers' saving capacity and investment possibilities. At the qualitative level, labour is usually more skilled in the northern countries, especially among young farmers. In the southern and eastern countries the general level of training is still lower, despite major efforts; this handicap curbs the efficiency of guidance structures and hampers the access of farmers to responsible positions in farmers' organizations. The way to agricultural intensification lies through the extension of modern techniques and the means to acquire them.

Land-tenure issues are also extremely diverse, and a broad variety of land-tenure or agrarian reforms exists in the Mediterranean, ranging from simple plot consolidation or regrouping of plots to the management of most farmland through collective forms of agriculture.

Lastly, institutions associated with the technical and economic guidance of the sector vary as to their nature and their capacity to contribute to food and agricultural growth: co-operatives or agencies managed by farmers with state financial assistance and fairly broad autonomy of action, more or less compulsory state-managed co-operatives, etc.

2. The agro-food sector in the scenarios

The agro-food part of the Blue Plan scenarios was designed mainly to explore:

- land use;
- water use;
- agricultural intensification and pollution;
- activities upstream and downstream from agriculture.

Although the role of agriculture in the socio-economic development of the Mediterranean as a whole up to 2025 is unlikely to be subject to major reversals, since the factors of inertia prevail over the factors of change, the narrowness of the margins for decision should not lead to the conclusion that all policies will produce the same results. The Blue Plan scenarios each provide a logical matrix of development options which make it possible to cover amply the range of possibilities. Some reference-points can be identified in four of them to illustrate the differences between the scenarios.

(a) Modelling the agro-food sector in the light of the scenarios

The development of agricultural production and national agro-food systems in the Mediterranean region can be understood from the current situation and the recent past, in terms of either the internal dynamics of agricultural production or the dynamics of certain key elements of the agro-food system. Methods vary and it is important to choose those most relevant to set objectives and to the quality of information that can be gathered. The objectives were basically to understand better the extent of the impact of foreseeable agricultural development on the environmental components most affected—namely, inland water and the soil—in a number of Mediterranean countries, particularly those to the south and east.

In the specialized model developed, the starting-point was a set of equations, termed 'production functions' in macro-economics, which link production at national level to a number of factors such as, in this case, land (the soil), irrigation (water), agricultural machinery, fertilizers (and their impact on water pollution), and labour.

Simulated agricultural production is in fact an aggregate figure: the quantity of each agricultural product harvested is multiplied by a deflated price, and additions are made for all products (it was not possible to study output in detail, product by product, although a number of individual values were estimated for 2000). An increase in the value of agricultural production can therefore be obtained in two ways: either by an increase in the quantities of certain crops harvested, or by the replacement of lower-priced products with higher-priced ones. In the first case there is an intensification of agriculture without any basic change in the national production system (as in the T trend scenarios), whereas the second case, over and above any possible intensification, involves a specialization linked with increased trade, within the logic of the A alternative scenarios.

The first production factor is the surface area

cultivated annually, and the area under permanent crops (orchards, vines, etc.), excluding fallow land and rough grazing. The extension of the surface area under cultivation could result from either land clearance or a reduction of fallow land. In both cases any extension leads to a reduction of grazing land and the disappearance of its richest areas. It should be noted that the ratio of agricultural production to cultivated area corresponds to yield, or productivity, per surface-area unit.

Special attention was given to surface area under irrigation. It should be observed that areas recorded as under irrigation differ widely as to the type of irrigation in service, some using flood water or winter irrigation, others having complete control of water throughout the year. The prospective study assumes complete control in the future, ensuring 10,000 m³/ha, sufficient for efficient irrigation and good agronomic results. Any use of water-saving techniques would be reflected by an increase in real irrigable surface areas.

The use of NPK fertilizers has also been included, regardless of their kind and form of application. Methods of use do not necessarily combine efficiently to exclude wastage. Moreover, the distribution of fertilizer on crops is not homogeneous, and this factor must be considered above all as an indicator of intensification and the use of industrial inputs. It therefore also indicates the extent to which agriculture is linked to the general development of the country and its industry, the chemical industry in particular.

The introduction of mechanization is important. It is not clear how intensively the tractor stock is used. In the industrialized countries there is often over-mechanization linked to specific farming practices, private ownership, etc. In the less industrialized countries a considerable part of the stock is often immobilized due to breakdowns and to the fact that spare parts are not immediately available. Mechanization should anyway be considered as an indicator of agricultural intensification through the use of industrial inputs; in addition it represents a link with the development of upstream industrial activities.

The agricultural labour force as a factor of production can reflect to some extent the state of intensification through labour. But this factor also partly contributes to consistency in the interpretation of results with respect to the general level of economic development and to specific problems such as rural exodus, urbanization, etc.

Lastly, the model took into account possible

advances stemming from better use of existing techniques and their improved efficiency (selected seeds and high-yield varieties, observance of the calendar for agricultural tasks, appropriate location and apportioning of fertilizer inputs, etc.), through a 'technological multiplier'. This factor is above all linked to the alternative scenarios, which assume technological transfers and technical co-operation among Mediterranean countries. It takes into account performance comparisons, results of experiments, and ecological similarities in the various scenarios and for different countries.

Projections have been drawn up for 2025 (the year 2000 was usually deduced by geometrical interpolation, except when an intermediate exogenous value was available) for four scenarios—T2 worst trend, T3 moderate trend, A1 reference alternative, and A2 integration alternative—for two groups of countries:

- Morocco, Tunisia, Libya, Syria, Spain, Italy, and Turkey, for which there were acceptable descriptive equations;
- Algeria, Egypt, France, Greece, and Israel, for which it was not possible to determine a production function.

The first step for the countries in both groups was to set a level of agricultural production, scenario by scenario, for 2000 and 2025. For EEC member states this level reflects assumed market constraints; for the others a country's known potential was taken as a basis. Then the size of the agricultural labour force was estimated according to the mechanisms of agricultural income trends per worker (in relative terms, compared to the average income per worker in the economy); these mechanisms amount to an assumption that the agricultural exodus is discouraged when income per agricultural worker reaches a given level.

When production functions were available, they were used to estimate factor demand, basically land and fertilizers or machinery. The coefficients of these functions were set at their assumed value in a state of equilibrium. The multiplier coefficient which simulated technical progress was given different values for the southern and eastern countries on the one hand, and the northern countries on the other. For the first group it was given the value of 1.5 for the reference alternative scenario A1, and 2.5 for the integration alternative scenario A2, in 2025. These values were respectively 2 and 1.5 for the northern countries, the highest value for the members of the European Community being attained in A1, where markets and trade are the broadest.

To conclude on the subject of methods and hypotheses, it can be said that the compromise between a purely technical analysis of agricultural potential in each separate land unit (a huge task for such a heterogeneous set of countries) and greater degree of formalization or modelling (with the risks associated with the remoteness of the horizon) is justified basically by the fact that formalization serves mainly to guide the evaluation of agronomists or economists.

(b) Findings of the agro-food scenarios

Table 10.2 gives some of the findings by country, by scenario, and for the two horizons 2000 and 2025 (together with 1980 reference values for comparison purposes). Information here will be confined to a general outline of projections for the countries south and east of the Mediterranean basin as a whole, and for the countries north of the basin.

(i) Countries south and east of the Mediterranean basin

In this set of countries the worst trend scenario T2 stands out from the other trend and alternative scenarios. For the sake of consistency, low agricultural growth (even decline in one country) has been linked with the T2 scenario's general hypothesis of slow economic growth. The agricultural labour force was estimated so as to keep the income gap between agriculture and the other sectors to a level close to that of 1980. Rural exodus therefore remains low, although this scenario assumes the highest rate of population growth: the labour force (all sectors) for the countries south and east of the basin as a whole thus approaches 100m., from a starting-point of 26m. in 1980. The agricultural labour force, although declining fairly fast compared with the total economically active population, still amounts to 15 m., higher than the 12.5m. in 1980. So there is a slight increase in production with a large labour force, in other words a weak growth of productivity, equal on average to 1.4 times its initial level in the region. This average conceals extreme cases, such as one country where the 2025 level is scarcely higher than that of 1980 (this is in no way intended as a forecast, but merely a matter of extending the hypotheses to their limits).

However, estimates indicate a significant increase in yields per hectare, even for the most disadvantaged countries: by a factor of 1.7 in Morocco and 2.6 in Syria between 1980 and 2025. This

Table 10.2 Some findings of the agricultural scenarios for 2025, compared with 1980

	Agricultural value added (1975 $m.)	Yield value added ($1,000/ha)	Irrigated land (%)	Fertilizer (kg/ha)	Productivity ($1,000/worker)
(a) Countries with production functions					
Spain					
1980	10,535	0.514	14.8	77	4.7
T2	10,637	0.780	24.4	148	15.3
T3	11,045	0.794	26.1	136	23.5
A1	35,556	1.781	22.5	299	28.7
A2	29,810	1.458	19.6	298	24.5
Italy					
1980	16,717	1.344	23.1	175	7.0
T2	16,717	1.478	30.4	300	29.0
T3	17,553	1.666	40.9	300	35.4
A1	33,029	3.171	43.2	350	45.2
A2	20,754	2.544	49.0	350	34.1
Turkey					
1980	11,400	0.399	7.2	47	1.1
T2	19,995	0.873	11.3	151	2.0
T3	22,407	2.023	28.9	199	3.7
A1	29,843	3.009	40.3	203	5.0
A2	49,389	3.846	31.1	211	5.0
Syria					
1980	1,328	0.233	9.6	23	1.3
T2	3,617	0.612	11.6	187	1.0
T3	4,309	0.749	14.3	187	1.5
A1	5,808	1.165	20.1	234	2.1
A2	8,961	1.361	15.2	249	2.7
Libya					
1980	413	0.199	10.7	35	3.5
T2	648	0.335	13.2	250	4.3
T3	648	0.345	13.6	250	8.5
A1	1,058	0.531	12.9	250	10.1
A2	1,613	0.899	14.3	250	10.1
Tunisia					
1980	800	0.168	3.3	15	1.3
T2	1,832	0.331	4.2	200	2.8
T3	1,939	0.333	5.0	200	3.1
A1	3,303	0.573	5.6	200	4.7
A2	4,203	0.932	8.9	200	5.6
Morocco					
1980	2,008	0.251	6.4	28	0.7
T2	2,099	0.437	15.9	250	0.7
T3	4,309	0.545	12.1	280	1.7
A1	7,275	0.828	14.2	280	2.7
A2	9,635	1.291	16.7	280	2.8
(b) Countries without production functions					
France					
1980	20,072				10.17
T2	20.072				41.69
T3	21,076				49.71
A1	33,119				60.71
A2	27,097				46.63

	Agricultural value added (1975 $m.)	Productivity ($1,000/worker
Greece		
1980	3,555	2.44
T2	3,555	29.11
T3	3,733	35.36
A1	11,909	45.21
A2	10,665	34.05
Israel		
1980	765	7.17
T2	1,603	21.06
T3	1,954	26.70
A1	2,258	30.25
A2	2,371	28.30
Egypt		
1980	4,094	0.69
T2	8,188	1.29
T3	9,826	1.53
A1	12,282	2.04
A2	15,148	2.06
Algeria		
1980	1,223	0.59
T2	612	0.39
T3	1,223	0.90
A1	4,281	1.46
A2	5,504	1.59

BOX 10B. **Some results from the Moroccan and Tunisian models**

The models make it posible to explore the very dissimilar conditions in these two countries, endowed with very different natural resources (specially in the case of water). Water is scarce in Tunisia, and the surface area under standardized irrigation is at most 400,000 ha, compared with 1,250,000 in Morocco.

In these two countries the T3 moderate trend scenario produces maximum pressure on land: about 9 ha per agricultural worker in Tunisia, compared with 3 in Morocco, where population growth is stronger. The result of the scenario is an expansion of cultivated land, although this is doubtful even if it were combined with minimum agricultural employment: in Tunisia a 22 per cent increase in surface area under cultivation as compared to 1980. Clearly these are extreme cases, but on the whole they illustrate the fact that, without technical progress, even a not very ambitious growth objective is inaccesible (doubling of production in Morocco, multiplying by 2.4 in Tunisia). Correlatively, it is interesting to observe that the two alternative scenarios, which have production objectives for 2025 that are 3.6–5.2 times higher than in 1980, require a much smaller surface area—about 5–10 per cent less than the 1980 level for the A2 scenarios in both countries.

In view of its water resources, it is not surprising to see that Morocco achieves a much greater intensification than Tunisia, at least in absolute terms. Compared with the situation in 1980, however, output in Tunisia is 6.6 times higher, whereas it is only 6 times higher in Morocco. Analysis of mechanization and fertilizer consumption indicates the price to be paid for the lack of water: a bigger increase in the other inputs (land, fertilizer, and tractors). The overall evaluation brings out the fact that, excluding a stagnation which is difficult to consider (T2 scenario), the most important parameter—even for a country comparatively rich in water, like Morocco—is the rate of technical progress.

In both countries the least favourable situation for the environment (pressure on resources and pollution) is that explored in the T3 scenario: growth combined with technical stagnation. The most favourable situation corresponds to the most ambitious production objective, solely because the technical progress assumed in this scenario (A2) simultaneously minimizes the use of land, fertilizers, and mechanization. This objective, however, can only be achieved if irrigation approaches its maximum potential in 2025; this is the second conclusion to be drawn.

increase is the result of an expansion of irrigated surface area as a percentage of total surface area—amounting, for example, to 16 per cent in Morocco and 12 per cent in Syria—combined with a strong shift towards mechanization and the use of fertilizers, more than 8 times the level per hectare compared to the base year.

Nevertheless, Tunisia and Libya display characteristics found in other scenarios, associated with the very small size of the agricultural labour force, especially in Libya, which relieves pressure on land. If the findings for these countries are compared with the former ones, it can be observed that the model leads to a substitution of capital for labour: the number of machines per 1,000 ha is 57 in Tunisia and 66 in Libya, compared with 28 in Morocco.

Moderate trend scenario T3 and reference alternative scenario A1 illustrate hypotheses of distinctly higher general and agricultural production in an atmosphere of commercial exchanges which, despite their differences as regards the role of Europe, are similar in one aspect, namely a price structure conducive to trade rather than self-sufficiency. As a result, agricultural value added more than doubles or triples by 2025 compared to the base year, with a smaller agricultural labour force in the T3 scenario than in the worst trend scenario T2, about the same size in the A1 scenario. Briefly, agricultural productivity, hence income per worker, is distinctly higher in these scenarios: more than double in T3, a little less than triple in A1 for the region as a whole.

Yields per hectare would double in T3, triple in A1, with peaks of three- to fivefold increases for Syria. These yields are obtained either through a rise in mechanization, e.g. in the Maghreb, or through a considerable expansion of the irrigated surface area (Syria). An exogenous factor simulating technological progress must be added for the A1 scenario, justified by the effect of trade combined with financing from Europe for research and training activities. The typical features of Tunisia and Libya are again apparent, average yields being lower in these two countries than elsewhere because of lack of water; high productivity per worker is then obtained partly through a reduction in the size of the labour force and, as in the previous scenario, through a more pronounced substitution of capital for labour.

In the integration alternative scenario A2, higher agricultural output is aimed first of all at self-sufficiency. In this kind of scenario, development economic policy as a whole is assumed to be geared to encouraging small and medium-sized enterprises in order, among other things, to establish as large a population as possible in rural areas, while waiting for the growth of industrial employment in the cities. Despite the higher level of production, productivity per worker advances little beyond the level of the reference alternative scenario A1, because of the large number of agricultural workers.

The technological performance assumed by the model is reflected by very high yields per hectare. In Morocco and Syria they reach on average those of Italy at present, and in Tunisia and Libya are nearly double those of Spain today. This level of intensification is not only the result of irrigation and the use of industrial inputs, whose levels are indeed high but barely exceed those of the A1 scenario. In this case an optimization of technological progress was assumed in particular, based on training and the quality of agricultural research, orientated equally towards traditional agriculture and modern farming. This progress enables farmers to improve their use of machines and industrial inputs and irrigate more efficiently, all factors contributing to a reduction of the impact on the environment. This trend is supported by extension institutions and agricultural credit, and by a remunerative price structure for produce for both domestic consumption and export.

(ii) Countries north of the Mediterranean basin

In the trend scenarios T2 and T3 agricultural production (imposed exogenously in the model) is at a standstill in the Mediterranean countries of the European Community (Spain, France, Italy, and Greece) because of market constraints. In the other countries, Turkey in particular (included with the northern countries in this section), production advances strongly in the moderate trend scenario T3, a little less in the worst trend scenario T2.

In the reference alternative scenario A1, in which the countries south and east of the basin exchange manufactured goods and market-garden produce for cereals, the special market these countries offer for cereals and animal products could account for a doubling of European Community production. In the integration alternative scenario A2, Community production falls off somewhat compared to the A1 scenario. In the other countries production triples or even quadruples in the two alternative scenarios, to reach its maximum.

The agricultural labour force also follows the different trends in the European Community member states and the other countries north of the basin, chiefly because of demographic features specific to the latter, especially Turkey. In the EEC member states the agricultural labour force drops from 11 per cent of the total working population in 1980 to 2–4 per cent in 2025. In Turkey the agricultural labour force falls from 53.5 per cent of the working population in 1980 to 21 per cent in 2025 in the T2 scenario, and to 14 per cent in the T3 scenario, but accounts for 26 per cent in the A2 scenario. The scale of the reduction, although significant, cannot be compared to that of the EEC countries. As a result, productivity levels still differ considerably in 2025.

The effects of technological progress are also different in the two subgroups of countries. In Spain, for instance, the Common Agricultural Policy (CAP) produces both a rapid contraction of the area under cultivation and a reduction in the size of the agricultural labour force, the combined effect of which is to keep a density of 5–6 workers per 100 ha. The intensification process is vast, with a quadrupling of industrial inputs per hectare compared to the base year (reaching 110 machines per 1,000 ha) and irrigated surface areas amounting to 20–6 per cent of arable land. In Turkey, on the other hand, potential production in the A2 scenario could equal or even exceed that of Spain, but with four to six times more agricultural workers, hence a substitution of capital for labour—indicated by the density of machines and fertilizers per hectare— one-third lower than in Spain. Factors in these proportions suggest farming practices mid-way between horticulture and the mechanized farming existing in the European Community. In other words, yields per hectare in Spain and Turkey are fairly close, but obtained with widely diverging technologies.

On the basis of these scenarios it is estimated that the consumption of chemical products (fertilizers and pesticides) in the Mediterranean coastal countries will double in 2000 compared to 1980. The southern and eastern countries, where consumption would triple or quadruple, would catch up with the northern industrialized countries, where an increase of a factor of 1.4–1.5 is expected. In 2025 a rough estimate would be a threefold increase in the basin, varying from five- to sixfold in the least industrialized countries and doubling in the industrialized countries as compared to 1980.

Tractors, i.e. motorization, will increase by a factor of 1.5–2 in 2000 and by less than 3 in 2025, with considerable differences between the north, where the rise would be by a factor of 1.5 in 2000 to 2 in 2025, and the southern and eastern

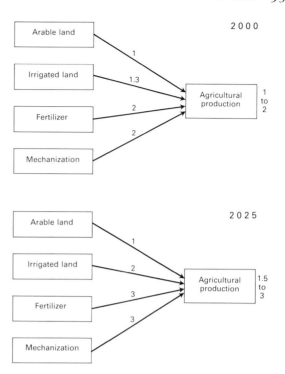

FIG. 10.3 Estimate of increase in use of production factors, 2000 and 2025, for the Mediterranean countries as a whole (current situation = 1)

Source: Blue Plan (M. Labonne and J. Royer).

countries, where the increase would be in the region of three- to fivefold in 2000 and five- to eightfold or more in 2025. Two diagrams, one for 2000 and the other for 2025, highlight the growth in the rough estimates of the main variables on the scale of the Mediterranean basin (Fig. 10.3).

(c) Profiles of change

Changes in the north will stem above all from increased yields, in the region of 50 per cent, on the basis of already significant output. Areas under cultivation will tend to contract, crop substitution or change of location taking place according to price variations and institutional provisions for marketing. In the southern and eastern countries the dynamics of domestic demand and population pressure will result in an increase in the surface area seeded and planted, and yields will also rise. Variations will depend on crops and their technical and economic performance.

Thus, increase in yield and expansion of crop areas can be expected in the south and east for dry-farmed cereals (wheat, barley); crop areas and yields will also grow rather fast for irrigated maize, either for fodder or grain. The development of rain-fed tree-farming will be backed up by motor-ization in some areas and the improvement of farming practices. Oil-crop production will be sup-ported by an expansion of crop areas and improved yields, particularly for oil-seed. For fruit and ve-getables under irrigation, growth could stem from a combination of higher domestic demand and the opening of foreign markets, with the surface area devoted to citrus fruits remaining static.

For other produce, the fact that crop areas do not expand corresponds to an adjustment to high-profit produce: thus in the case of cotton the search for commercial quality (long fibre), prevails over the increased output of an indifferent product. After the sugar boom of the 1970, it is likely that the surface area devoted to beetroot will not increase for a while, in view of possible improved yields and the price of sugar on the international market.

The contraction of grazing and fallow land will entail changes in extensive stock-farming. Since demand for milk and meat becomes more urgent, stock-farming will use increasing amounts of cereals or cultivated fodder (which will assume a fairly important position in crop rotation in irrigated districts) to supplement animal feed. For some breeds feed-lot farming will boost the already large market share they supply, based largely on imported feeds.

In some scenario options, particularly in the alternative scenarios, the value of production would rise rapidly because high value-added products would become important (intensively produced meat and dairy products, fruit and vegetables, competitive on the international market on account of their quality).

The profile of Mediterranean agriculture in 2000 and 2025 will therefore, in all scenarios, be one of intensified activity using more and more capital, but with varying efficiency and success and with a significant impact on the environment.

3. Agro-food trends and the environment

(a) Agro-food industrialization

The salient factor in coming years in the Medi-terranean world—as elsewhere—will be the in-creasing industrialization of the agro-food system. This means that agriculture itself will be making increasing use of industrial inputs, and that output will undergo various processing operations prior to consumption. The agro-food system will therefore form part of a broader industrial system, above and below the production stage, and this integration will become stronger regardless of the type of scenario. In fact, there will be a wider difference between future agro-food situations and the present situation than among the various scenarios for a given period. The largest technological leap is likely to occur in southern and eastern countries, where in the next twenty to thirty years industrial consumption by the agricultural sector will draw level with consumption observed at present in countries north of the basin.

Incidentally, fertilizer consumption and the use of tractors, as presented for the scenarios, are in fact only two indicators of the degree of industrial penetration into agriculture. A remarkable feature is that industrial consumption is not proportional to production results; whereas a clear progression appears in production levels, which rise from T2 to A2, use of fertilizer and tractors does not follow on the same scale. The technical capacity of the agricultural production system to use industrial inputs to the best advantage, and in general to adopt technological innovations, must be emphasized, as well as the efficiency of institutions organizing this sector. The mastering of agricultural development factors other than technical ones remains a major objective for progress, as any attempt at agricultural intensification, poorly mastered and executed, would result in wasted money and effort, and also probably further indebtedness among peasant farmers lacking any significant investment resources.

Industrial activity downstream of agriculture will be stimulated by changes in life-styles, mainly as a result of urbanization. Storage, packaging, pro-cessing, transport, and distribution of produce will expand fast, even if an agricultural policy en-couraging small-scale food production near urban areas (market gardening, fruit, minor stock-farming) and local trading were to be energetically implemented.

All this activity will affect the environment be-cause of the energy, water, and other types of consumption required and the resultant pollution. A fivefold increase or more in agro-food activities by 2025 should be envisaged in countries south and east of the basin, possibly at a faster rate than overall industrial development. If insufficient, local or national supplies could be supplemented by imports.

In the northern countries downstream agro-food industries will continue their growth, but at a slower rate than in the other countries, and tending towards greater product sophistication rather than major increases in processing capacity. The pollution caused by downstream industries in industrialized countries is unlikely to increase much.

Countries to the south and east are more vulnerable than northern ones to the increase in pollution and environmental pressures arising from development of the agro-food sector. Land-based pollution stemming from the massive use of fertilizers would be the most obvious outcome, even if innovations, such as using the ability of plant-roots to fix nitrogen directly from the air after inoculation, lead to savings in this area. In fact, the ability to use inputs appropriately will be a determining factor in the possibility of intensification at a lower cost in terms of pollution.

As regards other ways of reducing food-industry pollution, several lines of research are at present being followed up: use of waste as raw material for other products, such as animal feedstuff, fertilizers, plastics, etc. (e.g. use of lactoserum—whey—a cheese-making by-product); improvement of separating methods, in particular diaphragm techniques; use of biotechnologies.

One aspect of agro-food development that needs to be considered is 'soil-less' production. This can involve both plants (tomatoes and large-scale greenhouse horticulture) and animals (poultry, milk, eggs); characteristic of the method is effective control of the production process, an advanced level of technology, and a completely external source of inputs, which justifies the use of the term 'soil-less'. Hence, there can be a considerable degree of flexibility in locating these activities (like food-processing industries) either near centres of supply or of consumption. And yet in all cases they quickly become large-scale and their effluent causes pollution unless removal or reuse of waste is properly organized. When, in addition, soil-less units are concentrated around urban areas, the problem can become quite serious.

The rising demand for animal products will increasingly be met from intensive feed-lot livestock units, which may be virtually the only source of supply by 2025, relying to a considerable extent on imports. Clearly the major lines for the rational establishment of units should be planned to avoid any error, supplemented if possible, in southern and eastern countries, by the reuse of effluent. In northern countries demand will grow far less quickly, and soil-less production can be more dispersed, in so far as a substantial proportion of supplies will come from domestic sources.

However, information is still too fragmentary to go beyond the speculative stage. Moreover, the isolated nature of pollution sources, and problems in identifying the type of pollution (e.g. antibiotics, plastics) and volume discharged into the environment, make any nationwide or regional prospective calculation for each kind of production very difficult. Some figures provide an idea of the volume of pollution discharges. For instance, as regards battery or penstock breeding, one fowl in a battery cage produces around 20 per cent of its own weight in waste matter every year.

(b) Variations in uncultivated plant cover and land use

Land is a specifically agricultural production factor. In the past, the area under cultivation tended to increase overall as a result of demographic pressure, for many years absorbed mostly by the countryside. Agriculture, particularly if there is a lot of communal land or small holdings, acts as a 'shock-absorber' for employment. The tendency in this case is then for the development of a more intensive use of land, notably by an increase of areas under cultivation or permanent crops, to the detriment of pasture land, rough grazing and ranges, fallow land, forests, and wetlands. This trend reflects population pressure on natural resources in societies where technical resources are poorly developed and increase in output comes from greater use of the land factor.

The recent past has seen a movement away from this general trend towards expansion of farmland, in countries with the capacity to use and deploy more intensive capital-based techniques to a significant extent, mainly by using industrial inputs, such as fertilizers, pesticides, machinery, and specialized irrigation techniques. As already emphasized, this capacity to use and produce industrial inputs has to be related to a country's general level of development, its mastery of production techniques, and its saving and investment possibilities. The methods and general level of work-force training and guidance should also be mentioned.

The possibility of using more capital in agriculture thus evolves as jobs are created in other sectors of the economy; beyond a certain threshold agriculture no longer needs to play a dominant role in absorbing employment: the unduly intensive farming of marginal land drops sharply.

This situation has been reached in the last few years in countries north of the basin. In France, for instance, the phenomenon has long been under way in the Mediterranean region, strictly speaking, while it is very recent in Spain and Greece. In the south,

Libya, because of its oil income and small population, displays the same pattern as countries to the north as regards trends in areas under cultivation.

In other southern and eastern countries the sharp increase in irrigated areas expected in the future will not prevent areas under cultivation or crop-land from expanding within a margin of between 0 and 10–20 per cent between 1980 and 2000, depending on the country and the scenario, a figure which could reach 5–30 per cent in 2025. In general, one type of scenario does not further an increase in cultivated land more than another. The moderate trend scenario T3 and the alternative scenarios would appear to use the most land. But on any assumption pressure will remain high on un-cultivated plant cover until 2025 in southern and eastern countries; and yet in these countries the area under cultivation (including fallow land) is nearly always greater than the area suitable for farming.

In addition to the risk of a spread of sterile land through soil erosion or salinization of irrigated land (see Chapter 18), there is the more general phenomenon of soil impoverishment and changes in water-flows.

Apart from clearing new land, surface area can be extended at the expense of fallow, land left to rest in a rain-fed farming system. The practice of fallowing restores some of the soil fertility. However, the soil's rainwater storage capacity reaches a lower level than with true 'dry farming' methods. In fact, fallow land is usually not worked, and becomes covered with spontaneous weed growth, all the more easily as weed-killer is not in general use. Other consequences of the contraction of un-cultivated plant cover involve the reduction of grazing land and a drop in quality in terms of fodder-unit capacity.

Until recently desert regions with low agricultural productivity, together with fallow land, were used for extensive sheep-raising, sometimes with seasonal transhumance. These long-established practices are likely to decline at the same time as the reduction of grazing land, sometimes even faster, because when a single factor in transhumance disappears, the overall capacity of the system is affected.

With the reduction of grazing land, in surface area and quality, the supply of mutton will dwindle and it will not be easy to counterbalance this loss by more intensive methods. This means that feed-lot stock raising, particularly of poultry, will have to play a more important part, with the concomitant increase in imports of animal feedstuff, mainly grain and protein-rich ingredients, a process which will swell port activities.

(c) Chemical inputs

(i) Fertilizers

Fertilizers used in agriculture are not completely absorbed and spread pollutants in the environment. If concentrations become too heavy, they may make ground water unfit for consumption and create problems for the domestic water supply. In the case of insufficient leaching, soil quality is also threatened (risk of salinization in dry climates). The two main elements concerned are nitrogen and phosphorus, and more specifically:

● *Nitrates.* Being highly soluble, they percolate into the soil and either accumulate in ground water or are conveyed into rivers with run-off water.

● *Phosphates.* Virtually insoluble, they are carried (in the same way as potassium from potash fertilizers) with the eroded sediment to which they are adsorbed. In addition, phosphate fertilizers contain trace toxic elements (e.g cadmium), likely to accumulate in the soil or in tissue over the long term.

The European countries, alerted by the recent fast degradation of the drinking-water resources in intensive farming and stock-breeding areas, caused mainly by the increase in the amount of nitrates in the water, have begun to have a better knowledge— if not complete control—of the harmful effects of fertilizers in temperate climatic conditions with heavy rainfall and run-off. In the countries south and east of the Mediterranean basin, especially those which tend to be arid, climatic features are likely to alter the appearance and development of these phenomena, and the threshold level of an en-vironment's reaction to massive fertilizer inputs may be lowered.

The discharge of nutrients into the sea comes either from natural inputs, in dissolved or particulate form resulting from leaching and soil erosion, or from artificial inputs, fertilizer spread on agricultural land. The amount of natural inputs is higher when the use of fertilizers in a given watershed is moderate (the case of the southern and eastern shores of the basin in 1980). Conversely, the amount of artificial discharge rises with the volume of run-off (the case of the north-west part of the basin). In Tunisia, for example, the discharge of nitrogen into the sea in 1975 was five times higher (in weight) than the total consumption of nitrogenous fertilizer for agricultural purposes; in Italy, on the other hand, discharge

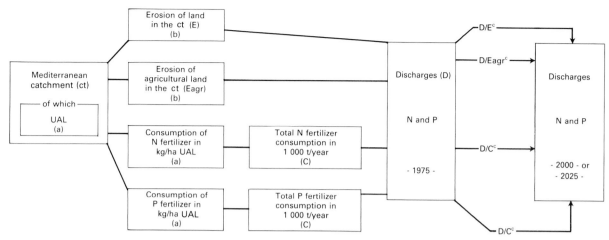

Fig. 10.4 'Agricultural-based phosphorus and nitrogen discharge' chain

C = N or P consumption; D = N or P discharge.
 [a] Variant with the Blue Plan agro-food scenarios.
 [b] Variant with the findings of the Blue Plan 'soil erosion' scenarios.
 [c] Variant according to the scenarios. Ratios are arranged in the order: T2 > T3 > A1 (to reflect the general hypotheses of the scenarios).

Note: All calculations were based geographically on the Mediterranean watersheds of the coastal countries (except for Egypt and Libya, not included in this exercise). Findings are grouped under three sets of countries:

Northern shore: Spain, France, Italy, Yugoslavia, Albania, Greece;
Eastern shore: Turkey, Cyprus, Syria, Lebanon, Israel;
Southern shore: Tunisia, Algeria, Morocco.

during the same period was equal to only half of agricultural consumption. It is therefore impossible to distinguish among the amounts of nitrates, phosphates, and potash reaching the sea those of natural origin and those introduced by human activity (which could be of urban origin, such as phosphates from detergents).

An 'environmental chain' covering discharges of agricultural origin (phosphorus and nitrogen) has been devised (Fig. 10.4) in order to understand better the influence of the various factors. It uses the following basic data:

 • utilized agricultural land (UAL), including arable land, temporary crops, and permanent grass-land, excluding range-land, in the Mediterranean catchment area of each country;
 • consumption of nitrate and phosphate fertilizers for each country (in this case national averages, the only data available);
 • the ratio between nitrogen and phosphorus discharges into the Mediterranean Sea (FAO statistics, 1977) and the amounts of nitrogen and phosphorus consumed in the watershed.

The prospective exercise, based on trends of the various indicators since 1965, and especially since 1975, and using the findings of the agricultural part of the Blue Plan scenarios, involves mainly the application of multipliers to the basic data (UAL of catchment area and NPK fertilizer consumption per hectare) for 2000 and 2025 for the three representative scenarios: worst trend scenario T2, moderate trend scenario T3, and reference alternative scenario A-1. The volume of nitrogen and phosphate fertilizer consumed is assumed to be stable. These trends reflect the 'plus' or 'minus' provided by the efficiency of fertilizer management (notably as regards application) and erosion control (suspended particles in particular being 'carrier agents' for phosphorus and to some extent for carbon of organic origin).

Images obtained from the scenarios correspond to two aspects of environmental problems related to fertilizer consumption:

 • input of nitrogen and phosphorus compounds into the Mediterranean Sea (in thousands of tonnes), contributing to land-based pollution in coastal areas;
 • the amount of fertilizing elements introduced each year into the environment.

A fairly accurate estimate could be made of total

consumption, but in view of the various approximations and/or uncertainties discharge figures are much less reliable.

For the countries south and east of the basin the increases in fertilizer consumption anticipated in all the scenarios are such that they overshadow all other indicators (crop area, soil erosion, etc.). Variations are introduced through the management, conservation, and control of fertilizer spreading, making it possible to reduce discharge. Thus, in T2 discharges may rise by a factor of 4 or 5, whereas in A1 they may fall.

(ii) Pesticides

The general term 'pesticides' encompasses many chemicals, also called 'pest control' products, classified by major family: insecticides (DDT, HCB, aldrin, and other organochloride compounds, organophosphates, etc.), seed dressings (organomercurial compounds, etc.), herbicides (2, 4-D, MDPAZ, 2-, 4-, 5-T, triazines, carbamates, etc.), rodenticides, etc.

Used in agriculture, industry, and the home, they are increasingly widespread in all environments. Some of the more chemically stable products become concentrated in the food-chain, as far as man, in whose tissue they accumulate (DDT is at present found in mother's milk in some parts of the Mediterranean basin).

Increasingly varied and complex insecticides can affect animal populations (fish, shellfish, aquatic invertebrates, birds, insects, etc.), natural balances, and the genetic heritage, and vary depending on the species and environments contaminated, application techniques, doses and frequency of use, form (granules, powder, liquid), etc.

Unfortunately, few data are available on the matter: they are published by FAO or some countries (figures, expressed in active-component equivalents or in prepared-product weight, cannot be compared or added). Nevertheless, growth-rates for the Mediterranean countries indicate a trend similar to that for the use of NPK fertilizers. On the other hand, growth in the consumption of some very stable and accumulable pollutants (e.g. DDT) has slowed down, even halted in some countries (because of prohibition on use), after a period of steady growth from 1974 to 1980, which was particularly high because consumption levels in the countries ten years ago were low or irrigation became more important.

It is very difficult to establish forecasts for environmental pollution from pesticides, especially because their development in the host environment is still very poorly understood. There is an overall similarity to trends of other inputs required for agricultural intensification (fertilizers, irrigation); but data on the consumption starting-point are inadequate.

4. Mediterranean fisheries

(a) Present situation

The coastal population's requirements for marine products are high, in the region of 4 m. t per annum. For many years now they have not been met by the Mediterranean alone. From 1938 to 1955 the catches of edible species in the Mediterranean strictly speaking (excluding the Black Sea) amounted to approximately 500,000 t per annum, and fluctuated around 700,000 t per annum from 1965 to 1973, according to FAO. They gradually rose to 1,047,000 t in 1985—a 48 per cent increase since 1973—but scarcely over one quarter of the demand. It is interesting to note that while catches in the Mediterranean are not large and amount only to 1.2 per cent of world catches, their commercial value is important since it amounts to 5 per cent of the world figure.

The countries north of the basin currently take 78.5 per cent of the total catch, compared with 21.5 per cent for those in the south and the Levant. In 1985 the leading producer country was Italy (420,000 t), followed by Spain (140,000 t), Greece, Tunisia, Turkey, and Algeria, the other countries or regions each fishing less than 50,000 t. Aside from a small amount of tunnies, all catches in the Mediterranean were taken by coastal countries.

Nevertheless, these data should be taken cautiously. Part of the Mediterranean fisheries is still very much a craft industry; many boats, often of low tonnage and based in a large number of ports and shelters, frequently unload their catch in sites lacking statistical supervision. In addition, door-to-door sales are still common, with products escaping all control. As a result, the catches may be underestimated by about 30 per cent, and even much more than that in some cases, among others in many countries where small-scale coastal fishing is practised.

With regard to resource conservation it must be stressed that the withdrawal from available stocks is not confined to the species unloaded, the only ones taken into account in official figures: it also includes the undersized or unmarketable fish thrown back into the sea. These rejects may be considerable, amounting to 40–50 per cent of catches and up to 70 per cent in some cases. This is a serious problem for the rational use of living resources (not specific to the Mediterranean), which must be carefully taken into account in any development prospective study.

Mediterranean fishery resources are used unevenly. The demersal varieties, highly prized by consumers, are generally exploited to the maximum and even beyond. Thus, they cannot be expected to contribute significantly to the growth of production. On the contrary, measures must be taken to preserve stocks, particularly through fishery supervision and protection of their reproduction and growth zones. In contrast, small pelagic species are insufficiently exploited in some regions, due basically to the fact that they are less appreciated by consumers. A special effort should therefore be made to develop the exploitation of these species, which—along with those to be produced through aquaculture, if expectations are confirmed—could provide the basis for a substantial increase in catches.

It should nevertheless be recognized that the resources of the Mediterranean Sea will never be sufficient to meet the ever-increasing demand stemming from both the considerable population growth anticipated, especially on the southern shores, and tourist pressure. Fishery policy should therefore aim at the use of limited fishery resources under optimal biological and economic conditions. Only international co-operation can develop a policy of this kind and ensure its successful application. This collaboration already exists, as demonstrated by the achievements of the General Fisheries Council for the Mediterranean (GFCM); it should, however, be enlarged and those bodies whose priority objective is the future of the Mediterranean's living resources should be even more closely linked to it than at present.

(b) Tentative future outlook

In view of the current situation described above, trends should be assessed in terms of the Blue Plan scenarios. Considering reference trend scenario T1 and worst trend scenario T2, which favour national strategies in a harshly competitive world environment, it seems that the evolution of living resources and their mostly unrestricted use would continue in the current fashion. In the short and medium term, a relative increase is likely in tonnages taken by fishermen seeking a maximal catch in species with a high market value, due to the upgrading of fishery equipment stemming from increased profits and the exploitation of new deeper fishing zones, intensifying to some extent withdrawals from already seriously mistreated stocks.

Accordingly, the period of prosperity for fishermen is likely to be followed by a down-turn, which will speed up until uncontrolled exploitation and the lack of any environmental protection lead to the virtual disappearance of fishery resources and an inevitable crisis in the fishing industry. This increase in the productivity of fishing fleets should peak, then decline for various reasons, mainly the over-exploitation of both demersal and pelagic stock and a deterioration of the environment entailing a loss of living resources (although this deterioration could be controlled locally, as seen from the reference scenario).

On the other hand, a different trend can be anticipated in the light of reference alternative scenario A1, and particularly integration alternative scenario A2. Fisheries would benefit from the envisaged concertation of international or interregional efforts (as recommended continuously by the GFCM) and specific development measures, thus helping to prevent the depletion of stocks and intense competition for output by suitably adjusting catches to existng resources. In this kind of scenario, the causes of deterioration in the marine environment seem to be better controlled, and resources, better managed and so more productive, are able to contribute substantially to meeting the requirements of the population.

(c) Aquaculture

The target of economic balance encourages coastal countries to develop aquaculture. The current situation is as follows: Mediterranean fish-farm production in 1978 was estimated at approximately 26,500 t, basically of species with a high market value. The trend up to 1992 indicates a 65 per cent increase over the current figure. It is difficult to assess whether this initial effort will be continued, but it should be possible considering that more than 1m. ha of coastal areas could be devoted to this activity, that many brackish lagoons are very productive, and that climatic conditions are favourable in the Mediterranean, which moreover benefits from the existence of high-level research institutes in this field.

Aquaculture was originally extensive. Semi-intensive aquaculture developed later, with the

Table 10.3 Brackish water basins in the Mediterranean countries

	No. of water basins	Surface area (ha)	Depth (m)	Salinity (%)
Spain	2	28,400	2.0–7.0	36.8–52.0
France	6	31,500	3.0–10.0	10.0–40.0
Italy	41	137,500	0.25–28.0	2.0–40.0
Yugoslavia	3	14,200	1.0–18.0	0.5–8.0
Greece	14	400,000	0.2–2.0	3.0–40.0
Turkey	15	45,200	1.0–23.0	3.0–50.0
Cyprus	3	4,040	—	12.0–48.6
Israel	4	2,400	0.5–2.5	0.7–5.0
Egypt	8	278,880	0.5–3.0	1.2–40.0
Tunisia	6	74,500	1.4–12.0	4.0–60.0
TOTAL	102	1,016,620		

Source: Blue Plan (D. Charbonnier, 1988).

enrichment of water from inorganic fertilization, artificial stocking with alevins caught in the natural environment or produced in hatcheries, and the improvement of fishing in both directions of fish migration.

Lastly, the Mediterranean, particularly because of its favourable climate, lends itself to intensive aquaculture, carried out in bays on the coast, floating cages in deep lagoons, or more generally in deep and sheltered areas along rocky coasts. Aside from aspects related to semi-intensive farming, this kind of aquaculture is characterized by control of the life-cycle of a species, hence its reproduction, nutrition, and pathology. Aquaculture in the open sea, a possibility that is beginning to be examined, also seems to have great potential.

5. Some conclusions and issues for appraisal

Intensification of agricultural production will have to be stimulated in the countries south and east of the basin, in conditions made more difficult by heavy population pressure. Ratios between agricultural labour and the industrial inputs required for this intensification vary according to the scenario. The more intensification is based on industrial inputs (fertilizer and tractors in particular), the more the production of these inputs has to be integrated into the general process of economic development and the growth of industrial production. This is certainly one of the major issues that needs to be solved, especially if the inertia related to the application of this kind of policy is taken into account.

Pressure on natural resources and the envir-onment will be considerable in the trend scenarios, and remains substantial but better controlled in the alternative scenarios. Water requirements in some countries will be such that urban water will have to be recycled for subsequent use in agriculture, and agricultural water will itself have to be recycled. Aside from these problems of quantity and availability, however, water also poses the problem of quality, linked to the massive use of fertilizers and pesticides. At present the spread of these pollutants in the environment is comparatively less well known in the countries south and east of the basin than in the countries north of the basin, where they nevertheless present growing problems.

More serious yet is the pressure on soil (as examined in Part IV), to the extent that questions arising about the long or very long term cannot today receive answers which could relieve concern.

When and how will the EEC's Common Agricultural Policy evolve? What agro-food development options will be chosen by countries south and east of the basin? What kind of intensification? What balance will be established between a minimum of self-sufficiency in food and greater participation in international markets, in so far as these develop in an atmosphere conducive to a multipolar world? And how can the overriding short- and medium-term production objectives be reconciled with the necessary conservation of resources, since efforts produce visible results only over a time-span of decades? Exploration of the agro-food sector of the Blue Plan scenarios clearly confirms that along with—and because of—population pressure, agricultural policy will remain a major factor in any environment/development prospective study in the Mediterranean basin.

11 The Industrial Readjustment

The Mediterranean countries' industrial production (manufacturing and mining, excluding energy products), which in 1950 accounted for approximately 3 per cent of world production, underwent spectacular development up to the early 1980s (more than 10 per cent of world production). Part of this production was carried out on Mediterranean coasts, the extent varying according to the country (section 1).

The major trends and hypotheses of economic growth analysed in the second part of the report provided the starting-point for the basic hypotheses of the industrialization scenarios (section 2). Considerable differences exist between the countries north of the Mediterranean basin, which will continue their restructuring process, and countries south and east of the basin, whose industrialization will have to keep pace with the vigorously growing needs of populations in full expansion.

Some of the anticipated sectoral developments and their impact on Mediterranean environments are then described in more detail (section 3). From now to the year 2000 current trends are likely to continue, but the countries south and east of the basin will play an increasingly important role in traditional industry compared with that of the northern countries, as the projections for 2025 clearly indicate. The outlook for technological change in some sectors and its possible effect on environmental protection are also examined.

Forecasts are different in the capital goods industry, whose technological development will long be dominated by today's industrialized countries. This prospect in no way excludes the rapid growth of this branch in the less industrialized countries with a capacity for the dynamic assimilation of technology. Nevertheless, the development factors of these industries raise some queries (section 4).

1. Mediterranean industry: past and present

(a) Industry in the Mediterranean countries

The period 1945–85 was characterized by a spec-tacular industrialization process in the Mediterranean coastal countries. These countries now provide approximately 14 per cent of world industrial production (8 per cent excluding France), whereas this figure was approximately 5 per cent (excluding France) in 1929 according to a League of Nations survey, and had fallen to around 3 per cent in 1950. As indicated in Table 11.1, growth of the manufacturing sector between 1960 and 1980 was 6.9 per cent per annum for countries south and east of the Mediterranean basin, compared to 5.7 per cent for those in the north. This growth dipped between 1980 and 1985, slightly for the group of southern and eastern countries, whose average annual growth-rate remained at 6.4 per cent, more noticeably for the northern group, in which it settled at 0.9 per cent per annum.

If the industrialization level is measured by the percentage of manufacturing value added in the Gross Domestic Product (corrected for mining for the major hydrocarbon producers, such as Libya

Table 11.1 Growth of the manufacturing sector 1960–1985 (% p.a.)

	1960–80	1980–85
North		
Spain	7.7	1.8
France	5.1	−0.3
Italy	5.2	1.2
Malta	5.1	−0.9
Yugoslavia	7.0	2.7
Greece	8.6	0.1
Turkey	7.8	6.8
Cyprus	6.4	4.3
South and east		
Syria	4.5	
Israel	6.4[a]	3.8
Egypt	6.0	8.1
Libya	14.3	9.2
Tunisia	8.1	7.2
Algeria	7.1	8.9
Morocco	7.6	0.6

[a] 1965–80.

Sources: 1960–80: Blue Plan data-base; 1980–85: UN Statistical Office.

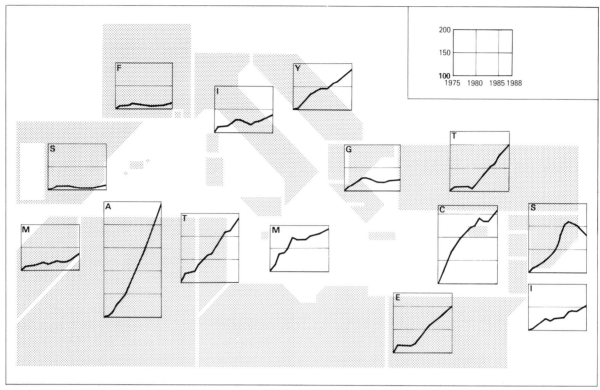

FIG. 11.1 Industrial production, 1975–1988 (1975 = 100)
Source: UNIDO.

and Algeria), the following ranking is obtained for 1985:

20 per cent and over: Spain, France, Italy, Malta, Turkey, Yugoslavia;

15–20 per cent: Cyprus, Greece, Israel, Lebanon, Morocco;

10–15 per cent: Algeria, Egypt, Tunisia;

Less than 10 per cent: Libya, Syria.

Figure 11.2 gives indications of the main industrial branches in the Mediterranean countries. The total share of the two traditional industries, agro-food and textiles, is declining in the north, where it accounts for only 30 per cent, but is growing in the south and east, where it ranges between 40 per cent and 60 per cent.

This ranking nevertheless highlights the persistent imbalance between the two sides of the basin, despite the vigorous industrial growth observed in the southern and eastern countries. The northern countries (including Turkey) still accounted for approximately 95 per cent of total manufacturing value added in the basin in 1985, and three countries alone accounted for 85 per cent of the total (France, Italy, and Spain).

(b) Industry in the Mediterranean regions

If, however, industry in the Mediterranean regions alone is considered, rather than national aggregates, northern predominance is reduced, as indicated in Table 11.2 and the short summary below.

Table 11.2 Value added in the manufacturing industry, 1983 (1980 $000m.)

	Entire country	Mediterranean area
Spain	56.00[a]	18.00[a]
France	173.00	9.70
Italy	120.00[a]	60.00[a]
Yugoslavia	19.51	7.00[a]
Greece	6.51	6.50
Turkey	14.26	3.50[a]
Syria	2.34	1.50[a]
Egypt	8.95	8.50[a]
Libya	0.76	0.75
Tunisia	1.29	1.30
Algeria	6.06	6.00
Morocco	3.17	0.20[a]

[a] Estimates.

Source: Blue Plan (J. Giri, 1986).

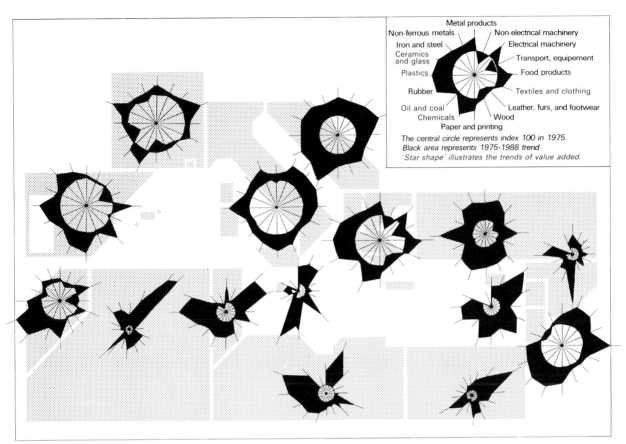

FIG. 11.2 Industrial structures in the Mediterranean countries: Trends 1975–1985. The above diagram allows one to follow structural trends by country and to compare countries within the region. Only some industrial branches have been explored in detail by the Blue Plan (e.g. steel or cement).

Source: UNIDO/Blue Plan.

● *Spain*. With the decline of heavy industry along the Cantabrian coast, the role of Catalonia in Spanish industry has grown. The region now provides a quarter of the industrial value added, most enterprises being concentrated in the province of Barcelona. The province of Valencia is also playing an increasing role, with strong industrial expansion, and is attracting immigration from other Spanish provinces.

● *France*. Despite physical planning efforts and a certain 'heliotropism' among the French, the Mediterranean region is still under-industrialized. The industrial importance of the entire region cannot compare with that of Barcelona alone.

● *Italy*. Italian industry is concentrated outside the Mediterranean regions as such, in Lombardy, the country's leading industrial region (the Milan area provides almost a quarter of domestic production), and in the Piedmont. The rest, about half the value added, is scattered over the coastal provinces.

● *Yugoslavia*. Slovenia and Croatia are the two most industrialized republics. Despite physical planning efforts, the north–south imbalance persists and a large proportion of industry is found in the Danube basin, especially in the Save valley.

● *Turkey*. Industrial production is concentrated mainly along the shores of the Black Sea and the Sea of Marmara: Istanbul alone accounts for at least 30 per cent of the country's industrial activity. A small part is found in the upper basins of the Tigris and the Euphrates. Several industrial centres have developed on the Mediterranean coast: İzmir is the second largest industrial area in the country, providing 15 per cent of domestic production.

● *Syria*. Part of industry is situated inland, in closed basins with no outlet to the sea, and another part lies in the Euphrates basin, which flows into the Arabian–Persian Gulf.

● *Egypt*. Most industrial production is concentrated on the Mediterranean coast, in the Nile delta and lower valley.

● *Libya, Tunisia, Algeria.* Most industry (except mining) is situated in the Mediterranean coastal regions.

● *Morocco.* The industry located in the Mediterranean province is insignificant, limited to the three centres of Tetuan, Nador, and Oujda. The principal area of production is in the Atlantic basin, with 55 per cent concentrated in Casablanca.

To complete this review by country, some major sections are described below, chosen for their current or potential impact on the environment.

(i) Mining (excluding energy)

The value of mining production in the Mediterranean countries was in the region of 1978 $3,500m. in the mid-1980s, i.e. less than 1 per cent of the Mediterranean value added, or approximately 5.5 per cent of world mining production. Only part of this mining production (about 40 per cent) involves the Mediterranean basin: bauxite in France, Yugoslavia, and Greece, chromite and boron in Turkey, iron ore from the Sierra Morena in Spain.

(ii) Iron and steel industry

Steel production in the countries of the Mediterranean basin in 1984 was 70.9m. t (62.7m. t in the north, 8.2m. t in the south), of which 37m. t came from the Mediterranean regions (north 31.9m. and south 5.1m.) (Table 11.3).

Among the most important points to be noted are:

● the development of the iron and steel industry

in the Mediterranean since 1950, when it had previously been limited to Italy;

● a falling-off in production, which started in France in the early 1970s (1974: 27m. t; 1986: 17.9m. t) and has recently affected Italy (1984: 24m. t; 1986: 22.9m. t) and Spain (1984: 13.5m. t; 1986: 12m. t), whereas production continues to grow in other countries, especially Yugoslavia and Turkey;

● the existence of unused production capacity in three countries: France, Italy, and Spain (production of 53m. t for a capacity of 80m. t);

● the fact that French and Spanish production has remained largely concentrated in the Atlantic basin despite planning efforts: the Fos complex in Mediterranean France was to produce 10m. t p.a. but only produces 3m. t; the Sagunto complex, set up in 1972 on the Spanish Mediterranean coast, has been sacrificed in order to maintain production on the Cantabrian coast, despite the advantages of the site.

(iii) Cement industry

Cement production was 157.2m. t in 1984/85 (113.7m. in the north ; 43.2m. in the south) of which 94.4m. t came from the Mediterranean regions (north 72.5m. and south 21.9m. (Table 11.4).

To be noted are:

● the very vigorous development of this industry throughout the Mediteranean basin since 1950;

● a falling-off in production in France—by about

Table 11.3 Steel production, 1984 (m. t)

	Total	Mediterranean basin
Spain	13.5	1.0[a]
France	18.9	3.0
Italy	24.0	24.0[b]
Yugoslavia	5.4	3.0
Greece	0.9	0.9
Turkey	4.3	1.2
Syria	1.0	1.0
Egypt	1.0	1.0
Tunisia	0.1	0.1
Algeria	1.8	1.8

[a] 0 in 1985 after closure of the factory as Segunto (Valencia).
[b] Main producers are 4 major complexes on the sea: Cornigliano (Genoa), Piombino, Bagnoli (Naples), and Taranto; with about 5m. t produced in small electrical steel factories of the Brescia region.

Table 11.4 Cement production, 1984/1985 (m. t)

	Total	Mediterranean basin
Spain	30.6	19.0
France	22.1	2.1
Italy	38.3	38.3
Yugoslavia	9.6	3.0
Albania	1.0	1.0
Greece	13.1	13.1
Turkey	17.6	4.0
Cyprus	1.1	1.1
Syria	3.6	2.1
Lebanon	2.0	2.0
Israel	1.9	1.9
Egypt	4.1	4.1
Libya	0.6	0.6
Tunisia	2.8	2.8
Algeria	5.3	5.3
Morocco	3.5	1.0

Source: Blue Plan (J. Giri, 1986).

one third—in a few years; Italy has just been affected (10 per cent decline);

● the strong exporting position of Spain (12.6m. exported in 1984) and Greece;

● the existence of unused production capacity, not only in France but also in countries like Turkey.

Much of the Spanish and Yugoslavian cement industry is situated on the Mediterranean coast, with factories 'on the water', so as to dispatch a high proportion of their production by sea. Greece also has three large cement works on the water's-edge (Patras, Athens, and Thessaloniki). Most of the cement works in the other countries are also close to the sea. Exceptions are France, with very modest production capacities in the Mediterranean basin, and Morocco, where cement works are distributed between the Mediterranean basin (Oujda, Tetuan) and the Atlantic basin (four plants).

(iv) Other industries

Similar analyses of the refining and petrochemical industries (ethylene, propylene, and benzene) show like concentrations in the countries in the north, although sometimes less pronounced. A few large plants for these branches are being constructed or launched (for example, a production capacity of 300,000 t of ethylene and 140,000 t of propylene in İzmir). The same pattern recurs with other products, such as polyethylene, vinyl chloride, and polystyrene, perhaps with more attenuated contrasts between north and south. The picture of industrial distribution between north and south changes if the production of sulphuric acid, superphosphates, and ammonia is also taken into account:

● In 1984, the production of sulphuric acid in the Mediterranean regions (not at the national level)

reached 5,483,000 t (Table 11.5), 2,724,000 t in the north and 2,759,000 t in the south. In the north production is almost entirely concentrated in Italy, and in the south in Tunisia.

● Production figures for superphosphates in the Mediterranean regions amounted to 489,000 t in the north and 569,000 t in the south.

● For ammonia the figures are 2,240,000 t in the north and 2,655,000 t in the south (Mediterranean regions).

2. Major trends and industrialization prospects

(a) Major trends

Some additional information is needed to complete the observations and hypotheses identified in the summary presentation of the scenarios for the major industrial development trends in the Mediterranean countries.

For the Mediterranean countries of the European Community the major trend would be, in the best of cases, a growth in production and employment at the same rate as GDP growth for food and agriculture, primary processing (metal-working, heavy chemicals), and light industry (textiles, leather, unsophisticated metallurgical products). Only the capital goods and consumer durables industries should have a growth-rate higher than that of the GDP (from 1.2 to 1.5 times higher than the growth-rate of the economy). In these sectors the 'high technology' branches hold the most potential: electronics, informatics, telematics, and, to a still minor extent, biotechnologies (pharmaceuticals, fertilizers, seeds, etc.). Upstream these industries are bringing about a radical and already noticeable change in the materials produced by primary processing industries (high-quality steel, specialized ceramics, processed silicium and rare elements).

The decline of the traditional industries in the north is often explained by competition from industrializing countries, more especially those where the dynamics of industry and marketing are the most vigorous. This factor is indeed important and it is likely to become more so, contributing to competition among producers not only on the domestic market, but also on that of third countries, thus hampering exports from the north. But this factor only adds to other internal considerations concerning both supply and demand. The steel coefficient (volume of steel per unit of final product,

Table 11.5 Sulphuric acid production, 1984 (000 t)

	Total	Mediterranean basin
Spain	3,400[a]	—
France	4,518	74
Italy	2,650	2,650
Yugoslavia	1,300	—
Turkey	349	—
Egypt	44	44
Tunisia	2,715	2,715

[a] Mostly in the region of Huelva (i.e. Altantic basin), where pyrite mines exist.

Source: Blue Plan (J. Giri, 1986).

or GDP unit) continues to diminish to the extent that in 2000 1 t of steel will probably render the same service as 2 t did in 1970. This development seriously affects the iron and steel industry, and derives from a number of factors, including the improvement of steel quality, often stimulated by competition with other materials (plastics, aluminium), or by price trends outside the branch concerned. Oil prices in the 1970s, for example, induced the motor-car industry to reduce the weight of vehicles in order to cut down on fuel consumption. Finally, a factor clearly related to demand should not be overlooked, namely market saturation for mass-consumption end-products. Over and above the major economic disorders occurring since the mid-1970s, this phenomenon is probably at the origin of the slow-down of industrial growth-rates in the major industrialized countries. Therefore the relative or absolute decline of the iron and steel, cement, and heavy chemicals industries in the northern coastal countries seems inevitable, even in the case of economic recovery. Possible shifts in this major trend will be seen in the scenarios.

Industrialization prospects for the countries south and east of the Mediterranean basin (including Turkey in this analysis) are quite different. The so-called light industries are likely, at least initially, to experience the highest relative growth, for at least two reasons: the fast expansion of domestic markets, resulting from both population growth and rising per capita income, and comparative advantages for exports. But the size of the foreign market, which differs from one scenario to another, is likely to vary considerably, as will be seen further on. In time, however, these industries will lose high growth-rates to other branches (after 2000 in the Maghreb, earlier in Egypt).

Agro-food industries will no doubt reach their maximum growth-rate before light industry, including those involved in cereals processing. This comparative decline can be assessed by the share of the agro-food industry in industrial value added: 52 per cent in Egypt and 58 per cent in the Maghreb in 1980—the proportion could be closer to 40 per cent in Egypt and 50 per cent in the Maghreb in 2025, which in no way excludes absolute growth, more or less vigorous depending on the scenario.

On the other hand, industries involved in the primary processing of industrial raw materials should enjoy steady growth throughout the period, with a rate comparable to that of industrial value added. The capital goods and consumer durables industries would therefore benefit from the comparative decline of the agro-food and light industries. This hypothesis is valid, however, only in so far as conditions exist for the growth of the primary processing industry, namely, a capacity for the dynamic assimilation of technology, backed up by efforts in research and development and the training of skilled labour, together with external conditions conducive to technology transfer, in turn dependent on the general hypotheses of the scenarios.

(b) The industrialization scenarios

In the trend scenarios the countries south and east of the Mediterranean basin have to face up to international competition. Two examples of this hypothesis are given below, based on either weak world growth, as in worst trend scenario T2, or strong world growth, as in a moderate trend scenario T3, the reference trend scenario T1 lying midway between the two. Growth multipliers for the periods 1980–2000 and 1980–2025 are compared with the multiplier observed for the period 1980–85 (Table 11.6).

The slowness of industrialization, especially in the worst trend scenario T2, results from two factors. The first is that competition on the world market will require southern and eastern countries, as well as those in the north, to undertake a radical restructuring of existing enterprises, set up in the more favourable conditions of previous decades. In the trend hypotheses export is a prerequisite for continued overall economic growth, considering limited sources of financing. The second factor is precisely the difficult search for industrial investment financing. Any possibility of external financing is linked to solution of the debt problem, which is likely to shackle industrial development, especially in Egypt and the Maghreb countries.

The original feature of reference alternative scenario A1 is to act effectively on the two factors mentioned above. First of all, long-term agreements between the European Community and the countries south and east of the Mediterranean basin mean that market shares open up for manufactured products from the southern and eastern countries. An idea of the possible penetration of their products into north Mediterranean markets can be obtained from comparison with the penetration of light industry products from South-East Asia into the North American market since the 1970s (over 60 per cent of textiles, for example). It could be envisaged that these market shares will prompt northern industrialists to associate with southern

Table 11.6 Industrial growth (trend scenarios)

	1980–85 (observed)	1985–2000 T2	1985–2000 T3	1985–2025 T2	1985–2025 T3
Multipliers for manufacturing value added:					
Morocco	1.0	1.7	2.1	4.9	8.2
Algeria	1.5	1.0	1.5	2.6	6.1
Tunisia	1.4	1.4	1.9	7.6	11.5
Libya	1.6	2.6	5.3	12.0	40.0
Egypt	1.5	1.2	1.3	2.9	5.1
Syria	0.9	1.6	1.8	4.0	8.6
Maghreb (3)	1.3	1.3	1.7	3.4	5.8
Sector multipliers for all Maghreb countries:		1980–2000		2000–25	
Agro-food		1.0	1.5	3.0	6.0
Heavy industry		1.8	2.3	7.1	12.3
Light industry		2.2	2.7	5.8	9.4
Capital goods		1.7	2.0	4.3	6.1
GDP		1.7	2.0	4.3	6.1

Note: Heavy industry = primary processing of industrial raw materials; capital goods = mechanical and electrical industry (processing equipment and consumer durables, including transport equipment).

Source: Blue Plan (J. Giri, 1986).

exporting industries, leading to transfers of capital and technology which should facilitate the launching of new businesses and at least partly attenuate financial obstacles.

However, the A1 scenario lacks one major aspect assumed in the integration alternative scenario A2, namely, an internal network of dynamic, employment-generating small and medium-sized enterprises, which provide a basis for many sectors, notably through subcontracting from mechanical and electrical industry assembly plants. This component coincides well with two other general features of the integration alternative scenario A2: a physical planning policy concerned with the development of both small and medium-sized towns and a training policy orientated towards increased productivity in the rural areas.

With respect to foreign trade, the previous hypothesis of a preferential market in the north for manufactured products from the south and east gives way to one of long-term economic co-operation agreements between neighbouring countries or countries with cultural affinities (Maghreb, Arab countries, etc.). Growing industrial complementarity between these countries induces them to absorb reciprocally a large part of their exports, in which case the world market would account for only a small portion of their trade. It can also be assumed that the creation of these large markets will act

as a strong incentive for direct investment from transnationals in the northern countries, a source of financing and also a source of technology transfer, considering the markets' stronger negotiating position.

The hypotheses of the alternative scenarios are depicted by the multipliers in Table 11.7, ensuing from both vigorous world growth and the interplay of various economic agents. Considering the time-span necessary for effects to be felt on industrial growth, results are much more evident in 2025 than in 2000. The figures in Table 11.7 could seem optimistic compared with those of Table 11.6 for the trend scenarios. The case of the Maghreb is given here as an example, but the results for Egypt would be quite similar. It can be seen that from now to 2000 the agro-food industry would grow more slowly than the GDP (e.g. 1.6 compared with 2.2 for reference alternative scenario A1), and that the growth-rate of the primary processing and capital goods industries would be roughly equivalent to that of GDP. For this comparatively close horizon, only light industry (textiles, clothing, leather, plastic goods, metal furniture, etc.) grows definitely faster than GDP. For a further horizon like 2025, all the industrial sectors grow faster than GDP in the alternative scenarios, whereas in the trend scenarios growth of the agro-food industry lags behind that of GDP. The primary processing industry advances at the same

Table 11.7 Industrial growth (alternative scenarios)

	1980–85 (observed)	1985–2000 A1	1985–2000 A2	1985–2025 A1	1985–2025 A2
Multipliers for manufacturing value added:					
Morocco	1.0	2.0	2.1	8.8	11.1
Algeria	1.5	1.5	2.2	8.2	10.5
Tunisia	1.4	2.1	2.2	13.2	22.7
Libya	1.6	5.9	5.9	38.9	40.0
Egypt	1.5	1.6	1.8	6.4	9.4
Syria	0.9	2.0	2.1	14.4	19.8
Maghreb (3)	1.3	1.7	2.0	7.8	10.8
Sector multipliers for all Maghreb countries:		1980–2000		2000–25	
Agro-food		1.6	1.9	7.5	12.2
Heavy industry		2.2	2.5	12.5	16.8
Light industry		3.0	3.5	13.1	16.3
Capital goods		2.2	2.6	15.9	23.9
GDP		2.2	2.6	7.4	9.5

Note: Heavy industry = primary processing of industrial raw materials; capital goods = mechanical and electrical industry (processing equipment and consumer durables, including transport equipment).

Source: Blue Plan (J. Giri, 1986).

rate as light industry in the alternative scenarios, which is not the case in the trend scenarios. However, the strongest growth is in the capital goods industry, regardless of the type of scenario.

The logical pattern of industrial development therefore implies in the long run the construction of a capital goods industry, the only way for a country to free itself of structural trade deficits and to maintain control of its growth; this nevertheless raises a number of questions which will be brought up in section 4 of this chapter. For a long time to come, however, exports from the countries south and east of the Mediterranean will have to rely on light manufactured goods and the intermediate goods resulting from the primary processing of raw materials.

3. Selected industrial sectors: prospects and environmental impact

(a) Mining

(i) Prospects

The future of extractive industries (excluding energy) in the Mediterranean basin depends on the following features:

● General conditions on the world market for mineral raw materials are the first consideration.

As mentioned above, the current period is one of overabundance due to the 'crisis' in northern industries and the fact that evolving production techniques imply lower industrial consumption. In the medium term (about ten years) this situation will probably not be reversed. In the longer term the growth of needs in the less industrialized countries may bring, if not a shortage, at least tension and a sustained rise in world market rates for some raw materials.

● Specific features of the Mediterranean basin play an important rule. As regards most useful metals and mineral substances, the basin is an 'old' mineral region which has been prospected for 2,000–3,000 years. It is likely that new large-scale undertakings will be carried out in regions of the world where there has been less exploration, and also in regions where environmental problems are less acute. The only mineral for which the basin is in a privileged position is phosphates. Morocco possesses 70 per cent of known world reserves to date (but deposits lie on the Atlantic side of the country). Proven reserves in Tunisia are far less extensive and, unless there are new discoveries, its production should decline at the beginning of the twenty-first century.

Over the period from 1985 to 2000 Mediterranean mining is likely to remain at a standstill. After 2000, fresh expansion is more likely to occur in the countries south and east of the basin than in the northern countries.

(ii) Environmental impact

Recent decades have been marked by considerable advances in the mechanization of ore extraction and quarrying, both in opencast and underground mines (including coal-mines, in the energy sector). Progress in excavation and conveyor machinery in particular has made it possible to use opencast mining techniques at ever greater depths, which would previously have required underground extraction. This trend, which is hardly favourable for the environment, seems likely to continue. The two main impacts on the environment, in addition to the extent of excavated areas, are dust emission and exposure to the atmosphere of rocks that had been buried for millions of years under quite different physico-chemical (pH) conditions, with the concomitant risk of soil and aquifer pollution.

For very deep deposits, underground mining will remain the only possible method. Since working conditions are still generally very arduous, in spite of mechanization, the possibility of fully robotized excavation or the on-site processing of ores is often mentioned. Such technological changes are unlikely to come into effect before 2000.

Biotechnologies should occupy a growing place in post-extraction ore-processing for enrichment, alongside existing physico-chemical technologies. It is difficult at the moment to assess the consequences of these changes for pollution. Pollution caused by mechanical preparation of ore (breaking and crushing) will not be much affected. On the other hand, biological pollution could replace chemical pollution. Will it be easier to control? The answer is by no means clear.

Lastly, the specific problem of sludges deriving from mineral processing, which on several occasions have disturbed certain Mediterranean maritime areas, should also be mentioned ('red sludges' from bauxite and ilmenite processing plants).

(b) Iron and steel

(i) Prospects for change

The decline of this industry in France, Italy, and Spain has not yet come to an end. The European Economic Community has programmed further reductions in production capacities. Competition from new producers like Korea, Brazil, and Venezuela is likely to continue, and Spain in turn will probably have to reduce its production to a level closer to that of its domestic consumption. In all, France, Italy, and Spain will probably have to bring down their production to under 50m. t per annum and their Mediterranean production to below 25m. t per annum.

A substantial recovery in the iron and steel sector at the world level is unlikely to occur before 2000. Beyond 2000, developments will depend chiefly on technology, notably on the role to be played by new materials. The range of possible futures is very broad: from a new downturn to a new acceleration. But it is unlikely that the production level of the 1970s will be surpassed. Under these circumstances, the opening of a new industrial pole for iron and steel in the Mediterranean, or the strengthening of an existing one, seems highly unlikely for north of the basin before 2000 and doubtful beyond.

The situation is totally different in the other countries. Steel production for the Arab countries as a whole, for example, was about 40 kg per capita in 1986, whereas the industrialized countries in the basin produced between 200 and 400 kg per capita for domestic consumption. Allowing for a moderate advance which would bring production to 60 kg per capita in 2000, installed capacity should reach about 10m. t in 2000 (which, given the projects under way in Egypt and Libya, is probably a low scenario). Allowing for production consumption of 140 kg per capita in 2025, capacities should attain 33m. t. Clearly, regional co-operation, such as that envisaged in the alternative scenarios (integration alternative scenario A2), would greatly facilitate the expansion of steel industries in this subregion, and in any event the evolution of materials has to be carefully taken into account after 2000.

Turkey produced just under 90 kg per capita in 1985. Assuming that its production will rise to 120 kg in 2000, and to 250 kg in 2025, existing installed capacity should be 8m. t and 18m. t respectively. Yugoslavia is in a situation similar to that of Spain: it is an exporting country and produces about 165 kg per capita for domestic consumption. Its capacity should not change scale before 2000. Beyond, as in the industrialized countries, trends will depend on technology.

Whatever the assumptions, a shift south and eastwards in the centre of the steel industry seems very probable. Up to 2000 the north is likely to dominate the industry. Beyond 2000, at a more or less distant period of time, depending on the scenarios, the situation should be reversed, with the south gaining importance. By way of an example, a production of 100 kg of steel per capita would correspond to low economic growth, as in worst trend scenario T2, whereas 200 kg of steel per

Table 11.8 Steel production (average scenario) (m. t crude steel)

	1985	2000	2025
Italy, France, and Spain (Mediterranean regions)	28.0	24	24
Yugoslavia, Greece	4.0	7	7
Turkey	4.5	8	18
Mediterranean Arab countries	4.0	10	33

Source: Blue Plan (J. Giri, 1986).

capita would correspond to strong growth, as in alternative scenarios A1 or A2. An average scenario can be constructed with these hypotheses (midway between reference trend scenario T1 and moderate trend scenario T3), as shown in Table 11.8.

There have been no technological changes in the last quarter of a century in the steel industry. Of course, there have been very important technological modifications, such as the increase in the size and automation of blast-furnaces, conversion of cast iron into steel with pure oxygen, or continuous casting of steel. But these modifications have occurred within the framework of existing methods, without the appearance of any really new techniques. The steel industry in the world at present is still divided basically into:

- the conventional integrated system of coking blast-furnace—converter—continuous casting —rolling: this is the process currently used for most of the output in the Mediterranean basin;

- the electric steel plant, using scrap iron from the steel industry itself, from the metallurgical industry, or from salvage; it is most widely used in Italy ('Bresciani').

Direct reduction of iron ore with natural gas has not yet developed to any extent (about 2 per cent of world steel production). Conventional steelmaking has evolved towards giant-scale operations. This trend now appears to have stopped, whereas electric steel plants have developed through increasing the number of small-scale units.

Most experts consider that the period of relative immobility in steel-making processes, if not in techniques, is drawing to an end, and that a real change may be coming in the medium term. It is unlikely that any more conventional steel mills will be built, except in special cases. New plants will be either installations using pre-reduction processes, and particularly direct reduction, now highly competitive, or else electric plants using scrap and sponge iron obtained by direct reduction. This process will usually involve a mixture of hydrogen

and carbon monoxide, produced by the reforming of natural gas. This means that countries with gas, of which there are many in the Mediterranean basin, should be well placed to use this new method. It is not impossible that a number of conventional plants might in the medium term be forced to convert to this technology in order to remain competitive. Although involving small quantities, this is an instance of the new areas of use of natural gas.

(ii) The steel industry and the environment

Steel production is one of the industries that cause most pollution and nuisances of all kinds. Considerable progress has been achieved in controlling pollution, particularly in conventional steel plants, by far the most polluting. This pollution comes mainly from the coking unit, responsible for much of the air pollution (emission of large quantities of smoke during changing of furnaces and removal of coke) and water pollution (phenols and heavy metals in washing water); but the blast-furnace, converter, and rolling mill also contribute. In fact progress in controlling pollution was achieved only at high— even very high—cost, at present a handicap for the

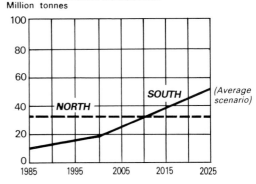

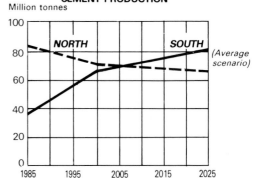

FIG. 11.3 Two industrial activities in the Mediterranean to the year 2025

Source: Blue Plan.

least-polluting steel plants, which have to face severe international competition. In such plants 20–25 per cent of overall investments are for anti-pollution installations, while 7–8 per cent of running costs are for their operation.

The technological changes mentioned above should have a positive impact on the environment:

● In the long term, coking and its accompanying pollution should disappear. This will nevertheless take time, and meanwhile pollution can be reduced, notably by replacing standard coke with 'moulded coke', although, as already mentioned, this requires large investments.

● Direct reduction plants working at fairly low temperatures (900 °C, non-smelted iron) should be less polluting than blast-furnaces.

● For the many remaining sources of air and water pollution (arising from reduction, the electric furnace, and the rolling mill) it may be possible to eliminate gas, filter dust, and collect the metals in washing and cooling water. However, all this will involve significant investments and higher running costs.

● Lastly, the steel industry will be moving towards manufacture of complex or even hyper-complex products and alloys. These products will entail little pollution, at least from a quantitative viewpoint. But they may lead to the release into the environment of small amounts of dangerous substances, either continuously or following an operating failure.

The steel industry will therefore probably undergo radical technological change, which will mean a less polluting industry than in the past, as long as the necessary heavy investments are made for environmental protection, and provided that anti-pollution installations function—not always the case today—in all countries. Finally, although the volume of 'ordinary' pollution is likely to decrease, the risk of pollution by toxic substances (accidental or 'extraordinary' pollution) will increase.

In the very long term, it is not impossible that an even more radical change in the steel industry may occur, with 'bio-steel-making', in which bacteria, making use of solar energy, would extract iron directly from the ore. This cold extraction would certainly be less polluting than present hot extraction methods (although the question of possible biological pollution remains open) and the Mediterranean basin could well adopt a technology of this kind. Before 2025?

(c) Cement industry

(i) Mediterranean prospects

The position of the cement industry and building materials generally speaking is fairly similar to that of steel. In the medium term, there is little likelihood that Spain, France and Italy will be able to maintain their production at the present level of 90m. t per annum. A recovery in consumption is possible in France (where there has been a sharp drop). Spain will probably have difficulties in maintaining its present level of exports, whereas the southern countries will equip themselves with cement production capacities. It is fairly probable that a certain saturation of needs will occur, especially in Italy, which has a very high production level, almost 700 kg per capita (in France it is 400 and in the United States 300).

Greece (13m. t) is the second biggest European exporter after Spain, and supplies the Middle East. It may face serious problems in a fairly distant future, however, and may be obliged to reduce its production. Turkey (17m. t) has surplus capacities and is encountering increasing difficulties with exports. These surpluses will soon be reabsorbed by the rising population, and production is likely to exceed 20m. t in 2000, perhaps reaching 35m. t in 2025.

Compared with these countries, production for all of the southern countries from Morocco to Syria is only 22m. t per annum, or slightly under 200 kg per inhabitant. Eventually, however, the balance of production should be restored. A production of 230 kg per capita should lead to a capacity of 40m. t in 2000. Egypt, for example, where production capacity is old and inefficient and demand is increasing rapidly, plans to raise its capacity to 20m. t as early as 1990. A scenario of 40m. t may well be a low one (T1, T2): in an average scenario (T3) production should lie more between 45m. and 50m. t in 2000. In 2025 a production of 300 kg per capita would lead to a capacity in the region of 70m. t, which would doubtless also enter into an average scenario (Table 11.9).

The cement industry, like steel, has not undergone any profound technological change in recent decades. The upright batch-kilns still common after the Second World War have gone. Production is now carried out entirely in continuous rotary kilns. Contrary to the steel industry, no technological change is at present envisaged for the cement industry. Cement is very cheap: production naturally requires a large amount of energy, but the raw

Table 11.9 Cement production (average scenario) (m. t)

	1985	2000	2025
Sapin, France, Italy (total)	90.0	75	75
Of which Mediterranean basin	60.0	50	50[a]
Yugoslavia	9.6	12	10
Greece	13.0	8	5[b]
Turkey (total)	17.0	20	35
Of which Mediterranean basin	4.0	5	9
Arab countries	22.0	45	70

[a] A lower scenario (approx. 40m. t) can be envisaged.
[b] Only if Greece can keep a comparative advantage and maintain, at least partially, its exports.

Source: Blue Plan (J. Giri, 1986).

materials, limestone and clay, are in plentiful supply and inexpensive to extract. No new process seems able to compete with the present way of processing materials. The 'fluidized bed' technique has been used in a few works (Japan and Australia), but it is suitable only for very small plants, producing about 50,000 t a year. It is hard to imagine the development of such plants in the Mediterranean basin, where markets are much larger. Research into the use of plasma flares also seems unlikely to come to fruition quickly and its outcome is uncertain.

The real technological change, in fact, would be to use new materials in concrete (such as fibres) to improve its mechanical properties and substantially reduce the quantity of cement needed; or to develop a completely new binder, which could compete with conventional cement in the manufacture of building materials. A tonne of concrete at present contains from 300–350 kg of cement. Is there any hope of a new product, such as a resin, which would be almost certain to cost more per kilo than cement, but of which perhaps only 100–150 kg would be enough for a material with properties similar to concrete, or even better? In the medium term, the answer to this question appears to be negative. In the longer term, any forecast is uncertain, in a field where the cost price of any new material is the dominant factor.

(ii) The cement industry and the environment

The cement industry used to be highly polluting, mainly because of the clouds of dust that it emitted. Many cement works have become far less polluting in recent years. Preparation of the kiln load, the actual kilns, and cooling and crushing of the clinker caused large amounts of dust to be emitted, and this used to cover the whole area around the cement works with a grey coating. The use of electrofilters has reduced this considerably. In France, for instance, pollution has gone down from 3 kg of dust (or more in the absence of any anti-pollution device) per tonne of cement manufactured in the 1950s to less than 0.5 kg in the 1980s. Despite this progress, the cement industry in France is still responsible for approximately 30 per cent of dust emitted by the whole of industry. In a number of countries the fixing of artificially low production prices does not encourage the recovery of this dust.

Considering the hypothesis of a status quo in production techniques, the prevention of pollution is possible in this industry, but future enforcement will depend on the standards laid down by governments and on incentives linked with price fixing. In northern industrialized countries levels will probably be further lowered and greater attention paid to the very fine dust and fluoride dust produced by firing, the exact effect of which on the human body is poorly known. Similar remarks could be made about other building-material industries, in particular tile-, brick- and ceramic-making, which also emit fluorides.

(d) Petrochemicals: heavy chemicals and fine chemicals industries

(i) Prospects

Installed refining capacity along the Mediterranean is in the region of 280m. t of crude per year. Several major petrochemical complexes linked to refineries are located along the Mediterranean, such as Tarragona in Spain, Lavera and Berre near Marseilles, Prialo and Gala in Sicily, Porto Marghera near Venice, Porto Torres in Sardinia, Ras Lanuf in Libya, and so forth.

A distinction should be made between:

- the heavy chemicals industry, using large installations to produce basic molecules, particularly ethylene, propylene, vinyl, chloride, etc., monomers for subsequent polymerization and production of numerous plastic products;
- the fine chemicals industry, using basic molecules to manufacture increasingly complex products.

The Mediterranean basin contains nearly 7 per cent of world capacity for ethylene and propylene production and 5 per cent for benzene (but nearly 8 per cent of refining capacity).

Future geographical distribution of petrochemicals in the Mediterranean basin poses far more complex problems than in the case of either steel or cement. The production of the major industrialized countries in the north is unlikely to increase in the medium term, and there may even be fresh reductions in capacity. On the other hand, two new types of industrial activities could eventually be implanted in the countries south of the basin:

- conventional petrochemical complexes using naphtha and possibly other products of the refineries situated close to the places of consumption (like the one that recently came on stream in İzmir);
- complexes based on so-called C2 to C4 hydrocarbons (ethane, propane, butane) associated either with either oil or gas deposits (like those that recently came on stream in Saudi Arabia).

The following scenario may be outlined:

- Production of ethylene on the Mediterranean shores of the three major industrialized countries in the north remains at a ceiling of 3m. t per annum, although a considerable, even sharp, drop is not to be excluded in the long term, if gas-based plants definitely prove more profitable than naphtha-based ones.
- Production capacities in the south and east in the region of 1m. t in 1987, taking into account the projects now being completed, will be developed:
  - either in the currently under-equipped consumer countries (Greece, Turkey, Egypt, Algeria);
  - or in the countries possessing oil and gas resources (Algeria, Libya, perhaps Egypt).

By a date which would be hard to fix, production in the south and east should attain the same level as, or even outstrip, that in the north. A south–south co-operation scenario, such as integration alternative scenario A2, should speed up this trend.

As regards technological prospects, most experts consider it unlikely that there will be any major modifications in the list of basic molecules manufactured by heavy chemistry. More specifically, polymerizable molecules are now known, and nothing new is to be expected in this field. This in no way means that plastics chemistry will not advance. On the contrary, there is expectation of:

- a major development of new technical plastics, made from known but little-used molecules, such as polycarbonates, polyphenylene oxides, polyvinylidenes, etc., the volume of which in manufactured goods is likely to rise from 3 per cent to 10 per cent before 2000;
- a considerable growth of new materials, designed for highly specific uses and made from basic polymerizable molecules, combined with one another or with a varied range of fillers

(such as mineral fibres to reduce the relative number of carbon and hydrogen atoms and increase the fire-resistance of materials), or else combined with other products, such as carbon fibres, glass-fibre metal alloys, etc.: in the long term there could be a kind of partnership between metallurgy and polymer chemistry, producing a specific industry.

(ii) Organic chemicals and the environment

Both kinds of organic industry—heavy chemicals and fine chemicals—cause pollution. The heavy chemicals industry is a nuisance because of the volume of discharges, which can seriously pollute surface and ground-water. Discharges from the fine chemicals industry are smaller in quantity but can be extremely toxic—as the cases of Seveso (dioxine) and Bhopal (methyl isocyanate) clearly show.

How will pollution connected with all these production processes evolve? With regard to heavy chemicals, substantial advances have been made towards controlling pollution in large complexes. During the last two decades awareness of the nuisances caused by chemical plants has spread, and major efforts have been made to develop less polluting installations, discharging fewer products into the air or water. One example is vinyl chloride monomer, the basic material for PVC, of which 2m. t are produced annually in the Mediterranean basin. European standards are now 0.2 kg of discharge per tonne produced (as plants are virtually hermetically closed), compared to a previous level of 30 kg.

Diverging developments are expected in the future: some new production methods will release very little pollution, others will involve high risks. A favourable trend which should continue is the increasing economic use of manufacturing waste. On the other hand, it seems virtually inevitable that the subsoil of major chemical sites will be polluted to a greater or lesser extent by water, oil, and sludge, whatever the precautions taken and despite the increasingly effective control measures used (super-absorbent products, discharging at depth, etc.). On the whole, though, the heavy chemicals industry—experiencing limited growth—will improve its control of pollution, as long as standards aimed at both ordinary pollution and the risk of accidental pollution are set and observed.

In the fine chemicals industry, manufacture of the toxic products or intermediate products will certainly not disappear. However, more efficient methods will become available to remove the polluting agents from effluent—for example, by using semi-permeable membranes and, later on, bio-technologies. Moreover, research chemists are now aware of pollution, and take it into account in the design and development of processes for manu-facturing new products. The trend towards avoiding the use of solvents by turning to aqueous emulsions, hydrodilutable techniques, or reagent diluents in the manufacture of inks, paint, and adhesives, etc. is one example. The fine chemicals industry, expected to develop vigorously in the Mediterranean basin, should therefore be less polluting in general, except for a small number of products that could cause accidental pollution.

Concerning 'pollution' by used plastics, it is likely that in future packagings will become biodegradable, but many products designed for specific use may remain non-biodegradable and not very heat-degradable at low temperature, therefore difficult to eliminate. No doubt provisions will have to be made for the separation and processing of these used materials in special plants.

(e) Inorganic chemicals industry

(i) Prospects

In tonnage, fertilizers represent an important part of this industrial sector. Fertilizer consumption is close to saturation in the most industrialized coun-tries (where certain soils are even over-saturated with inorganic fertilizers), whereas the prospects in the less industrialized countries are immense, as shown in the Blue Plan scenarios. In the medium term it seems likely that production on a world scale will enter into a new phase of growth—lower, however, than that of the period from 1950 to 1980.

In the Mediterranean basin the production of ammonia is already well into its shift south and eastwards. Installed capacity in Turkey and Algeria is more than 2.6m. t per annum, far more than the installed capacities on the Mediterranean shores of France, Italy, and Spain (1.85m. t per annum). Capacities are expected to increase considerably in Syria (Homs), Turkey (partly in Istanbul, partly in İzmir), Egypt (but in Suez, on the Red Sea), Algeria, and Israel, so that the overall capacities installed in the Mediterranean regions of these countries should soon exceed 4m. t per annum in the 1990s. In the longer term it is likely that—barring an unexpected technological development—the production of ammonia will be concentrated in the oil- and gas-producing countries, as the level of production

depends closely on the consumption of nitrogenous fertilizers.

The production of superphosphates will also prob-ably be concentrated in the countries possessing large deposits of natural phosphates. Major de-velopments in this industry should not be expected along the shores of the Mediterranean; a decline seems likely in the long term. This decline will have repercussions on the production of sulphuric acid, which is widely used by the fertilizer industry.

Lastly, there is the production of chlorine, both an inorganic chemical product and a basic product of the organic chemicals industry. The chlorine industry is still mainly concentrated on the north shore of the Mediterranean, but it should experience the same shift south and eastwards as petro-chemicals.

The inorganic chemicals industry will probably not evolve technically as quickly as the organic chemicals industry with respect to products or manufacturing processes. But minor technological change is to be expected in many sectors, some of which will have considerable effects on pollution.

(ii) Inorganic chemicals and the environment

The chlorine industry is currently the biggest con-sumer of mercury (mercury cathodes for the elec-trolysis of saline solutions) and is also responsible for the largest discharges of mercury in terms of weight. Technological change is expected involving cathodes made from titanium, platinum, and other metals. Until these new technologies are operational, mercury discharges can be reduced substantially by treating the water used to cool and wash regenerated mercury.

In the fertilizer industry, three processes cause most pollution:

● *Ammonia*. Pollution from the production of ammonia and ammonitrates comes from the release of ammonia, mostly into water. Discharges can be reduced considerably by altering processes for purifying synthetic gas.

● *Sulphuric acid*. Pollution in the contact process in general use at present comes mainly from the cooling water.

● *Phosphoric acid*. In addition to producing mineral salts and ammonia, the manufacture of phosphoric acid generates very large amounts of gypsum powder (4.75 t of gypsum per t of P_2O_5); it is generally not used and has to be stored.

In addition, all natural phosphates also contain fluorides, and their conversion into simple or triple superphosphates releases fluorinated products, which must be prevented from spreading.

A real change would be the general introduction of direct fixing of nitrogen by bacteria living in symbiosis with cultivated plants, something that would call for a reappraisal of the nitrogenous fertilizer industry. However, potash and phosphate fertilizers would still be needed to compensate for the removal of minerals contained in crops. Would the phosphate fertilizer industry be affected by the replacement of present chemical processes by other processes, mainly biological (which make natural phosphates, virtually insoluble, soluble and thereby capable of assimilation)? At present this question cannot be answered.

(iii) Chemistry, biotechnologies, and the environment

Apart from the possibility of replacing chemical processes with biological ones, biotechnologies could play a major role in controlling pollution downstream of the inorganic and organic chemicals industries. Several laboratories are studying specific enzymes, which could transform pesticides, chlorine compounds (mainly dioxines), phenols, nitrogen oxides, cyanides, etc. into non-toxic molecules. Other enzymes could extract the mercury or chrome ions to include them in non-dangerous or easily separable complex molecules. None of this research may come to fruition, but in the medium and long term vast possibilities seem to be opening up for the depollution of industrial effluent by biological methods.

(f) Paper pulp

(i) Prospects and state of the art

Owing to the lack of plentiful raw materials on the spot, the chances of expansion for this sector in the Mediterranean basin are poor (a large part of Spanish production is located in Galica and French in the Aquitaine). Virtually all paper pulp produced in the world is made from plant fibre. Two main groups of processes are used for pulping:

● *Mechanical processes*. The new process of crushing with rotary grinders supplies good-quality pulp, but not very strong. Since the 1970s two variants, the thermomechanical process and the thermo-chemical-mechanical process, provide higher-grade pulps, suitable for newsprint.
● *Chemical processes*. These are increasingly common, the main technique being bisulphate processes and in particular the kraft process, which provide very strong paper for packaging.

(ii) Interaction with the environment

The rotary grinding process causes little pollution. New mechanical processes are unfortunately worse in this respect, causing water pollution and air pollution deriving from volatile woody components created during processing. Chemical processes pollute both water and air to the extent that the paper pulp industry has long been considered as one of the most polluting. But in the face of mounting awareness of the public since the early 1970s, a considerable effort has been made to reduce pollution in existing plants (easier for air pollution than for water pollution), or to build a new, less polluting plant. Currently and in the medium term pollution control in this sector is a matter of deployment of resources.

In the long term it seems that vegetable fibre will remain the raw material for paper pulp, since it is difficult to compete with its very low cost (compare the case of cement). On the other hand, it is not unlikely that less polluting processes will be developed and disseminated.

(g) Other industries

Observations will be confined to three fairly different examples, to give a representative sample of the situation.

(i) The aluminium industry

Electrolysis releases fluoride compounds which have disastrous effects on vegetation within a radius of several kilometres around a plant. There does not seem to be any hope of a medium-term technological change in this field: work undertaken to extract aluminium from clay seems unlikely to lead in the near future to any method that would be economically competitive with the present process. The slower growth of aluminium consumption world-wide will indeed make it less urgent to make use of ores other than bauxite. On the other hand, fluoride pollution can be reduced considerably:

● by using pre-baked anode tanks;
● by retaining fluoride dust, not only in the tanks, but in workshop ventilation circuits, either by electrofilters or by more efficient dry-purification processes.

(ii) Tanneries

Leather industries are traditionally important in Spain—the leading world exporter of leather and leather goods—in Catalonia and the provinces of Valencia and Alicante; and in Italy, in Tuscany,

Lombardy, the Marches, etc. They are less important, but not insignificant, in Turkey, in the region of İzmir, in Greece, around Athens and Thessaloniki, in Egypt, in Alexandria, etc. Tanning has always been a highly polluting industry, discharging large amounts of effluent, which is of course biodegradable, but the process is slow and produces many nuisances. Modern tanning processes, such as chrome tanning, have considerably reduced tanning time, but have added chemical pollution to biological pollution. In several countries use is made of automated processes, 'short baths' to reduce the volumes discharged, or effluent treatment, in order to combat this pollution.

(iii) Electronics

Handling minute quantities of materials compared to those used in many traditional industries, keeping a severe watch on any impurities incompatible with product quality and reliability, these 'white-coat' industries would at first sight appear to be less threatening for the environment. And yet the example of Silicon Valley in the United States, where the microchip industry has produced problems of toxic waste, shows that this is not always the case. This example illustrates the concerns aroused by the 'new pollutions' and/or trace substances (micropolluants) in the air or water, whose effects on human health are still not fully grasped, and which are not yet subject to systematic regulation. However, this example and the above analysis of relationships between the various industrial sectors and the environment clearly show the difficulties in carrying out a prospective study in this field.

4. Conclusions and issues for appraisal

First of all, a widespread tendency can be identified which characterizes interaction between industrial development and the Mediterranean environment over the coming decades:

● In industrialized countries north of the basin, routine, 'ordinary' pollution produced by traditional industries has probably passed its peak and will be better controlled and reduced, provided that the authorities impose increasingly strict standards and make sure that they are observed, and that the necessary investments are available. On the other hand, the risk of accidental 'extraordinary' pollution will probably increase in many industries, whether old or new: fine metallurgy, fine chemicals, biotechnology industries, electronics, etc.

● In the less industrialized countries south and east of the basin, where certain production capacities will increase considerably, as indicated, the problem of investment will be fundamental. In some cases choices will be made easier by the competitiveness of new 'environment-friendly' processes, as with natural gas in the steel industry. North–south co-operation, as envisaged in the alternative scenarios, could also play a major role.

With regard to the spatial distribution of industry, emphasis has been laid on growth discrepancies between the north and south for the three major industrial branches: agro-food, primary processing industries producing intermediate goods, and light industry producing most non-durable consumer goods (including textiles). Since the countries south and east of the Mediterranean have far higher growth-rates for these industries than the northern countries, spatial distribution will inevitably be inverted between these two groups of countries in the fairly long run.

Basically, this shift is linked to the differing dynamics of domestic markets. It will occur through the creation of new enterprises in the southern and eastern countries, which in this case cannot be described as a 'delocation' of industry. Another reason for the shift, however, which differs according to the scenarios, is changes in foreign trade, the northern industries losing ground either on their home markets or on those of third countries, to the benefit of southern and eastern Mediterranean industries. The term 'delocation' is then more suitable, especially since the establishment of enterprises would be financed partly by northern transnationals banking on southern exporters, thus setting up a true north–south transfer of activities. Even in the scenario most favourable to this kind of transfer (reference trend scenario T1) this would be a minor cause compared with the slow erosion of the northern position due to the continued advance of southern industries under the pressure of population growth and rising standards of living.

In many cases this geographical shift in industrial siting will occur beyond the Blue Plan horizon, but it will certainly be under way by 2025. This shift should be stressed especially because its impact on the environment and spatial distribution and organization of populations will be crucial: concentration in the major urban agglomerations or a balanced distribution between these and small or medium-sized towns (as in integration alternative scenario A2, for instance). At the local or regional level, the choice of industrial sites and the possibility of planning suitable waste and effluent treatment facilities on them offer ways to limit pollution and its effects.

The case of the capital goods industries should be considered separately. In fact possible trends in these industries are not as easy to foresee as in traditional industry, and this leads to a number of queries. Among these industries, those which involve the use of high technology are the source of a continuous renewal of techniques, a movement which spreads by degrees throughout the capital goods and consumer durable industries, in fact even to all industries. The textile industry, for instance (considered here as a light industry), is undergoing radical transformation with the automatic control of machinery and workshops; the new materials industry in fact belongs to the raw materials primary processing sector, and so forth.

The first query is, therefore: is it correct to assume the rapid growth of these industries outside the most industrialized countries on the basis of the demand for capital goods? Do not the features of the high technology industries create obstacles to the construction of new capital goods industries outside a small group of countries? In fact it can be observed that high technologies quickly spread to other industrialized countries, and this diffusion is already under way in industrializing countries with a capacity for the dynamic assimilation of technology, as can be seen by computers manufactured in Brazil, Korea, Taiwan, etc. So there is no reason to think that this spread of knowledge will be constrained.

In the future, however, its prerequisites will be more difficult to meet than at present. These are:
- accumulation of know-how concerning enterprise creation and management;
- sufficient concentration of skilled labour;
- well-organized research and development;
- link-ups with transnationals for technology transfers.

The geographical distribution of capital goods industries would therefore depend on the capacity of countries to master these factors. The general hypotheses of the alternative scenarios facilitate the access of the countries south and east of the Mediterranean basin to technology, but other conditions would also have to be met.

A final query is worth considering. Since new technologies save on raw materials and so are fairly independent of natural resources and also existing transport networks, does this not offer a fresh opportunity to the under-industrialized Mediterranean provinces of both the northern and southern coastal countries, such as eastern Andalusia, the French Midi, and the Italian Mezzogiorno, remote from major European industrial centres?

These considerations lead back to the harsh conditions already mentioned for the establishment of new poles of industry, illustrated moreover by the fact that few new poles of capital goods industries have been created in Europe since the end of the First World War. This kind of pole cannot be established by individual action, but by an overall policy and the dynamism of a network of enterprises working together and interrelated over the long term.

12 Energy Outlook

Both consumption and production of commercial energy in the Mediteranean countries have evolved considerably over the past few decades, peaking in the northern countries, while continuing to grow in the south, admittedly from fairly low levels after the Second World War (section 1).

The scenario hypotheses for the energy sector (section 2) include both the range of national strategies and possible trends in the international context for supplies (especially fossil fuels). The international market is particularly important as regards energy, and this chapter contains a number of references to it.

On the basis of these hypotheses, a number of trend and alternative scenarios have been established (section 3) related to the general economic hypotheses.

Interactions between the energy sector and the Mediterranean environment have been broken down into the hydrocarbon sector (section 4) and electricity generation (section 5), concluding with potential impact on the climate ('greenhouse effect'). Clearly it is better to have knowledge about polluting emissions and the directly destructive effects of the energy sector than about the indirect and/or distant effect, and in fact it is very difficult to compare two totally different processes, such as the use of coal or of nuclear energy for electricity generation, on the basis of their environmental impacts alone.

Whatever the scenario, a number of fundamental issues remain. These are briefly reviewed at the end of the chapter (section 6).

1. Energy in the Mediterranean basin

Both consumption and production of commercial energy throughout the Mediterranean basin have changed radically in the past decades and, among other factors, have been deeply marked by the oil crises of 1973, 1979, and 1985.

(a) Consumption

Energy consumption for the Mediterranean basin as a whole has developed remarkably since the end of the Second World War: over sixfold between 1950 and 1985 (an average annual growth rate of 5.3 per cent). In 1950 total consumption of the Mediterranean basin countries was virtually equivalent to that of Spain alone at present. Nevertheless, there is a very large difference between the countries in the north (from Spain to Greece) and the countries in the south and east of the basin (from Morocco to Syria, together with Turkey), although this difference is gradually being effaced. Up to the end of the 1960s consumption in the northern countries accounted for more than nine-tenths of the total. It is currently less than 80 per cent (for a total of a little less than 600m. t oil equivalent ('toe').

The growth of consumption in the chief countries in the north has tended to peak (especially in France, the largest consumer in the region, where the value for 1984 was still 3 per cent below the maximum reached in 1979), whereas that in the southern and eastern countries continues. Between 1970 and 1985 the increase in total commercial energy consumption averaged only 2.8 per cent per year in the countries north of the basin, and 7.2 per cent per year for the countries along the southern and eastern shores, admittedly starting from far lower values.

Very significant structural differences in consumption exist between the two shores in addition to these quantitative differences. Almost all the coal produced, for example, is consumed by the countries in the north, where it still represents about 20–25 per cent of energy consumption (nearly 50% for countries like Greece and Yugoslavia) and by Turkey. It is usually less than 5 per cent in the southern and eastern countries, although this situation could change shortly because of electricity generation requirements.

In both the north and the south oil remains the chief energy source. Some countries which import the greater part of their supplies have made considerable efforts, particularly since 1979, to reduce

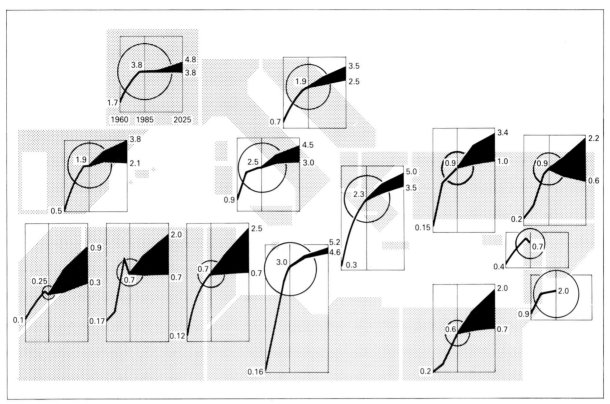

FIG. 12.1 Energy consumption per capita: Trends 1960–1985 and extreme scenarios 1985–2000 (toe per capita). Circles are proportional to 1985 consumption. The range of increase in per capita consumption is much wider for the southern and eastern countries depending on the various scenaros.

Source: Blue Plan/UN.

their oil consumption. Between 1979 and 1985, for instance, France reduced its oil consumption by more than 27 per cent (oil imports now account for less than 50 per cent of total energy consumption), Italy 18 per cent, Spain 10 per cent, and Greece 6 per cent, in a context of stabilization or decline in total energy consumption. In the southern and eastern countries, where oil consumption remains paramount, it nevertheless dwindled from 90 per cent to approximately 75 per cent of the energy balance, despite the strong growth of total energy consumption.

Except for France, where uranium has largely replaced heavy fuels for the thermal generation of electricity, the shift—absolute or relative—from oil has generally been towards natural gas. The consumption of natural gas has increased sharply throughout the basin, rising from roughly 20m. toe in 1970 to nearly 80m. toe in 1985, in other words a growth of almost 9.5 per cent per annum despite the fact that consumption is still comparatively weak (or nil) in some countries (Malta, Greece, Turkey, Syria, Lebanon, Israel). It should be noted that the

share of hydrocarbons—oil plus natural gas—was comparatively stable between 1970 and 1985: in the region of 65–70 per cent for the Mediterranean basin as a whole, but over 90 per cent for the south), slightly higher than the world average (about 60 per cent).

One of the major trends over past decades has been the strong growth in electricity consumption in all countries: growth-rates were usually higher than those of energy in general, in turn higher than the economic growth-rate for most countries (Table 12.1), except in the most industrialized countries, where the energy growth-rate plunged spectacularly after 1979 (effect of the growing importance of the tertiary sector in the economy and energy-saving efforts). Thus, between 1970 and 1985 electricity consumption growth-rates in France and Spain were over 5 per cent (but about half that in Italy for institutional reasons), nearly 8 per cent in Egypt, 9 per cent in Morocco and Turkey, 11–13 per cent in Tunisia and Algeria (equal to doubling every five or six years), over 15 per cent in Syria, and nearly 22 per cent per annum in Libya (doubling every

Table 12.1 Average annual growth-rates of GDP, total energy consumption, and electrical energy consumption, 1960–1980 and 1980–1985 (%)

	1960–80			1980–85		
	GDP (1975 $)	Energy consumption	Electricity[a] consumption	GDP (1975 $)	Energy consumption	Electricity[a] consumption
Spain	5.71	7.89	9.24	1.37	0.32	2.68
France	4.62	4.73	7.83	1.12	0.41	5.87
Italy	4.14	5.84	6.09	0.92	−0.62	−0.18
Yugoslavia	5.78	5.62	9.94	0.66	2.24	4.41
Greece	6.30	10.07	12.17	1.31	3.66	4.14
Turkey	5.32	10.80	13.24	4.78	5.87	8.38
Syria	7.70	10.14	12.44	3.54	7.52	13.78
Lebanon	5.60	5.42	7.53	0.00	0.76	−5.52
Israel	6.93	6.74	8.81	0.00	3.88	4.61
Egypt	6.40	6.37	10.36	7.44	7.76	5.64
Libya	17.90	18.20	21.10	−5.12	11.87	11.07
Tunisia	6.41	10.53	11.52	4.06	4.30	7.54
Algeria	3.73	12.52	8.77	4.67	−3.15	11.50
Morocco	6.84	7.60	8.23	2.56	1.72	7.32

Source: AIEA/Blue Plan.

[a] These data represent electricity production rather than consumption. The figures differ only for electricity importers or exporters, such as Italy (importer) or France (exporter).

three and a half years). Libya in fact holds the Mediterranean 'record', as it increased its electricity consumption by a factor of more than 200 between 1950 and 1985. In the southern and eastern oil- and gas-producing countries in particular, electricity consumption, very low after the last war, increased rapidly after 1970.

Non-commercial energy consumption is currently estimated at between 25m. and 30m. toe per annum, with little fluctuation. This represents, for 1980, an average of 4–5 per cent of total energy consumption, but the figure varies considerably from one country to another.

(b) Production

Total commercial energy production in the countries of the Mediterranean basin increased nearly ninefold between 1950 and 1985, but, unlike the steady growth in consumption, production rocketed in the 1960s (Libyan oil production, for instance, soared from 0 to more than 160m. t in a few years), followed by decline in the 1970s. Between 1970 and 1985 total energy production rose from 344m. toe to 412m. toe (but dipped to 290m. toe in 1975). This trend results mainly from a significant reduction in oil production (above all in Libya), an increase in the production of gas and primary electricity, and virtual stagnation in coal production. Mediterranean energy production represents only 4.8 per cent of the world total. The difference of more than 150m. toe (1985) between consumption and production is covered by imports from non-Mediterranean coun-

tries (Arabian–Persian Gulf, Nigeria, North Sea, etc.).

Roughly 70 per cent of coal production (about 77m. toe in 1985) is concentrated in the countries north of the basin: France (falling sharply), Yugoslavia, Spain, and Greece, and also in Turkey (increasing in these last countries but often with low-grade coal).

Approximately 95 per cent of primary electricity generation is concentrated in the countries north of the basin, contributing nearly 50 per cent of their total energy production balance. Hydroelectric power is produced in France, Italy, and Spain, followed by Yugoslavia and Turkey. In the south the only country which counts in this respect is Egypt, with the Aswan dam. Commercial geothermal energy is produced in Italy (installed capacity 519 MWe, with 43 power-plants) and Turkey (20 MWe and 2 power-plants). Nuclear power is produced in four countries: France (50 plants in 1987, or more than 85 per cent of total nuclear power in the Mediterranean), Spain, Italy, and Yugoslavia (one 660 MWe plant).

In 1985 oil and gas accounted for nearly 56 per cent of all the energy produced in the Mediterranean basin (43 per cent for oil, 13 per cent for gas).

In 1986 the southern and eastern countries produced more than 90 per cent of Mediterranean oil. The main producers—and exporters—in the south are Libya, Algeria (both with about 50m. t in 1986) and Egypt (41m. t), followed by Syria (nearly 10m. t) and Tunisia (5m. t). However, the comparative positions of these countries differ as regards reserves: at 1986 levels Libya (in fact producing at a very reduced capacity), with a reserves/production ratio of more than sixty years, is one of the major oil producers in the world, whereas Algeria and Egypt each have only some fifteen years of production left. In the north, Spain, France, Italy, Yugoslavia, Greece, and Turkey are all producers, but in a very minor way—1–4m. t per annum; and the north as a whole represented less than 9 per cent of the Mediteranean total in 1986.

The situation is somewhat different for natural gas, with 30 per cent of total production coming from the northern countries, where production usually started earlier and has the advantage of proximity to consumer markets. In 1986 70 per cent of Mediterranean gas was produced by the southern countries. In fact a distinction has to be made between gas associated with oil (the case with Libyan gas, for instance) and 'dry' or unassociated gas (the case with Algerian gas). In the north, Italy is the main producer (nearly 15,000m. m³ in 1986), followed by France, where production (at Lacq) is falling. The largest gas producer is in the south: Algeria, seventh largest producer in the world in 1986, with 35,000m. m³.

Table 12.2 summarizes a number of data on energy consumption and production in the countries of the Mediterranean basin.

2. Hypotheses for the energy scenarios

(a) The international supply context

In order to meet their energy requirements, most countries supplement their domestic resources with purchases of oil, coal, natural gas, uranium, and even, more recently, electricity, on the international markets (Italy, for instance, currently imports approximately 10 per cent of its electrical consumption, sold to it by France and Switzerland, among others). Excessively strong growth of energy consumption at the world level could lead to tension on these markets, considering limited resources or the time needed to install additional production capacity, as was the case with oil in the 1970s.

Unlike mineral resources, for which supply prospects are quite promising because of technological progress and geological abundance (as stressed in Chapter 11), questions are regularly raised about the life-span of some energy resources, starting with oil, but also uranium and natural gas. So, regardless of prices and their impact on economic development, because either imports are a burden or exports represent a source of financing, it is important to explain the hypotheses concerning energy resources used in the construction of medium- and long-term development scenarios at the international, regional, or national levels. National or regional scenarios

Table 12.2 Energy consumption in the Mediterranean countries, 1960 and 1985

	Total consumption 1960 (m. toe)	Total consumption 1985 (m. toe)	Per capita consumption 1985 (toe)	Per capita electricity consumption[a] 1985 (kWh)	Total production 1960 (m. toe)	Total production 1985 (m. toe)
Spain	16.07	74.56	1,935	3,227	11.00	32.05
France	77.19	198.47	3,634	5,967	43.10	90.08
Italy	46.26	139.57	2,436	3,171	19.58	29.16
Yugoslavia	13.48	44.95	1,942	3,185	12.02	29.95
Greece	2.78	22.64	2,260	2,798	0.79	12.31
Turkey	4.12	42.65	865	676	2.88	25.28
Syria	1.01	9.97	949	696	—	10.17
Lebanon	0.74	2.21	528	508	—	0.27
Israel	1.98	8.49	1,998	3,692	0.13	0.06
Egypt	5.12	27.60	588	531	3.45	52.73
Libya	0.22	11.07	3,070	2,266	—	54.83
Tunisia	0.50	4.62	652	568	0.02	6.72
Algeria	1.86	16.76	771	565	8.93	76.73
Morocco	1.21	5.72	261	319	0.52	0.98
TOTAL MEDITERRANEAN COUNTRIES	172.54	609.28			102.42	421.32

Source: IAEA/Blue Plan.

[a] These data represent electricity production rather than consumption. The figures differ only for electricity importers or exporters, such as Italy (importer) or France (exporter).

cannot be formulated without specifying these hypotheses. And the scenarios naturally have to take into account interchangeability of resources. The possibilities for substitution vary according to the end use; motor-car or aviation fuel, for instance, currently has no commercial substitute; conversely, electricity or heat can be produced from virtually any source (hence occasionally fierce competition on some markets).

In 1985 world commercial energy consumption was approximately 7,400m. toe. Oil provided about 38 per cent of it, ahead of coal (nearly 31 per cent), natural gas (20 per cent), and primary electricity (hydraulic, geothermal, and nuclear, 11 per cent). World energy consumption rose by an average of 4.2 per cent per annum between 1965 and 1975, and by 2.2 per cent per annum from 1975 to 1985, a particularly disturbed period for the world economy. Assuming an average growth of no more than 1 per cent per annum, the world consumption level would exceed 11,000m. toe in 2025; with a growth-rate of 2 per cent per annum (comparable to the population growth-rates given in the chapter on population), it would exceed 16,000m. toe, i.e. more than double the current amount. These figures provide an idea of the scope of the energy supply problem as from early next century.

(i) Oil

According to most experts, oil will stay in first place at least until 2000, providing 30 per cent or more of the world energy supply. Proven reserves are in the region of 95,000–100,000m. t (98,200m. in 1986), or slightly more than thirty years of current consumption. The Mediterranean countries possess some 5,000m. t, i.e. 5 per cent (Table 12.3). About 11,000m. t are found in the socialist countries, which are thus comparatively self-sufficient. A little over half, 53m. t, are located in the Middle East.

Beyond the reserves, in any event globally insufficient to reach 2025, potential resources are very poorly known: nevertheless, these are the resources that will make it possible to reach or go past 2025, or, in the final analysis, will determine the length of the 'oil era' (along with non-conventional oils, known even less and usually very expensive). As regards the quantity of oil remaining to be discovered, the following values were selected for the Blue Plan scenarios, although they are somewhat arbitrary, combining physical and geopolitical assumptions (figures for some Mediterranean countries are given in Table 12.3).

- 36,000m. t or a dozen extra years (2030) for the reference trend scenario T1 and worst trend scenario T2, as the international situation is adverse to oil prospection and production;
- 55,000m.–60,000m. t for moderate trend scenario T3;
- 80,000m.–120,000m. t for the alternative scenarios (although the probability of reaching the latter figure is in the region of 5 per cent) as international co-operation furthers oil prospection and optimal production.

Two possible levels of world production have been associated with these different estimates for oil reserves and resources:

- 3,000m. t per annum. This is somewhat higher than production over the past few years, but slightly lower than the maximum production of more than 3,200m. t in 1979. With a world population of roughly 8,200m. in 2025, this hypothesis of stagnating world production means declining average per capita 'availability', in the order of 370 kg per annum in 2025, compared to a little over 580 in 1985. This sort of hypothesis corresponds to reference trend scenario T1 and worst trend scenario T2.
- 3,500m. t per annum. This is about 20 per cent more than in 1985. This hypothesis corresponds to moderate trend scenario T3, and alternative scenarios A1 and A2, with stronger economic growth and a better atmosphere of international co-operation.

Whatever the scenario, virtually all Mediterranean countries will have to face the major issue of oil supply. And whatever the hypothesis concerning resources, the potential reserves and resources of most Mediterranean oil producers, with the exception of Libya, are likely to become depleted during the second period of the scenarios, i.e. between 2000 and 2025, an event which will greatly affect their economic development prospects in the medium and long term.

(ii) Natural gas

Overall, natural gas came into use much later than oil (after the Second World War), and some Mediterranean countries, like those mentioned above, have not started to use it yet. With 10^{14} m^3, or about 60 years' worth of consumption, world and Mediterranean natural gas reserves (Table 12.3) are steadily growing. Considering that this fuel is flexible to use and has environmental advantages, it is likely that there will be vigorous development

Table 12.3 Energy reserves and potential resources in the Mediterranean basin

	Oil			Natural gas			Coal	
	Reserves (m. t)	R/P years	Potential resources (m. t)	Reserves (Gm³)	R/P years	Potential resources (Gm³)	Recoverable reserves (m. tce)	Potential resources (m. tce)
Spain	4.7	2.6	n.a.	22	64.00	n.a.	883.0	542
France	31.0	10.6	n.a.	35	8.10	n.a.	381.0	—
Italy	130.0	50.1	n.a.	225	15.20	n.a.	39.0	n.a.
Yugoslavia	36.0	8.6	n.a.				16,570.0	n.a.
Greece	3.2	2.6	n.a.				3,000.0	n.a.
Turkey	19.0	8.1	n.a.	13	28.60	n.a.	4,857.0	3,138
Syria	201.0	20.8	n.a.	118	875.00	n.a.		
Egypt	616.0	15.1	135–270–1,650	250	56.50	200–600–1,700	52.9	n.a.
Libya	3,120.0	63.2	500–800–2,000	595	127.90	200–500–1,500		
Tunisia	238.0	43.4	135–270–1,200	90	44.30	100–300–1,000		
Algeria	660.0	13.2	70–200–700	2,978	85.60	200–500–1,500	43.0	
Morocco				4	50.00	n.a.	45.0	n.a.
TOTAL MEDITERRANEAN COUNTRIES	5,065.0	29.7	900–1,600–5,600	4,329	65.66	700–1,900–5,700	27,871.0	

Key: R/P = number of years of proven reserves at current production rates.   n.a. = not available

Sources: *World Oil* for oil reserves; *Oil and Gas Journal* for gas reserves; US Geological Survey for potential oil and gas resources; World Energy Conference for coal.

in this sector during the coming decades. The energy scenarios have started to explore this possibility.

(iii) Coal

Coal reserves and resources are considerable: several million million tonnes, equal to several hundreds of years' worth of current consumption. Since coal is also a low-priced product as a result of highly sophisticated extraction techniques (used in the United States, Australia, South Africa, Colombia, etc.), it may play an increasing role at the world level, particularly in thermal power production, for which it is or will be in competition with nuclear energy. There is not much coal in the Mediterranean: virtually none at all in the southern countries; more, but of low grade, in the northern countries (Spain, France, Yugoslavia, Greece) and Turkey. In addition to its effects on the climate, greater than those of oil and gas, its environmental impacts still need to be solved. It also requires rather large-scale transport infrastructure, currently more than sufficient, but which would need considerable future investment in the case of strong growth. Some scenarios explored the steady growth of coal use in the world and in the Mediterranean basin, of coal trade, and consequently of its maritime transport, as well as its impacts on the environment.

(iv) Nuclear energy

After an impressive start in the 1960s, the production of nuclear energy has slowed down considerably with regard to commitments (if not to the opening of plants commissioned five or ten years ago). With an installed capacity of a little over 50 GWe, France has become the second biggest nuclear country after the United States, and the Rhone is doubtless one of the most 'nuclearized' rivers in the world. In the Mediterranean, Spain lags quite far behind France (6.5 GWe). The other countries have adopted a 'wait and see' attitude, especially since the accident at Chernobyl.

World reserves and resources of uranium seem to be quite sufficient for the coming decades. In the longer term, after 2000 or 2010, the need may arise to adopt other production techniques, such as breeders. Assuming that an acceptable, and accepted, solution can be found for the permanent storage of nuclear wastes, some experts mention the possibility of a 'second nuclear age', using new reactors, which might start after 2000.

(v) New or renewable energy sources

Despite a considerable world potential sometimes estimated at 7,000m.–8,000m. toe per annum, or the equivalent of current world energy consumption, and undeniable advantages for the environment, renewable energies (geothermal, wind energy, biomass, solar energy with its different exploitation possibilities, etc.) are finding it hard to make a breakthrough, although they regularly arouse interest. The drop in oil prices has placed a curb— which is not quite rational—on research and development efforts in most countries.

There is still hydraulic potential in many countries, including Turkey, Greece, Yugoslavia, Italy, and Spain, but only to a minor degree in the other countries east and south of the Mediterranean basin. Geothermal power is already exploited in Italy, as well as Turkey (where it has interesting potential), Greece, France, and Yugoslavia.

Solar energy has considerable potential in the countries south and east of the Mediterranean basin (due to a combination of abundant sunshine and vast desert regions not too far from inhabitated areas), but its exploitation on a significant scale in relation to energy needs requires, under present conditions, interventionist policies, such as those partly assumed in the alternative scenarios. Moreover, it should be noted that the major trend towards urbanization (analysed elsewhere) is more conducive to concentrated forms of energy production rather than dispersed or decentralized forms. On the other hand, decentralized production could offer attractive solutions for scattered dwellings. Some Mediterranean countries, such as Israel, have achieved remarkable results in specialized sectors, using solar energy for sanitary installations (65 per cent penetration rate); Crete uses it for tourist requirements; and so on.

With regard to biomass, the traditional use of fuel-wood still plays an important role in the southern and eastern countries. The trend envisaged by, for instance, FAO for the consumption of fuel-wood is a serious concern both from the energy viewpoint and from that of the protection of soil and water resources (see Box 12A).

(b) National strategies

The hypotheses first focus on national energy consumption growth-rates in relation to the economic growth and industrial hypotheses, then on the possible structure of supply in terms of the international context described above and national strategic choices: supply cost in the light of the market situation, a fairly high degree of international

BOX 12A. **The fuel-wood problem**

The problem of fuel-wood, which it had been hoped would soon be solved, has become more acute with the high price of commercial fuel and increasing population pressure. Many countries throughout the world are already experiencing a shortage, others are in a state of crisis and may be suffering increasing deficits by 2000. The problem is threefold: it concerns forests, energy, and ecology. As it becomes increasingly difficult to obtain fuel-wood, resources not directly related to the forest, such as agricultural waste, will probably play an important role as substitutes; this will then reduce its availability as organic soil supply and make wider use of fertilizers necessary.

Fuel-wood needs are estimated at between 0.5 and 1 m³ per person per annum for cooking food and heating water (not including needs in many craft industries in rural areas).

According to a study undertaken by FAO, the Mediterranean countries along the southern and eastern shores can be classed in three groups:

- non-consumer countries (or countries using fuel-wood only to a minimal extent per capita): Cyprus, Israel, Libya, the last two having no forests;
- low-consumer countries (from 0.05 to 0.1 m³ per inhabitant per annum): Lebanon, Egypt, Syria;
- high-consumer countries (from 0.2 to 0.8): Tunisia, Morocco, Algeria, Turkey (the last three—and the Lebanon—being mountainous countries where needs in fuel-wood are likely to be at least 1.5 m³ per inhabitant per annum in certain zones).

	Average level of fuel-wood requirements (m³ per inhabitant p.a.)	Rural population concerned in 2,000m. inhabitants	Total requirements (000 m³ p.a.)	Total availability (000 m³ p.a.)	Deficit (000 m³ p.a.)	Per capita deficit (m³ p.a.)
Lebanon	0.10	3.1	310	220	90	0.029
Egypt	0.03	30.6	908	415	493	0.016
Syria	0.05	12.8	640	368	272	0.021
SUB-TOTAL		46.5	1,858	1,003	855	
Tunisia	0.50	9.2	4,600	2,974	1,626	0.17
Morocco	0.80	23.1	18,480	7,580	10,900	0.47
Algeria	0.80	23.9	19,120	6,713	12,407	0.51
Turkey	0.80	40.6	24,480	20,331	4,149	0.30
SUB-TOTAL		96.8	66,680	37,598	29,082	
TOTAL		143.3	68,538	38,601	29,937	

The accompanying table shows that by 2,000 over 140m. persons will be affected by a deficit approaching 30m. m³.

As productivity, without degradation, lies in the region of 0.5–1 m³ per hectare per annum, the extent of the surface area involved, or the risk of degradation, i.e. over-exploitation of existing forest, is very high.

dependency, choices between growing dependency and low-cost supply or between the medium and long term, incentives for saving energy, and advantages or disadvantages for the environment.

The overall assumption of weak energy growth for the most industrialized countries in the Mediterranean basin, which have already attained comparatively high energy consumption levels per capita (between 2,000 and 4,000 koe per annum, the case in France and Italy) allows these countries little margin for manœuvre, especially up to 2000, considering the equipment programmes under way. The scenarios for these countries therefore diverge little and only show marked differences after 2000.

The future is more open for the other countries north of the basin with comparatively low energy consumption per capita, between 1,000 and 2,500 koe per year, such as Spain, Yugoslavia, Greece, and Cyprus, where development requirements and possibilities are still fairly high, with a wider range of choice.

The countries south and east of the basin, except Libya, have fairly low per capita consumption levels, varying between 300 and 1,000 koe per year (compared with the world average of about 1,300 koe per year), since their consumption is largely based on hydrocarbons, as mentioned above. Whether consumers or producers, their future trends

BOX 12B. **Energy statistics and methodology**

Bearing in mind consistency and availability for the Mediterranean countries as a whole, the United Nations energy statistics series were chosen as the starting-point, despite some inconvenience caused by the fact that they are published three years after the date they cover. With regard to consumption, these statistics give final forms of energy source (except for losses and non-energy uses), indicating the thermal equivalent (1 kWh = 84.5 goe) of primary electrical energy (hydraulic, nuclear, geothermal). This convention was adapted for the calcuations in the scenarios (production equivalence: 1 kWh = 222 goe). In some cases, and when there was no apparent contradiction, specialized statistics were also used (e.g. for reserves, resources, etc.).

A small model was constructed in the macro-economic scenarios to explore possible energy trends, on the basis of the growth-rates of total consumption by country and of electrification (with a ceiling when necessary for the share of electricity in national energy balances). The distribution of consumption—then production—by source was calculated by logical trend extrapolations and/or by hypotheses concerning growth and expected availability based on reserves and potential resources, taking into account additional determining factors usually derived from other sectors (such as the development of iron and steel and cement industries, major energy consumers; trends for the motor-car stock and transport; specific fuel consumption, refining structures, etc.).

Supply structures were calculated from the trends and potential of domestic production by source, on the basis of both reserves and potential resources, differentiating between them according to the scenario.

depend considerably on the world market for oil and gas. The scenarios can therefore be very open and very contrasted, and explore a wide range of different possible futures.

In all cases, in the north and in the south and east of the basin, it has been assumed that the trend towards electrification would continue, average to strong in the north, strong to very strong in the south and east. This assumption is very significant for energy development in the Mediterranean countries, regarding both required investment and possible supply structures. Its importance is such that several extreme variants of the scenarios have been explored in order to study the consequences of virtual concentration on a single source for electrical generation (nuclear or coal).

Whether for energy consumption or for electricity development, the growth-rates chosen could seem modest compared with the performances of many countries during the past decades, even in comparison with the rates of some socio-economic plans under way or in preparation. But it should be recalled that the rates used are average rates over long periods (fifteen and twenty-five years successively) and that various pressures will apply to put a brake on world consumption, including probably action on prices.

3. Findings of the energy scenarios

(a) Trend scenarios

The trend scenarios reflect a certain degree of continuity as regards consumption and supply trends, with low penetration of new and renewable energies, which nevertheless increase from the worst trend scenario T2 to the moderate trend scenario T3 (the T1 trend scenario usually lying midway between these two diverging scenarios).

In the worst trend scenario T2, weak economic growth means low energy growth, and limited investment resources curb electricity growth. Total energy consumption rises from a little over 600m. toe to nearly 900m. toe in 2025, an annual average growth of 1.02 per cent for forty years (compared with an average growth of 5.3 per cent between 1950 and 1985). The countries north of the basin consume about 65 per cent of total energy in the region but their growth-rates were lower than average (only 0.48 per cent per annum), and some countries make virtually no progress. At this rate per capita consumption rises little, and even falls in some countries south and east of the basin, with an energy consumption growth-rate lower than the population growth-rate (this rate is assumed to be the highest in the T2 scenarios).

Total electricity consumption grows faster than energy consumption, with an average annual rate of 1.6 per cent, reaching 1770 TWh. Per capita consumption rises in all countries except one. Consumption increases much more in the southern and eastern countries (by nearly 300 per cent) than in the northern countries (where the increase is only 75 per cent).

Supply structures change little. Oil consumption, which in 2025 still accounts for about 40 per cent of the total energy supply, rises for the basin as a whole from 300m. to 360m. t, peaking or falling in the northern countries. World production is at a standstill, with irregular prices, which is not very conducive to energy planning (the overall tendency is to rise); towards 2010—15 the 'bottom of the barrel' becomes visible for some Mediterranean producers (Tunisia, Egypt), which induces the consumer countries able to do so to turn to other sources. As this scenario is not conducive to international trade, countries with domestic coal resources, such as Spain, Yugoslavia, Greece, and Turkey, continue to develop them. Total coal consumption, supplemented in the southern countries with coal imports, for electrical generation among other things, rises from 100m. toe to 175m. toe, but anti-pollution devices are not always installed (partly because of their cost). Use of natural gas grows slowly, virtually at the same overall Mediterranean rate as coal, but this time to the benefit of southern and eastern producers. The growth of primary electricity is hampered by the cost of investment: maximum hydraulic potential is far from being achieved in the north and in Turkey. The nuclear energy programmes under way are completed; programmes start up again slowly after 2010 (commissioned after 2000).

Overall, this scenario is at first sight not very conducive to the use of renewable sources of energy: weak economic growth, low energy growth, irregular oil prices, inadequate international scientific and technological co-operation, few incentives on the part of governments, etc. The main use of solar energy is to generate hot water for hygienic use, an application fairly widespread in the Mediterranean basin (households, hotels and lodgings, hospitals, etc.); there are a few applications of photovoltaic cells (e.g. in communication relay stations).

Conversely, moderate trend scenario T3 postulates strong economic growth, bringing about high energy and electricity consumption. This scenario also assumes that more attention is paid to the environment, a phenomenon fostered, on the one hand, by the renewal and/or development of the productive equipment but, on the other, curbed to some extent by an economic dynamism which tackles the most urgent matters first or postpones consideration of some constraints till later.

Energy consumption grows strongly, at an annual average rate of nearly 2.2 per cent, to reach close on 1,500m. toe in 2025, almost 2.4 times the current level. In fact, growth is stronger during the first half of the period, weaker after 2000 for the countries north of the basin, and weaker in general after 2010. With an average annual growth-rate of 4.4 per cent throughout the period (compared with 1.25 per cent for the north), the southern and eastern countries virtually catch up with the north in 2025, with 47 per cent or so of the total energy consumed (a similar catching-up process to that depicted for heavy industry, indeed linked to it to some extent). Electricity consumption also surges forward for the basin as a whole (level of approximately 2,800 TWh). At the end of the period the south and east consume more than one third of the total.

Per capita consumption of both energy and electricity increases, and for many countries south and east of the basin in 2025 it nears the current consumption of the northern Mediterranean (2,800 kWh per annum for Greece in 1985, 3,200 for Spain, 6,000 for France, compared with 10,000–20,000 for north European countries). The gap narrows, especially as consumption in the north rises more slowly or reaches a ceiling.

This kind of growth naturally resorts to all sources of supply, under constant pressure. Although the share of oil in Mediterranean supplies would be reduced to 33 per cent in 2025, its absolute value would rise by nearly 60 per cent, to approximately 490m. t. This is made possible by increased world production (in turn deriving from much more intense prospection), a widespread improvement of on-land and offshore techniques, also use of some domestic sources such as oil shale, existing in several Mediterranean countries, and better co-ordination between the countries of the Mediterranean region and those of the Arabian–Persian Gulf.

Increased oil production and technological advance lead to the strong growth of production and consumption of natural gas, whether or not associated with and dependent on oil production. The increased number of oil and gas pipelines enables some non-producing countries or small producers to benefit from transit through their countries, especially in the case of natural gas. Natural-gas consumption rises by a factor of 4.5 in forty years (an average annual growth-rate slightly under 4 per cent), taking over from oil, which peaks, and at the same time enjoying particularly advantageous conditions in the Mediterranean basin.

In this scenario primary electricity reaches virtually its maximum level, as hydraulic potential is exploited more than 60–70 per cent, geothermal energy is developed from Yugoslavia to Turkey, and nuclear energy starts up in the southern and eastern countries after 2000 in the context of international co-operation agreements.

Coal demand for electricity production and industrial needs is such that domestic production reaches its highest level, and even then imports are required, as total consumption exceeds 300m. t. Solar energy enjoys more favourable conditions (without yet reaching the optimum ones in the alternative scenarios), among other things on account of the industrial climate conducive to innovation: hot water for hygienic and industrial purposes, greenhouses for intensive agriculture, crop-drying, incipient use of photovoltaic cells in isolated locations, and the spread of solar units (for electricity and heat) for dispersed dwellings.

(b) Alternative scenarios

The strong economic growth and north–south and south–south co-operation assumed in the alternative scenarios, as well as incorporation of the environment in decision-making procedures and in the choice of technical processes, are reflected in different ways in the energy sector:

● Preference is given to apparently less polluting sources of energy such as natural gas and renewable energies, starting with solar, hydraulic, wind (etc.) energy. These scenarios rely heavily on gas: gas benefits from efficient and constantly advancing technology, which tends to diverge from oil technology. Renewable energies assume increasing importance in these scenarios but would probably not realize their full potential until after the horizon of 2025. Their development is furthered by north–south technological co-operation in the case of the A1 scenario and by the activity of small or medium-sized enterprises in the A2 scenarios. Finally energy savings are systematically encouraged.

● These 'gas-orientated' scenarios are based on a high level of trade, north–south in the A1 scenarios, and south–south in the A2 scenarios—'south' being understood in broad terms, including in some cases the Arabian–Persian Gulf region or sub-Saharan Africa (gas pipeline networks).

● This option of natural gas, especially for countries south and east of the basin, partly constrains the development of nuclear energy, which starts off more slowly in this region, as a 'wait and see' attitude is assumed.

● Oil remains important in absolute terms, especially because of the prevailing atmosphere of international and intra-Mediterranean co-operation; its days are numbered, but its decline can be planned and optimized.

● The biggest difference with moderate trend scenario T3 concerns coal, whose consumption would be scarcely higher than that for the worst trend scenario T2 (i.e. about 200m. toe, a large part of which would be for industrial purposes). When it is used for electricity generation, power-stations are equipped with the most efficient depolluting devices, or use new combustion processes such as fluidized beds or resort to gasification. But this does not solve the problem of CO_2, considered sufficiently alarming to elicit international measures for controlled coal use, without going to the point of banning it altogether.

These hypotheses lead to overall Mediterranean consumption of a little under 1,600m. toe in 2025 and to electricity consumption very similar to that in moderate trend scenario T3. Per capita consumption is a little higher because of the population hypotheses, with smaller populations in the southern and eastern countries in this kind of scenario (up to 10 per cent lower than in T2, as these two trends coexist). Natural gas, with 580m. toe, outstrips oil (510m. toe). The two sources combined still equal 68 per cent of the total, the southern and eastern countries consuming a little under half.

The alternative scenarios assume that co-operative and very interventionist solar research programmes will have borne fruit by 2000, contributing to increasing penetration after this date, with possible variations depending on whether it involves decentralized thermal solar energy, decentralized electrical solar energy (small autonomous units), or centralized electrical solar energy, the latter required for significant penetration in the very large-scale electrical generation sector.

Decentralized solar energy (thermal and electric) is widespread in the two alternative scenarios, and serves most of the dispersed dwellings in southern and eastern countries not linked to distribution networks (5–10 per cent of the total population); it is also widely used in agriculture (water-pumping, crop-drying, etc.), and in small decentralized enterprises that are fairly low energy-consumers. This penetration of solar energy into the rural world contributes to solving the fuel-wood problem, along with the distribution of liquefied petroleum gas (LPG) at the beginning of the period.

Since environmental needs and very large co-operative research programmes foster the production of large-scale photovoltaic solar energy (third-generation photocells), it progresses vigorously in the southern and eastern countries, with huge technological and financial backing from the northern countries, but not excluding future energy imports. However, achieving 7 per cent of 3,000

TWh or 10 per cent of 2,000 TWh by 2025 requires growth-rates in the region of 25 per cent per annum as from 2000, a considerable pace that can only be envisaged in the context of particularly goal-orientated programmes.

4. Oil development and the environment

Between the crude-oil or gas field and the consumer of fuel oil or another other oil or petrochemical product lies a long chain of operations, which can extend physically over several thousand kilometres, whose main links are prospection/exploration, production, transport, processing, possible further transport, distribution and end use. Since the products handled are fluid, often inflammable, sometimes explosive, and of variable toxicity, the risk of loss and/or environmental contamination exists to varying degrees at each step. Much of the amount lost or spilt in coastal regions returns to the sea through infiltration or run-off, and contributes to hydrocarbon-related pollution. However, serious efforts are made to prevent accidents or reduce their consequences and risks are minimized under normal operating conditions.

Only two significant aspects for the Mediterranean sea and its coastal regions will be examined here: offshore exploration/production and refining. Maritime transport will be reviewed in Chapter 14.

(a) Mediterranean offshore exploration and production

Offshore oil operations in the Mediterranean are not very extensive, contrary to what might be suggested by a quick look at a map of the concessions granted (involving 115 companies). Depending on the year, a score of mobile drilling rigs are in operation, 3 per cent of the total number in the world, compared with 13–14 per cent in the North Sea. In 1984, for instance, approximately 95 wells were drilled off nine Mediterranean countries (excluding work in the Gulf of Suez in Egypt), more than 60 per cent of them on the Italian continental shelf. The main areas of activity are the Adriatic, the Ebro shelf, the plateau between Sicily and Tunisia, the Gulf of Gabes, the Nile delta, and the Aegean Sea. Offshore oil production was around 5.5m. t in 1984, coming from Spain (42 per cent), Tunisia (30 per cent), and Greece (28 per cent).

The three operations that have the greatest po-

tential effect on the environment are exploration, production, and removal of extracted oil (the case of natural gas where operations are not toxic is somewhat different). In addition to these operations and their possible impact on the marine environment, there are associated installations on land for services and management and the terminal where the oil or gas arrives. These installations, usually located on the coast, are either completely new or based on existing ports, and their size depends on the scale of prospection and exploration operations.

How are prospects likely to evolve in the Mediterranean basin in coming decades, against the background of the economic development scenarios? Three facts have to be taken into account: geological potential, the international context, and national energy and oil development strategies.

Regarding geological potential, oil and natural gas have certainly been found on the Mediterranean continental shelf, but in small deposits, and for the moment there is no question of a major oilfield. Some experts consider that the particular configuration formed by salt domes represents a deep-sea potential. Since drilling costs increase faster than depth, giant oilfields would have to be found to justify operations at great depth, something very much dependent on technological progress. The possibility of a 'Mediterranean Texas' or 'Mediterranean North Sea' seems remote, unless a major discovery changes the picture some day. An attractive discovery quickly has a multiplier effect and can transform a fairly inactive area into a major oil region, with a large increase in the number of activities both at sea and on shore.

The international context operates through world oil prices (there are thresholds for technical costs), overall demand for hydrocarbons, the 'atmosphere' conducive or not to prospection, and the possibilities of technological co-operation. As regards prices, for instance, the effect of the fall in 1986 was to reduce the number of offshore drilling operations in the world by more than half. National strategies face choices, partly political, on whether to develop and use certain domestic resources or not, and whether to resort to internal financing or open up to international oil companies, etc.

Worst trend scenario T2 is on the whole quite unfavourable to amplification of prospection efforts in the Mediterranean, even less than reference trend scenario T-1, in which activities continue roughly at present levels, without any significant change in technologies.

Moderate trend scenario T3 is associated with a significant increase in energy demand in countries in the Mediterranean basin, particularly to the south and east, hence the need to make optimal use of all available energy resources, beginning with oil. In this scenario Mediterranean offshore exploration expands in the 1990s through the efforts of international companies. Technology continues to advance, mainly in three areas: prospection (where measurements taken during drilling and the use of information technology increasingly reduce the risk of 'dry' wells); production equipment installed directly on ever deeper sea-floors, served by robots; and all technologies related to gas on sea and land, which are developing continuously and contribute to the increasing penetration of gas.

The alternative scenarios display a higher level of technical and financial co-operation among all coastal countries: many joint enterprises actively explore the Mediterranean, searching for oil and, increasingly, natural gas too, which undergoes spectacular development, based on the most efficient techniques, designed to protect the marine environment. At the peak of activity, 100–120 annual drillings could be carried out, both on the continental shelf and in the high seas.

(b) Refining

Refining is an essential link in the oil-chain. It is a complex operation culminating in a range of very different products, from LPG to heavy oils and asphalts, and including various fuels and major petrochemical intermediate products (ethylene, pro-

pylene, benzene, etc.). Each product requires specific physico-chemical operations, carried out in industrial plants that can handle millions of tonnes a year and incur the risk of routine or accidental pollution, and of accidents (explosions, fires, toxic substances, etc.).

World refining capacity in 1986 was about 3,650m. t of crude per annum, down by about 11 per cent on the 1980 peak. A little more than 12 per cent, 461m. t, was located in Mediterranean countries (Table 12.4), down on average by about 20 per cent on 1980 (a 43 per cent drop in France, 38 per cent in Italy, 18 per cent in Spain, these three countries still accounting for 67 per cent of the Mediterranean total). This capacity was well in excess of requirements, since the amount of oil refined was less than 300m. t.

Installed refining capacity on the Mediterranean shoreline was around 280m. t (Fig. 12.2), also lower than what it was in the early 1980s (over 315m. t, but only 220m. t of oil refined). Whereas Italy, France, and Spain have reduced their refining capacities, several countries south and east of the basin—Algeria, Turkey, and Egypt—have increased theirs. These refineries are usually located on the coast, linked to the arrival of crude oil by sea or the redispatch of products (often by inland pipelines in the countries north of the basin).

Existing surplus capacity and the peaking of oil consumption expected for countries north of the basin in the various scenarios suggest that refining capacities should continue to contract at the same time as refining structure changes, with an increase in (expensive) conversion of heavy products into

Table 12.4 Refining capacity of Mediterranean countries, 1970–1985 (000 t.)

	1970	1973	1978	1980	1981	1982	1983	1984	1985
Spain	34,800	43,700	76,100	78,100	76,100	76,100	76,100	68,900	64,400
France	116,500	153,900	169,040	166,050	158,282	140,970	118,390	109,600	106,800
Italy	150,200	188,670	211,600	195,600	196,100	172,200	149,300	145,300	135,000
Yugoslavia	12,500	11,900	20,200	20,200	20,200	20,200	14,800	14,800	14,800
Albania	1,800		3,200	3,700	3,700	3,700	3,700	3,700	3,700
Greece	4,625	7,125	20,170	21,310	21,260	21,020	18,400	19,500	19,500
Turkey	7,375	14,475	16,830	16,830	18,300	23,280	23,620	23,600	23,600
Cyprus		600	750	750	800	770	770	770	800
Syria	2,950	2,950	11,100	11,100	11,610	11,390	11,390	11,390	11,390
Lebanon	3,000	3,000	2,640	2,590	2,590	2,590	2,590	850	850
Israel	5,600	6,000	9,710	9,460	9,460	9,460	9,460	8,500	8,500
Egypt	8,500	9,000	12,500	14,540	14,540	16,960	18,500	18,500	21,200
Libya	500	500	6,500	6,500	6,500	6,500	6,500	15,200	17,000
Tunisia	1,000	1,000	1,690	1,690	1,690	1,690	1,690	1,690	1,690
Algeria	2,875	5,790	5,790	21,900	21,900	21,900	21,900	21,900	21,900
Morocco	1,650	2,900	3,590	7,700	7,700	7,700	7,700	7,700	7,700
TOTAL	353,875	451,510	571,710	578,020	570,732	536,430	484,810	471,900	460,830

Source: Comité Professionnel du Pétrole (French oil industry statistics).

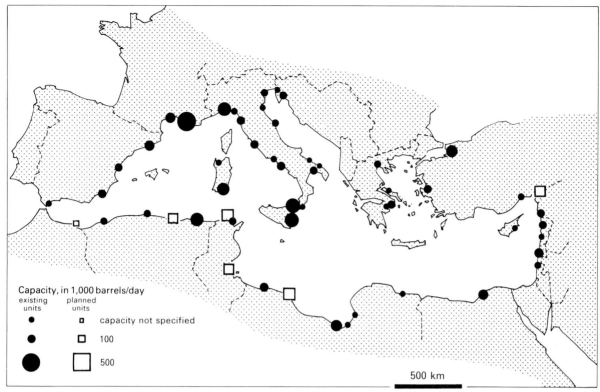

FIG. 12.2 Refineries on the Mediterranean coast

light products, fuels and fillers for petrochemicals. South and east of the basin, refining capacities are likely to increase considerably and could more than double by the start of the next century, both for domestic market needs and for product exports, gradually replacing crude exports. Much of this increase in capacity will probably be obtained by extending existing plants; the demand for new coastal sites could be confined to a few large complexes (refineries, petrochemicals, harbour dispatching installations, for example, in the event of large offshore discoveries).

Considerable efforts have been made to reduce and/or eliminate environmental impact. According to a CONCAWE (Conservation of Clean Air and Water in Europe, an association of European refiners) survey, for instance, the weighted average volume of liquid effluent discharge was reduced by a factor of 20 between 1960 and 1970 (from 6.37 to 0.38 m³ per tonne of crude processed) in European refineries, and their weighted average hydrocarbon content was reduced by a factor of 60 in the same period (from 56 to 0.92 kg of hydrocarbon effluent per 1,000 t of crude processed). In addition to hydrocarbons, waste water contains oils and fats, phenols, ammonia, dissolved or suspended solids,

sulphur, chromium, etc., and may be acid or basic; after treatment effluent contains only very low concentrations of these various pollutants.

In 1975, at the time when the Barcelona Convention was being prepared, UNEP estimated that the sixty refineries located on the Mediterranean coast discharged about 20,000 t of oil per annum into the sea. This figure has no doubt now to be scaled down, since the discharges were usually linked to old refineries with high water consumption and no advanced effluent treatment.

Even though there is no such thing as a 'typical refinery', since plants differ in scale, crudes processed, their sulphur content, processes used, and the specific processing units installed depending on the required product range, UNEP (in its 1985 energy reports) provides the following scales for atmospheric effluents per million t of crude processed: 820 t of sulphur oxide, 700 t of nitrogen oxide, 170 t of carbon monoxide, 1,200 t of organic substances, 90 t of ammonia, and 100 t of dust (figures based on a 25m. t per annum refinery).

Site coverage may vary between 1.5 and 35 ha per million tonnes of crude processed; these figures could be twice as much if safety zones are taken into account. Water requirements vary between 100 and 2,000 m³ per million tonnes of crude processed, as equipment cooling is usually carried out in closed circuits.

5. Electricity generation and the environment

In the Mediterranean basin electricity is generated from a wide variety of sources: chiefly coal, oil, gas, nuclear, hydraulic, and geothermal. Several quite different processes can be used with the same power source: steam turbine, gas turbine, combined cycle, etc. With the same process, the degree of concern for environmental protection and pollution control can range from a minimum to the adoption of the most sophisticated techniques (dedusting, smoke treatment, etc.), which are currently in full development. This illustrates the difficulty of any prospective study of the environment stretching over fifteen years, let alone forty. Work was therefore confined to drawing attention to some trends, identifying possible major changes, and reflecting on a few figures.

The main sources of electricity generation in the Mediterranean basin are:

- coal, often replaced by fuel oil (especially in non-producer countries), but which is making a 'come-back' because, among other factors, of its low price compared to fuel oil (less true since 1986);
- fuel oil, which has considerably declined since the oil price increases in the 1970s;
- natural gas, still little used except in two countries (Algeria and Italy), but which could be considerably developed (envisaged among other things in the alternative scenarios);

- nuclear energy, concentrated in a few countries for the moment, but an option which remains open after 2000;
- hydraulic power, which still has development potential in some countries.

The following paragraphs will focus on thermal generation in particular, on the basis of coal or uranium, although renewable energies are also considered.

(a) Coal

All scenarios foresee the continued expansion of electricity in many countries, based partly on coal, at least up to 2000, a trend which will grow stronger after 2000 in the trend scenarios (competing with nuclear energy in some countries), and give way to other sources (natural gas and renewable energies) in the alternative scenarios. Coal requirements for electricity generation add to industrial needs (the iron and steel industry in particular, cement works, etc.). As Mediterranean total coal production capacity is lower than demand, part of the coal consumed will have to be imported, entailing the development of specialized infrastructure.

Domestic production of most coal-producing countries in the Mediterranean (except France) is increasing and should continue to grow during the coming decades. But, as indicated in Table 12.5, this usually involves medium- or low-grade coal (lignite), with high ash or humidity content, sometimes produced in opencast mines that may have a serious impact on the landscape (before possible rehabilitation when seams are exhausted), and on ground-water resources (the case of Greece, for example).

Coal can be imported either to each power-plant or on a national basis, possibly through one or more

---

BOX 12C. **Coal in Spain**

Spain possesses anthracite reserve, mainly in the north, and black and brown lignite (which can be extracted in opencast mines). Coal output supplies 24 per cent of primary energy production and 65 per cent is used to generate electricity (40 per cent of electricity is generated from local or imported coal). Ash content is usually quite high, between 30 and 50 per cent, and will reportedly increase further with mechanized underground mining, raising serious problems for washing operations, which lose their effectiveness. This is one of the factors encouraging research into new processes for using coal.

To replace or increase present electricity capacities of nearly 11,000 MWe, it is estimated that between 600 and 1,000 MWe of coal-fired generating capacity (part of which will have to use coal imports) need to be installed each year from 1995 to 2020.

A major study programme has been launched, concerned among other things with the possibilities of using various fluidized-bed combustion processes (circulation or high-pressure). There are plans to turn an old conventional power-station, at Escatrón (Saragossa), into a testing station for these fluidized-bed processes.

Source: 1986 World Energy Conference.

Table 12.5 Domestic coal production in the northern Mediterranean countries, 1986

	Bituminous coal (m. t)	Lignite (m. t)	Equivalent (m. toe)	Difference 1986/1985 (%)
Spain	15.9	23.7	17.8	+12.6
France	14.4	1.9	10.2	−15.7
Italy		2.0	0.3	—
Yugoslavia	1.4	68.1	20.8	+35.9
Greece		35.9	4.9	+39.4
Turkey	3.5	33.5	14.0	+94.4

Source: British Petroleum statistics.

break-bulk ports carefully sited on the Mediterranean (there are projects in Turkey, Malta, etc.). This solution would encourage the use of large bulk carriers (200,000 t or more compared with 50,000–150,000 t today). After 2000, within the context of the trend scenarios, tonnages of coal carried by shipping in the Mediterranean could gradually exceed those of oil. Coal-dust emitted during various handling operations and storage is estimated at approximately 1 per thousand of the tonnage shipped.

Coal-fired power-stations are at present the major source of atmospheric pollution: CO_2, SOx, NOx, CO, hydrocarbons, dust, trace heavy metals, radon, etc. They also produce large amounts of polluted liquid effluent (sulphuric acid, organic matter, chlorides, phosphates, borons, etc.), and solid waste, ash, and recovered flying ash. Considerable efforts are now being made in the United States, the United Kingdom, Sweden, and also in Spain, Yugoslavia, Turkey, and elsewhere, to reduce this pollution and develop 'clean' ways of turning coal into electricity.

A certain degree of priority has been given to dedusting, to the reduction of sulphur emissions, and now to the problem of nitrogen oxides (the second largest source of pollution after the motor car). Regardless of the preference for low-sulphur coal, processes can be divided according to whether they aim at:

● cleaning coal before use;
● dispersing gaseous effluent in high chimneys (in the region of 200 m), a sulphur-reduction method now considered outdated (Stockholm Conference in 1982 on acidification of the environment);
● desulphurizing flue gases, with the transfer of sulphur into another medium to remove it (over a hundred processes known today using dry or wet methods; the wet processes, requiring large amounts of water, may pose problems in countries where this is scarce, as in the south and east of the Mediterranean; and in addition, the annual production of sludge—approx 100,000 m^3 for a 600 MWe power-plant—without lime treatment, may be unacceptable in densely populated regions);
● eliminating nitrogen oxides.

Dust and particle elimination techniques are at present fairly well mastered (except perhaps for the problem of micrometric dust), with the use of four processes: cyclone separators, hydraulic dedusters, electrostatic precipitators (yields over 99.5 per cent, even up to 99.9 per cent), and bag filter devices. The most promising processes are based on either fluidized-bed combustion, in which sulphur compounds are fixed by lime, or prior gasification of coal.

The main problem is related to the production of solid waste deriving from the extraction and use of coal, especially in densely populated regions. The extent of the problem can be grasped by observing that the European coal industry produced 205m. t of solid waste in 1980, of which 170 m. t of coal residue and 35 m. t of ash, as compared to 90m. t of urban waste.

It is possible that 'clean' processes will gradually be marketed during the 1990s. The future of coal for electrical generation may even depend on it to some extent. OECD experts currently estimate that these processes increase the investment for a coal-fired thermal power-station by 15–20 per cent, and the price of the kWh generated by 20–5 per cent. These costs are high, and give rise to hypotheses or different choices in the light of the various scenarios.

If depolluting processes are not developed, 12.5m. t of SOx, 3m. t of NOx, 900 t of dust, and 46,000 t of hydrocarbons would be released every year into the Mediterranean skies, if 1,000 TWh of the 2,000–3,000 TWh of electricity consumed in 2025, within the context of the scenarios, were to be generated by power-stations of the present type. Whatever the case may be, between 1,100m. and 1,300m. t of

BOX 12D. **Lignite in Yugoslavia**

Together with hydroelectric power, Yugoslav lignite reserves are one of the country's main resources. The slightly inclined deposits vary in thickness from a few metres to a hundred metres, so that opencast mining is possible, using powerful machinery. Present techniques produce approximately 19m. t of lignite a year, containing up to 54 per cent humidity, high ash content, only about 0.6 per cent sulphur, and with low heating capacity (6.3–11.3 MJ/kg). Future opencast mines could produce between 15m. and 30m. t per annum.

More than 86 per cent of present output is used in thermal power-stations, and the rest, from the Kossovo basin, is gasified (producing 450m. m³ town gas, using the Lurgi process) or dried (Fleisner process) for domestic use.

At the end of 1985 forty turbines had a total installed capacity of 7,670 MWe. Of these, 52 per cent were 200- to 300-MWe turbines, but they comprised 74 per cent of capacity. Some 2,500 MWe extra capacity was under construction using 350- to 614-MWe units. These were to be fitted with anti-pollution devices, to meet the requirement of an average 0.15 mg SO_2 per m³ (peaking to 0.5 mg SO_2 per m³ per hour). Electric filters, with a smoke-dedusting efficiency of 99.5 to 99.8 per cent, are already being manufactured in the country.

Source: 1986 World Energy Conference.

CO_2 will be released into the atmosphere every year.

Figures would be somewhat different for oil-fired stations, but without changing orders of magnitude; they would be much less for natural gas, which is a major argument for its increased use.

(b) Nuclear energy

Of all the uses envisaged for nuclear energy when it was first developed (from sea-water desalinization to 'peaceful' explosions to build canals or increasing hydrocarbon production from low permeability formations), only electrical generation has become a reality, and on a large scale: some sixty plants in the Mediterranean countries (about half on the Mediterranean coast and in its watershed), equal to an installed capacity of about 50,000 MWe, out of a world total of 380 plants and 280,000 MWe installed capacity.

The nuclear cycle, from uranium in the ground to the end consumer of electricity, is, as in the case of oil, rather complex: mining of uranium and processing of the ore (often low grade, hence considerable amounts of solid waste), enrichment in isotope 235, manufacture of fuel assemblies, reactor operation, and, depending on the case, very long-term storage of the spent fuel or, in the event of recycling, radiochemical reprocessing, re-conditioning of the fuel, and storage of waste. Such a cycle involves risks of pollution and/or accidents of two kinds: 'conventional' (and safety performances are in most cases among the highest in all branches of industry), and radioactive. In normal operation, radioactive pollution at each stage of the cycle is below—often well below—the very strict standards laid down. In fact, nuclear energy can be given as an example of an industry that has endeavoured to incorporate all environmental constraints into its development (whether public opinion considers this to be sufficient or not is another matter). There is still the question of accidents, the most serious of which can involve (in order): reactors, reprocessing plants, carriage of radioactive material, and storage facilities. The most serious accidents fall under a new category of accidents with very low probability (even infinitesimal but not completely nil) and large-scale potential consequences, comparable to some extent to natural disasters. Lastly, regarding very long-term storage of radioactive waste, technical solutions have been proposed but have not yet been adopted on an industrial or market scale, or as a definitive solution.

Nuclear power-stations produce the largest amount of solid radioactive waste compared with other stages of the nuclear cycle. There are two kinds:

● There is the so-called 'process' waste linked to operations, such as filters and traps, mainly ion-exchange resins, by far the most active and perhaps containing caesium (which means planning for a 300-year storage period, six times its half-life). Resin radioactivity varies considerably depending on the circuit in which the resins are used, between 800 curies and a few tenths of a curie per m³. In volume resins amount to only 8 per cent of waste, but 80 per cent of radioactivity.

● Secondly, there is the so-called 'technological' waste, deriving from maintenance work, which can usually be compacted to some extent; radioactivity is in the region of 0.04 curies per m³, rising to 0.2 curies per m³ after compacting in 200-litre drums.

Average waste production for a 900 MWe plant

with a pressurized water reactor is estimated at 173 m³ (volume) and 1,150 curies (radioactivity).

Scenario hypotheses assume a total of about a hundred nuclear plants of 1,000 MWe on average in worst trend scenario T2, and 150 plants in the moderate trend scenario T-3 with strong economic and energy growth (125 or so 1,000 MWe plants in the intermediate trend scenario T1) for all the Mediterranean countries. About half these plants are on the coast. The amount of uranium required has been estimated at 21,000 t per annum (intermediate case), i.e. the equivalent of 57 per cent of world production in 1986, equal (for instance) to 28m. t of 0.1 per cent U_3O_8 uranium oxide ore, which means considerable extraction activity. Without reprocessing, 3,000 t per annum of spent uranium—containing 27 t of plutonium—will have to be stored. Reprocessing of the spent fuel would produce some 350m. curies a year of long-life fission products (figures taken from UNEP Energy Reports).

A simple exercise would be to assume that all electrical power-stations commissioned from 2000 would be nuclear in order to estimate the pressure on uranium resources, the number of plants needed, total amount of radioactive waste produced, etc.; this means roughly tripling the above figure.

In contrast, a 'Swedish' solution (freeze on nuclear energy and no replacement of decommissioned stations) was also explored, in order to assess possible impacts on other sources, including coal, oil, gas, and renewable energies. For instance, if coal had to meet the requirements of virtually all electrical generation in reference scenario T1 in 2025, consumption (excluding industrial and/or household needs) would be close to 1,000m. t. This is another way of looking at the acute problem of electricity growth in the Mediterranean basin.

(c) Renewable energy

Aside from fuel-wood widely used in the Maghreb and Turkey, renewable sources of energy are basically water, solar, and wind. Observations will be confined to a few comments on the environmental impact of renewable energies, as their stage of development—hence acquired experience—cannot be compared with that of the two previous energy sources and is insufficient for accurate estimates in the case of significant use.

(i) Hydraulic power

Some countries, like Yugoslavia, Greece, and Turkey, still have a large potential for hydraulic installations, which has been taken into account in the scenarios. Dam construction could lead to the flooding of agricultural land, sometimes even entire villages; it also disturbs the migration and reproduction cycles of some fish species, may further increase soil erosion, and may cause the erosion of beaches through sediment retention; lastly, it deteriorates the quality of water in the reservoirs.

With respect to accidents, a bursting dam is also a low-probability hazard, but with disastrous consequences. With 'small-scale' hydraulic power-generation based on the installation of micro power-stations, a careful comparison should be made between the low amounts of electricity generated on the one hand and the risk of site alteration and impact on wild life and plant life on the other. Ecologists have often stressed—even with regard to climate—the disadvantages of a series of micro power-stations.

(ii) Solar energy

A distinction has to be made between:

● *Passive solar energy*. Its nuisances are more aesthetic than otherwise.

● *Active solar energy*. Occasionally there is some risk of leakage and/or of the fluid used catching fire (especially in industrial installations).

● *Thermal solar electricity* (types of power station at Odeillo, Targassonne, and Corsica in France, Almeria in Spain, and other installations in Italy, Turkey, Israel, etc.). One feature is the extent of the area needed to collect sun-rays, which could have an impact on the biotope or the local micro-climate. Hazards may be related to the high-temperature fluids used (pressure, temperature, toxicity). Water requirements for the conventional thermo-dynamic cycle may also cause problems in the countries south and east of the Mediterranean basin.

● *Photovoltaic solar electricity*. It seems to be the most promising process for fairly large-scale use and it would also have fewer environmental impacts, although these are difficult to assess at present because of lack of experience on a large scale and over a long period.

In the scenarios a comparison was made, for example for Egypt, between six 1,000 MWe nuclear power-stations in 2025 and 'solar ponds' (a technology now available, and attractive on account of its integrated storage system, enabling electricity to be produced as and when needed, not only during strong sunshine, though unfortunately with low output). To produce the same annual amount of electricity, a solar pond of about 2,250 km² would be needed, roughly half the size of Lake Nasser at the Aswan Dam. The use of photovoltaic cells could reduce this area by a factor of 2–5. As regards domestic use, and even if the overall figure is not very meaningful, solar energy offers clear advantages, particularly for areas of scattered dwellings, not connected or poorly connected to the electrical distribution network.

(iii) Wind energy

This energy source is a very attractive proposition for small islands. It is already widely used for pumping in Sicily, in the Balearic Islands, etc. Nuisances are essentially related to noise, in necessarily exposed (and windy) sites, especially for major installations. Rotor disintegration, or loss of part of the airscrew, may also be a hazard.

(d) Impact on water and sites

With regard to thermal power-stations (conventional or nuclear), there should be no confusion between water consumed by evaporation and water removed, to be restored to the cold source (at a temperature some 10 °C higher), since they vary considerably, depending on the method of cooling used, as shown in Table 12.6.

Application of these coefficients to the conditions of reference trend scenario T1 for countries south and east of the basin (from Morocco to Turkey, where development of electricity generation will be greatest, comparatively speaking, but where water resources are scarce) suggests that, in the case of open-circuit power-station cooling, removals in 2025 will be in the region of 120,000m. m³ per annum, slightly more than 100m. of which will evaporate; with closed-circuit cooling (towers), removals will be 7,000m.–13,000m. m³ per annum, nearly 1,500m. of which will evaporate.

Comparison of these figures with the amounts of water potentially available and with the requirements of other sectors, as well as with the

geographical distribution of populations (coastal urbanization) and industrial and tourist activities, suggests that most electrical power-stations south and east of the basin (only Turkey, and Egypt to some extent, possess a certain margin for manœuvre) will be established on the Mediterranean coast, as is already the case for most existing power-plants (Fig. 12.3).

Generally speaking, coal-fired stations, both in the north and south, are located on coalfields or nearby, especially in the case of low-grade coal, which is difficult to transport, or near the point of import by sea, i.e. on the coast.

Although a number of existing sites will be extended to house more powerful plants (several units per site), the problem of choosing sites will become increasingly difficult, and have many impacts on the coast and the Mediterranean environment, since the average surface area of a thermal power-station can range from 50 to 150 ha.

The average temperature increase for the Mediterranean as a whole, corresponding to about 2,000–3,000 thermal TWh for 1,000–500 electric TWh, would naturally be negligible. However, the effect could be significant at a regional level: on some sections of coast, up to 2–3 m offshore, the sea could be heated by 1–2 °C, with possible repercussions on fish reproduction and nurseries.

In addition, in order to prevent the attachment of organisms (such as mussels) inside the cooling-water circuit, chlorine (stored in a liquid form) or bleach has to be continuously injected into the discharge circuits during certain periods of the year. To avoid cumbersome transport and storage, hypochlorite can also be produced through electrolysis of sea-water (a process systematically used in France for nuclear power-stations). The optimal injection rate can only be established on a site-by-site basis after on-site studies lasting a year or two. The amount of organic and ammonia components in sea-water is in fact a dominant factor. The optimum solution is attained when the risk of plancton and micro-organism

Table 12.6 Average specific water consumption of power-stations (l/kWh)

Type of unit	Open-circuit cooling		Closed-circuit cooling	
	Consumption	Evaporation	Consumption	Evaporation
Classic 600 MW	145	1.00	10–20[a]	1.35
Nuclear 900 MW	165	1.55	3[b]	2.10

[a] Without purifying.
[b] With purifying.

Source: Électricité de France.

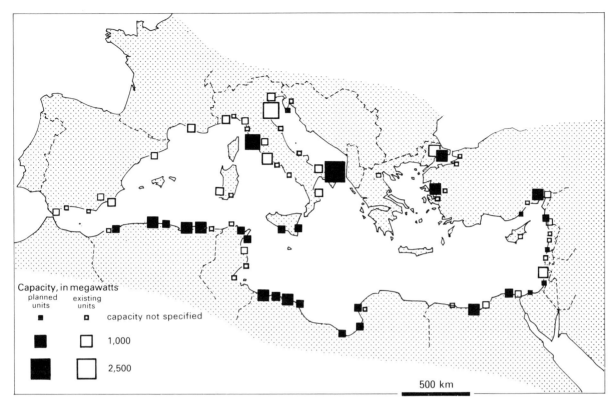

FIG. 12.3 Thermal power-stations on the Mediterranean coast. Only plants close to the coastline are shown.

mortality is minimized while complying with set objectives.

(e) Climatic impacts of energy

The climatic impacts of energy production and use may be felt at various levels. They may be local (alteration of micro-climates, smogs), regional (acid rain, heat releases), or global ('greenhouse effect' of flue gas). As energy production and consumption increase, some of these effects may shift to another level. In addition, at each of the levels considered, environmental effects can produce feedbacks, usually negative, on development (e.g. effects of acid rain on plant cover, and thereby on the water-cycle; or on soil composition and micro-fauna, and thereby on fertility).

As for the possible results of heating-up of the world climate by the greenhouse effect, because of the build up of CO_2 and other industrial gases (e.g. freons), the Mediterranean basin will of course be only a modest contributor. The repercussions felt in the region could, on the other hand, be considerable (rise in the sea-level, changes in rainfall and evapotranspiration, modification of the hydrological regime, etc). Confirmation of the hypotheses of this heating-up and its global repercussions should lead to reassessment of the conditions in which fossil fuels are used and to restrictions or ceilings on their use throughout the world. Along these lines, it should be recalled that the ratios among the amounts of CO_2 emitted are in principle $75 : 65 : 43$, depending on whether coal, oil, or natural gas is used. This could be a major additional argument in favour of natural gas, helping to gain several decades in tackling the problem, considerations which partly led to the strongly 'gas-orientated' hypotheses in the alternative scenarios. But it could also advocate a nuclear 'come-back' which does not produce carbon dioxide, associated with as intensive as possible a use of solar and other soft energies.

6. Conclusions and issues for appraisal

At a constant per capita consumption level, with no appreciable improvement in standards of living and no goal-orientated energy-saving programme, the mere population effect leads to an overall Mediterranean consumption of between 800m. and 900m. toe in 2025 (compared with 600m. in 1985).

These are roughly the values and conditions assumed in the worst trend scenario T2. Any improvement in standards of living is reflected by overall higher consumption levels for the Mediterranean basin as a whole. In any event, fairly significant amounts are involved, which raises many questions.

One of the first queries concerns the 'energy-saving margins' that enabled many industrialized countries to limit and even reduce their energy consumption after 1973. In fact, the Mediterranean countries of Europe cannot be compared to the northern countries of Europe or other major industrialized countries, whose levels of consumption, or over-consumption, they are still far from equalling. Their energy-saving potential seems to be lower, which is not a reason to overlook it. The southern and eastern countries consume comparatively little and their economic and social conditions scarcely permit concerted, long-term energy-saving efforts. With these considerations in mind, it seemed that this energy-saving potential is unlikely to be a determining factor in most scenarios, although it could play an increasingly important role in the alternative scenarios.

The inertia of behaviour and the durability of installations and processes have led to hydrocarbons being assigned a continuing role in the scenarios, while stressing some of their special features in the Mediterranean basin. Concerning oil in particular, rather than analysing annual consumption levels it is perhaps more important to examine cumulated consumption between 1985 and 2025: 13,000m.–16,000m. t, compared with 5,000m. t of current reserves in the Mediterranean countries, and their 2,000m.–6,000m. t of potential resources. This will give rise to an acute supply problem, considering the difficulties of finding a substitute for this energy source. During the first quarter of the next century the world will without doubt pass through a true 'energy transition' period, but it is very difficult to envisage what it will be like: this is the second question mark.

Will coal prevail? On the one hand it would be hazardous to extrapolate on the basis of the current favourable situation of plentiful cheap low-sulphur coal; knowledge of reserves and resources is in fact insufficient to make a valid estimate of potential over half a century. On the other hand, environmental problems (including that of CO_2) cast a shadow over the medium- and long-term future. Hence the possible interest of natural gas.

The central problem of electricity consumption and generation remains. Considering the levels anticipated, the question of which energy sources will be used is a major one. Bearing in mind construction time (five to ten years) and the life-span of installations (thirty to forty years or more), this indeed calls for a fifty-year prospective view. No doubt all possible sources without exception will be resorted to for several decades yet. But what happens afterwards?

With regard to environmental impacts, paradoxically and making due allowances, the less energy that is available, the more inappropriately it is used: the efficiency of installations is poor and often accompanied by strong impacts. The example of fuel-wood is well known: output/consumption ratio of a few percentage points, smoke emissions, and forest degradation as a result of over-exploitation (this subject is examined in Chapter 17).

The scenarios and the study of water availability indicate that power-station cooling requirements will increasingly lead to the location of these plants on the coast in the southern and eastern countries. At the anticipated production level, it would not be easy to install some 200 thermal power-stations (average size 600 MWe) on a 400-m strip of coast suitable for development (and highly desirable), and this matter calls for the integrated planning of all national coastlines.

Lastly, the disturbance of biophysical processes caused by the cumulative effects of energy consumption could be a more serious threat to the well-being—even long-term survival—of mankind than the direct toxic effect of effluent.

It is therefore clear that meeting long- and medium-term energy needs in the Mediterranean basin will require the mobilization of all efforts:

● *financial.* Some studies (IIASA) have shown that in the next decades the industrialized countries will have to devote 2–3 per cent of their GDP (direct and indirect investments) to their energy system, as new techniques (nuclear, offshore drilling, deep gas, non-conventional oil, 'clean' fossil-fuel electricity generation, renewable energy) are increasingly capital-intensive. In the case of the less industrialized countries, about 6–7 per cent of GDP will be devoted to energy development.

● *Institutional and organizational.* These are needed to deploy the resources for a kind of development which, irrespective of the processes chosen, can only be on a large scale.

● *Technological.* Advances since the end of the Second World War have indeed been spectacular, but the possibilities for progress and innovation remain wide open.

13 The Futures of Tourism

The first part of this chapter reviews the recent and current situation of tourism in the Mediterranean basin: the development of international tourism has made this region into the world's leading tourist area and domestic tourism is constantly evolving; both are concentrated largely on the coast. Section 1 also analyses the economic impacts of tourism and suggests a classification of tourists in order to help understand the impact of this activity on the Mediterranean environment.

The study revealed that all the Mediterranean countries were envisaging the development of their tourist activities. Section 2 examines growth potential up to 2000 in the context of the macroeconomic development scenarios, while section 3 extends this analysis up to 2025, making the simplification required by this more distant horizon.

Whatever the scenario, tourist 'pressure' is likely to be increasingly strong, chiefly on the Mediterranean coast. Will tourism know how to treat the environment, considering that harmony with surroundings is vital for tourist development? This aspect is studied in section 4, by analysing in turn site coverage and use of the coastline, water consumption, and physical and socio-cultural pressures. This section concludes with a semi-quantitative consideration of the medium- and long-term tourist potential of Mediterranean countries.

Lastly, section 5 draws a number of conclusions from the scenarios and pinpoints some of the issues that may occur to Mediterranean officials and decision-makers.

1. Past and present

Long reserved for an élite disposing of time and money, tourism in the twentieth century has become a social phenomenon of the industrialized countries, entailing the migration of increasing numbers of holiday-makers each year. The factors which have encouraged the development of mass tourism are chiefly:

- growing urbanization, calling for periodical escape from this particularly restrictive environment;
- the rise in living standards, meaning that a smaller share of household income is devoted to basic needs and more can be spent on leisure;
- the development of transport, whether individual (motor car) or collective (trains, aeroplanes, boats);
- the social organization of labour, recognizing workers' rights to paid holidays, the reduction of working hours, and the increase of free time, etc.

Many features have contributed and still contribute to the tourist attraction of the Mediterranean, in particular: the geographical proximity for tourists from northern Europe, the climate, especially linked to bathing, the beauty of landscapes and natural sites, the exceptionally rich cultural heritage left notably by the great civilizations of antiquity—the very foundations of the present Western world—and more recent historical ties which have fostered the habit, even created a tradition, of interregional and international exchange and travel.

(a) Development of international tourism 1970–1984

International tourism involves travellers who cross one or several borders for leisure purposes. Data from countries about tourism are not usually homogeneous, and statistical data from the World Tourist Organization (WTO) have been used as much as possible. WTO provides information communicated to it by national tourist offices in the different countries. A few definitions and units of measurement are given in Box 13A.

The world market grew from 160m. to 341m. international tourists from 1970 to 1985, an increase of 113 per cent in 15 years, with an average annual growth-rate of 4.88 per cent (derived from Tables 13.1). This last figure masks considerable differences depending on the year:

- During periods of very strong expansion

BOX 13A. **A few definitions**

Visitor: any person travelling to a country other than the one where he normally resides, for any reason other than that of exercising a remunerated profession. This definition covers two categories of visitors: tourist and tripper.

Tourist: temporary visitor spending at least 24 hours in the country visited for purposes of leisure (pleasure, holiday, health, study, religion, sport) and/or business (mission, conference, family).

Tripper: temporary visitor spending not more than 24 hours in the country visited.

Hotel lodgings: hotels, motels, boarding-houses, and inns.

Other lodgings (or extra-hotel): youth hostels, camping sites, children's homes, holiday villages, rented rooms, villas or apartments, spas.

Units of measurement:

Arrivals: data refer to the number of arrivals of travellers and not to the number of persons. The same person paying several visits to a particular country over a given period will be counted as a new arrival each time.

Guest-nights: the number of nights spent in the different types of lodgings. If two persons travel to a country and stay five nights in that country, this corresponds to ten nights' accommodation. These data refer to hotels and assimilated institutions, i.e. hotels, motels, boarding-houses, and inns, or to accommodation as a whole, hotels, assimilated institutions, other lodgings (camping sites, holiday villas, apartments, etc.)

Average length of stay: this is expressed in number of days or nights.

Receipts from international tourism: these are defined as the receipts a country derives from payments made in currency by foreign tourists for consumer expenditure, i.e. goods and services. They do not include receipts from international transport.

Expenditure of international tourism: this is defined as consumer expenditure, i.e. related to goods and services, incurred by persons residing in the country concerned for tourism purposes. It does not include payment of international transport.

Number of beds: this refers to the total capacity in beds of the different types of lodgings (hotel and other); 1 bed = 1 person lodged.

Source: WTO.

growth-rates reached 8 per cent (1971, 1977, 1978) and even 9 per cent (1975, 1984).

● During periods of low growth the number of tourists increased by only 4 per cent (1980), 3 per cent (1974, 1976, 1981), or 1 per cent (1983), or even fell by 1 per cent (1982).

These figures, for a fifteen-year period in which an economic slow-down and two oil shocks occurred, already elicit two comments:

● The international tourist market varies greatly from one year to another.

● The need for or habit of tourist travel is such that even major economic difficulties have no lasting effect on the sector.

The countries in the Mediterranean basin, taken globally, accounted for nearly 35 per cent of the world tourist market in 1984, and it was the leading 'tourist basin' in the world. In the fifteen years under review the share of the coastal states fluctuated between roughly 33.5 per cent and 39 per cent.

In numbers of tourists, the Mediterranean market rose from 58m. in 1970 to 117m. in 1986, an annual average growth-rate of 4.48 per cent, slightly lower than that of the world market. Interannual variations were sharper: 11 per cent increase in 1972, 6.2 per cent drop in 1974 (whereas the world market rose by 3 per cent). Fluctuations in the Mediterranean market do not follow those of the world market too clearly.

The country-by-country analysis (devised from Table 13.1 and Fig. 13.1) of the number of foreign tourists shows, in addition, that between 1970 and 1986 all countries experienced an increase:

● The average annual growth-rate was above or equal to 10 per cent in four countries (Cyprus, Egypt, Greece, and Tunisia), denoting very strong expansion for this sector of activity.

● Five countries experienced steady growth in this sector, with an average annual rate ranging between 5 per cent and 10 per cent (Turkey, Malta, Israel, Morocco, and Syria).

● Only six countries had a moderate rate of growth for foreign tourism, ranging between 3 per cent and 4 per cent. These are either countries which had

Table 13.1 Number of International Tourists in the Mediterranean countries, 1970–1986 (000s)

	1970	1971	1972	1973	1974	1975	1976	1977	1978	1979	1980	1981	1982	1983	1984	1985	1986
Spain	15,320	17,330	20,430	22,000	19,400	19,800	18,500	21,000	24,600	24,000	22,500	23,800	25,300	25,583	27,176	27,477	29,910
France	18,130	19,280	21,520	23,510	23,580	25,710	26,960	26,265	26,846	28,763	30,100	31,340	33,467	34,018	35,429	36,748	36,080
Italy	14,188	14,418	15,111	14,670	14,200	15,500	16,505	18,500	19,193	21,918	22,087	20,036	22,297	22,140	23,043	25,047	24,672
Malta	171	179	150	211	273	335	340	362	478	618	729	706	511	491	480	518	574
Yugoslavia	4,749	5,243	5,142	6,149	5,454	5,834	5,572	6,116	6,387	5,966	6,410	6,616	5,955	5,947	7,224	8,436	8,464
Greece	1,407	1,981	2,436	2,846	1,956	2,840	3,672	3,961	4,532	5,233	4,796	5,034	5,033	4,778	5,523	6,574	7,025
Turkey	446	494	595	807	387	1,201	1,336	1,268	1,222	1,057	865	997	1,026	1,178	1,717	2,230	2,079
Cyprus	127	179	228	264	150	47	180	178	217	297	353	421	547	621	737	814	901
Syria	409	547	429	441	504	678	723	970	823	914	1,204	1,043	831	836	976	986	986
Lebanon	900	1,242	1,281	1,070	1,606	1,555	100	122	109	118	118	—	—	—	—	—	—
Israel	419	618	680	604	570	559	733	894	959	1,009	1,116	1,090	949	1,043	1,076	1,243	1,160
Egypt	348	406	528	512	440	730	984	1,004	1,052	1,064	1,253	1,376	1,423	1,498	1,560	1,518	1,311
Libya	77	133	166	258	296	241	145	126	164	118	126	126[a]	126[a]	126[a]	126	126	120
Tunisia	411	608	780	722	716	1,014	978	1,016	1,142	1,536	1,602	2,151	1,355	1,439	1,580	2,003	1,502
Algeria	236	226	237	250	249	296	185	242	260	266	290	320	280	285	409	407	347
Morocco	747	823	1,062	1,341	1,205	1,242	1,108	1,428	1,477	1,436	1,475	1,567	1,815	1,877	1,944	2,180	2,128
TOTAL MEDITERRANEAN	58,085	63,707	70,785	75,655	70,986	77,582	78,021	83,452	89,459	94,313	94,974	96,683	100,916	101,855	109,000	116,307	117,259
WORLD	160,000	172,000	182,000	191,000	197,000	214,000	221,000	238,000	256,000	269,000	279,000	288,000	285,000	287,000	312,000	334,000	341,000

[a] Estimate.

Source: WTO Statistical Yearbooks (and Blue Plan).

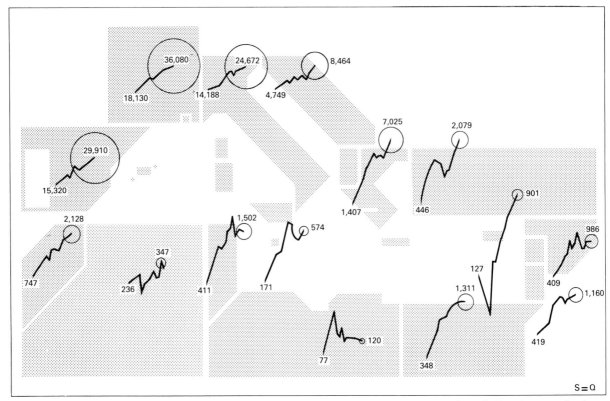

FIG. 13.1 International tourists in the Mediterranean countries: Trends 1970–1986 (000s). Tourists trends show irregularities arising from economic or other circumstances.

Source: Blue Plan.

experienced a period of very strong tourist expansion in the 1960s (France, Spain, Italy, Yugoslavia) or countries which had no active tourist development policy (Algeria, Libya).

Over the years, some Mediterranean countries went through periods of very sharp acceleration (up to nearly 300 per cent for Cyprus in 1976) and deceleration, which in no way alters the overall result.

In addition to the number of tourists, a guest-night is generally regarded as the basic unit of measurement that lends coherence to statistics and analyses of tourist demand. The number of guest-nights is also used to measure the average stay per tourist. It is estimated that the 108m. international tourists in 1984 'consumed' approximately 890m. guest-nights in hotels and other lodgings in the Mediterranean countries. The length of stay varied between twelve days (Malta) and two days (Syria), the average length being 8.2 days.

Table 13.2 provides a breakdown, by country of origin, of international tourists visiting the Mediterranean countries as a whole for the years 1975, 1980, and 1985. It can be observed that the main

country of departure is Germany, that the United Kingdom and the Benelux countries vie for second place, and that the share of France, a country of both departure and destination, is comparatively high. Northern Europe (Germany, Benelux, the United Kingdom, and the Scandinavian countries) accounts for between 50 per cent and 60 per cent of the Mediterranean tourist market.

With respect to host countries, the three north-western countries (Spain, France, and Italy) receive between 70 per cent and 80 per cent of international tourism (this percentage seems to have stabilized recently), followed by Yugoslavia and Greece. The remaining 10 per cent is shared among all the other countries, some of which experienced spectacular growth.

The seasonal nature of tourist frequentation, which poses a very serious problem as regards employment, accommodation, and effect on the host population, is more or less pronounced, depending on the country, with its impact on investment and management. Apart from Algeria, Israel, Egypt, and to a lesser extent Syria, most of the Mediterranean countries are affected by a high concentration of

Table 13.2 International tourism in the countries of the Mediterranean basin, 1975, 1980, 1985

Country of origin	Visits to Mediterranean countries					
	1975		1980		1985	
	000s	%	000s	%	000s	%
Germany	11,595	19.0	22,753	24.0	26,687	22.9
Belgium	3,297	5.4	7,913	8.3	5,012	4.3
Scandinavian countries	2,949	4.8	3,295	3.4	4,465	3.8
Spain	2,691	4.4	3,304	3.5	3,805	3.3
France	6,924	11.4	8,876	9.4	9,751	8.4
Netherlands	3,319	5.5	6,237	6.6	6,535	5.6
United Kingdom	6,975	11.4	11,014	11.6	15,524	13.3
Italy	2,685	4.4	3,248	3.4	6,594	5.6
Switzerland	2,150	3.5	4,543	4.8	6,450	5.5
Other European countries	5,273	8.6	8,622	9.0	9,969	8.5
Canada	624		819		1,275	
and		8.0		6.0		8.3
USA	4,274		4,956		8,368	
Other American Countries	821	1.3	1,655	1.7	1,759	1.5
Arab Countries	2,550	4.2	3,520	3.7	5,033	4.3
Other countries	4,809	7.8	4,019	4.2	5,257	4.5
TOTAL	60,936		94,774		116,484	

Source: WTO (and Blue Plan).

tourist visits during the summer quarter (up to 70 per cent of international tourists in Yugoslavia, for instance). Furthermore, during the high tourist season there are peak periods lasting from a few days to one or two weeks, when the inflow is greater and can even exceed total lodging capacity by 20–30 per cent.

The emergence and development of organized tourism have been both a factor and a cause of the growth in mass tourism, with the introduction, among other things, of all-inclusive rates and the setting-up of dynamic distribution channels. Organized travel currently represents a large portion of international tourist arrivals in some countries: in the region of 80 per cent for Malta and Cyprus, 67 per cent for Greece, 50–60 per cent for Tunisia and Turkey, 48 per cent for Spain, etc. (1985 figures).

Lastly, changes in transport methods, with the rapid expansion of the private motor car and commercial aviation, have made a decisive impact on international tourism. Table 13.3 indicates the trend since 1970 in international tourist arrivals in the Mediterranean countries in terms of principal means of transport. Air tourism rose sharply; growth in recent years has exceeded all expectations and has

caused the congestion of air corridors, considerable routing delays, and the saturation of a number of airports, reproducing the overloading of some major road routes.

(b) Domestic tourism

As regards data and information, domestic tourism raises more problems than international tourism, and the estimates of national experts have been used when homogeneous data, from the international viewpoint, were unavailable. Thus, in the following analysis, more importance should be given to proportions and rough estimates than to absolute figures.

In 1984 departure rates within national borders for the populations of the various Mediterranean countries ranged from 8 per cent (Egypt and Turkey, according to Blue Plan estimates) to 64 per cent (France). This rate, or the number of persons travelling at least once compared with the total population (persons travelling several times are only accounted once), depends quite clearly on several factors, such as a country's level of development, per capita income, the importance of the public sector, social measures and benefits, etc. But it also

Table 13.3 Trends in means of arrival of international tourism, 1970, 1980, and 1985

Destination countries	Air			Land (road and rail)			Sea		
	1970	1980	1985	1970	1980	1985	1970	1980	1985
Spain	22	24	29	71	72	68	7	4	3
France	9	17	15	85	77	77	6	6	8
Italy	8	9	9	91	77	77	1	2	2
Greece	52	62	69	24	19	14	24	19	17
Cyprus	91	94	91	—	—	—	9	6	9
Yugoslavia	2	5	6	97	92	91	1	3	3
Malta	94	96	94	—	—	—	6	4	6
Israel	87	81	75	2	8	12	11	11	13
Syria	7	25	27	93	72	72	—	3	1
Turkey	46	24	33	48	43	47	6	33	20
Egypt	75	79	74	20	13	15	5	8	11
Tunisia	77	69	59	16	26	38	7	5	3
Algeria	58	67	85	37	0	6	5	33	9
Morocco	31	46	45	29	30	36	40	24	19

Source: WTO statistics.

depends on social and cultural factors, as illustrated by Yugoslavia and Israel (approximately 30 per cent of holiday departures). In some countries, like Algeria and Morocco, holiday travel to family and friends is apparently not taken into account in the data supplied to the Blue Plan, so the number of domestic tourists has probably been systematically underestimated.

The total number of domestic tourists was estimated at 105m. in 1984 for the whole of the Mediterranean countries, and the corresponding figure for guest-nights is 2,310m. The seasonal nature of domestic tourism is extremely clear in France (73 per cent of domestic tourism occurs in the summer quarter), Italy (64 per cent), and Yugoslavia (56 per cent), with its consequences (congestions, over-equipment, etc.).

Although domestic tourism is particularly hard to delimit, it offers substantial development potential, as only two Mediterranean countries seem to have had a departure rate above 50 per cent (France and Italy) and half the countries (in the south and east) had rates apparently under 20 per cent.

(c) Tourism in the Mediterranean coastal regions

Efforts were made to calculate the number of domestic and international tourists staying in Mediterranean coastal regions, the proportion of which varies enormously from one country to another. In France, for example, 18 per cent of international tourism and 19 per cent of domestic tourism concerns the Mediterranean coast. In Tunisia, both

these figures seem to exceed 80 per cent, whereas in Yugoslavia apparently over 90 per cent of international tourists take holidays on the coast. The attraction of the Mediterranean coast seems to depend on the geographical origin of the tourists, their motivations, and the tourist appeal of the rest of the country. It was estimated that 51m. foreigners and 45m. nationals spent their holidays in Mediterranean coastal regions in 1984, equal to about 1,400m. guest-nights.

One of the basic features of Mediterranean coastal tourism is its concentration in zones devoted largely or almost solely to tourism, and for the time being there are no signs of either decline or incipient saturation. The Italian and French Rivieras (Liguria and Côte d'Azur), where tourism virtually came into being, are still regions of prime importance. In the past forty years other coastal regions have joined these precursors, and tourism now concerns virtually all Mediterranean countries:

- Spain: a succession of tourist zones, the Costa Brava, Costa del Sol, Costa Blanca, Costa Dorada, and of course the Balearic Islands, the leading Spanish tourist region;
- France: the Languedoc–Roussillon coast, which changed into a major and highly structured tourist region in twenty years;
- Italy: the Costa Smeralda (Sardinia) and, among other places, Rimini, virtually the archetypal tourist resort;
- Yugoslavia: tourism has spread along the entire coast, with a heavier concentration in Istria near Rijeka, in Dubrovnik, and on the Montenegro coast;

- Greece: the Athens region and some islands which have become powerful poles of attraction;
- Cyprus and Malta: almost entirely devoted to tourist activities;
- Turkey: the region of İzmir and Antalaya, and the Bodrum peninsula;
- Syria: the Tartus region;
- Israel: all coastal regions unoccupied by industry or ports are intended as leisure areas;
- Egypt: Alexandria and the west coast, the country's leading coastal tourist region;
- Libya: the region of Tripoli and Cyrenaika;
- Tunisia: Djerba, Nabeul-Hammamet, and Monastir rank among the famous tourist destinations;
- Algeria: Zeralda, Tipaza, and Andaluses, poles of tourist development;
- Morocco: Mediterranean tourist activity is concentrated in the region of Saida, Al Hoceima, Tetuan, and Tangiers-Malabata.

On the Mediterranean coast itself the trend towards building residential hotels and flats rather than conventional hotels and the development of cruising tours with passengers lodging on board should be underlined.

(d) The economic impacts of tourism

Tourism plays a sometimes important role in both the balance of payments and employment. In 1984 the contribution of international tourism to GDP averaged 6.5 per cent in the Mediterranean countries as a whole. This contribution exceeded 10 per cent in some countries, like Israel, Cyprus, and Malta, and approached this level in Spain, Italy, and Tunisia. It was more modest for heavily industrialized countries like France, or where development has been fairly recent.

Revenues from tourism covered a considerable portion of imports: up to 27 per cent in Spain, between 10 per cent and 20 per cent in Cyprus, Malta, Tunisia, Greece, Israel, Morocco, and Italy. In this last case, the tourist balance would offset 80 per cent of the food deficit or cover one third of hydrocarbon imports. In Morocco tourism is the second most important source of foreign exchange.

Employment in the tourist sector is particularly hard to pinpoint. According to the findings of a specific model, the share of the labour force working in tourism was over 10 per cent in Israel, and varied between 6 per cent and 3 per cent in countries like Malta, Italy, Spain, Tunisia, Yugoslavia, Greece, and even France. Moreover, the large share of the

underground economy in the tourist sector should be stressed, although it is unfortunately almost impossible to quantify. Undeclared activities chiefly concern lodgings (furnished rooms or bed and breakfast) and some services, like catering and small building trades, not forgetting currency exchange in certain countries. Lastly, it would be interesting if the diverging number of tourists from one year to the next could be expressed in terms of jobs and incomes in order to form a more accurate idea of the possible repercussion on the economy of the country concerned.

(e) Qualitative aspects of tourism: holiday styles

Efforts have been made to arrive at a qualitative distribution of tourists/holiday-makers in the Mediterranean, by attempting to pinpoint their favourite activities, usual choice of accommodation and general attitude towards organization of their holiday period. The purpose was to link each kind of tourist to specific impacts on both their natural and their social and cultural environments. The six 'typical portraits' of holiday-makers are those intent on:

- *adventure*: the oldest kind of tourist, who travels for discovery and self-discovery, off the beaten track, but not necessarily outside organized groups;
- *relaxation*: these tourists prefer to stay in a chosen spot rather than visit a region, and seek sun, sea, and sand;
- *culture*: this group enjoys touring a district or country and gives priority to culture in the broad sense (communication, discovery, encounters, learning, etc.);
- *congresses*: here tourism is a matter of meetings, conferences, symposia, or incentive travel;
- *health*: this covers the sporty type of tourist who chooses to stay in a place to practise sport intensively, to follow a course of treatment, or to get back into shape;
- *recreation*: such a tourist comes, goes, and also stays in places, but with a spirit of initiative, aware of nature, looking for dynamic, organized activities and entertainment.

A Delphi survey (in two stages) was carried out among Mediterranean experts to test the validity of this approach and to verify assumptions concerning the distribution of holiday-makers for 1985 and possible trends up to 2000 and 2025. The findings indicated that the proposed distribution for 1985

Table 13.4 Categories of tourist in the Mediterranean countries, 1985 (%)

	North[a]	South and east[b]
Adventure	10	4
Relaxation	40	80
Culture	25	8
Congresses	1	1
Health	7	2
Recreation	17	5

  [a] Spain to Greece inclusive, plus Israel.
  [b] Turkey to Morocco, excepting Israel.

Source: Delphi survey.

was likely in general terms, and would be as shown in Table 13.4. This distribution gives only a general idea of holiday styles, and the societal analysis should be carried out more thoroughly (as in other sectors). It already indicates, nevertheless, that it is necessary and important to reflect on the diversification of supply so as to respond in the best way possible to the different holiday styles adopted.

2. Tourism in the scenarios: horizon 2000

The prospective study of tourism in the Mediterranean was carried out country by country, then globally (all Mediterranean countries) for the five Blue Plan scenarios. Findings were sometimes aggregated for four regions:

- 'north-west': Spain, France, and Italy;
- 'southern Europe' (and assimilated): Yugoslavia, Greece, Israel, Cyprus, and Malta;
- 'eastern Mediterranean': Turkey, Syria, Lebanon, and Egypt;
- 'Greater Maghreb': Libya, Tunisia, Algeria, and Morocco.

An attempt was also made to identify as far as possible findings concerning the coastal regions of countries bordering the Mediterranean.

Estimated average annual growth-rates for the number of tourists vary from 1.45 per cent to 4.1 per cent depending on the country. It should be stressed that these estimates are comparatively modest compared with the hypotheses selected for other studies for 1990 or 1995, which vary from 4 to 9 per cent per annum for international tourism. The overall results by major region are given in Tables 13.5 (for 2000), 13.6 (for 2000 and 2025 aggregated), and 13.7 (for coastal zones). Fig. 13.2 illustrates the findings for international tourism.

(a) The trend scenarios

Reference trend scenario T1, based on the hypothesis of a continuation of the present trend in an unfavourable economic context, shows an imbalance in tourist development for the various Mediterranean countries, and between international and domestic tourism.

With an average annual growth-rate of 2.3 per cent, this hypothesis gives 308m. tourists in 2000 in the countries as a whole. International tourism increases faster (3.3 per cent per annum) than domestic tourism (1.17 per cent). In addition, this economic context does not permit improving the balance of international tourism among the different regions of the basin. The three countries in the

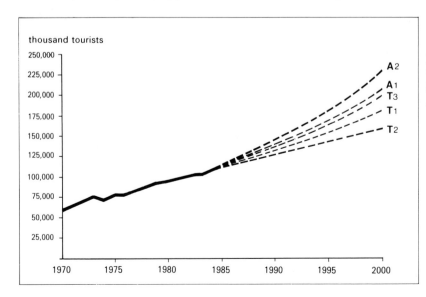

FIG. 13.2 Number of international tourists in the Mediterranean basin: Scenarios

Source: Blue Plan.

Table 13.5 Tourism in the Mediterrnean countries (numbers, distribution, economic impact): Horizon 2000

Scenarios	International tourism			Domestic tourism			International and domestic			Tourism as % of GDP	Increase of employment in tourist sector (%)
	No. of tourists (m.)	Geographical share		No. of tourists (m.)	Geographical share		No. of tourists (m.)	Geographical share			
		m.	%		m.	%		m.	%		
T1	181			122			308			5.2	8–11
(a)		136.4	75.4		86.0	67.7		222.4	72.2		
(b)		29.7	16.4		13.0	10.2		42.7	13.8		
(c)		7.1	3.9		18.0	14.2		25.1	8.1		
(d)		7.8	4.3		10.0	7.9		17.8	5.7		
T2	162			106			268			5.6	11–14
(a)		123.5	76.2		80.5	75.9		204.0	76.1		
(b)		24.9	15.3		10.8	10.2		35.7	13.3		
(c)		6.5	4.0		9.0	8.5		15.5	5.7		
(d)		7.1	4.5		5.7	5.4		12.8	4.7		
T3	199			151			350			6.1	14–17
(a)		148.3	74.5		100.2	66.4		248.5	71.0		
(b)		34.9	17.6		15.3	10.2		50.2	14.3		
(c)		8.0	4.0		22.0	14.5		30.0	8.5		
(d)		7.8	3.9		13.5	8.9		21.3	6.0		
A1	207			166			375			5.7	17–20
(a)		147.7	71.6		111.1	66.1		258.8	69.0		
(b)		37.1	18.0		17.3	10.3		54.4	14.5		
(c)		9.3	4.5		25.0	14.9		34.3	9.1		
(d)		12.2	5.9		14.6	8.7		26.8	7.1		
A2	227			182			409			5.7	20–23
(a)		158.8	70.0		115.8	63.6		274.6	67.1		
(b)		43.1	19.0		19.4	10.6		62.5	15.2		
(c)		11.5	5.0		27.5	15.2		39.0	9.5		
(d)		13.6	6.0		19.3	10.6		32.9	8.0		

Key: *(a)* Spain, France, Italy; *(b)* Yugoslavia, Greece, Malta, Cyprus, Israel; *(c)* Turkey, Syria, Lebanon, Egypt; *(d)* Libya, Tunisia, Algeria, Morocco.

Table 13.6 Tourism in the Mediterranean countries (numbers, growth-rates): Horizons 2000 and 2025

	International tourism			Domestic tourism			Total Mediterranean tourism		
	m.	Growth 2000/1984 (%)	Av. annual growth-rate 1984/2000 (%)	m.	Growth 2000/1984 (%)	Av. annual growth-rate 1984/2000 (%)	m.	Growth 2000/1984 (%)	Av. annual growth-rate 1984/2000 (%)
Horizon 2000									
T1	181	67.7	3.28	127	20.4	1.10	308	44.6	2.30
T2	162	50.1	2.57	106	0.5	0.04	268	25.8	1.45
T3	199	84.4	3.90	151	43.3	2.20	350	64.3	3.10
A1	207	91.8	4.10	168	59.4	2.96	375	76.0	3.60
A2	227	110.0	4.76	182	72.6	3.47	409	92.0	4.10
	m.	Growth 2025/2000 (%)	Av. annual growth-rate 2000/2025 (%)	m.	Growth 2025/2000 (%)	Av. annual growth-rate 2000/2025 (%)	m.	Growth 2025/2000 (%)	Av. annual growth-rate 2000/2025 (%)
Horizon 2025									
T1	312	72.3	2.20	169	33.0	1.10	481	56.2	1.80
T2	265	63.5	1.98	114	7.5	0.30	379	41.5	1.40
T3	344	72.8	2.20	230	52.3	1.69	574	64.0	2.00
A1	357	72.5	2.20	305	81.5	2.40	662	76.5	2.30
A2	409	80.0	2.38	349	91.7	2.63	758	85.3	2.50

Source: Blue Plan (Lanquar and Figuerola, 1986).

Table 13.7 Coastal tourism, 1984, 2000, 2025

	Tourist Nos. (m.)			Guest-nights				
	IT	DT	Total	IT		DT		Total (m.)
				m.	av.	m.	av.	
1984	51.0	44.7	95.7	418.2	8.2	983.4	22.0	1,401.6
2000					8.7		23.3	
T1	85.4	53.9	139.3	743.0		1,256.0		1,999.0
T2	76.4	45.0	121.4	664.0		1,048.0		1,712.0
T3	94.0	64.1	158.1	817.0		1,493.0		2,310.0
A1	97.7	71.4	169.1	850.0		1,663.0		2,513.0
A2	107.0	77.3	184.3	930.0		1,801.0		2,731.0
2025					8.2		22.0	
T1	147.0	72.0	219.0	1,205.0		1,584.0		2,789.0
T2	125.0	48.0	173.0	1,025.0		1,056.0		2,081.0
T3	162.0	98.0	260.0	1,328.0		2,156.0		3,484.0
A1	168.0	130.0	298.0	1,377.0		2,860.0		4,237.0
A2	193.0	148.0	341.0	1,582.0		3,256.0		4,838.0

Key: IT = international tourism; DT = domestic tourism.

Note: International tourism in coastal regions is estimated at 47.2% of total international tourism in Mediterranean countries; domestic tourism in coastal regions is estimated at 42.5% of total domestic tourism.

Source: Blue Plan (Lanquar and Figuerola, 1986).

north-west still absorb just over three-quarters of foreign tourists. Only southern Europe substantially increases its share of the market, receiving 16.4 per cent of foreign tourists, whereas the number of domestic tourists doubles in the eastern Mediterranean and the Greater Maghreb (18m. holiday-makers respectively). The number of jobs in tourism grows only from 8 per cent to 11 per cent in total, although wages increase. The share of tourism in the Mediterranean GDP is 5.2 per cent.

Along the coast, tourist flows rise from 95m. to nearly 140m. domestic and international tourists (average increase of 2.2 per cent per annum). The relaxation group is the largest in this scenario, with 40 per cent of holiday-makers. They seek, first and foremost, sun, sea, and sand, and are not always fully aware of the quality of the natural and cultural environment. Continuation of this trend also implies that the seasonal nature of tourism becomes more pronounced, i.e. that pressure at peak periods increases considerably. All this combined indicates that this scenario leads to a considerable deterioration of the environment: spread of ugly, shoddy accommodation, encroachment on natural areas, congested access routes, more and more parking lots, etc.

Worst trend scenario T2 unfolds in a context of harsh economic competition, which tends to handicap the weak and serve the strong. Domestic tourism, remaining virtually at its 1985 level, is the first victim, as the stagnation—even regression—

in living standards will not allow Mediterranean populations to take longer holidays or more leisure time. International tourism continues to grow, but only slightly (2.5 per cent per annum), accounting for 162m. tourists in 2000 for the countries as a whole.

The outcome of this scenario, with heightened international competition to win or retain comparatively flagging market shares, is the setting-up of very well targeted tourist products designed for a wealthy élite and to a less extent for prosperous executives seeking appropriate forms of recreation. The adventure and health groups may therefore increase considerably in this scenario. In line with the spirit of competition, the improvement of tourist products causes a growth in employment of between 11 per cent and 14 per cent (with, however, low salaries to remain competitive), and the impact on the GDP is proportionately weaker than at present: roughly 5.6 per cent.

This comparatively pessimistic scenario, quite the contrary of a scenario of tourism for all, implies great disparity in the quality of accommodation: on the one hand luxury complexes for up-market international tourism, and on the other modest lodgings for domestic tourism and down-market international tourism. Striking contrasts can be observed in the impact of tourism on the natural environment. Luxury élitist tourism is not necessarily destructive in actual fact, and in some cases, paradoxically, can contribute to safeguarding

BOX 13B. **Egypt: qualitative aspects of the consequences of tourism development in the Blue Plan scenarios**

Reference trend scenario T1 involves two major changes:

- the opening of new destinations in the country to receive more than double the present number of visitors;
- the completion of projects to improve infrastructure networks and tourist amenities.

The new destinations will follow three directions:

- along the Nile valley towards the newly exploited archaeological sites, which is expected to lessen the pressure on Luxor and Aswan and attract newcomers from the 'cultural' group;
- along the Mediterranean coast and the Red Sea, to answer the needs of the 'relaxation' and 'health' groups;
- around the oases in the western desert combining desert and greenery, which particularly attract the 'adventure' and 'recreation' groups.

The improvement of infrastructure and tourist equipment creates certain problems:

- In the new tourists centres along the Nile valley tourists' needs are added to those of the constantly growing resident population. Needs not only mean consumer goods, but also networks, building sites, services, etc.
- The coastal zones receive domestic and international tourists at the same time and in the same place, increasingly at the expense of space and with negative effects on the environment.
- In the oases, influences tend to be felt in the socio-economic area. In order to respond to tourist needs, goods have to be imported from other governorates because of the limited production in the zone. As a result, the local population develops new types of consumption and in addition traditions and customs risk being commercialized.

In this scenario the coast will not be faced with serious problems of saturation before horizon 2000 and probably horizon 2025. But costly investment is needed for infrastructure and equipment.

Worst trend scenario T2 has disquieting consequences for the less developed countries, which include Egypt, because it assumes the development of international tourism with high standards. To meet the requirements of these tourists, the country will have to import consumer goods and equipment which local production cannot supply. The economic benefits of tourism are doubted by the local population, which also finds the disproportion between the development of international tourism and the stagnation of domestic tourism hard to accept. The public feels that it is being deprived of the right to enjoy the tourist amenities of its country and has to pay a very high price in terms of damage to the environment and risk of pollution.

Moderate trend scenario T3 brings a new flow of tourists, but from the 'cultural' group, which poses the crucial problem of the very dense frequentation of archaeological monuments and sites, fragile tourist products *par excellence* because even the slightest damage is irreversible

Reference alternative scenario A1 allows the less developed countries to apply strict measures for the protection of the environment.

Integration alternative scenario A2, which assumes considerable domestic tourist demand, is purely hypothetical in the case of a developing country, at least until 2000.

Source: Mr Sayed Moussa (Blue Plan).

---

unspoilt sites for the pleasure of a few people. Conversely, in the zones reserved for mass tourism the results can be disastrous: overcrowding, ugliness, destruction of the landscape, cheap facilities, hence increased pollution etc.

It must be stressed, however, that the total number of tourists is the lowest in this scenario and that the Mediterranean area as a whole is therefore less affected in any event. This is particularly true of the coast, where tourist pressure is scarcely higher than at present (20m. more).

Moderate trend scenario T3 is based on the hypothesis of economic recovery, with the beginning of a long-term view. Economic growth means higher income, hence more holidays. Domestic tourism consequently shows good results. In this scenario

overall, Mediterranean tourism in 2000 reaches 350m. visitors, an average annual growth-rate of 3.1 per cent. The market share of the three north-western countries falls slightly (71 per cent of the whole area), while the shares of the other three regions increase: southern Europe 14.3 per cent, eastern Mediterranean 8.5 per cent, Greater Maghreb 6 per cent. Domestic tourism, at 2.2 per cent per annum, grows less quickly than international tourism (3.9 per cent). As commercial competition is less keen, holiday styles evolve and the accent is on culture and the historical and cultural heritage. The cultural group (26 per cent) increases more than the others, but the relaxation group is still the largest (38 per cent).

This scenario is doubtless the one most conducive

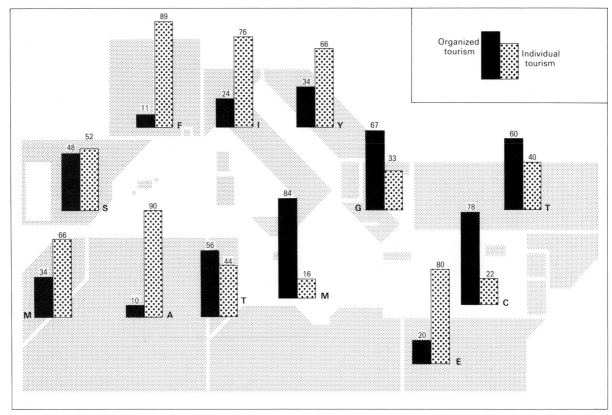

FIG. 13.3 Type of tourism, 1985 (as percentage of international tourist arrivals)
Source: WTO/Blue Plan.

to innovation in the field of information and communication, in response to growing demand. Imagination is likewise discernible in the creation of new tourist products ('aqualands', pleasure-grounds, theme-parks, etc.), which serve as substitutes for beaches and other sites that have become saturated and/or have lost some of their appeal. In economic terms, the share of tourism in GDP is high (6.1 per cent), and the increase in employment ranges from 14 to 17 per cent.

On the other hand, the environment is not taken sufficiently into account, nor is intra-Mediterranean co-operation. The sector is dynamic, but there is no overall view, and real safeguards are lacking: no real co-ordination, no proper long-term reflection, a 'sprinkling' of bilateral aid, duplication of facilities, unrestricted exploitation of natural resources without appropriate regulations, etc. This scenario, finally, is the least favourable for the Mediterranean environment, especially the coast, with 158m. tourists flocking to the seaside. This saturation (and even excess) may induce tourists spontaneously to change their kind of leisure demand, making this scenario just as unstable, though for other reasons, as worse trend scenario T2.

(b) The alternative scenarios

From the economic viewpoint the multipolar world structure makes some degree of Mediterranean autonomy possible.

Reference alternative scenario A1 assumes a reorientation of north–south trade in the Mediterranean, with the European Community acting as a driving force and better development conditions in the countries south and east of the Mediterranean basin. Under these circumstances Mediterranean tourism reaches 375m. visitors, an annual average growth-rate of 3.6 per cent. Although declining in comparison with the trend scenarios, the share of the three countries in the north-west remains considerable (69 per cent). The position of southern Europe remains unchanged compared with the T3 scenario, whereas the eastern Mediterranean and the Greater Maghreb show signs of improvement (9.1 and 7.1 per cent of Mediterranean tourism respectively).

The A1 scenario fosters domestic tourism, because of a better rate of economic growth, which rises on average by 2.9 per cent per annum to reach 168m. holiday-makers. International tourism, however, is still more dynamic, with 207m. arrivals (growth-rate of 4.1 per cent per annum). Employment increases from 17 to 20 per cent by 2000, and the share of tourism in GDP is in the region of 5.7 per cent.

In this scenario, the 'relaxation' group is again the largest (30 per cent), but the 'cultural' group (28 per cent) is close behind and the 'recreation' group grows considerably (22 per cent). Half the holiday-makers are therefore people who are sensitive to their own culture and that of others, to the quality of their leisure and to that of their environment. Governments are fully aware of the importance of tourism in the context of balanced economic growth because of its impact on employment and the creation of wealth, and on the organization of leisure time. Accordingly, staggered holidays become a reality, which makes the growing number of tourists perfectly bearable, particularly the 169m. tourists on the coast and in coastal regions.

Very strict standards are applied in respect of the environment, so that all these tourists can be accommodated, fed, and entertained. However, constant vigilance must be the keynote, with the most imaginative management techniques brought in to help, particularly as regards accommodation (whose capacity is currently under-utilized, as is plainly shown by the correlation index in Table 13.8). It is a matter of finding ways in which existing resources can be better employed and building only where resources are inadequate.

Table 13.8 Supply/demand correlation index for tourist accommodation in the Mediterranean, 1984 (%)

	Annual correlation index[a]	Correlation index in peak months[b]
Spain	26	40
France	36.5	54
Italy	30	45
Malta	36	54
Yugoslavia	30	46
Greece	30	45
Turkey	104	156
Cyprus	10	15
Syria	42	64
Israel	42	63
Egypt	42	64
Libya	60	90
Tunisia	42	63
Algeria	26	39
Morocco	42	63

[a] = (total beds × 300)/total guest-nights.
[b] = (total beds × 30)/15% total guest-nights.
Source: Blue Plan (Lanquar and Figuerola, 1986).

In the integration alternative scenario A2, domestic tourism expands vigorously as departure rates in the southern and eastern countries catch up, in response to these countries' sound economic situation. International tourism is composed mostly of visitors from the Mediterranean region itself. The total number of tourists reaches 409m., an average annual growth-rate of 4.1 per cent. With 44.5 per cent of the total, domestic tourism considerably narrows the gap with international tourism. In fact, domestic tourism experiences its strongest average annual growth-rate (3.47 per cent), although international tourism remains dynamic: 227m. foreigners (average annual growth-rate of 4.76 per cent). Regional distribution evolves towards a better-balanced share of the Mediterranean market among the four groups of countries (north-west 67 per cent; southern Europe over 15 per cent; eastern Mediterranean 9.5 per cent; Greater Maghreb 8 per cent).

This scenario gives a certain priority to the enhancement of the natural, cultural, and historical heritage, with a consequent expansion of the cultural group (30 per cent). It is also the one with the strongest development of social tourism, and that of clubs and associations, for the purpose of study and social advancement, which contributes to the education of the 'relaxation' group (36 per cent) and its trend towards a less passive and 'predatory' style of holiday. The impact of tourism on GDP is roughly the same as in the A1 scenario, and the growth of employment ranges between 20 per cent and 23 per cent.

This high number of tourists encourages the authorities and tourists themselves to take measures to avoid potential saturation. Along the coast, for instance, there are more than 180m. tourists. It is virtually compulsory to stagger holidays and also (probably) to split them: going away more often but for shorter periods. The most modern techniques are used for accommodation and facilities. Lastly, in this scenario of change, not only economic but also of attitudes, the tourists themselves become more aware of the value of goods and people, which should facilitate the reception of large numbers of tourists without too much harm to the natural and human environment.

3. Tourism at horizon 2025

The overall approach for the period 2000–25 is the same as for the previous period, with a few differences:

● The sound economic growth in the alternative scenarios brings about a rise in living standards, especially in the countries south and east of the Mediterranean basin, and in turn the growth of domestic tourism.

● Similarly, the countries in southern Europe attain high levels of GDP per capita, comparable to those of France and Italy at present, which stimulates the growth of intra-regional international tourism.

● In worse trend scenario T2, growth recovers somewhat in the southern and eastern countries, restoring some degree of dynamism to domestic tourism, which nevertheless remains at a comparatively low level.

● International tourism continues to grow faster than domestic tourism in the trend scenarios, but tends to settle down. Indeed, it seems difficult to go beyond a certain level of departure rates (roughly 70 per cent).

For horizon 2025 only overall results are available, not for the four regions (Table 13.6 above). Compared with the situation in 1984, the multiplier of tourist numbers varies from 1.7 in the T2 scenario to 3.5 in the A2 scenario. The corresponding number of tourists, 379m. and 758m. respectively, must be taken with caution, as in the other scenarios for the 2025 horizon. The same applies to the number of guest-nights in Table 13.9, which varies from almost 4,700m. for T2 scenario to a little over 11,000m. for the A2 scenario.

With these reservations, the following comments may be made:

● Tourist numbers in the reference trend scenario T1 and the moderate trend scenario T3 are very high: 481m. and 574m. In view of non-restrictive government policies where environment and planning are concerned, the impacts on the environment are naturally considerable: haphazard land-use,

destruction of rare and fragile coastal ecosystems by the building of infrastructure and tourist amenities, breaking up of landscapes by second residences, etc. The spread of planning errors committed in recent years can be witnessed throughout the Mediterranean coast.

● The worst trend scenario T2, with only 379m. tourists, 114m. of whom are domestic, paradoxically remains the most 'favourable' for safeguarding landscapes and natural and historic sites. Its most worrying impacts are at the social and cultural levels, owing to the dualism in the two ways of life: on the one hand the idle rich spending their holiday in 'dream-spots' reserved for their sole use and, on the other, the disadvantaged groups, unable to pay for a family holiday or obliged to take one under poor conditions. The sight of wealthy tourists has very negative effects on the values of the host society, with a consequent rise in para-tourist delinquency (theft, prostitution, etc.). This situation is naturally unstable and may lead to revolt and the reappropriation of reserved areas.

● The number of tourists is the highest of all in the alternative scenarios. But goal-orientated government policies for planning (leisure-time as well as space) and balanced economic development allow for these flows of tourists to be absorbed without undue conflict.

Furthermore, the harmonious organization of leisure for such huge numbers of tourists can scarcely be contemplated otherwise without causing serious damage: over-saturation, uncontrolled building, etc. Governments have virtually no choice but to implement planning policies of this kind.

Table 13.9 Number of guest-nights for international and domestic tourism, 2000 and 2025

Scenarios	2000: guest-nights (m.)			2025: guest-nights (m)		
	IT[a]	DT[b]	Total	IT[c]	DT[d]	Total
T1	1,570	2,960	4,530	2,560	3,720	6,280
T2	1,410	2,470	3,880	2,170	2,510	4,680
T3	1,730	3,520	5,250	2,820	5,060	7,880
A1	1,800	3,910	5,710	2,930	6,710	9,640
A2	1,970	4,240	6,210	3,350	7,680	11,030

[a] Average stay = 8.7 days.
[b] Average stay = 23.3 days.
[c] Average stay = 8.2 days.
[d] Average stay = 22 days.

Source: Blue Plan (Lanquar and Figuerola, 1986).

4. Interactions between tourism and the environment

The study of the interactions between tourism and the environment in the Mediterranean focuses chiefly on three aspects:

- consumption of resources (land and water);
- pollution and waste;
- physical and socio-cultural pressures.

But it must be recalled that, owing to lack of data (especially statistical information), some analyses had to be limited to the national level, without being able to grasp specific trends in the coastal regions themselves.

An attempt has been made to analyse the 'tourist potential' of each country in relation to the physical and human environment, although the lack of data is even more pronounced than for the socio-economic study. Consequently, only a few simple indicators have been used to illustrate the importance of tourist activities on the Mediterranean environment and to explore the coastal countries' tourist potential.

(a) Site coverage and use of coastal land

The impact of tourism on land resources can be studied on the basis of prospects for accommodation capacity and the number of guest-nights identified by scenario, bearing in mind that tourism uses both accommodation facilities and amenities for sport, cultural, or recreational activities. It is estimated that the different kinds of tourist lodgings cover an average surface area of 40 m² per bed for hotel accommodation, 70 m² per bed for additional lodging (including gardens and parking lots in both cases).

Table 13.10 provides an estimate of tourist accommodation capacity and corresponding site coverage for all the Mediterranean countries in 1984. This shows that 90 per cent of hotel and additional lodging capacity is in the north-west region of the basin. Altogether, about 2,200 km² were used by specifically tourist accommodation in the countries of the Mediterranean basin. If this surface area is doubled to take account of urbanization regulations and necessary infrastructure (such as service roads etc.), total site coverage amounts to about 4,400 km².

Table 13.10 Capacity and site coverage of hotels and other lodgings, 1984

	No. of hotel beds (000s)	Site coverage (1,000 m²)	No of other beds (000s)	Site coverage (1,000 m²)
Spain	840	33,600	8,923	624,610
France	1,590	63,600	10,894	762,580
Italy	1,598	63,920	5,854	409,780
Malta	14	560	41	2,870
Yugoslavia	319	12,760	1,127	78,890
Greece	323	12,920	324	22,680
Turkey	68	2,720	182	12,740
Cyprus	27	1,080	137	9,590
Syria	23	920	71	4,970
Israel	65	2,600	162	11,340
Egypt	48	1,920	218	15,260
Libya	9	360	24	1,680
Tunisia	72	2,880	77	5,390
Algeria	27	1,080	37	2,590
Morocco	59	2,360	152	10,640
TOTAL	5,082	203,280	28,223	1,975,610

Note: The different types of tourist lodging (hotel and other, including related areas) occupy an average surface of 25–100 m² per bed:

rented, self-catering accommodation	50 m² per bed
hotels	30 m² per bed
youth hostels	30 m² per bed
holiday villages	100 m² per bed
camping and caravan sites	50 m² per place
car-parks	20 m² per place

The average reached is 40 m² per bed for hotel accommodation and 70 m² per bed for other accommodation.

About 50 per cent of hotel and other types of accommodation is situated in the Mediterranean coastal regions, a total of 2,200 km² of urban development for tourist use. This consumption of surface area, although not too significant compared with the size of the national territory, is considerable within the coastal regions themselves. It is equivalent to 2,200 km of densely urbanized coast 1 km deep, or 4,400 km of densely urbanized coast 500 m deep.

For horizon 2000, and despite the considerable rise in the number of international and domestic tourists, about 40m. tourist beds should be available in the Mediterranean countries, which assumes an average growth-rate of 20 per cent compared with the current situation. The supply/demand correlation index (Table 13.8) reveals the under-utilization of hotel and para-hotel facilities. The most likely trend will be towards better management, with few new installations (or rather a rough balance between new installations and the abandoning of obsolescent ones) except in the south and east, particularly in the alternative scenarios. In the scenarios of weak economic growth the over-occupation of some accommodation will continue to coexist with the under-utilization of others. Site coverage, however, will be greater, especially on the assumption that quality will improve, as notably in the alternative scenarios. Total coverage could reach 8,000 km² for the countries as a whole. This might also be the case of moderate trend scenario T3, which implies very dynamic tourist development. In the coastal regions 4,400 km² would consequently be used specifically to accommodate tourists.

(b) Water consumption

Here too, accommodation capacity and the number of guest-nights have been chosen as indicators. Water consumption is not strictly equivalent to withdrawals, as it depends on the efficiency of the network, nor to the volume of waste water discharged, which depends on the rate of connection to sewage systems.

The hypotheses of domestic water consumption chosen for the scenarios, in litres per person per day, are as follows (assimilating tourists to the urban population):

	1984	2000	2025
International tourism	250	300	300
Domestic tourism	150	175	200

These hypotheses are based on weightings. In fact, a luxury hotel can consume over 600 litres of water

Table 13.11 Estimate of tourists' annual water consumption in Mediterranean countries, 1986, 2000, and 2025 (m. m³)

	International tourism	Domestic tourism	Total	Multiplier coefficient[a]
1984	222.5	346.5	569.0	
2000				
T1	472.2	517.8	990.0	1.7
T2	422.7	42.8	854.7	1.5
T3	513.3	615.6	1,129.0	2.0
A1	540.0	684.9	1,225.0	2.1
A2	592.2	742.0	1,334.2	2.3
2025				
T1	767.0	743.6	1,511.0	2.6
T2	651.9	501.6	1,153.5	2.0
T3	846.0	1,012.0	1,858.0	3.2
A1	878.0	1,342.0	2,200.0	3.9
A2	1,006.0	1,535.0	2,541.0	4.4

[a] Taking 1984 as the base-year.
Source: Blue Plan (Lanquar and Figuerola, 1986).

per tourist guest-night, whereas a camper will use very little. It has also been assumed that water consumption by international tourism will increase no further after 2000, whereas that of domestic tourism will continue to grow until 2025. Estimated annual consumption is given in Table 13.11, on the assumption that these hypotheses are valid for all the scenarios.

The results show that worst trend scenario T2 is the most sparing of water, with consumption increasing by 50 per cent in 2000 and doubling in 2025 compared with the situation in 1984. Integration alternative scenario A2 entails a strong increase in consumption, 340 per cent in 2025 compared with 1984. In this scenario, however, co-operation among states and the long-term view have a favourable effect, and the reuse and recycling of water become a reality. This is not the case with moderate trend scenario T3, where the risk of wastage is real in view of increased consumption, multiplied by 2 in 2000 and by 3.2 in 2025 compared with 1984, in a very dynamic economic context but one still little concerned with the optimal use of resources.

One of the effects of water consumption by tourists is a lowering of the ground-water level through over-pumping (the case in the Hammamet region in Tunisia, for instance), leading to a 'social waste-land' or the abandoning of cultivated land. In coastal regions this phenomenon could be aggravated by the infiltration of seawater, making the aquifer salty (in the Balearic Islands, some resorts on the Spanish coast, etc.).

Table 13.12 Solid waste and waste water from tourism in Mediterranean countries, 1984, 2000, 2025

	Solid waste (000 t p.a.)	Waste water (m. m³ p.a.)
1984	2,880	341.4
2000		
T1	4,986	594.0
T2	4,265	512.8
T3	5,774	677.4
A1	6,285	735.0
A2	6,835	800.5
2025		
T1	8,786	906.6
T2	6,553	692.0
T3	11,032	1,115.0
A1	10,600	1,332.0
A2	12,134	1,525.0

Source: Blue Plan (Lanquar and Figuerola, 1986).

(c) Waste and pollution

Waste has been studied on the basis of tourist guest-nights for solid waste and water consumption for liquid waste.

(i) Solid and liquid waste

The initial hypothesis for solid waste was an average production of household refuse of 0.9 kg per day per tourist. In the medium term, because of the spread of packaging, this figure was brought up to 1.1 kg in 2000 for all the scenarios. In 2025 there would be a further increase to 1.4 kg per day per tourist in the trend scenarios, whereas a stabilization at the 2000 level would occur in the alternative scenarios. In the latter case most waste would be biodegradable or recyclable. The findings are given in Table 13.12. For liquid waste, it was estimated that waste water represents 60 per cent of domestic water consumption. This percentage remains constant for all the scenarios. The composition of waste specific to tourists is also important: solid packaging (related to consumption pattern), nature of waste-water flow (e.g. type of detergent, for instance).

(ii) Pollution

The effects of tourism on noise, atmospheric pollution from exhaust fumes, or pollution of coastal waters could not be quantified for lack of homogeneous statistical series for all countries of the Mediterranean basin, especially as these effects combine with those from other sectors of activity.

● *Noise*. Air and road transport increase sound pollution. The tourist trends examined above show that this kind of nuisance will increase at least until 2000, partly because of the number of tourists using air transport. Over the period 2000 to 2025 the level of sound pollution should stabilize if technical innovations lead to the construction of quieter aircraft, which has in fact been the trend for the past ten years. Similarly, tourism contributes to noise from urban sources, which is becoming increasingly difficult to tolerate. Public authorities can do a great deal to reduce sound nuisances: regulations at source (for light vehicles, among other things), siting of roads and aerodromes, sound-proof screening, maintenance of silent zones, instruction, and incentives of all sorts.

● *Atmospheric pollution* from exhaust fumes (see Chapter 14) is considerable in the countries with very high tourist inflows and where arrivals are usually by road. This type of pollution is concentrated along the major motorway access routes, as well as in the receiving areas. Spain, France, and Italy are especially affected by this problem, as is Yugoslavia, where the percentage of international arrivals by road (86 per cent) is the highest in the Mediterranean basin and concentration on the coast is very heavy in the summer. In these countries the situation may well deteriorate in the short and medium term owing to the increase in the number of tourists, even when new compulsory depollution systems are taken into account. The countries in the south and east, where international arrivals by road are significant (Syria, Turkey, Morocco), will also be affected by this problem. The construction of transit roads far from inhabited areas could help to remove nuisances.

● *Pollution of coastal waters* through the discharge of waste water from tourism adds to that from the discharge of the resident population. Effective depollution rates for each country would have to be available in order to discern trends, which is not yet the case. In France the current real rate of depollution for total discharge is 27 per cent in Provence–Côte-d'Azur and 42 per cent in Languedoc–Roussillon. In 1990 these rates will attain 47 and 49 per cent respectively.

The arrival of increasingly larger tourist populations in some areas could lead to pollution with noticeable effects on health, justifying epidemiological surveys and the publication of the levels of water quality, as is already the practice in several Mediterranean countries. In areas with high tourist inflows (beaches near urban areas, among others) special attention should be given to the cleanliness of sand and to the disposal systems of pleasure boats

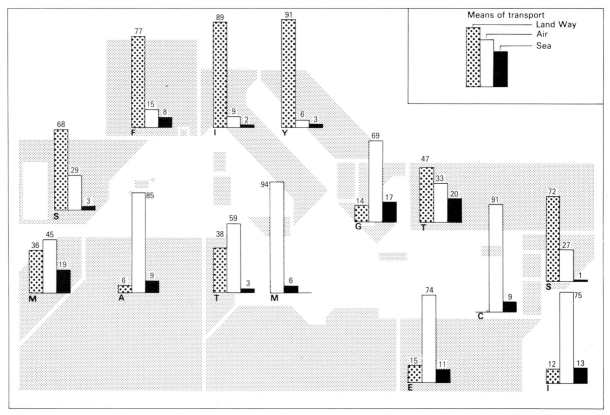

Fig. 13.4 International tourist arrivals by means of transport, 1985 (as percentage of international tourist arrivals)
Source: WTO/Blue Plan.

(in ports, inlets, and bays which receive many visitors during the summer period).

(d) The physical and social pressure of tourism

Tourist pressure on the area was measured according to two indicators:

- tourist density or number of tourists per km²;
- tourist pressure along the coastline, or number of tourists per km of coast.

Although very imperfect, the second indicator has been used in the absence of data on the surface areas of beaches, which would have provided more specific information on 'bathing density'. Both indicators concern Mediterranean coastal regions during the peak month (20 per cent of the total numbers of domestic and international tourists visiting the Mediterranean). To gauge the 'social pressure' of tourism on the local population, the ratio chosen was that of the number of tourists during the peak month compared with the resident population.

Table 13.13, for reference year 1984 and for 2000 in the case of reference trend scenario T1,

shows that overall tourist pressure was weak and that it rises only very slightly in 2000. Contrasts are sharper when each country is taken separately, as illustrated by a few examples:

- The heaviest tourist density is in Malta, five times higher than in Spain (in second position), and this ratio will have risen further by 2000.
- On the other hand, use of the coastline is heaviest in Spain, both in 1984 and in 2000, and this country combines the heaviest use of the coastline with considerable tourist density and social pressure.
- Yugoslavia is experiencing the strongest social pressure, twice as high as in Spain (in 1984 and 2000). This perhaps explains the low increase observed and forecast for the number of tourists in this country.
- Syria is experiencing heavy tourist pressure on its land and coastline, but not on its population.
- Turkey and Egypt seem to experience low tourist pressure.

This kind of indicator of tourist pressure does not help to tackle the excessive numbers of visitors at archaeological and historical sites, especially acute

Table 13.13 Indicators of tourist pressure on coastal regions, 1984 and 2000

Mediterranean regions	1984			2000 (T1 scenario)		
	Tourist density (tourists/km²)[a]	Density on coast (tourists/m)[b]	Social pressure (tourists/inhabitants)[c]	Tourist density (tourists/km²)[a]	Density on coast (tourists/m)[b]	Social pressure (tourists/inhabitants)[c]
Spain	62.0	2.30	0.41	84.0	3.10	0.47
France	56.0	1.50	0.46	76.0	2.00	0.52
Italy	20.0	0.60	0.10	25.0	0.70	0.13
Yugoslavia	52.0	0.40	0.89	69.0	0.50	0.94
Greece	13.0	0.10	0.14	31.0	0.20	0.32
Turkey	5.0	0.10	0.05	9.0	0.20	0.07
Malta	316.0	0.70	0.26	696.0	1.60	0.52
Cyprus	17.0	0.20	0.23	32.0	0.40	0.39
Syria	51.0	1.20	0.18	101.0	2.30	0.18
Lebanon	—	—	—	—	—	—
Israel	51.0	1.20	0.07	79.0	1.80	0.09
Egypt	1.0	0.40	0.02	1.6	0.70	0.02
Libya	—	—	—	—	—	—
Tunisia	10.0	0.30	0.08	19.0	0.70	0.12
Algeria	4.0	0.20	0.02	8.0	0.40	0.02
Morocco	6.0	0.60	0.08	13.0	1.30	0.10
TOTAL MEDITERRANEAN COASTAL REGIONS	15.6	0.41	0.14	23.0	0.61	0.17

Note: 0.20 in the following calculations denotes the estimated 20% of tourists staying in coastal regions during the peak month.

[a] $\dfrac{\text{number of tourists} \times 0.20}{\text{km}^2 \text{ surface area of coastal regions}}$

[b] $\dfrac{\text{number of tourists} \times 0.20}{\text{m coastline}}$

[c] $\dfrac{\text{number of tourists} \times 0.20}{\text{resident population}}$

Source: Blue Plan (Lanquar and Figuerola, 1986)

in places like Luxor or Venice (where municipal authorities are considering setting up a system to restrict the number of visitors). This problem also concerns natural sites, such as some islands which are particularly attractive in the summer (nature reserves like Port-Cros, Greek islands, etc.). Over-frequentation implies very negative and even destructive impacts, notably through trampling, and visitors' breath or artificial lighting in confined or underground areas. Once begun, the degradation of this wealth is irreversible. Those responsible are well aware of the dangers of excessive tourist inflows and are seeking solutions still far from clear-cut.

(e) Potential for tourism

On the basis of the criteria described above and other wide-ranging ones, such as the climate (annual hours of sunshine), air-transport infrastructure (passenger unloading capacity), a country's cultural and natural riches, supply of tourist accommodation (hotel and para-hotel capacity), the level of additional activities (restaurants, bars, sports facilities, casinos, etc.), an effort was made to define 'tourist potential', representing either assets or possibilities for tourist development in each Mediterranean country in the light of various scenarios. For this purpose a 'potentiality index' was tried out, based on a weighted average of the indicators listed below. This approach, which needs to be carried further, made it possible to undertake an initial evaluation of tourist development potential at horizon 2000 for the four regions defined earlier.

The interest of this approach lies in making a dynamic connection between these indicators, which all have an influence on one another. To take the example of Spain, the following features can be noted:

- a climate more attractive in summer than in winter;
- already high tourist density;
- an extensive coastline, but already very full in summer;
- very high accommodation capacity;
- a very high level of additional facilities;
- good air-transport infrastructure;
- well-exploited cultural wealth;
- already heavy social pressure.

These observations show that Spain can take steps to improve the quality of the services offered and to diversify them as there are no problems of quantity and that to preserve its attraction for tourists the authorities should in any case be careful about the risk of seasonal saturation.

The reverse of the Spanish example could be valid for Egypt and Turkey, which have:

- a dense population able to receive very large numbers of tourists;
- in the case of Egypt, attractive climatic assets for two departure zones (northern Europe and North America in winter and spring, Arab countries in summer);
- an extensive and under-utilized coastline;
- archaeological and historical treasures;
- very low accommodation capacity;
- transport infrastructures needing improvement.

Both these countries consequently have a very high tourist development potential, which materializes in the T3 scenario and becomes even more of a reality in the alternative scenarios.

The trends envisaged in the T1 and T2 scenarios imply a lowering of potential in the three north-western countries because seasonal saturation is not relieved in these scenarios; according to the criteria selected, this area can barely advance any more. Its potential remains stable in the other scenarios. Southern Europe increases its potential in all the scenarios except the worst trend scenario T2, where it stagnates.

At any rate, this study of tourist potential is a good illustration of the difficult balance required in order to ensure economically profitable, socially harmonious, and ecologically acceptable tourism. However, since tourism needs a good-quality environment, it can contribute to some extent to improving and conserving it, to the spread of criteria regarding living standards, to the enhancement of natural and cultural sites, and can become a real driving force for environmental protection.

5. Conclusions and issues for appraisal

All the scenarios indicated a considerable development of tourism in all the Mediterranean countries. One of the most important issues for the future is that of better geographical distribution among the host countries, which could lead to an improved balance among the four regions studied. The necessary facilities will have to be constructed so that the three regions currently receiving fewer tourists may increase their share of the market (while preserving as far as possible their natural wealth). The moderate trend scenario T3 illustrated the risk of this kind of increase in the absence of co-ordination and planning. Moreover, will the most frequently visited countries in the leading region accept this diversion, or would they try to keep their share of the market? And, in the same vein, how will the Mediterranean countries of the European Community react when the Single European Act comes into force in 1993, leading to a huge redistribution of goods and persons, which could pave the way to the expansion of installations (with north European capital) in areas like Sardinia, the Greek islands, etc.?

One aspect of this international competition is the search for the new kinds of amenities or leisure styles to attract a different class of tourist. There is the example, shifting from conventional amenities, of the encouragement given to lightweight yachting facilities, such as dry ports (in France marinas are too often 'parking lots' where, according to statistics, boats only go out seventeen days a year), or to camping or hiking. In a completely different style, there are the amusement parks, which, perhaps poorly designed or targeted, have not been as successful as their promoters expected.

Another query is related to the emergence of domestic tourism in a number of countries south and east of the Mediterranean basin, among others those with a high population growth-rate and with good or strong economic growth. Will this kind of tourism, which usually starts with holidays at home (particularly difficult to account for in statistics), develop according to the European model, based on new accommodation capacity whose rapid growth could conflict with the quality of and respect for the environment and landscapes?

Mention can also be made of the problem of social segregation, which runs counter to the spirit of intermixing of populations through tourism. The worst trend scenario T2 depicted it in the form of luxury tourist 'islands'. But it could also take other shapes, between domestic and international tourism.

Along with geographical distribution, there is also 'temporal' distribution or 'time-planning'. The scenarios clearly indicated the importance of the problem, without really suggesting any solution, since the difficulties to overcome are so vast. Will national development policies, by taking into account the economic, social, and cultural issues of tourism, manage to avoid the concentration of holidays in the peak period? This problem is perhaps one of the most important and most urgent: congestion on roads, and in air corridors and airports, which recently reached the highest levels ever, and the ensuing risk to life, provide an initial idea of the scope of the problem and the decisions to be taken.

Yet it is striking to observe in this respect that the highest number of guest-nights, i.e. a little over 11,000m. in the integration scenario A2, could already be absorbed today by the total lodging capacity of the Mediterranean countries (33m. beds), if it were occupied 365 days a year (which would provide 12,000m. guest-nights). This is naturally an unrealistic assumption, but it provides an idea of the importance of staggering holidays.

Lastly, from the environmental viewpoint, one of the most worrying aspects is the excessive number of visitors to historical and some natural sites.

On the other hand, it seems that most of the other impacts of tourism could be brought to an acceptable level by thorough study and above all the planning of development goals, by realistically taking stock of the advantages and disadvantages involved, and by using integrated planning methods.

14 Transport in the Mediterranean

The prospects for transport are closely linked with those for intra-Mediterranean trade, for trade between the region and the rest of the world, and for the traffic (mostly oil tankers) which passes through the Mediterranean. The volume of merchandise and passenger flows and the dynamics of the infrastructure work required vary considerably with the hypotheses of the different Blue Plan scenarios. But prospects are still dependent on the physical and historical features of the Mediterranean regions. The first section identifies some trends in the light of the various scenarios.

The review of interactions between transport and the environment can be tackled by grouping transport activities into four categories (section 2), each representing different types of impact, if only in terms of the host environment or the kind of pollutants emitted or nuisances provoked:

- land transport (road, section 2 (*a*); rail, section 2 (*b*));
- maritime transport (section 2 (*c*));
- air transport (section 2(*d*)).

Special attention has been given to maritime transport because of its importance for the Mediterranean Sea itself and for all the coastal activities related to it.

Some issues for appraisal conclude this chapter.

1. General prospects by scenario

(*a*) Some trends and factors of change

Maritime transport, strongly established in the region from time immemorial, will change radically during the next forty years. How will port facilities harmonize with road and river infrastructure in the hinterlands?

There is a considerable difference between maritime transport infrastructure in the countries north of the basin (from Spain to Greece and, partly, to Turkey) and that in the southern and eastern countries. Development during the first industrial age led to the emergence of a distinction between the following two categories of port:

- *Peninsular ports*. Some of these may play a strategic role or a role in redeployment, either at the national level (like the Piraeus) or, more often, at the international level (like Naples or Barcelona). Some have already launched into a process of reconversion together with industrialization (e.g. Augusta or Taranto).
- *Deep-bay ports*. These are more important (e.g. Marseilles, Genoa, Venice, Thessaloniki), and have benefited from the political and economic situation and from a significant transport infrastructure. In particular, they have a much more extended hinterland than the peninsular ports. The Suez Canal, opened in 1869, contributed to their development.

France, Italy, and Spain assumed a prominent role in sea traffic, which was heightened with the integration of these countries into the European Community.

The overspill effect, and also a certain degree of monopolization on the part of the major deep-bay port complexes, were strengthened by the appearance of new, efficient technologies related to 'combined carriage',* itself increasingly linked to the multinational organization of the economy (cf. the role of the predominant urban metropolises), interconnected through high-level service operations. Tied to the intercontinental traffic system, the Mediterranean has become increasingly dependent on external momentum and strategies. A major Mediterranean port like Fos-sur-Mer, for example, faces very strong competition from Rotterdam (numerous lines and services are offered) and other North Sea ports, despite its special facilities for handling containers. This keen competition is likely to grow. The Channel Tunnel may provide a fresh impetus to the efficient road–rail combinations serving Europe, and encourage the Mediterranean part to fuse increasingly with the future structure of northern transport.

---

*A legal term referring to the global contract covering all the transport components intervening between the starting-point and the destination, before breaking of bulk. Maritime transport, one of the links of this multiform chain, has, to some extent, become commonplace.

Another example of external influence is the link-up between the Mediterranean and the outlet of the Danube, through the Dardanelles. The north–south eastern road route is slowly materializing: 'the 10,000-kilometre road' which should connect the Polish port complex lying on the Baltic Sea (Gdansk-Gdynia) to the Persian Gulf through the Bosporus and Anatolian plateau, with its Iraqi and Iranian branchings, is being undertaken by sections in the various European states concerned.* The Soviet Union is developing important international ports on the Black Sea. These are all changes which, without being spectacular, are gradually materializing and will have an effect on Mediterranean Europe's 'transport' system.

The southern and eastern coast too will develop on the basis of a few break-bulk points, mostly connected with the north-west coast. Bulk goods transport will continue to progress, and the growth of combined carriage will no doubt be the main innovation in the next two decades.

The proportion of food and agricultural products (grains, meat, etc.), coal, and manufactured goods in Mediterranean transport should rise and, as a result, all the leading port complexes are likely to be enlarged. Whereas medium-sized ports may decline, the major ports will be extended with satellite or off-loading facilities (like Fos with respect to Marseilles), and some new ports may be constructed for very specific products.

As regards tonnage, ports on the southern and eastern shores are likely to expand the most in the coming decades (related to the development of industry and energy). A very large increase in the range of products and services offered is expected and many processing activities will be established.

Pressures exerted will be even heavier because they will be both stronger and faster; this will certainly be the case in southern and eastern countries. Impact will depend on economic, technological, political, and financial measures taken at the national and international level as well as at the regional or local level. The Blue Plan scenarios are therefore differentiated by the evolution of transport itself (starting with means of transport), and by measures taken to cut down pollutant emissions or discharges into the atmosphere, water, or soil, to reduce noise and other nuisances, and to protect sites and social and cultural patterns.

*Four Mediterranean countries are involved: Italy (98 km), Yugoslavia (1,700 km), Greece (960 km), and Turkey (nearly 3,000 km). Launched in 1977, this project (TEM: Trans-European Motorway) should be finished at the start of the 1990s.

(b) Trends according to the scenarios

(i) Reference trend scenario T1

While traditional trade-flows develop, profound changes take place in terms of logistics. The two north-west Mediterranean countries—France and Italy—which to some extent are in a dominant position with regard to Mediterranean trade, both within the basin and with the rest of the world, are mainly orientated towards northern Europe; 40–50 per cent of their trade is with the countries of the European Community.

Trade favours the north–south orientation of transport routes. The more coherent infrastructure networks in the northern regions, in both France and Italy, tend to be mutually strengthening, and international land transport (road and rail) remains important. The North Sea–Mediterranean link is basically ensured by road (except for bulk). In the countries south and east of the basin the polarization brought about by Europe (more than 50 per cent of trade) produces a more coherent infrastructure network on the coast and the development of ports, furthered by economic relations which encourage maritime transport. In this context the ports of Tarragona, Barcelona, Marseilles, Genoa, Trieste, Venice, Rijeka, Piraeus, Thessaloniki, and Volos ensure the link with the East and Africa, where Morocco's Atlantic seaboard is even more closely linked to the Mediterranean through works like Jozf Lasfar. There is renewed interest in the western and northern-eastern tips, somewhat neglected up to now, because of the deployment of road traffic on either side of the straits (Gibraltar, Tangiers, Bosporus).

In both the northern and the southern and eastern countries, attempts occasionally made at physical planning and the balanced development of transport infrastructure only produce results when economic parameters prevail, regardless of opportunities arising from circumstances. In this respect, the development of motorized transport leads to the expansion of networks which more or less incorporate basic economic and social needs.

This scenario does not pay any special attention to the environment. This means that the negative impacts of transport on the environment will grow (increased pollutant emissions, formation and dispersion of photo-oxidants, noise, air, and water pollution from hydrocarbons, increasing risks of accidents, etc.), nevertheless leading to the necessary action for the reduction of emissions and nuisances, with a lagging behind on the part of other countries compared with the European Community.

(ii) Worst trend scenario T2

Because of keen international competition among the major industrialized countries, the idea of a Mediterranean area tends virtually to disappear. Trade-flows are characterized by the concept of transport chains and routes, information technology, and new organizational techniques which give priority to shippers rather that to transport operators and locate decision-making centres on the outskirts of the Mediterranean basin.

● *The northern shore of the basin.* The role of France and Italy, which continues to influence Mediterranean trade and transport, is less strong than in reference trend scenario T1, mainly as a result of very lively competition between the various countries of Western Europe. The interest of some European countries in the East European and Middle Eastern markets furthers the development of the Danube route. The Black Sea–North Sea link then facilitates a greater internationalization of the capital already committed along the corridor, which diverts part of the traffic hitherto going through the Mediterranean. The '10,000-km road' gradually materializes, increasing the volume of north–south traffic coming from (and going to) Western and Eastern Europe. At the same time the search for transport security prompts the development of other routes and the strengthening of the traditional Rhone–Rhine–North Sea, Rhone–Channel, and Italy–North Sea routes. Competition is fairly keen between different means of transport.

Transport infrastructure develops within the context of short-term plans, more operational and flexible enough to cope with unpredictable and frequent policy changes. The concepts of economies of scale and flow management tend to reduce the number of ports. Transport techniques also develop in accordance with the same concern for adaptability and safety. Thus, containerization continues to expand, but not as much as the use of 'ro-ros' (roll-on, roll-off vessels), a special handling process. At the same time true 'dry ports' compete with sea ports under the impetus of new techniques. Thus, for example, river-maritime transport facilitates the development of traffic to Lyons and in the Rhone valley, with its effects on the physical, economic, and social environment. Another example is the Perpignan vehicle port, impelled by the vitality of Catalonia and the growing importance of Barcelona.

● *The southern shore of the basin.* The economy is even more outward-orientated, reflected by the development of major ports and large coastal industrial zones. The development of land infrastructure involves the major routes, commercially justified in an international outlook and orientated in the direction of hinterland–Mediterranean coast, but does not prevent the parallel development of coastal navigation. The concept of physical planning tends to fade in the face of plans for siting the most productive and profitable short-term investments. In the south and east polarized development favours the coast, with main infrastructure facilities scaled down to minimum.

Worst trend scenario T2 thus envisages a considerable strengthening of road traffic, along with its nuisances and pollution, to the detriment of rail and sea transport. In both the north and south the increase in the vehicle stock, especially commercial vehicles, the development of infrastructure, and the rise in the volume of trade are accompanied by even more damaging effects on the environment because decisions and investments prefer the short-term above all, and the search for quick profitability tends to sacrifice both the natural heritage (landscape, natural areas) and the quality of the environment (particulate and gaseous pollutants, noise, congestion, etc).

(iii) Moderate trend scenario T3

Compared with the reference trend scenario T1, awareness of the Mediterranean's potential—with the need to protect this market—leads to the organization of better-balanced relations, with an incipient long-term view. A major infrastructure mesh—the national network routes, supplemented by secondary infrastructure linking the countries as a whole—seeks a more effective use of human resources (through better spatial distribution), and of land and subsoil resources.

The fabric of land infrastructure (mainly road) is strengthened in all countries as a result of increased economic activity. In the north of the basin regionalization and decentralization efforts help to fill out the existing network. In the south and east the economic development of the hinterland requires the expansion of roads, motorways, and, in some cases, railways to feed the area. While traditional, but reorganized, exchange routes still predominate, new structurizing routes are developed. National and international air transport expands vigorously and requires the construction or enlargement of airports in the southern and eastern countries.

In the countries south of the Mediterranean basin the development of the hinterland begins to take priority over that of the coastal regions, with infrastructure linking the two areas within the context of an economic and social development plan furthering economic, social, and cultural decentralization. Ports develop, often through the extension of existing infrastructure. The creation of new ports helps to bolster the major existing industry–port complexes. In addition, the number and capacity of airports, which have become essential to keep pace with (or promote) hinterland development, are rising (which implies an expansion of national fleets).

Still in the south and east of the basin, the major imbalance between road and rail is gradually attenuated by the development of rail traffic and, therefore, of the necessary infrastructure whenever it is economically and socially justified. Since rail is suited to the long-distance transport of weight cargo—important for a number of developing countries—this encourages a certain degree of rail standardization in some southern and eastern countries. Navigation has the opportunity to develop on the coast.

The development of infrastructure in the southern and eastern countries is nevertheless curbed by the cost, while international loans do not encourage the long-term view and tend to prefer road transport.

Significant efforts are made in countries north of the basin (partly under pressure from European Community directives), then in the southern and eastern countries, to reduce atmospheric pollutant emissions related to transport (NOx, CO, particulate matter, lead, etc.). However, the structure and age of the vehicle stock (tourist and commercial vehicles) and the time required to renew it cause considerable delay, even as the volume of traffic continues to increase.

(iv) Reference alternative scenario A1

In this scenario Europe is stronger and as such acts as the commercial negotiator for the other individual Mediterranean countries. Trade develops between north and south, with possibly competition among some of the southern countries.

The countries of southern Europe, in particular France, Italy, and Spain, are the special partners of North Africa (mainly the Maghreb). The spatial development of ports is better balanced, both at the national and international level, since the creation of an economically integrated Europe becomes a reality.

The Mediterranean Sea becomes to some extent a transit zone in an economic and transport area covering the whole of Europe and Africa. More or less well-knit transport networks would provide the structure for this area (especially in the A1 alternative scenario, in which a permanent link with Gibraltar would be established, the Sicily–Italy links would be enlarged, etc.). This kind of structure, in addition to the stimulus of economic and social development, would help minimize spatial and environmental impact.

In this kind of scenario necessary measures are taken and actively applied to reduce emissions and nuisances through the use of less polluting technologies, less polluting and low consumption vehicles, and better traffic management (e.g. speed limits), ultimately improving the quality of air in urban and rural areas. Europe imposes its standards for environmental protection to some extent, and helps to absorb the extra cost.

In this scenario the imbalance in the network configuration remains considerable between the countries north of the basin and those south and east: there is a better-integrated meshing in the north in the context of a European physical planning policy (a major international north–south and east–west turntable in Sicily, for instance, involving Europe, Africa, and the Middle East). On the other hand, countries assume a role as intermediaries and transit areas towards the Sahelian and West African countries. External financing and loans favour the north–south routes. Logistic support can nevertheless be undertaken to make the role of middleman more active and productive.

(v) Integration alternative scenario A2

Country groups are formed in the south and east of the Mediterranean basin on the basis of economic complementarity (human and natural potential, agriculture, industry, etc.). These behave as partners for Europe, in the context of better-balanced commercial relations. Horizontal relations are furthered between economically viable regional bodies.

Relationships favouring south–south links are gradually set up. As a result, land-based infrastructure develops, such as the bypass across the high plateaux in Algeria linking Morocco to Tunisia and then further on to Libya, Egypt, and the Middle East. Major investments, set within a long-term and large-scale perspective, thus with no immediate result, may cause a drop in the commercial GDP in the initial stage. Coastal navigation expands rapidly and existing air links are strengthened (business travel, tourists, freight, and workers).

Within the European Community the south European countries do not always benefit from partnership with countries south and east of the basin, which curbs infrastructure development compared with reference alternative scenario A1.

In a subsequent period intra-Mediterranean trade recovers within better-negotiated frameworks in which the notion of complementarity and the need for co-operation prevail. The role of southern country groups as intermediaries between Europe and Africa is maintained, to the benefit of the partners as a whole. South European regions regain the important role which derives from their geographical position with respect to the southern and eastern Mediterranean.

Infrastructure develops more consistently in vertical directions, linking the hinterland to the coast, and the countries among themselves. Some major hubs are formed at interconnections between different transportation means and at the terminals of international, national, regional, or local spokes. These nodal points are determined within the context of a physical planning policy which exceeds national boundaries.

This kind of situation could encourage, in an ultimate stage, the economically viable grouping of countries to the north, south, and east of the Mediterranean basin, regardless of the groups to which countries individually already belong.

2. Prospects by means of transport

After an overall analysis of possible transport trends according to the different kinds of scenarios, it is worth reviewing the major forms of transport, which all have a rather special kind of relationship with the environment.

(a) Road transport and the motor-vehicle stock

The Mediterranean basin is one of the world regions which was a relative latecomer to road mobility: the relief and inclination towards the sea acted as a curb. The growing importance of road transport for the movement of both goods and passengers has nevertheless led to a policy for the development of new land routes for trucks and motor-cars. Many road and motorway 'terminals' were established on the northern shore, as well as a motorway network started in Italy in the 1930s and now developed mainly in Spain and France, but gradually reaching the other countries. The relationship between the growing density of networks and the growing intensity of flows, of commercial vehicles in particular, is at the origin of this process.

Trends in the vehicle stock reflect as much population growth as the expansion of overland exchanges and rising incomes. Table 14.1 illustrates, among other factors, the recent vigorous growth of the vehicle stock in the southern and eastern countries, nevertheless still far from reaching the 'saturation'-point observed in the northern countries. Unlike the latter, where rail had won the bulk of major flows during the first industrial era, the impact in the southern and eastern regions may come mostly from roads. In 1970 Spain, France, and Italy represented slightly over 90 per cent of the total. In 2000 Spain, France, Italy, and Greece (the four EEC countries) will represent no more than 61 per cent of the total, and in 2025 less than 50 per cent. At that time the levels of vehicle ownership will exceed 200 per 1,000 inhabitants in most countries.

The extremely rapid progress of road traffic inevitably means thinking in terms of the planning of

Table 14.1 Growth of the Mediterranean countries' motor-vehicle stock, 1970–2025 (000s)[a]

	1970	1980	2000	2025
Spain, France, Italy, Greece	29,360	51,402	73,966	83,077
Yugoslavia, Turkey, Cyprus, Malta, Israel	1,527	4,478	19,992	35,801
Syria, Lebanon, Egypt	366	945	11,580	25,355
Libya, Tunisia, Algeria, Morocco	783	2,250	14,945	30,430
TOTAL	32,036	59,075	120,483	174,663

[a] Average scenario (reference trend T1 or moderate trend T3).

combined transport systems, from sea to land (road and rail) and air, with one underlying concern: taking into account all communication technologies, which in turn provide a decisive impetus for the development of transport networks.

(i) Site coverage and impact of road networks

Outstandingly flexible, road transport ensures door-to-door service and usually requires less investment than other kinds of transport. There is a major north-south imbalance in the Mediterranean road network: in the north networks are comparatively dense and interconnecting, and include a growing motorway network (of the 13,958 km of motorways existing at the beginning of the 1980s, 13,176 were in the three north-western countries—Spain, France, and Italy); in the south and east networks are less developed (serving the major cities in particular), and road connections with neighbouring countries remain inadequate. Road infrastructure requirements in these countries are therefore considerable.

In the mid-1980s, according to the International Road Federation (Table 14.2), the total length of the road network in the Mediterranean basin countries was over 2m. km (all roads included), of which nearly three-quarters lay in the three countries north-west of the basin. Among the countries in the south and east, Turkey was in the lead, followed at some distance by Algeria and Morocco.

Table 14.2 Total length of roads in Mediterranean countries, 1987 (km)

	Length
Spain	318,020
France	804,940
Italy	301,580
Malta	40
Monaco	50
Yugoslavia	119,610
Greece	34,500
Turkey	320,600
Cyprus	11,680
Syria	28,100
Lebanon	7,100
Israel	4,950
Egypt	32,240
Libya	>20,000
Tunisia	27,370
Algeria	72,100
Morocco	59,200
TOTAL MEDITERRANEAN	2,162,000

Source: International Road Federation.

The Egyptian network seems rather small, but this is partly due to the very idiosyncratic geography of the country.

The scenarios have adopted the growth of the Mediterranean road network in the light of the economic development hypotheses and assumed physical planning policies. Growth in the countries north of the basin, and especially in the three north-western countries, would be comparatively weak, rising from 1.6m. km at the beginning of the 1980s to 1.7m. or a maximum of 1.9m. km in 2025. The latter figure in fact corresponds to the integration alternative scenario A2, in which the hypothesis of a population increase in the countries to the north of the basin was explored.

The growth of road networks in the countries south and east of the basin is comparatively much higher, since the total length could be multiplied by a factor of 3.2 and even a maximum of 4.3 in 2025 compared with the beginning of the 1980s. The maximum for the countries south and east of the basin would be close to 2m. km in the reference trend and moderate trend scenarios (T1 and T3), about 11 per cent longer than the road network in the northern countries (although the per capita kilometre density would still remain lower). The alternative scenarios attribute slightly lower figures to the countries south and east of the basin in 2025, partly because of the better spatial organization assumed in these scenarios. These increases may seem very large, but it should be stressed that road transport is likely to be the main beneficiary of economic and social development, as rail network development depends on the growth of weight cargo and the choice of strategies as regards means of transport.

Since these estimates include all roads (secondary, national, main, motorways), it is more difficult to calculate site coverage. Experts have suggested using an average width of 20 m (including verges and considering, for example, that a six-lane motorway is 100 m wide). Table 14.3 summarizes the results of the scenarios for the length of networks and their site coverage. According to the scenarios, these will amount to between 63,000 and 75,000 km^2 in 2025 for the countries of the Mediterranean basin as a whole (the equivalent of the combined surface area of virtually all the large Mediterranean islands). Between 10,000 and 20,000 km^2 could be located in the Mediterranean regions as such.

The major impacts of this kind of road network on the environment (usually difficult to quantify) are:

Table 14.3 Total length and surface area of Mediterranean roads (scenarios)

Scenario	Length (000 km)		Surface area (km²)	
	2000	2025	2000	2025
T1				
N	1,668	1,703	33.360	34.060
S	902	1,974	18.040	39.480
TOTAL	2,570	3,677	51.400	73,540
T2				
N	1,668	1,703	33.360	34.060
S	939	1,457	18.780	29.140
TOTAL	2,607	3,160	52.140	63,200
T3				
N	1,708	1,768	34.160	35.360
S	1,352	1,974	27.040	39.480
TOTAL	3,060	3,742	62.500	74,840
A1				
N	1,708	1,768	34.160	35.360
S	1,305	1,812	26.100	36.240
TOTAL	3,013	3,580	60.260	71,600
A2				
N	1,754	1,929	35.080	38.580
S	1,305	1,812	26.100	36.240
TOTAL	3,059	3,741	61.180	74,820

Key: N = north; S = south and east (including Turkey).

- pollution of surface water and ground water from run-off (hydrocarbons, used oil, etc.);
- the alteration of water systems during road construction;
- competitive use of land, especially in densely populated areas, and the effects of degradation and of dividing up districts, agricultural land, and wild-life and plant-life habitats (motorway layout sometimes expropriates the best agricultural lands in the region—e.g. the A8 motorway in the Var, France);
- the extraction of road-building material;
- abandoned dumps, demolition materials, and road-work waste (especially from motorways);
- the risk of structural defects appearing in old or worn road infrastructure;
- noise, even more of a problem when roads run through urban areas.

Generally speaking, the layout of new land routes should be studied more carefully. As agricultural land is limited in the Mediterranean basin it should be treated carefully, and some traffic could be channelled into the hinterland. But above all it is vital to avoid the tracing of roads and motorways in the immediate vicinity of the coast, and in particular to forgo decisively the construction of coast roads in all regions still preserved.

(ii) Emission of pollutants by road transport

The nature and scope of the environmental impact produced by road transport depend on trends in:

- the stock of vehicles in circulation (tourist and commercial vehicles);
- the volume of traffic (assessed in number of kilometres covered per vehicle per year);
- the road network (estimated in length of roads).

Emissions of pollutants by road transport comprise mainly nitrogen oxides, carbon monoxide, poorly burnt hydrocarbons, and particulate matter, all of which involve considerable risks for health and ecological balance (including that of forest and crops). Atmospheric pollutant emissions, particularly nitrogen oxide (NOx) and sulphur dioxide (SO_2) from road traffic, depend on a large number of factors, which can be grouped into three categories:

- the characteristics of the vehicle: type (private vehicle, commercial vehicle), engine capacity, fuel used (petrols, diesel), age, etc.;
- use of the vehicle, in particular mileage on different stretches (built-up areas, roads and motorways in open country, traffic speed);
- the typical emissions of each vehicle expressed in g/km, which depend on the vehicle's characteristics and conditions of use (to simplify, average speed over distance covered can be used as an indicator).

Total pollutant emissions have tended to rise because of the increasing size of the vehicle stock. The only effective way to combat the formation and hence the dispersion and accumulation of photochemical oxidants in urban and rural areas is currently to reduce the combined emissions of hydrocarbons and nitrogen oxides.

With regard to NOx, accurate information is not available everywhere. In France, where total NOx emissions have been stable for fifteen years, the proportion contributed by road transport has nevertheless risen from 49 per cent in 1973 to 70 per cent in 1986—from 8.6m. t of NOx per annum to 11m. t of NOx per annum. About half these emissions come from private petrol-run vehicles; one third is produced by commercial diesel vehicles.

In the case of SO_2 emissions, the share of transport is very low (7.2 per cent) compared with industrial or power-plant boilers, but is growing in comparative terms. Traffic in France emitted 114,000 t of SO_2 in 1986 (compared with 128,000 t in 1980); 90

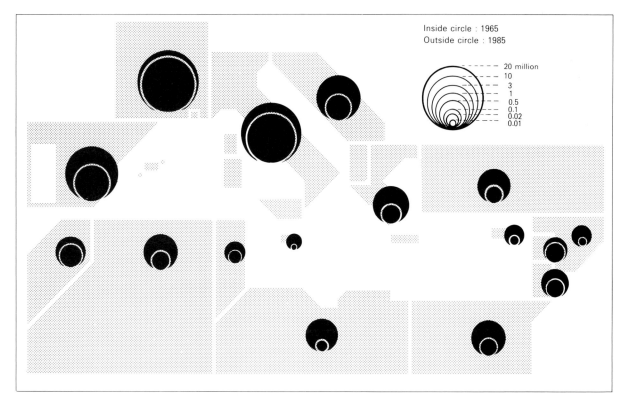

FIG. 14.1 Number of tourist vehicles: Trends 1965–1985
Source: UN.

per cent of these emissions come from diesel vehicles, particularly commercial vehicles, mainly over inter-city stretches.

In Italy, as in France, transport has become the biggest emitter of particulate matter (43 per cent in France, 56 per cent in Italy—69m. t in France in 1986 and 229m. t in Italy in 1984), for a stock of about 20.5m. vehicles in both countries.

It is estimated that 90 per cent of carbon monoxide in the air deriving from human activities comes from the transport sector, especially motor vehicles.

The technological trends of motor vehicles, stemming in particular from the concern to save fuel, have tended recently to favour the direct-injection diesel engine; unfortunately it is considerably more polluting than the petrol engine. Conversely, gas (LPG) propulsion is an interesting innovation.

Chain reactions, in the presence of sunlight, between the nitrogen oxides, hydrocarbons, and oxygen produce photochemical oxidants (or photo-oxidants), defined as compounds with a high oxidizing capacity, among which ozone (O_3) is the most widespread (others include: hydrogen peroxide, peroxyacetylnitrate—PAN, peroxybenzoylnitrate—PBzN, etc.). Photochemical pollution of the atmosphere causes eye irritations (as well as increased vulnerability to infection), the deterioration of plants and materials, and visibility-reducing smog. These photochemical oxidants, about half of which are formed by road traffic in cities or heavily populated industrial zones (high pressure furthers the process), are likely to be transported by the wind over very long distances and accumulate in less populated areas, where they are a threat to the environment: plant life, crops, the forest, etc.

The smog prevailing in some cities and the effects of photo-oxidants (in the Mediterranean these pollutants seem more serious than acid rain) are relatively recent phenomena, and it is difficult to assess all their consequences. In addition there is the nuisance of congestion and the stress caused by traffic, heading towards saturation-point, not to mention the price to be paid in terms of road accidents (if traffic conditions and vehicles in 2025 resemble those today, there will be some 180,000 deaths a year in the Mediterranean coastal countries as a whole).

Table 14.1 indicates that the stock of all vehicles in the Mediterranean countries almost doubled between 1970 and 1980 (from 32m. to 59m.) and would no doubt double again between 1980 and 2000 (to 120m.), to exceed 170m. in 2025. The biggest increase will occur in the countries south and east of the basin, where the vehicle stock could rise from 8.5 per cent of the total in 1980 to more than 47 per cent in 2025.

These figures vary little from one scenario to another because the rate of motorization depends on the level of economic development: lower development levels correspond to slightly larger populations.

If private vehicles alone are considered (83 per cent of the total in 2025), fuel consumption would peak around 2000 then fall (by about 5 per cent) until 2025 because of the slow-down in the growth of the motor-car stock and the reduction in specific consumptions (estimates were made with averages of 8.5 l/100 km in 1980, 6 l/100 km in 2000, and 4 l/100 km in 2025).

In 2000, road transport activities in the Mediterranean basin could release about 3.6m. t of NOx and 8m. t of hydrocarbons, excluding particulate matter (whose composition is often toxic), carbon monoxide, and toxic organic components (mutagens, teratogens, carcinogens) present especially in the urban environment. Emissions could decrease after 2000 either because of technological progress and reduced fuel consumption alone, or because of regulations. In fact, the impact of nitrogen oxides on the quality of air in urban and rural environments was recently proven to be stronger than expected (particularly because of their role in the formation of photo-oxidants).

Expected results from technical advances to improve the energy output of vehicles and from the introduction of unleaded petrol will nevertheless be delayed by:

- lengthening of the useful life of vehicles;
- the time-span (10–12 years) for renewing the vehicle stock.

At the same time the introduction of road management energy policies (speed limits, anti-noise barriers, controls, etc.) would have a more immediate impact on safety and the quality of transport.

(b) Rail

Considering the historical importance of the sea itself and the uneven relief, as well as numerous conflicts (and therefore disruptions) between countries during the past century and a half, rail has not played an important role in the Mediterranean region. Road haulage is a decisive competitor for merchants over short, medium, and even long distances. Air transport, expanding vigorously over the past twenty years, also affects the prospects for rail, although new technologies (high-speed trains) could create the conditions for a renewed vigour in the railways.

The rail network varies from one country to another, denser in the north than in the south (60 km of rail per km² in France and Italy; about 10 km per km² in the south and east), and is generally in decline; small unprofitable lines are being closed down in several places. The state of the network and rolling stock is also very different depending on the country, as is the level of electrification (in the region of 10 per cent in Algeria, 30 per cent in Yugoslavia, 40 per cent in Morocco, and 50 per cent in France and Italy, for example).

Passenger traffic has nevertheless increased between 1970 and 1980; it rose from 112,000m. passengers-km to 138,000m. It grew by 22 per cent in the northern countries (where at the same time the population increased by 6.5 per cent) and by 26 per cent in the southern and eastern countries (a figure virtually identical to that of population growth).

As regards merchandise, the tonnage transported (about 135,000m. t-km) has fallen for the past fifteen years; already in 1975 merchandise traffic accounted for no more than 12 per cent of traffic transported in Spain, 17.7 per cent in France (compared with 40 per cent ten years earlier), and 35 per cent in Yugoslavia.

It seems that no significant quantitative changes can be expected in the future. Nevertheless, some new factors may intervene:

- the development of a European high-speed network, probably towards Spain and northern Italy;
- use of the train for some intercity stretches where the road network is congested or even saturated;
- the connection with Sicily;
- the possible integration of the Maghreb network, resulting from co-operation between the three North African countries (particularly in the integration alternative scenario A2), with a possible extension to Libya (a possible Tunis–Tripoli link has been studied); this linkage, extended as far as Egypt, has moreover already been advocated by the Union of African Railways, established in 1972;
- the possibility of rail links towards Morocco and Algeria if the Gibraltar tunnel or bridge materializes.

Concerning relationships with the environment, the railway system, in tonnage transported or in passenger-km, is the most economical in energy use and the least polluting.

It should be observed, however, that infrastructure development (very inflexible), formerly linking mainly the hinterland and the sea (thus the use of hinterland resources during the colonial period), usually involves coastal plains, already under heavy pressure (intensive agriculture, urbanization, industry, tourism), but where nevertheless rail would contribute to relieving the volume of road traffic and avoiding an increase in saturation-points.

(c) Maritime transport

Sea transport has played a vital role in trade among Mediterranean countries and between them and the rest of the world from time immemorial. In fact, air transport has wrested a growing share of trans-Mediterranean passenger traffic from sea routes only over the past thirty years. Moreover, this traffic has grown to such an extent that the routing of passengers by ship—now mostly car ferries—is still an indispensable supplement to the aeroplane during the summer holiday period.

Overland pipelines, whether those of the Middle East or south-west Europe, also compete with maritime transport by shortening the distances between loading and unloading ports. As regards Mediterranean traffic, however, they have so far tended rather to promote growth, since these ports are located on the Mediterranean Sea. Up to the horizons selected for the Blue Plan, therefore, maritime transport will continue to play an irreplaceable role in the trade of Mediterranean countries, particularly if it involves the routing of weight cargo, large volumes of liquid, and dry merchandise, or even massive passenger traffic during seasonal migrations.

(i) General features of maritime transport in the Mediterranean

Ships passing through the Mediterranean Sea are involved in many kinds of traffic, which fall into three main geographical groups: traffic between coastal states, traffic with its departure- or arrival-point in a coastal country port, and traffic crossing the sea to form a link between the Atlantic, the Black Sea, and the Red Sea—through Gibraltar, the Bosporus, and the Suez Canal—with no commercial port of call. From the economic viewpoint, only the first two categories should normally be considered as Mediterranean traffic as such because they are directly related to the economic activity of the coastal states. The third group, however, cannot be ignored, considering its overall volume and the large proportion of hydrocarbons in its cargo, with its potential pollution hazards.

Mediterranean maritime traffic, by category of merchandise, comprises a very large hydrocarbon tonnage: crude oil, refined products (including liquefied petroleum gas), and liquefied natural gas (recently experiencing competition from the trans-Mediterranean gas pipeline through the strait of Sicily), equal to about half of the 600m. t unloaded in Mediterranean ports. This figure should be compared with that of the volume of world maritime transport, 3,300 m. t in 1985, of which 1,200m. t are oil and derivatives—36 per cent of the total. The share of hydrocarbons in Mediterranean traffic is therefore higher than the world level, especially considering transit traffic.

Another feature of maritime transport in the Mediterranean Sea is the imbalance between the western and eastern parts of the basin. The activity of the north-western countries (Spain, France, and Italy) produces the largest share of traffic in the region as regards tonnages of merchandise loaded and unloaded. In contrast, the economic activity of

---

BOX 14A. **The Suez Canal: some figures**

The Suez Canal was opened in 1869.

Total length (Port Said to Port Tawfiq): 162.5 km.
Depth. 9.5 m (future: 23.5 m).
Capacity of fully loaded ships: 150,000 tdw (planned 250,000 tdw)

| | *1985 traffic* | | |
	North–south	South–north	Total
No. of ships	10,235	9,556	19,791
of which tankers	*1,758*	*1,616*	*3,374*
Goods traffic (1,000 t)	105,695	151,901	257,596
of which oil and oil products	*12,262*	*81,792*	*94,054*

the southern and eastern countries is more modest and maritime traffic in the eastern Mediterranean is more a matter of necessary routeing, including routeing to the ports on the western shores, than of the requirements and resources of the coastal countries, since the oil loaded on their shores comes mostly by pipeline from non-Mediterranean countries.

Despite the importance of national coastal navigation for countries like Italy, Greece, Yugoslavia, Turkey, and even Tunisia, which accounts for about 20 per cent of port traffic for the region as a whole, the active fleet in the Mediterranean is used above all for international links. Nevertheless, it is very difficult to define a 'Mediterranean fleet' because the concepts of a flag, of financial and technical supervision, and of commercial operations do not coincide.

At any time there are in the Mediterranean freighters or passenger ships employed in national coastal navigation, usually under the flag of the country concerned; freighters and ferries maintaining regular lines between Mediterranean countries, usually under the flag of one of them; ships on these lines also serving third countries, some of them under the flag of these countries; tankers, bulk carriers, and tramp freighters, effecting transport to order and coming from or going to one of the coastal countries, that may be under any flag, particularly flags of convenience; and lastly vessels of all kinds and nationalities in transit, which do not stop at ports in the region except possibly to pick up or put down a pilot. The problem is even more complicated because some countries, like France, Spain, Morocco, Egypt, Israel, and Turkey, have several seaboards, and their ships do not necessarily operate out of their port of registry. It should also be noted that the Greek fleet, flying the Greek flag, has world-wide activities which are far from being concentrated in the Mediterranean. This is even more true of ships placed under flags of convenience—Panama and Liberia in particular—by Greek ship-owners, the most important of whom are moreover based in London or New York, while maintaining links with their home country. It should also be noted that some small states in the Mediterranean region have 'opened' their flag to ship-owners who do not have their business headquarters in the country, thus enabling their fleet to reach a tonnage out of proportion with their share of Mediterranean maritime transport.

As at 1 July 1987, according to *Lloyd's Register of Shipping*, all the 10,369 ships navigating under flags of Mediterranean coastal states were equivalent to a fleet drawing 58.3m. gross registered tonnes (GRT), with a lading capacity of a little over 98m. t, 14 per cent of the world total in terms of GRT and number of units, and 15 per cent in terms of lading capacity.

The distribution of this capacity by economic categories of countries was as follows:

- 30 per cent for the countries north-west of the basin: Spain, France, and Italy;
- 55 per cent for Yugoslavia, Greece (representing alone 44 per cent of the total Mediterranean flags), Turkey, and Israel;
- 10 per cent for countries whose flags are very largely 'open': Gibraltar, Malta, Cyprus, and Lebanon;
- 5 per cent for the industrializing countries south and east of the basin: Morocco, Algeria, Tunisia, Libya, Egypt, and Syria.

It can thus be observed that the distribution of transport capacity among Mediterranean flags scarcely corresponds to the different countries' share in the region's maritime trade, a trend which is on the rise—because of difficulties for the more developed countries in continuing to operate ships under their own flags and interest of the less developed countries in financing the expansion of their merchant fleets. This situation has nevertheless disadvantages as regards combating Mediterranean pollution, for the coastal states are in a better position to ensure compliance with regulations when their ports are visited by their own ships.

(ii) Hydrocarbon transport in the Mediterranean

- *Oil and refined products.* Geographically, the Mediterranean is located between the world's largest oil-producing area, the Middle East, and two of the main consuming regions, Western Europe and North America. The main flow of loaded tankers crosses it from east to west starting from the Suez Canal or from Middle Eastern pipeline terminals and heading either towards the Atlantic through the Straits of Gibraltar or towards the north-west ports of the basin, where the large refineries and the pipeline heads feeding central European refineries are located.

Another form of east–west traffic, although much smaller, runs from the Soviet Black Sea ports; this usually involves refined products heading for southern Europe, but also, beyond Gibraltar, to Cuba. In addition, there is transversal traffic: from North Africa, near consumption centres, towards southern Europe and, via Gibraltar, Western Europe, and from the Suez Canal and the east Mediterranean

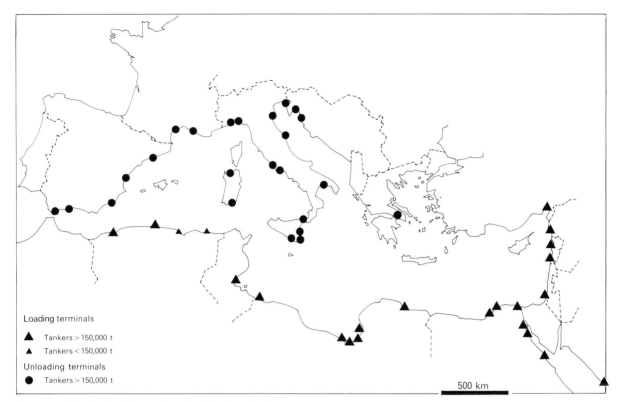

FIG. 14.2 Tanker loading and unloading terminals
Source: Comité Professionel du Pétrole/Blue Plan.

pipeline terminals towards Balkan Europe or the Danube regions, passing through the Bosporus.

Crude-oil traffic is declining considerably compared with the situation at the end of the last decade, before the second 'oil shock'. Globally, nearly 1,500m. t were transported in 1979; in 1985 this figure had decreased to 870m., a drop of 42 per cent. Since then falling oil prices have caused a considerable recovery, and it is estimated that over 960m. t of oil were transported by sea in 1987—still 36 per cent less than in 1979. On the other hand, transport of oil products is much more stable, and rising slightly: nearly 218m. t in 1979, over 300m. in 1987.

The tonnage of oil cargo travelling through the Mediterranean is estimated at about 20 per cent of the world total, whether it is loaded or unloaded there or only in transit. Considering that the surface area of the Mediterranean Sea is only 0.7 per cent of the world's total maritime surface area, this tonnage illustrates the exceptional density of oil traffic in this virtually closed sea, and at the same time the vulnerability of the sea to the pollution and risk that oil transport cannot fail to cause.

It is generally recognized that most of the pollution

ascribable to ships is caused by ballasting in the high seas, and to a much lesser extent by accidents. The MARPOL Convention, which came into force in 1983, has nevertheless had a positive effect on the behaviour of tanker captains in this respect. It is clear that, as regards ships loading or unloading in Mediterranean ports, compliance with the convention will improve as reception facilities for hydrocarbon-laden ballast and tank-flushing water are installed. Nevertheless, 36 out of 52 ports located in 11 Mediterranean countries, reviewed in 1983, did not have the kind of facility required to meet the convention's stipulations. With respect to oil-spills at sea caused by accidents, there were 120 events in the ten years from 1977 to 1986, i.e. between 12 and 13 per annum, according to the Regional Oil Combating Centre (ROCC) in Malta.

The tanker fleet under flags of Mediterranean states comprised, as at 1 July 1987, 946 units, corresponding to 25.5m. GRT. The disproportion between the distribution of tanker tonnage by Mediterranean flag and the relative importance of each country involved in oil import or export in the region is even greater than that for the total fleet:

● The three north-western countries, the main importers, have only 27.8 per cent of the 'Mediterranean' tanker fleet, virtually equivalent to the small countries with 'open' flags, which have 27.5 per cent.

● Yugoslavia, Greece, Turkey, and Israel account for 40.2 per cent, Greece alone for 35.7 per cent, whereas the southern and eastern countries, although mostly exporters, whose fields of action are clearly more global than regional, only have 0.5 per cent.

Trends in the maritime transport of oil and oil products in the Mediterranean up to the Blue Plan horizons will depend on two factors. One is changes in energy consumption and in the role played by oil in meeting these requirements in importing regions located around the Mediterranean or served by maritime routes using it. The other is changes which may occur in oil resources in regions adjacent to the Mediterranean or in major producing zones. These modifications will naturally be affected by oil-price fluctuations.

The scenarios formulated by the Blue Plan do not imply a significant increase in overall oil requirements in the coastal countries of the Mediterranean basin. Nevertheless, comparative stability stems from the contrasting trends envisaged for consumption in the most industrialized northern countries, which would continue to decline, although more slowly than in recent years, and in the southern and eastern countries, which should rise fairly fast. Since the latter are themselves either producers or have Middle Eastern pipeline outlets nearby, this growth in their oil demand should not imply imports by sea, but could gradually reduce their exports towards the northern countries, which would tend to reduce intra-Mediterranean traffic. On the other hand, transit traffic through the Mediterranean, from the Middle East via the Suez Canal and pipelines towards north-west Europe and North America, could increase as North Sea and United States deposits become depleted.

The trend already noted in recent years towards a rise in the proportion of refined products in oil-traffic flows should continue, or even extend. In fact, a geographical redistribution of refining activities is taking place. After having been concentrated in the area of high consumption, refining is now developing close to producing regions, thus resuming initial practices to some extent.

In the future, therefore, a decline is likely in the average tonnage of tankers operating in the Mediterranean, since the optimal size for the trans-port of refined products is under 100,000 t lading capacity, whereas for crude it is close to or may exceed 200,000 t. This will result in an increase in the number of units using the Mediterranean for the same tonnage transported. Impact on the environment is difficult to assess because the risk of accidents at sea should increase in proportion, but spillages will involve lower tonnages. In addition, refined products have a different impact on the environment when spilled as compared to crude oil: they are generally more volatile and more soluble, but also possibly more explosive and/or toxic.

Lastly, the increase in the transport of refined products implies the construction of new ships which would have to meet the stipulations of international conventions. It is to be hoped that they will also be more reliable as regards propulsion, manœuvrability, and navigation, as a result of progress in automation and information technology, leading to the development of 'intelligent ships' which could avoid human errors.

● *Natural gas.* Algeria is one of the world's leading exporters of natural gas, and Libya also has large reserves of this non-polluting energy source. In order to be transported by sea, gas must first be liquefied at the loading port—an expensive operation (expensive likewise in energy)—and ultra-sophisticated ships with very high construction costs have to be used. Over distances not exceeding 3,000 km, underwater gas pipelines which convey methane in its gaseous state are a new and more economical means of transport, successfully introduced by the trans-Mediterranean gas pipeline between Algeria and Italy via Tunisia, the Straits of Sicily, and the Straits of Messina. Pipeline capacity is 12,000m. m³ per year, as compared to Algerian LNG exports by sea, currently approaching 20,000m. m³ per year. The gas pipeline project linking Algeria to Spain and the rest of Western Europe, with an underwater section whose length varies according to the path chosen, is again being reviewed and there is a good chance of it materializing before the end of the century.

The energy scenarios formulated by the Blue Plan envisage a growing role for natural gas at the world level and that of the Mediterranean basin in particular. The trend scenario T3 and the alternative scenarios assume that the transport of gas between producers in the south and possibly the east of the basin and consumers in the north-west will reach such volumes that the construction of new trans-Mediterranean gas pipelines will be inevitable. At the same time, LNG exports should expand towards the United States and perhaps Greece and Turkey.

Aside from the risk of explosion at liquefaction and regasification terminals, LNG transport by sea has few disadvantages for the environment, and the only serious accident recorded so far for a methane tanker—grounding on a rock in the Straits of Gibraltar—has demonstrated the solidity of these ships. This is an important argument for the expansion of LNG maritime transport. In contrast, the alternative often suggested, transforming gas into methanol and loading on ordinary tankers, would be more hazardous for the environment as this product is highly toxic.

(iii) Maritime transport of other merchandise

● *Transport of bulk goods.* After oil and refined products, the main goods transported by sea in volume, if not value, are iron ore, coal, and grain: in 1987 world traffic was estimated at 309m. t, 272m., and 182m. t respectively.

Among the 'major bulk' goods, iron ore and metallurgical coke (included with coals) are unloaded in large quantities in the countries north-west of the Mediterranean basin which have installed huge waterside steel complexes, such as those at Fos or Taranto. The drop in European Community steel consumption and competition from producers outside Europe have caused a drop in the unloading of ore and coke at European ports compared with registered tonnages a decade ago, despite the fact that coastal steel works have suffered less from the crisis than those—often older—established inland.

For the period considered by the Blue Plan, a substantial recovery of steel production in the European Community is unlikely (as seen in Chapter 11); in contrast, some currently industrializing countries south and east of the Mediterranean basin should develop their production considerably, probably by using the direct reduction technique based on natural gas. On this assumption, coke transport towards these countries would not expand; on the other hand, they should start importing iron ore as their domestic resources are insufficient in either quantity or quality.

Rather than metallurgical coke, the bulk of maritime transport in this category of weight cargo is composed of 'steam coal', used mainly for electricity generation. The Blue Plan scenarios imply the vigorous growth of electricity consumption in the countries south and east of the basin, where the production capacities to be created will be mainly thermal. Along with heavy fuel-oil and natural gas, coal will certainly play an important role, especially in countries with insufficient hydrocarbon resources,

a fortiori on the assumption of a considerable rise in oil prices. Coal transport is therefore likely to increase in the Mediterranean.

Since the region has comparatively little coal or high-grade iron ore, weight cargo traffic heading for Mediterranean ports comes from outside the basin: the USSR, the United States, South Africa, and Australia for coal; the west coast of Africa, India, Brazil, and Canada for iron ore. These imports from distant sources are the subject of contracts for high tonnages, which furthers the use of ore-carriers or high-tonnage freighters, most of them in the 'Panamax' category (70,000-t capacity), but some of them with a capacity exceeding 100,000 t, or even 150,000 t, in so far as reception ports have the necessary draught, storage space, and facilities for these large ships and the handling of their cargoes.

As regards grain, the countries on the south and eastern shores of the basin are already major importers, especially Algeria and Egypt. Anticipated population growth in these countries and their limited agricultural resources imply strong growth of these imports up to horizons 2000 and 2025, which will come chiefly from distant sources such as Argentina, the United States and Canada.

Considering the large number of grain-loading points, often located in ports with shallow draughts, grain traffic is broken down into smaller quantities and is usually transported by low-tonnage freighters ranging from a capacity of 20,000–30,000 t, rarely exceeding 50,000 t on average. Small tramp cargo boats are also used. In future, average tonnage should rise moderately.

Many other 'dry' goods are transported by sea in bulk: various ores, among which phosphates, bauxite, and manganese are the most important in terms of volume; natural or agricultural products such as wood, soya, and various oil-seeds; and, lastly, finished and semi-finished industrial products, such as cement and clinker, crushed or powdered chemicals, fertilizers, oil-cake, and other animal feeds.

'Liquid bulk goods', aside from hydrocarbons, are also transported: chemicals, vegetable oils, molasses, and even fresh water. Aside from the latter, which, exceptionally, has been exported from Provence to southern Spain during recent periods of drought and can be transported in ordinary tankers (well cleaned), these products, because of their physical or chemical characteristics or because they are foodstuffs, must be loaded on to small or medium-sized tankers, barely exceeding 20,000 t capacity, but divided into sections and installed with special equipment for the handling and storage of the liquids transported, either alternately or simultaneously.

All these kinds of transport exist in the Mediterranean, and, although many come from outside it, some originate there, such as phosphates and phosphoric acid exported by Tunisia (those coming from Morocco are loaded at its Atlantic ports), cement manufactured in Greece and Spain, or wines loaded in wine-storage ships leaving from Spanish, French, Italian, and Algerian ports. On the whole, however, the region is more an importer than an exporter of both 'lesser bulk goods' and 'major bulk goods', in order to meet the requirements of the processing industries located mainly north-west of the basin, and the food and animal-feed requirements in the south-eastern countries.

The scenarios formulated by the Blue Plan all envisage the more or less rapid industrialization of these southern and eastern countries. This will result in the growth of their bulk imports of raw materials and semi-finished goods, which will become increasingly varied as their industrial fabric diversifies. A similar phenomenon will occur in the case of the bulk transport of foodstuffs under the growing pressure of the requirements in these counties, which will not only expand globally as a result of population increase, but will also diversify, because of rising standards of living.

Thus, the maritime transport of lesser bulk goods should, like that of major bulk, experience rather strong growth in the Mediterranean up to the Blue Plan horizons, since the stagnation, even decline, in tonnage unloaded in the north-western ports would be amply offset by the increase in that handled by other ports. This will imply the rethinking of port installations in most of the southern and eastern countries, in order to receive and handle a much larger number of bulk carriers, whose size will tend to expand with the increase in traffic.

● *Perishable foodstuffs.* Citrus fruits and other fruit and vegetables exported by the countries south and east of the Mediterranean to Western Europe are generally transported by sea ('fruit' cargo ships installed with ventilated, refrigerated holds), as routeing by air is only justified for a few types of fragile fruit during periods when their value is very high. Because of the bulk break-points and temperature changes between the departure port and the arrival port, a quickly growing portion of perishable foodstuffs is loaded at the production site on to trucks, semi-trailers, or isothermal containers which, after crossing the sea in a ro-ro cargo ship

or container carrier, arrive at the major consumption centres by road. When these 'load units' are used in this way, goods do not need to travel by special ship and can fit into the flow of 'general goods' transported mainly by regular cargo lines.

Fruit and vegetables are currently very important exports in terms of value for some countries like Morocco and Israel, but, as illustrated by the example of Algeria, they may stagnate or decline in the future because of increasing domestic consumption and the limitations that scarce resources of water and arable land impose on production increases.

Few deep-frozen products are currently transported in the Mediterranean, aside from fish caught off the west coast of Africa by Greek and Egyptian deep-sea trawlers. Meat imports by countries south and east of the basin are rather low, but should expand vigorously during the period covered by Blue Plan scenarios, as in the case for other foodstuffs. For ritual reasons, however, cattle is imported on the hoof rather than as refrigerated carcasses and, unless special abattoir chains under the supervision of Muslim and Jewish religious authorities are organized in the exporting countries, it seems likely that this kind of transport will continue and that the large 'floating sheep-folds' which currently transport Australian and New Zealand sheep to the Middle East will also ply the Mediterranean.

● *General merchandise.* Transport in the Mediterranean has, from time immemorial, been characterized by the very broad variety of the goods transported, as proven by the inventories of cargo on recovered wrecks. The very broad category 'general merchandise' or 'miscellaneous' still accounts for the majority of port operations, considering how often cargo boats, usually from regular lines, call into port.

This merchandise is handled in either traditional packaging (bags, bales, drums, and boxes, increasingly placed on pallets), or closed 'load units'— twenty- and forty-foot containers, semi-trailers, and trucks. Three basic kinds of ship correspond to these packaging categories: the traditional shipping line cargo boat with several bridges, equipped with its own lifting mechanism, the compartmentalized container carrier, usually using port gantries, and the ro-ro cargo vessel with horizontal boarding for vehicles or semi-trailers (which also takes containers). There are also combined ships: polyvalent cargo boats and ro-ro container carriers.

Although one of the world's main container carrier routes, the one linking north-west Europe to Asia and Oceania, crosses the Mediterranean over its broadest width, between the strait of Gibraltar and the Suez Canal, the penetration of containers into Mediterranean traffic as such has been comparatively slow; of the 56m. 'twenty-foot equivalent' units transported by sea throughout the world in 1985, only 8 per cent were loaded or unloaded in Mediterranean ports.

In contrast, ro-ro cargo boats have gained ground over the past twenty years for intra-Mediterranean links, first of all for north–south connections and more recently for the routes crossing the basin along its length. In 1987, more than 100 regular lines offering ro-ro services crossed the Mediterranean and in particular the Adriatic in every direction.

Prospects for traffic in general merchandise vary greatly depending on the different scenarios formulated by the Blue Plan. A very global approach (which would have to be confirmed by detailed sectoral analyses) indicates, however, that in an initial stage the southern and eastern countries will greatly increase their imports of capital goods and transport equipment, while nevertheless increasing their domestic value added. In a second stage the increase will involve consumer goods and household equipment. In contrast, traffic in general merchandise in the ports north-west of the basin is already very high, and its growth prospects are more limited.

The growth of traffic in general merchandise between coastal countries and with the rest of the world will be accompanied by a growing concern for the productivity of maritime transport, which implies the increasing use of faster handling techniques such as containerization and ro-ro services. In the first case, introduction into ports south and east of the Mediterranean has been slow, sometimes for lack of equipment but especially because of the absence of the organization needed for the rapid flow of these load units in the port hinterland. These shortcomings may be remedied under the pressure of demand for the transport of goods which can be containerized on arrival or which come from industrialized countries outside the basin.

In fact, ro-ro traffic will predominate on intra-Mediterranean links, and although the use of containers will also develop, these units, like trucks and semi-trailers, will mainly be loaded on ro-ro cargo vessels and, outside the tourist season, on passenger ro-ros. As regards the latter, the rise in living standards expected in the countries south and east of the basin will tend to improve the balance of north–south tourist flows.

The expected increase in the number of cargo and passenger ro-ro vessels operating in the Mediterranean presents a special problem as regards hazards for the marine environment. In fact the expected growth in the transport of chemicals will be accompanied by a diversification in uses and destinations, which will inevitably increase the load borne by these ships of drums and road-tanks, whose contents are often highly toxic and sometimes poorly identified. And yet, because of their structure, with little transversal compartmentalization, ro-ro vessels are particularly prone to capsizing and sinking after a collision, grounding, or even the shifting of poorly stowed cargo in a very high sea.

Care should therefore be taken to ensure that these loads, hazardous for the marine environment, are, as far as possible, transported on other kinds of ship which are less unstable after a mishap. There is no possibility of excluding all these goods from ro-ro freight flows, but it should be rigorously ensured that in future these goods are loaded only on ships (yet to be constructed) which will meet the new international safety regulations currently in preparation—much stricter as regards the stability and floatability of drive-on, drive-off vessels than those hitherto applied.

(iv) Hazards for the marine environment

The expected development of maritime traffic in the Mediterranean implies, as has just been mentioned for ro-ro freighters, the tightening up of regulations on ship safety and pollution control, and also closer supervision of international regulations by port authorities and national navies, which are generally competent to organize monitoring in the high seas. Those responsible for maritime traffic, ship-owners and ship captains, should observe an increasingly strict discipline, especially those operating under flags of convenience from small countries which hardly have the means to supervise the application of international conventions.

It is currently estimated that more than 200,000 commercial vessels over 100 GRT cross the Mediterranean each year. At any moment there are about 2,000 of these ships at sea, of which 250–300 are oil tankers. This figure should grow considerably in the future, despite the trend towards increasing the tonnage of vessels, which accompanies the rising volume of traffic.

Traffic is already very heavy in some areas near major ports or near some obligatory crossing-points, such as straits or the Suez Canal. Fortunately, navigating conditions are usually easier than in other parts of the world because of the reliability of maps and marine signalling, weak tides and currents, and good visibility most of the time. Nevertheless, modern monitoring and assistance systems should be improved and the concerted efforts of coastal countries in this respect are increasingly required, especially since the transport of hazardous materials and of passengers is expected to increase during the period covered by the Blue Plan. The current frequency of 'events at sea' is about sixty a year, and they are most frequent near the Straits of Gibraltar and the Dardanelles, as well as in the waters east and south of Greece.

(d) Air transport

For the past twenty years air transport has considerably changed the geography of the Mediterranean basin. Distances have been shortened to the extreme; it used to take about three months to sail across the Mediterranean from east to west, nine days in a steam-ship a century ago; today the journey lasts four hours over the longest distance.

The existing rigidities of the air network, which still oblige passengers to transit through off-centre gateways such as Madrid, Paris, Belgrade, Frankfurt, Geneva, or Zurich, will gradually disappear and an intra-Mediterranean mesh will be formed, with many more direct links.

Currently, transport through the large airports is a reflection of the major agglomerations. In the coastal regions, Barcelona, Marseilles, Nice, Rome, Athens, Istanbul, Tel Aviv, Cairo, Algiers are all operational. And already the geography of airports is revealing other hubs—Malaga, Alicante, Palma and Ibiza, Corfu, Monastir, etc.—whose future is linked to tourism. Recreational aerodromes are opening up some regions. On the whole, accessibility is good, which explains, for example, why the hydroplane could not find its niche in the Mediterranean, even for low-capacity transport.

Freight, which still represents only one-tenth of the tonnage transported, is growing and is a considerable resource for airports. It is linked only partly to tourism; in one direction it involves the transport of high-value manufactured goods (electronic materials etc.), and, in the other, the transport of agricultural produce able to bear the cost of transport (early fruit and vegetables). Air transport in the Mediterranean, however, at present involves essentially passengers—professional people,

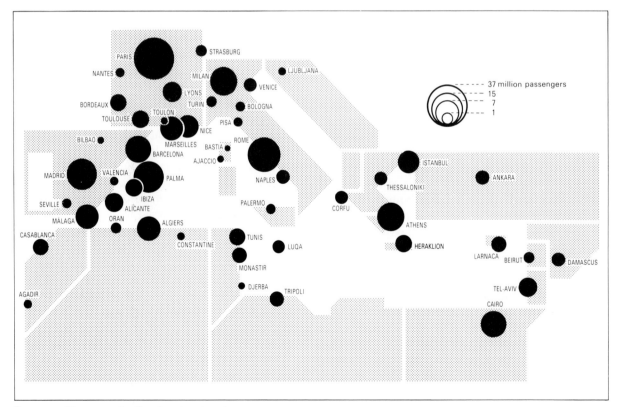

FIG. 14.3 Passenger traffic at main airports
Source: International Civil Airport Association (1984–87).

migrants, but above all tourists: the aeroplane is the way in for about 25 per cent of tourists. Naturally, this figure varies from one country to another, as seen in Chapter 13, but on the whole it is likely that the level will rise considerably during the next decade.

In addition to technological changes which will not fail to affect aviation (speed, safety, consumption, etc.), prospects for intra-Mediterranean air transport will no doubt be closely linked to relations among coastal countries and, in particular, to the growth of tourism. The annual average growth of air-traffic flows for the period 1985–2000 in an average scenario (T1) would be 4 per cent for the countries on the northern shore and 6 per cent for those on the southern and eastern shores.

The frequency of flights and the expansion of networks will lead to a growth in the size of fleets and the enlargement of many airports on the southern and eastern shores, as well as the creation of new airports, mainly at the regional level. The development of 'third level networks' will become necessary as a result of the strengthening of regionalization policies and interregional relations, considerable in the countries north of the basin in

all the scenarios—except perhaps for worst trend scenario T2—and in the southern countries in moderate trend scenario T3 and the alternative scenarios. But small airports will necessarily have to be profitable, since their activities rely on the economic dynamism of the region they serve.

The expansion of international tourism will require the development of gateways for long-range carriers. But as regards the growth of intra-European and intra-Mediterranean traffic (mid-range carriers):

● Either traffic-flows are or will be sufficiently large to justify the use of mid-range carriers, with direct flights; this will be the case of the main departure- or arrival-points for international tourism in the region. The growth of flows could be stabilized in the high season (staggering of holidays over several months is foreseen in the alternative scenarios, which will help to decongest airports and air corridors while ensuring increased cost-effectiveness of equipment).

● Or else traffic-flows are lower. Their services will operate via connection turntables and/or direct links, but in this case lines using smaller aeroplanes could not offer very attractive services (a rather high cost per seat, despite expected improvement). This

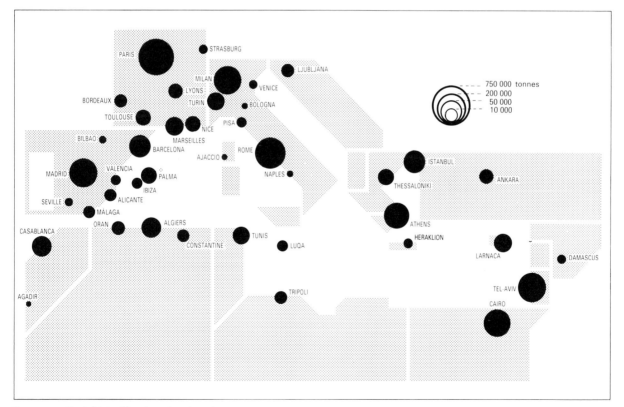

FIG. 14.4 Freight traffic at main airports
Source: International Civil Airport Association (1984–87).

situation corresponds more to the 'business' links which would develop with interregional relations.

Interactions between air transport and the environment concern both airports and aeroplanes. For airports, the problem of site coverage should be noted: the extension of existing congested airports (already started in Cairo) and also the establishment of new local or regional airports are to be expected (perspective studies will no doubt involve some major tourist sites, but the construction of new airports will be limited). Many airports have been built on the edge of the sea because of land use in coastal areas and efforts to avoid low-altitude flights over urban areas. It is to be hoped that precautions will be taken in the future to avoid some kinds of land-fill which destroy shallow waters or valuable wetlands.

Noise is inevitable around airports, but the outlook for this nuisance will largely depend on the continuation of the substantial progress already achieved for new aeroplanes (over the last fifteen years in particular). It will also and above all depend on the strategies and application of measures enacted by the land authorities; in order to counteract the speculative growth of housing, these authorities could envisage the development of economic zones linked to air transport and its activities.

The likelihood of congestion of air corridors and airports must also be tackled. This is already occurring as a result of the unexpected speed with which air traffic has expanded, and may grow worse during the few years needed to introduce corrective measures if this rapid growth continues.

In the next ten years a fleet of aeroplanes with a much larger capacity (over 400 passengers) may be introduced, involving the heavily used major airports or furthering high-density tourist routes. The trend will be towards reduced fuel consumption. For a more distant future, there is also, even now, the question of alternatives, such as engines running on liquid hydrogen. But in the medium term one of the major 'wastage' problems to be solved (waste of time, resources, and the quality of life) will be that of air congestion around certain airports.

3. Issues for appraisal

One of the first issues concerns trends in the distribution of various means of transport during the coming decades. Although the future of maritime transport seems to be fairly well delimited, it is much more open-ended for road and air transport, and 'unexpected eventualities' cannot be excluded for rail (high-speed trains, even ultra-high-speed trains). The 'energy consumption' factor, significant in the 1970s, has seen its importance reduced after the 'counter-oil-shock' of 1986, but what will be the case in ten or twenty years' time, when global energy consumption will have grown, transport will have increased everywhere, some energy sources will start to become scarce, and the greenhouse effect will have to be taken into account? Consumption efficiency is certainly rising along with technological advance, but increased speed always has to be paid for in energy. And the 'fuels of the future' which are sometimes mentioned—methanol, hydrogen, even electricity—are only derived energies which have to be produced, often with fairly low overall output, from available primary energies.

Will road transport in fact continue to grow, whether for goods delivered door to door, over distances exceeding thousands of kilometres, or for private transport, swollen by the growth of leisure time, the dividing up of holiday periods, the dispersion of housing, etc.? The countries of southern Europe, despite the congestion and pollution of cities (described in the case of Athens, for example, as a major ecological disaster) and the heavy and constant cost in human lives, continue to encourage their motor-vehicle industry, gradually followed by all the countries. And despite often considerable financial efforts, infrastructure (including parking possibilities in cities) cannot keep pace with traffic growth, a fortiori in the Mediterranean region with its compartmentalization, growing scarcity of space in coastal regions, etc. Will this lead to a segregation of traffic in time and/or space between trucks and private vehicles?

How will air transport face up to the growth in traffic observed over the last few years and more specifically the charter traffic partly responsible for the congestion experienced in 1988? Will it be through an increase in aircraft capacity, equivalent to promoting certain already overburdened routes to the detriment of a regionalization of traffic?

Lastly, modern telecommunications can in principle avoid some travelling for business or other reasons. Telecommunications in the Mediterranean basin are predominantly north–north links—north–south are weaker—reflecting to some extent economic ties. To what point, one may ask, will the foreseeable development of telecommunications in the coming years, with the widespread use of numerical transmission and the development of an entire optical-fibre cable network, affect travelling?

It is clear that the interactions between transport and the environment are complex. The problems of pollution (chemical and noise) are sometimes tackled through technological progress, but also through the application (sometimes difficult or poorly accepted) of now well-known technical solutions or through regulations which are only worth as much as the awareness of their target population or the supervisory capacity of their authors. Perhaps less attention has been devoted to the problems of site coverage and the location of infrastructure, an issue which would have to be tackled in the general context of national physical planning, especially for countries in which this kind of infrastructure will develop most vigorously.

These questions highlight the growing need for national and international co-operation on means of transport, which incidently raises the question— mentioned in the first section—of the location of decision-making centres in the ever-growing field of travel.

15 Urbanization

Cities have played a fundamental role in the history of the Mediterranean region. With their different functions they have, for more than two thousand years, foreshadowed an early form of urban network which is today an increasingly pronounced geographical characteristic of world urbanization. Places for exchange, sources of cultural identity, and shaping forces in the development of civilizations, the Mediterranean cities were formerly built on a scale commensurate with direct community life. Building materials and techniques determined the configuration of the buildings within the limits of a setting itself determined by the relief. Social and economic bonds were firmly established over long periods of time.

Although their societal and economic role is just as great today—and some 80 per cent of Mediterraneans will live in them within one generation, compared with only 40 per cent half a century ago—their size and configuration have turned them into conurbations, regulated in varying degrees. More than 200 million Mediterraneans are now concerned by the management of urban sprawl and the balance of urban life. Environmental problems, inevitable with the increasingly artificial nature of the urban framework, are more marked at the city gates in areas affected by 'suburbanization', but also in the very centre of cities, where congestion is frequent. Many Mediterranean cities are sick on account of problems arising from their size or their growth.

Without going into all the issues bound up with urbanization, the work done under the Blue Plan has been concerned with identifying some of the trends concerning the relations between growth and environment. They will be outlined here, taking into account the fact that the future will, it is true, depend on changes in size and scale or systems of growth, but just as much on the way in which city authorities will ensure that urbanization is kept under control and on the extent to which they will succeed. The stakes will be particularly high as regards the environment and the quality of life in coastal regions, which are increasingly becoming focal points of accelerated urbanization.

1. A look at the recent past: 1950–1988

The countries south and east of the Mediterranean basin have, since the mid-twentieth century, been characterized not so much by an evolution as by a real 'urban explosion': not only on account of the number of city-dwellers, but also because of the greater density of urban housing, peri-urban sprawl, the transformation of ways of life and consumer patterns, the daily scale of the commuting made necessary between the home and the place of work, and the nuisances of traffic jams and pollution. These developments have already generated numerous imbalances: excessive water consumption, wastage of agricultural land, congestion, disorganized building construction, ugly suburbs, and so forth.

(a) Urban dynamics

Between 1950 and 1985 the number of people in the world living in cities increased by 2.7 times, and it is reckoned that by the end of the century half the world's population will be so concentrated—78 per cent in the most industrialized countries and 40 per cent in the developing ones. In all the countries of the Mediterranean basin, out of a total population of 356m. in 1985, the urban population represented about 207m.—58 per cent of the population living in an urban district, compared with 43 per cent in 1950.

In 1950 Spain, France, and Italy together accounted for 70 per cent of the 91m. city-dwellers, and in 1985 still 52 per cent. Whereas the total population of the Mediterranean area increased by 168 per cent between 1950 and 1985, the urban population rose by 227 per cent. In the east and south the rates of urban growth and population growth are interconnected.

Spain, France, and Italy differ from the other countries in the Mediterranean area in regard to both the level of urbanization attained and present rates of urban growth (Greece and Yugoslavia occupy a specific, intermediate position). In order to bring out the contrasts more clearly, the Medi-

Table 15.1 Urban population in the Mediterranean basin, 1950–1980

	% of urban population			No. (m.)			Multiplier[a]	
	1950	1965	1980	1950	1965	1980	1965	1980
Region A	49.8	58.9	66.1	70	95	119	1.36	1.70
Region B	29.6	37.4	44.4	19	36	63	1.89	3.32
Region C	35.0	56.1	67.8	2	4	7	2.00	3.50
TOTAL MEDITERRANEAN COUNTRIES	42.9	50.9	56.8	91	135	189	1.48	2.08

Key: A = Spain, France, Italy, Greece, Yugoslavia; B = Turkey, Syria Egypt, Libya, Tunisia, Algeria, Morocco; C = Monaco, Malta, Albania, Cyprus, Lebanon, Israel.

[a] 1950 = 1.

Source: United Nations/Blue Plan.

terranean countries have been placed in three groups: the north-western countries, the southern and eastern countries, and a few 'intermediate' countries (Table 15.1).

During the period 1950–70 Region A (Spain, France, Italy, Yugoslavia, and Greece) underwent very marked urbanization, starting just after the last war and reaching a maximum in the 1960s; this was the result, first, of the rural exodus and the promotion of certain former rural districts, and secondly, of the natural growth of the population. During the period 1970–85 this trend continued in Spain, Greece, and Yugoslavia but slowed down in France and Italy.

The southern and eastern countries (Region B) comprised a total urban population of 20m. in 1950, representing some 30 per cent of the urban population of the Mediterranean area. In 1985 this population rose to 75m. (an increase of 275 per cent) and the rate of urbanization attained 47 per cent. This marked expansion of the urban population in the southern and eastern countries was caused by total population growth (multiplied by 2.4 during the period 1950–85) and by the increase in the rural exodus, whose contribution sometimes increased in certain cities to an annual rate of more than 3 per cent (Algiers, Cairo). The number of urban settlements and towns has sharply risen there since the 1960s as a result of the creation of new urban districts and the extension of urban boundaries. But this growth-rate of the urban population in the southern and eastern countries has not been matched by the urban development (development schemes and services) which should have accompanied it, nor by the creation of jobs. In other words, urbanization has preceded industrialization.

Intensive growth has on the whole occurred on existing sites. There have been very few 'new towns', and these have taken the form of deliberate extensions (Fos near Marseilles or development units in Israel) or of tourist developments (Costa Brava in Spain, Dalmatian coast in Yugoslavia, Languedoc-Roussillon in France). The essential part of the growth has been concentrated on existing cities, born of a combination of historical and geographical factors. Large-scale work has been carried out to allow for the growth of existing cities and to overcome handicaps (e.g. in respect of water resources), but even when earthquakes have occurred cities have been rebuilt on former sites.

The unequal evolution of the countries of the north and those of the south and east has been compounded by differences in economic (and urban) development between the various regions in each country, highlighting a certain type of special extension of urbanization around a particularly favoured urban axis (Istanbul-İzmir), often following a coastline (Casablanca—Rabat, the Tunisian Sahel, the region of Alexandria), or around a capital (Athens, Cairo, Algiers, Tunis). There is an increasing concentration of towns along the Mediterranean coast, with many conurbations in the north-west, from Barcelona to Genoa.

(b) The size of cities

Where size and urban functions are concerned, the situation in the countries of the north-west (Spain, Italy, France) contrasts, by the organization, scale, and diversity of the functions of the cities (industrial cities, ports, tourist centres, university towns, etc.), with the rest of the Mediterranean area. In those countries there is a relatively large number of regional capitals and small and medium-sized towns; there are about 130 cities with a population higher than 50,000 in Spain, and 100 in France—a density of 2–4 cities per 10,000 km².

In the south and east, the settlement pattern

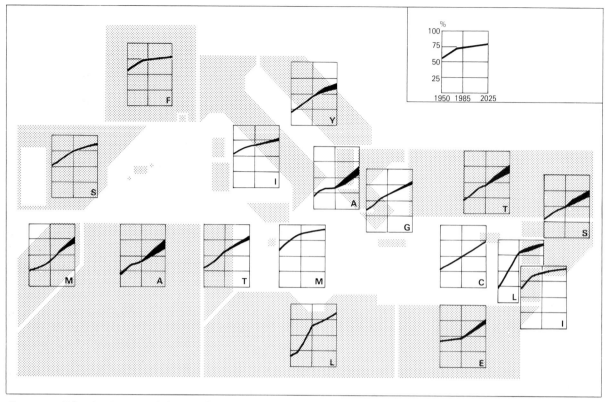

FIG. 15.1 Urbanization rates (%): Trends 1950–1985 and extreme scenarios 1985–2025
Source: Blue Plan.

reveals a relatively marked imbalance under the combined effect of the lesser relative importance of big cities and the presence of a capital, clearly separated from the other conurbations. Often between 30 per cent and 60 per cent of urban employment is concentrated in the capital, and the sphere of its economic influence extends over practically the whole of the territory. The other cities have a very limited area of influence. It may usefully be recalled that an unbalanced settlement pattern cannot but reflect very deep-seated structural imbalances. A strong movement in the direction of concentration aggravates the problems of urban development and weakens the locomotive effect on productive economic activities; it accentuates the disparity in the distribution of populations both between rural and urban regions and between different districts in the same city.

As for small and medium-sized towns, their number has greatly increased under the effect of administrative decentralization, which has been in progress since the 1960s in the inland regions, and new communication facilities. The distribution by size of those towns, according to their relative importance, confirms this situation.

A comparative analysis of the rate at which cities grow according to their size, at the national level, reveals that in a fair number of countries in the past few years it has been the medium-sized cities that have expanded most rapidly; in regions where population growth is slowing down, the population of certain big cities has decreased in size. If population movements are observed at district level, it is seen that the centres of the biggest cities tend to remain stable (Istanbul, Cairo, Tunis) or to suffer demographic decline (Rome, Marseilles) on account of a movement towards outlying residential areas and suburbs and peri-urban areas.

The development of increasingly rapid means of transport and of telecommunication media has largely contributed to the mobility of firms and industries that were formerly centralized in a small number of capitals or big cities. Higher standards of living and the demand for individual housing, the attraction of more open spaces and leisure facilities, and the recent decentralization of distribution services (supermarkets) have accelerated the movement away from towns and towards suburbs, particularly in the north-west.

Over the past decade, France and Italy have been

BOX 15A. Definitions of urban population	
	Definitions supplied by National Statistics Offices
Region A	
Spain	Localities of 10,000 inhabitants or more. Municipalities of 2,000 inhabitants or more.
France	Districts including an agglomeration of more than 200 inhabitants living in adjacent dwellings or not more than 200 m distant from one another, and districts where the majority of the population lives in a multicommunity agglomeration of this type.
Italy	Districts of 10,000 inhabitants or more.
Greece	Population living in municipalities and districts of over 100,000 inhabitants, including the 12 urban centres: Greater Athens, Greater Thessaloniki, etc.
Yugoslavia	Localities of 15,000 inhabitants or more; localities of 5,000–14,999 inhabitants with less than 30 per cent active in agriculture; localities of 3,000–4,999 inhabitants with less than 70 per cent active in agriculture; localities of 2,000–2,999 inhabitants with less than 80 per cent active in agriculture.
Region C	
Monaco	Total population of the district of Monaco.
Malta	Urban centre of Valetta.
Albania	Towns and other industrial centres of over 400 inhabitants.
Cyprus	Six district towns and suburbs of Nicosia.
Lebanon	Localities of 5,000 inhabitants or more.
Israel	All settlements of over 2,000 inhabitants excepting those where at least one third of the heads of household belong to the active civil population living off agriculture.
Region B	
Turkey	Population of localities situated within the municipal boundaries of the chief towns of the provinces and districts, including the centre of Istanbul.
Syria	Towns, district centres (*mohafaza*) and subdistrict centres (*mantika*).
Egypt	Chief towns of the governorates of Greater Cairo, Alexandria, Port Said, Ismailia, Suez; chief towns of frontier governorates; other chief towns of governorates and chief towns of districts (*markaz*).
Libya	Total population of Tripoli and Benghazi and urban sections of Beida and Derna.
Tunisia	Population living in districts, including the district of Tunis.
Algeria	All districts with a town, a rural town, or an urban agglomeration as chief town, including Greater Algiers.
Morocco	Population living in municipalities, autonomous centres, and other centres, including Greater Casablanca.

(i) The role of migrations

Large-scale migratory movements have occurred within the Mediterranean countries, reflected generally in urbanization, accompanied by a switch on the part of those actively involved in the agricultural sector to industry and to certain tertiary activities. These large-scale population movements, which started in the northern countries in the nineteenth century, gradually spread to the countries south and east of the Mediterranean, especially after the Second World War.

Population trends in Marseilles and Istanbul, for instance, clearly illustrate the dynamics of the major phases of these migrations. The population of Marseilles has increased sixfold in 150 years (from 111,000 inhabitants in 1801 to 640,000 in 1946). Likewise, Istanbul, starting with a population of 860,000 in 1945, attained 5,500,000 in 1985, which is more than six times as high.

In Mediterranean Morocco the attraction of the province of Tangiers (a major pole of industry and tourism) results in a positive overall migration balance for the rural area of nearly 16,000 between 1975 and 1982, whereas the other provinces show a deficit: Tetouan (−19,000), Chefchaouen (−12,400), Al Hoceima (−18,000), Nador (−19,000), and Oujda (−19,700). But even though the migration balances for these regions are negative, the fact remains that, from one census to another, the total population continues to progress as a result of natural growth. The majority of the migrants go off to the cities situated along the Casablanca–Fez urban axis.

In Tunisia the migratory component of the governorates of the district of Tunis and the north-west observed between 1979 and 1984, showing a surplus in Tunis (+8,000) and a deficit in the north-west (−6,400), represents more than a quarter of the natural growth of each of those regions, or respectively +27 per cent and −26 per cent.

The nature and scale of migratory movements have an obvious bearing on the spatial distribution of human beings and activities throughout the Mediterranean countries. The most spectacular population movements, by virtue both of their magnitude and of the economic and social problems generated by the urban growth to which they give rise, are those that start in rural areas and go towards urban areas. These movements seem to result at present more from the unequal development of different regions, changes in agriculture, and the inadequacy or indeed the absence of a non-agricultural rural economy than from the job op-portunities effectively offered by the urban labour market.

As for migratory movements towards foreign countries, apart from their effects on population levels and structures, the substantial income (deriving from the remittance of earnings by emigrant workers) received by a number of labour-exporting Mediterranean countries, mainly south and east of the basin, has profound implications for the rapid development of urbanization.

In the north the increase in urbanization indicators stems chiefly from immigration, whereas in the south and east the absolute increase in the urban population is largely due to explosive population growth.

(ii) Technological development

Economic transformations, especially economies of scale due to the concentration of production units and populations, largely explain the changes that have occurred in the Mediterranean cities within the space of a generation. However, technological changes play a central role in these developments. Some changes concern the economic function itself, and others are to do with urban forms or the context of the city.

The former category includes the new distribution and communication technologies. The first of these, connected with the rise of the motor car, lead to changes in trade (supermarkets in the suburbs), especially in the north-west; and the second, which announce a 'communication society', lead through computer technology and its offshoots to the emergence of a sector where, in some countries, the creation of jobs already exceeds industrial creations. Distribution and communication are the two growth-vectors of the 'tertiary' or 'quaternary' sector, whose development—even in countries where it is modest—is leaving the industrial sector far behind.

The new technologies do not merely have relations with urban functions: they transform cities in a variety of ways. Motor cars completely alter streets, which are so important in ancient Mediterranean cities, and the change is not for the better. Although the introduction of pedestrian precincts provides a means of to some extent withstanding the invasion of motor cars in the centre of towns and 'medinas', their impact is considerable in the case of city extensions, which involve considerable site coverage and destroy the landscape. New public transport technologies have for their part hardly progressed, and the experimental forms they might assume have remained in the experimental state for thirty or forty years.

Building techniques and materials have progressed considerably. As a result, construction work is carried out faster, urban centres can be renewed (for better and for worse), buildings mount ever higher, and areas can now be urbanized which previously could not be owing to the relief. But cities do not change in twenty years! Their physiognomy remains marked by their history and by their infrastructures: the water supply and sanitation systems are usually fifty or a hundred years old.

(iii) Land-use planning policies

Two types of policies have affected urban growth and especially the geographical distribution of cities. The first concerns the improvement of housing and what are called 'urban amenities'. Even though the factors contributing to the qualitative attraction of a city are not easily discerned, it has to be noted that some cities attract more than others. Mention may again be made in this connection of the attraction exercised by the cities on the coast; but the main point to be noted is the supply of accommodation and the quality of the buildings. Obviously no comparison can be made here between the various countries and there is a great gap in this respect between the north and the south.

In the countries north of the basin, at the quantitative level, the efforts made to improve the situation have on the whole been effective and most of the population are provided with decent accommodation and associated facilities. On the other hand, the measures taken to limit the growth of cities have seldom been successful, and the creation of new towns as a means of better distributing the population or in order to establish counter-magnets has been only partially successful.

In the countries of the south and east the population explosion and the rural exodus have led to an increasing number of people being crowded into the metropolises. Mass migration has overloaded the urban housing market, the labour market, and all the public services. This has brought in its wake a segmentation and a sort of loosening of the urban fabric, and has militated massively against economic and social development. On the whole, legal measures in the public or private sector have never been sufficient to cope with the demand. In addition, when private enterprise steps in, the inadequacy of the real-estate market makes for a situation in which it can benefit from a ground rent which rises considerably as urbanization proceeds apace and a well-to-do middle class emerges. The existence of a great variety of institutional means for regulating urban expansion and the efforts to promote subsidized housing have consequently not made it possible to control urban development in the countries of the south and east, as combined needs for such development largely exceed the real financial possibilities of households (housing) and public services (water, roads, sanitation, and transport).

However, while comparisons do not mean much between countries, they do at the national level, at least for those who migrate and are able to choose their residence. The Mediterranean conurbations and cities are therefore faced with a large number of problems, according to the general situation of each country. Thus, in the past twenty years the sudden growth of a number of large metropolises, from Istanbul to Casablanca, has generated fresh difficulties in respect of management and planning. The Cairo authorities, for instance, need to solve by the year 2000 the problems involved in providing housing and facilities for close on 1,000 additional inhabitants daily. The inadequacy of the means available to the countries of the south and the east to cope with their problems of housing and facilities, even minimally, has led to a form of urbanization very difficult to control and to the spread of spontaneous, makeshift, and illegal housing on the outskirts of cities.

The land-use planning policies decided upon at the national level, even when they are particularly strict (as in the cases of Algeria, France, the Italian Mezzogiorno, Yugoslavia, Israel, etc.), have not so far really affected individual choice. An urban policy decided upon at the national level may be able to avail itself of decisive incentives (investment assistance, location of activities, etc.). On the whole, however, it cannot be said that the urban strategy adopted for land-use planning has been sufficiently vigorous, and its practical results have been small in relation to the social and environmental issues involved.

2. Prospective trends in urbanization

In the light of the general framework of the scenarios, the basic hypotheses for the population scenarios and recent trends in urbanization observed in the different Mediterranean countries, a few broad lines for urbanization emerge. To start with, the proportion of the urban population will continue to increase in all countries, with a degressive increase until the attainment of a saturation level varying according to the society (in other words, the urban growth-rate will run counter to the level of urbanization).

This exercise in future studies is not easy for many reasons, relating to the following factors:

● It is difficult to define the urban population, what with thinning out over a given area, the development of outskirts and networks, 'rurbanization', and the introduction of the ways of 'city life' into small and medium-sized towns less and less tied to agriculture.

● The divergence between the population hypotheses has been deliberately left open.

● Little account has been taken of international migrations, which represent increasingly significant movements involving city-dwellers. The magnitude of these movements may attain a balance of 500,000 a year for the whole of the Mediterranean. These migrations, and especially repatriations, have a direct influence on housing construction (in terms of both scale and characteristics).

● There are difficulties with the size of the cities concerned by population movements (here it has been necessary to simplify and to assign the mean growth-rate to average-sized towns).

● There are many questions regarding societal trends.

● The structure of households will influence the types of housing.

● In attitudes towards work, changes in work-rhythms, and the evolution of employment the boundaries are less clearly marked than formerly— as with developments like part-time work and dual societies, whose importance is far more appreciable in the Mediterranean region than in northern Europe (for instance, the informal sector may in some towns be more developed than the formal sector).

● There are major changes in the standard of living—in particular, the use of income for forms of residence different from those of today: second homes often located on the coast, homes for retirement or future retirement, etc.

The results of the combinations of these scenarios are shown in Tables 15.2 and 15.3. It will be seen that overall, at the level of states, the urban population increases from 91m. in 1950 and 207m. in 1985 to 277m. in 2000 and 413m. in 2025 (T$_3$ scenario). Growth will be observed mainly in the southern and eastern regions, whose multiplier in relation to 1980 is shown to be 3.82 compared with 1.24 in the north-west regions. To give an idea of

the tremendous extent of urban growth in the cities of the southern and eastern countries, it can be said that the additional population of those cities will in forty years be equal to the present urban population of cities in the northern and eastern countries (Fig. 15.2)! The rate of urban growth in the southern and eastern regions would thus be some five times higher than that of the European cities at the height of their period of growth.

(a) The case of coastal regions

The evolutions considered up to now concern the entire territory of the countries bordering the Mediterranean. As regards the coastal regions of those countries, defined according to the criterion of territorial administrative units concerning the littoral, it is seen (Table 15.4) that the present urban population of those regions is 82m. and that, depending on the scenario, it will increase to a minimum of 106m. or a maximum of 113m. (T2) in the year 2000, and 155m. or 170m. in the year 2025. Here too, of course, most of the growth will be in the southern and eastern regions. Nothing indicates a future slowing down of the growth of the coastal regions and of the littoral fringe in particular. To what extent can this evolution be halted? All depends on the goal-orientated policy of states.

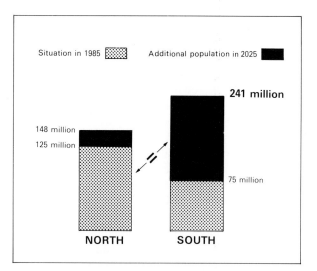

Fig. 15.2 Evolution of urban population, 1985–2025
   Northern countries: Spain to Greece (Region A)
   Southern countries: Morocco to Turkey (Region B)

The additional population foreseen in the cities south and east of the basin in 2025 would be equal to the current population of the cities in the north.
Source: Blue Plan.

Table 15.2 Urbanization rate in the Mediterranean, 1980–2025 (%)

| | Urbanization rate | | Scenarios | | | | | | | | | |
	1980	1985	T1 2000	T1 2025	T2 2000	T2 2025	T3 2000	T3 2025	A1 2000	A1 2025	A2 2000	A2 2025
Region A												
Spain	72.79	75.79	79.97	86.94	80.20	87.56	79.73	86.31	79.73	86.31	79.62	86.01
France	73.23	73.44	75.21	78.17	75.55	79.08	74.87	77.26	74.87	77.26	74.07	75.13
Italy	66.47	67.35	71.06	77.24	71.61	78.71	70.50	75.76	70.50	75.76	69.84	74.00
Greece	57.73	60.12	67.54	79.91	67.84	80.71	67.24	79.10	67.74	79.10	66.66	77.57
Yugoslavia	42.33	46.27	56.74	74.19	57.46	76.11	56.02	72.26	56.02	72.26	54.89	69.26
AVERAGE	66.11	68.31	72.63	80.65	72.63	80.65	71.65	78.39	71.65	78.39	71.36	75.91
Region C												
Monaco	100.00	100.00	100.00	100.00	100.00	100.00	100.00	100.00	100.00	100.00	100.00	100.00
Malta	83.14	85.30	89.35	92.38	89.35	92.38	89.35	92.38	89.35	92.38	89.35	92.38
Albania	33.43	34.05	39.94	58.30	46.50	67.26	39.94	58.30	39.94	58.30	39.94	58.30
Cyprus	46.31	49.47	59.69	73.73	59.69	73.73	59.69	73.73	59.69	73.73	59.69	73.73
Lebanon	74.77	80.08	87.99	91.83	84.56	92.03	87.99	91.83	87.99	91.83	87.99	91.83
Israel	88.58	90.27	93.34	95.58	92.62	96.54	93.34	95.58	93.34	95.58	93.34	95.58
AVERAGE	67.77	70.09	73.94	81.87	75.35	84.97	74.65	81.87	74.65	81.87	75.33	82.27
Region B												
Turkey	43.78	45.92	55.77	72.19	56.67	74.60	54.86	69.77	53.45	66.00	53.45	66.00
Syria	47.43	49.45	58.56	73.74	59.22	75.50	57.89	71.97	56.59	68.50	56.59	68.50
Egypt	44.69	46.37	56.37	73.05	57.21	75.27	55.54	70.83	54.25	67.37	54.25	67.37
Libya	56.62	64.46	72.15	84.96	72.30	85.37	71.99	84.55	71.87	84.22	71.87	84.22
Tunisia	52.32	56.76	65.48	80.02	65.84	80.96	65.13	79.07	64.65	77.81	64.65	77.81
Algeria	41.17	42.63	53.06	70.44	54.22	73.55	51.89	67.33	50.26	62.98	50.26	62.98
Morocco	41.28	44.80	55.85	74.26	57.06	77.50	54.63	71.01	54.17	69.78	54.17	69.78
AVERAGE	44.37	46.58	56.64	73.25	57.45	75.68	56.64	73.25	54.59	67.88	54.59	67.88
TOTAL MEDITERRANEAN COUNTRIES	56.76	61.61	63.95	75.98	64.46	77.58	63.97	75.50	62.91	72.36	62.96	71.88

Table 15.3 Total urban population in the Mediterranean, 1980–2025 (000s)

	1980	1985	Scenarios T1 2000	T1 2025	T2 2000	T2 2025	T3 2000	T3 2025	A1 2000	A1 2025	A2 2000	A2 2025
Region A												
Spain	27,200	29,200	33,500	39,000	33,600	39,300	33,700	39,700	33,700	39,700	34,900	44,500
France	39,300	40,100	41,500	41,100	41,700	41,600	42,800	45,100	42,800	45,100	43,200	47,700
Italy	37,900	38,600	41,100	41,400	41,400	42,200	41,300	43,300	41,300	43,300	42,200	46,800
Greece	5,570	5,940	6,810	7,640	6,840	7,720	7,020	8,530	7,020	8,530	7,190	9,410
Yugoslavia	9,410	10,700	14,000	18,500	14,200	19,000	14,100	19,300	14,100	19,300	14,200	20,100
TOTAL	119,000	125,000	137,000	148,000	138,000	150,000	139,000	156,000	139,000	156,000	142,000	167,000
Region C												
Monaco	26	27	30	36	30	36	30	36	10	36	30	36
Malta	306	327	373	424	373	424	373	424	373	424	373	424
Albania	913	1,040	1,640	3,370	1,910	3,880	1,640	3,370	1,640	3,370	1,700	3,790
Cyprus	291	331	455	665	455	665	455	665	455	665	455	665
Lebanon	2,000	2,140	3,180	4,790	3,060	4,800	3,180	4,790	3,180	4,790	3,370	5,460
Israel	3,440	3,840	4,950	6,560	4,910	6,630	4,950	6,560	4,950	6,650	5,340	7,760
TOTAL	6,980	7,710	10,500	15,800	10,700	16,400	10,600	15,800	10,600	15,800	11,300	18,100
Region B												
Turkey	19,500	22,600	36,400	66,400	38,900	78,400	35,900	64,100	33,300	53,900	33,300	53,900
Syria	4,170	5,190	10,400	23,400	10,800	26,800	10,300	22,900	9,630	19,200	9,630	19,200
Egypt	18,600	21,800	36,000	66,000	37,600	73,200	35,500	64,000	33,700	57,300	33,700	57,300
Libya	1,680	2,320	4,390	9,420	4,510	10,700	4,380	9,380	4,260	8,350	4,260	8,350
Tunisia	3,340	4,020	6,170	10,300	6,470	11,300	6,140	10,200	5,860	9,140	5,860	9,410
Algeria	7,680	9,260	17,700	35,700	18,800	41,600	17,400	34,100	16,200	29,300	16,200	29,300
Morocco	8,000	9,830	16,500	29,800	17,900	34,900	16,100	28,400	15,700	27,300	15,700	27,300
TOTAL	63,000	75,000	128,000	241,000	135,000	277,000	128,000	241,000	119,000	205,000	119,000	205,000
TOTAL MEDITERRANEAN COUNTRIES	189,000	207,000	275,000	405,000	283,000	443,000	277,000	413,000	268,000	377,000	272,000	391,000

Table 15.4 Urban population in coastal areas of the Mediterranean, 1985–2025 (000s)

| | | Scenarios | | | | | | | | | |
	1985	T1 2000	T1 2025	T2 2000	T2 2025	T3 2000	T3 2025	A1 2000	A1 2025	A2 2000	A2 2025
Region A											
Spain	11,177	13,899	16,770	14,230	17,685	13,684	16,277	13,684	16,277	14,023	17,800
France	4,810	5,416	5,606	5,216	5,468	5,564	6,314	5,564	6,314	5,773	7,033
Italy	27,923	29,850	30,429	30,346	31,228	30,149	31,408	30,149	31,408	30,855	34,210
Greece	5,261	6,595	7,391	6,167	7,490	6,781	8,209	6,781	8,209	6,939	9,033
Yugoslavia	1,404	2,069	3,049	2,464	3,560	2,257	3,693	2,257	3,693	2,272	3,743
TOTAL	50,575	57,829	63,245	58,423	65,431	58,435	65,901	58,435	65,901	59,862	71,819
Region C											
Monaco	27	30	36	30	36	30	36	30	36	30	36
Malta	327	373	424	373	424	373	424	373	424	373	424
Albania	1,040	1,640	3,370	1,910	3,880	1,640	3,370	1,640	3,370	1,700	3,790
Cyprus	331	455	665	455	665	455	665	455	665	455	665
Lebanon	2,140	3,180	4,790	3,060	4,800	3,180	4,790	3,180	4,790	3,370	5,460
Israel	3,840	4,950	6,560	4,910	6,630	4,950	6,560	4,950	6,560	5,340	7,760
TOTAL	7,705	10,682	15,845	10,738	16,435	10,628	15,845	10,628	15,845	11,268	18,135
Region B											
Turkey	5,300	8,083	15,858	9,357	18,673	7,816	14,775	7,380	12,996	6,944	11,218
Syria	415	832	2,340	972	2,948	824	2,061	773	1,890	722	1,728
Egypt	5,900	10,406	19,526	11,116	21,960	10,064	18,035	9,579	15,606	9,688	16,511
Libya	1,420	3,045	7,603	3,098	8,678	2,996	6,236	2,950	6,280	2,908	6,329
Tunisia	3,350	5,021	7,870	5,519	9,016	4,752	7,472	4,575	6,920	4,399	6,387
Algeria	5,520	10,000	17,708	11,187	22,162	9,341	16,297	8,560	14,221	7,774	12,145
Morocco	1,515	2,475	4,470	2,740	5,250	2,415	4,260	2,385	4,170	2,355	4,095
TOTAL	23,420	39,862	75,375	43,989	88,687	38,208	69,136	36,202	62,083	34,790	58,413
TOTAL MEDITERRANEAN COUNTRIES	81,700	108,319	154,465	113,150	170,553	107,271	150,882	105,265	143,829	105,920	148,367

The Blue Plan forecasts for the coastal population in the north, and especially in the south and east, indicate more rapid growth than that of the total population in scenario A2 for the northern countries, scarcely faster than that of the total population (or even slower) in scenarios A1 and A2 for the southern countries; they presuppose a strong and deliberate policy aimed at redressing the balance in favour of the inland regions. Similarly, the fact that, in the coastal region of the southern countries, in all the scenarios except one (T2) lower rates of urbanization are forecast than inland (while at present they would appear to be identical or slightly higher) reflects the need to take deliberate measures to reduce the problems of space, public facilities, and the environmental consequences of urban concentration in the coastal regions. The trebling of the coastal urban population of the southern countries envisaged by the Blue Plan, lower than that of the total urban population, presupposes a slowing down of the growth of the very large conurbations (Cairo, Istanbul, Alexandria, Beirut, Algiers, and Tunis) in the regions close to the coast, which would be redirected not to other places on the coast but to the inland towns of those countries.

Taking into account the geography of the littoral

and the scattered housing patterns outside cities, this urban growth of the coastal regions is considerable. It will present serious problems in respect of management and the environment.

(b) Growth according to the size of towns

The distribution of the growth of populations among the large metropolises or conurbations and small and medium-sized towns is of decisive importance: the answers to a number of environmental problems and the development pattern of a certain form of urban life will depend on the way in which this growth takes place according to the size of human settlements. At the financial level, it has been noted that in several countries of the world, when the population exceeds 100,000 inhabitants urban services cost more.

It is not easy to evaluate this distribution as it stems from the continuation of very long-established migration flows, from the importance of 'reservoirs of migrants'—the rural regions in particular—and from the lure of cities, where employment expectations play a significant role. It is also the result of land-use planning policies implemented at the national or regional level in favour of inland cities (the case of Algeria) or medium-sized towns to avoid

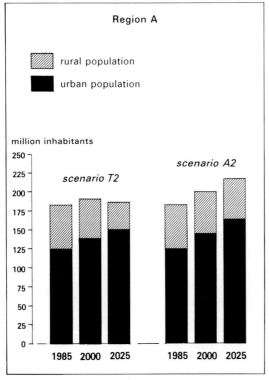

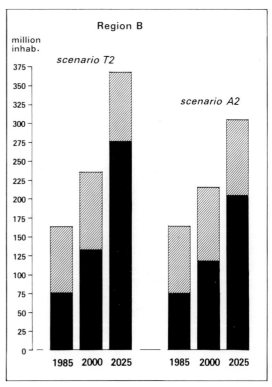

FIG. 15.3 Evolution of the urban population in Regions A and B: Scenarios T2 and A2
Source: Blue Plan.

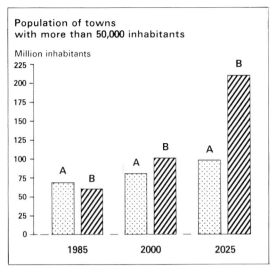

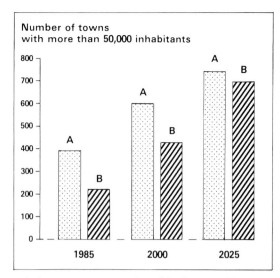

FIG. 15.4 Population and number of towns of more than 50,000 inhabitants in Regions A and B: Scenario T3
Source: Blue Plan.

congestion in the large metropolises, efforts which are not always justly rewarded.

Fig. 15.3 illustrates the extreme evolutions of the scenarios at the 2000 and 2025 horizons, corresponding to the worst trend scenario T2 and to alternative scenario A2. These two scenarios express the different redistributions of urban growth:

- the normative nature of alternative scenario A2, which provides for a balancing of the settlement pattern through:

  a reduction in the population growth of capital cities;

  a strengthening of the role of regional capitals; and

  the promotion of small and medium-sized towns;

- the contrasting 'laissez-faire' character of scenario T2, contributing to concentration around the major conurbations and to imbalances in the urban network.

Overall, the divergence between these two extreme scenarios is observed in all countries, although the factors contributing thereto vary in importance according to the country and major region. Some modulation is seen according to the type of scenario or development: 'megapolises' increasingly difficult to control for the trend scenarios, counter-magnets and promotion of small and medium-sized towns, with improved spatial distribution, for the alternative scenarios.

Figure 15.4 and Table 15.5 show, by way of example, trends in the populations and number of cities of more than 50,000 inhabitants in Regions A and B according to trend scenario T3.

Between the two extreme scenarios (respectively 377m. and 443m. persons living in cities in 2025, as against slightly more than 200m. today), there is a difference of 66m. city-dwellers—about six or seven cities of the size of present-day Cairo. And, naturally, there are also considerable differences according to the scenario in respect of homes provided with drinking water, electricity, infrastructures, and services, i.e. in respect of the quality of life (the black side of which involves a process of pauperization, eventually the creation of shanty towns, etc.).

The additional studies carried out for the development of the scenarios have shown to what extent the efforts made by most of the states south and east of the basin—albeit considerable—remain insufficient in view of the scale and urgency of housing needs. Even in the most optimistic scenario many factors need to be combined to bring about any appreciable improvement in situations in the future.

3. Urbanization and the environment

The continuation of urbanization in the Mediterranean area at the fast rate which appears in all the scenarios suggests a need to be increasingly attentive to the relations between urban development and the environment and to the decisive

Table 15.5 Population trends for towns with more than 50,000 inhabitants

Scenarios	T1			T2			T3			A1 and A2		
	No. of towns	Population (000s)	%ᵃ	No. of towns	Population (000s)	%ᵃ	No. of towns	Population (000s)	%ᵃ	No. of towns	Population (000s)	%ᵃ
Spain												
1985	103	20,743	70	103	20,743	70	103	20,743	70	103	20,743	70
2000	141	25,352	76	136	25,189	75	151	25,381	75	165	26,681	76
2025	172	31,145	80	164	31,036	79	188	31,460	79	214	36,106	81
France												
1985	100	12,919	31	100	12,919	31	100	12,919	31	100	12,919	31
2000	175	17,084	42	151	21,827	53	164	16,026	38	169	16,475	39
2025	157	15,966	39	149	21,555	52	203	18,391	41	233	20,174	43
Italy												
1985	130	21,616	56	130	21,616	56	130	21,616	56	130	21,616	56
2000	172	26,030	63	161	26,990	66	194	24,812	59	206	25,851	61
2025	176	26,402	64	169	28,101	67	229	27,037	63	269	30,469	64
Greece												
1985	8	4,614	78	8	4,614	78	8	4,614	78	8	4,614	78
2000	21	6,023	89	18	5,620	83	23	6,170	88	25	6,302	87
2025	27	6,949	91	23	6,623	86	32	7,808	92	37	8,567	92
Yugoslavia												
1985	38	5,565	53	38	5,565	53	38	5,565	53	38	5,565	53
2000	61	7,907	56	58	8,279	59	65	7,996	56	67	8,006	56
2025	79	10,737	58	74	11,437	60	86	12,300	64	88	12,454	62
TOTAL Region A												
1985	379	65,457		379	65,457		379	65,457		379	65,457	
2000	570	82,396		524	87,905		597	80,385		632	83,315	
2025	611	91,199		579	98,752		738	96,966		841	108,310	

		Towns	Urban pop.	%[a]	Towns	Urban pop.	%[a]	Towns	Urban pop.	%[a]	Towns	Urban pop.	%[a]
Turkey	1985	99	19,339	72	99	19,339	72	99	19,339	72	99	19,339	72
	2000	156	29,482	82	160	31,715	82	156	29,050	81	152	26,723	81
	2025	229	56,826	86	266	68,775	88	232	54,983	87	205	45,131	83
Syria	1985	13	4,100	79	13	4,100	79	13	4,100	79	13	4,100	79
	2000	25	8,458	81	25	8,808	81	26	8,368	81	26	7,544	78
	2025	49	22,274	95	48	25,555	95	51	21,927	95	76	18,375	96
Egypt	1985	38	17,658	81	38	17,658	81	38	17,658	81	38	17,658	81
	2000	85	28,797	80	81	30,312	81	98	29,580	83	92	27,929	82
	2025	112	58,622	88	109	65,750	90	121	57,205	90	116	51,240	90
Libya	1985	3	1,693	73	3	1,693	73	3	1,693	73	3	1,693	73
	2000	7	3,091	70	9	3,159	70	9	3,095	71	8	3,313	78
	2025	16	9,419	95	16	10,701	95	16	9,380	95	9	6,689	96
Tunisia	1985	9	2,131	53	9	2,131	53	9	2,131	53	9	2,131	53
	2000	25	3,455	56	29	3,637	56	26	3,452	56	25	3,272	56
	2025	42	6,708	65	47	7,548	67	42	6,665	65	40	5,973	64
Algeria	1985	24	5,809	63	24	5,809	63	24	5,809	63	24	5,809	63
	2000	55	1,223	68	55	12,818	67	55	12,595	72	54	10,922	67
	2025	137	33,565	94	141	39,326	95	136	32,036	94	135	27,387	93
Morocco	1985	27	7,545	76	27	7,545	76	27	7,545	76	27	7,545	76
	2000	52	13,132	79	53	14,261	79	54	12,756	80	54	12,732	81
	2025	80	25,371	85	83	29,873	86	84	24,116	85	83	23,308	85
TOTAL **Region C**	1985	213	58,475		213	58,475		213	58,475		213	58,475	
	2000	405	87,638		412	104,710		424	98,893		411	92,435	
	2025	665	212,785		710	247,528		682	206,312		664	178,103	

[a] i.e. percentage of the total urban population living in towns of more than 50,000 inhabitants.

factors affecting the way people live in urban settings. These relations will be far from identical from one country or situation to another, and the size of urban settlements will affect the 'design for living', which is more fragile in very big cities than in small and medium-sized towns.

In an attempt to show more clearly the effects of urban growth on the Mediterranean environment, it has been thought useful to examine a few essential factors in respect of environmental impact, namely: land consumption; water (supply and evacuation); waste; air and noise; urban planning and green spaces.

(a) Land consumption

One of the major effects of urbanization on the environment is the taking over of the rural or natural area previously encircling the heart of the city. Urban growth takes place not so much through the densification of existing urban nodes as through the phenomenon of urban sprawl, through spreading in ways that are often uncontrolled, encroaching on agricultural land which is sometimes of vital importance (as in the case of Egypt) or, more frequently, on the coastline itself, already highly coveted for other activities and whose preservation is essential both for the quality of tourism and leisure activities and for ecological reasons.

It is not easy to form a precise idea of the surface area consumed by urbanization. It may be defined as resulting from the urbanization *ex nihilo* of a rural area, from the transformation of an area occupied by rural dwellings, from the extension of the peripheral area of an existing urban settlement, from the filling in of built-up areas within a conurbation, from the utilization of former industrial sites, etc. Urbanized space comprises built-up areas and areas reserved for infrastructures, but also certain non-built-up areas such as cemeteries, sports grounds, parks and green areas, and even, in some cities, peri-urban forests. It also comprises in principle peri-urban agricultural land not being worked pending its reassignment, infrastructures outside the city but closely linked to it, such as airfields, refuse dumps, nearby motorways or bypasses, industrial waste land, etc.

Where they exist, statistics concerning the spatial dynamics of cities are often approximate. For the Mediterranean cities, especially in the southern and eastern countries, data concerning the consumption of space or all collective utilities are few and far between over a long period. Remote sensing is already providing quite precise monitoring, but the data will only be fully useable after a period of ten years, even if all the necessary tools are set up as of now.

The growth of land consumption in the future will result from three factors:

● In the first place there will be larger populations, particularly east and south of the basin.

● Secondly, there is the predicted higher standard of living, including the use of large unit areas for housing proper and community facilities (transport, leisure, social facilities, green areas, etc.). Per capita consumption of space increases as the standard of living goes up, and does so particularly in that the marginal propensity to consume space itself increases with income. This marginal propensity, which is high in the Nordic and Anglo-Saxon countries, is comparatively low in the Mediterranean countries, in both the north and the south.

Available data for the unit consumption of space generally correspond to needs observed in the OECD countries and a few developing countries. These data vary considerably: 40 m² per inhabitant for Cairo (this figure being reduced to less than 20 m² per additional inhabitant), 190 m² per inhabitant for the city of Madrid, and 450 m² for the area of Madrid (as compared with 750 m² per inhabitant for Los Angeles). For prospective studies in the Mediterranean basin, it is often helpful to start from relatively low levels of unit consumption (which may sometimes appear pessimistic) for the countries of the south and the east in order to determine minimal objectives for improving the standard of living. On the basis of these figures, ratios can then be used to ensure the maintenance of a level of health and well-being corresponding to the general level of development of each Mediterranean country.

● The third factor is the varying degree of control through town planning of urban growth and the forms it assumes: where a very strict policy is applied, the surface area used can be reduced by about 50–60 per cent, for an equal population growth.

A number of estimates have been made for the surface areas occupied by cities (according to the definitions above) at the horizons of 2000 and 2025. Unit surfaces per inhabitant have been kept constant for countries in Region A, in the order to 250 m². For Region B the 1985 figures, ranging between 40 m² for Egypt and Syria and 70 m² for Turkey, have been gradually increased, up to 100–125 m² per inhabitant, according to the scenarios, for most of the countries in 2000 (60–80 m² for Egypt, on

account of its specific constraints) and 125–150 m²
in 2025 (80–100 m² for Egypt). The lowest values
correspond to the reference trend scenario T1 and
the worst trend scenario T2, and the highest values
to the moderate trend scenario T3 and the two
alternative scenarios.

The prospects of urbanized areas in 2000 and
2025 are consequently fairly stable on average in
the countries north of the basin. But in the countries
to the south and east they increase according to the
scenario by a multiplier ranging from seven to eight
times the present average consumption for Region
B (with the multiplier being higher than 10 in the
case of some countries, like Algeria, where many
completely new towns should be created in regions
like the Hauts-Plateaux area). But despite these
figures (28,000–32,000 km² for all countries in
Region B in 2025), the surface area consumed by
urbanization is insignificant when compared with
the size of national territories (with the exception of
Egypt), especially if account is taken of the advances
in agricultural productivity. Such is not the case if
one considers not the whole of the territories but
only the coastal regions (cf. Chapter 20).

Irrespective of surface areas, mention should be
made of the topographic aspect of the land urbanized.
Many Mediterranean cities have spread to the hills
and mountains surrounding their original site, and
sloping land presents a number of risks of instability,
not to mention handicaps for modern buildings and
highway infrastructure. In the countries south and
east of the Mediterranean basin, and among others
in the countries of the Maghreb, the steepest slopes
have been urbanized by the most disadvantaged
populations, these spontaneous settlements generally lacking basic facilities. In 1972 a landslide in
a district of Constantine made it necessary to
evacuate 15,000 people.

(b) Water

The supply of drinking water is at present un-
satisfactory for approximately half of the urban
population of the southern and eastern countries.
The main question is whether urbanization is a
significant cause of the foreseeable critical situation
in regard to water supplies in certain countries. By
drawing on the quantitative data provided by the
sectoral studies for the Blue Plan, it seems possible
to reply in the negative where absolute values
are concerned. It is believed that urban domestic
consumption will rise in 2025, according to the
scenarios, to between 6.800 m. m³ (worst trend

scenario T2) and 7.800 m. m³ (integration alternative scenario A2) for countries north of the
basin, and to between 3.100 m. m³ (integration
alternative scenario A2) and 3.700 m. m³ (moderate
trend scenario T3) for the southern and eastern
countries. Even if rural domestic consumption and
touristic consumption are added, this gives fairly
modest percentages of total consumption, of the
order of 5–7 per cent, according to the scenarios.
Overall, agricultural needs are by far the most
significant and, in certain countries (Syria, Israel,
Egypt, Libya, Malta, Tunisia), may constitute a
stranglehold for development.

Although this is true in regard to total water
resources, the situation is different in reality, taking
into account the availability of facilities, and especially the priority assigned—in particular, to
drinking-water supplies for cities. This is the case,
for instance, in Algeria, and particularly for water
supplies for the city of Algiers. In 1967 the Algiers
area consumed approximately 80m. m³ of water
annually (65m. m³ of drinking water, 15m. m³ of
industrial water), brought from wells not very
distant from the city. In 1983 urban needs were
estimated at 150m. m³ a year, and the shortage in
supplies from the nearest sources led to the planning
of the vast twin project of Keddara-Beni Amrane,
in principle sufficient to meet needs at the end of
the 1980s, estimated at representing some 250m.
m³ a year. The needs of the conurbation in 2000,
however, have been estimated at some 540m. m³ a
year (including 450m. for the city-dwellers), and
this will call for fresh solutions, especially since the
existing ground water will be virtually depleted:
could these be other dams on the wadis of the
hinterland, recycling of waste water, desalination of
sea water? As extreme as it may be, the example of
the Algiers area illustrates the competition between
urban and agricultural needs, and the problem of
investment priorities.

The evacuation of sewage: drainage

In most of the southern countries, environmental
hygiene is insufficient and is linked to delays affecting
the housing stock and to the inadequate evacuation
of waste water. Diseases due to the water supply,
in particular cholera, typhoid, and dysentery, still
occur in the countries south and east of the Mediterranean, where some populations suffer from
insufficient food supplies or malnutrition. Many
studies denounce the inadequacy and poor quality
of the networks for water supplies and purification.

BOX 15B. **Environmental problems in the greater Cairo region**

Greater Cairo is composed of Cairo (east of the Nile), Giza (on the West Bank) and the adjoining areas north in Shubra-el-Kheima, and south up to Hawamdieh. This is a total densely populated area of 400 km² and more than 11m. people, with an additional 1½m. coming in and out every day. Population density averages 30,000/km², but in certain central districts it reaches 100,000/km². As regards crowding, Cairo is exceeded only by Calcutta and Bangkok. There are 250,000 residential houses and 1.5m. family dwellings. The first fresh-water distribution station was established in 1865. Now there are 17 major water stations, producing 3m. m³/day, 75 per cent of which comes from the Nile and 25 per cent from deep wells underground.

The first sewage system was established in 1911, and was handling 48,000 m³/day. There are now seven large sewage treatment stations collecting 2m. m³/day, which is about 90 per cent of the total effluent from the city. Thus, 200,000 m³ are absorbed underground, or left unpumped in the streets; and 30 per cent of the city area is not yet connected to the public sewage system. The shortcomings of the sewage and treatment system became obvious by the early 1980s. A provisional rescue project was started to strengthen and renew the 175 pumping stations and clean the major pipes—3,500 km long—of deposits which have accumulated over the years. A comprehensive sewage project was planned to meet requirements until the year 2000, when the population is estimated to reach 16.5m. On the east side a tunnel 5 m in diameter is to extend from the south to the north-east, with subsidiary feeding tunnels, to collect the sewage and then pump it into a large treatment plant before using the water to irrigate desert land. A similar project on a smaller scale is planned for the West Bank. At present only 15 per cent of the waste water collected is treated fully, while 25 per cent is treated partially and 60 per cent is carried raw for 200 km by open canals to Lake Manzalah and then to the sea.

Solid waste collected from Cairo is about 4,000 t/day from private houses, plus about 1,000 t from industry. It includes household garbage, refuse, building debris, and other. It is collected mostly by hand, horse- and donkey-cart, and heavy truck. Dry household garbage is composed as follows (in percentage):

paper	16
organic matter	60
metals	2
dust	2
glass	2
other	18

There is an intricate system of door-to-door daily collection, then transport to a central area at the outskirts, where the main components are picked by hand and recycled, or used as feed for pigs in nearby farms. There is a very autocratic system of management, which generates high income for the top chiefs, and very little for the rest of the workers. Several attempts have been made to devise more humane systems of garbage collection, but they have never worked as efficiently. Plastic bags are being distributed now at low cost to households to keep the garbage until the *zabbal* comes in the morning to take it. A special factory for the manufacture of these bags has been established by the Cairo governorate. Over the years there have been several projects to process solid waste into organic fertilizer, but they were not successful. The most recent is a factory established in Shubra district in 1985, processing 160 t a day; another with a capacity of 100 t a day is under construction in Salam district. It is hoped that a third of the garbage will eventually be processed in this way in the next five years.

Source: Egyptian national scenarios.

The problem of the evacuation of domestic sewage and of pollution flows to be treated will be dealt with in Chapter 20, and significant variations will be seen between the different scenarios.

If there is one area where the extrapolation of trends has little meaning for the environment, it is clearly that of the urban environment. The authorities responsible for a conurbation or a city can do a great deal to change the course of things, and in forty years the effect can be felt. Of course, the degree of effectiveness will largely depend on the funds earmarked for investments, but this is not by any means the only factor. Just as important is the way in which the environment is, from the outset, internalized in studies and town-planning documents. The presence of public-health specialists, biologists, meteorologists, and ecology specialists in town-planning teams is altogether decisive (and effectively assumed in the alternative scenarios). And also very important is the way in which specialized institutions are set up—preferably with responsibility for several administrative areas—for the management of water, waste, and sanitation (in other words the public, private, or semi-public 'secular arm'), to ensure management in a practical, day-by-day form.

(c) Solid waste

Urban households, distribution and service activities, and industrial enterprises produce solid waste. Their nature and quantity vary by type of city and neighbourhood and over time. They necessitate the establishment of services responsible for management and collection: destruction, recycling, utilization, and processing. These questions will be mainly dealt with in Chapter 20. The parameters involved, apart from urban growth and the pattern of consumption of households, are largely linked to the hypotheses of waste-management policy, whether in regard to waste discharge or to investments for recovery and processing.

It should be stressed that the creation of a large number of jobs can result from measures related to the evacuation and recuperation of solid wastes, to the saving of raw materials (salvaged) and to the rational use of energy (incineration, composting). In order not to transfer urban pollution of water and soil to urban pollution of the air (through evacuations and discharge from incineration factories), investment in 'clean' technologies, introduced into the processes used for the recycling and processing of solid waste, may reduce the effects produced in this area by half or even more.

(d) Air pollution and noise

The quality of the air in towns is a real problem in the Mediterranean, but of course it offers sharp contrasts due to meteorological conditions which vary greatly according to site, season, and degree of human concentration. By and large, the following points may be emphasized:

● The first decisive factor for the next twenty or thirty years is motorized traffic (cf. Chapter 14). Data show that in many cities, like Athens, where traffic has to be regulated (the stones of the Parthenon are already seriously affected), Cairo, Algiers, Rome, where private traffic has been forbidden in the town centre, etc., the hourly levels of 100–200 g/km^3 recommended by WHO are regularly exceeded, and can reach 300–400 g/km^3 or even 700 g/km^3.

● The second factor is the consumption of domestic energy for heating the home and for water. The development of electricity should make for real progress, especially in regions which up to now have been using coal with a high sulphur content or low-grade coal. The effort made in Ankara is exemplary in this regard, and the quality of the air in that capital will be very substantially changed by the measures taken in 1986 and 1987 to treat domestic coal.

Where domestic heating is concerned, the Mediterranean region is fortunate to have a temperate climate and to require only auxiliary heating in the winter. But many improvements will depend on the way in which buildings are put up in the future (active or passive architecture). The development of solar technologies, mainly for the heating of domestic water, already used especially in Greece, Italy, Turkey, and Israel, could be speeded up.

● Lastly, as industry is largely concentrated in or near conurbations, the atmospheric discharge from industrial activities is to be taken into consideration, especially in the southern and eastern regions, which, in the next forty years, should undergo significant industrial development.

The future of urban quality of life will hinge very strongly on town-planning policy in this regard and the means available to direct new structures to selected sites so as to minimize their effects. Before any installation scheme, studies in environmental micro-meteorology would be needed to reduce the impact of industry.

Noise, which is often linked to activities that pollute the air, is one of the nuisances most keenly felt in cities: domestic appliances, noises from neighbours and from within apartment blocks, and the background noise of road traffic. If measures are not taken, one can expect a doubling of the noise level within twenty years. But preventive action is possible, particularly at the source (fixed or mobile sources). This action may take the form of building regulations but will largely depend on the Mediterranean populations' awareness of this nuisance.

(e) Urban planning

Spontaneous tendencies in the territorial distribution of populations will largely determine the forms of the settlement pattern in the Mediterranean countries. The challenge is to achieve the growth of large conurbations in harmony with that of small and medium-sized towns which might increase in size with no change in category.

Increasing mobility, social changes, and the intense redistribution of the population towards the cities are only part of the picture where regional disparities are concerned (which is a problem of fundamental importance for the environment). The other side of the picture should also be examined, the spatial redistribution of the population in respect of the coastal area (and, broadly, at the scale of what was defined in Part I as 'Mediterranean regions').

Regulatory town planning, but especially operational town planning, will be altogether decisive for the future of cities; frequently action will have to be 'made to measure'. The Blue Plan is a comprehensive and quantitative prospective study. But, even quantified, the future will depend on the policies carried out in the field, at the level of the conurbation or network of towns, at the level of city centres and neighbourhoods. This is what may be understood as land-use 'micro-planning'. This type of planning, this attention given to all that constitutes the design for everyday living, is not a luxury reserved for towns that have already overcome the main hurdle. It is something else, involving architecture, colours, and the participation of the people, particularly the young. These considerations should be stressed, especially when the concern is with budgetary choices. Attention to the quality of urban life, to the proper use of urban facilities, and to the protection of amenities, of trees and green spaces in cities, as well as to the conservation of historic centres, costs relatively little and may prove extremely productive in respect of societal balance, security, and health. In this connection, 'cost–benefit' analysis in terms of urban management and health, for instance, as conducted in certain cities of the world, could be a useful exercise in the Mediterranean region.

Generally speaking, as great as is the importance attached to gardens in Mediterranean culture, the type of urbanization in the Mediterranean has not led to the development of 'nature in the city'. Here again, then, one can only note the diversity of situations. For a prospective study in this regard, the statistics available hardly provide enough data (in contrast with northern Europe) to quantify the surface area of green spaces incorporated into towns and suburbs.

The creation of large conurbations will, however, make it increasingly necessary to offset increased urban density *in situ*. The demand for green spaces, for spaces for young people, for sport crowds, and for spaces where people can meet will tend to become more pronounced with the declining function of the street, formerly so important and still so today in small towns, but increasingly taken over by motorized traffic. The tradition of Mediterranean gardens for private use or for the use of small communities will have to develop in such a way as to integrate higher densities; and when thought is being given to gardens and parks, account should also be taken of plant pathology in the Mediterranean area—e.g. diseases affecting town trees such as planes and cypresses.

The future of cities in the Mediterranean depends first and foremost on the efforts made at the national level (e.g. land-use planning) or at the municipal level. The efforts to be made regarding building, urban transport, landscape protection, and the quality of architecture stem primarily from the policies implemented *in situ*, which, as far as possible, involve local populations in the endeavours to improve their living environment. They also depend on the institutions set up, often on the initiative of states: boards serving several districts, waste-processing agencies, agencies responsible for water, air, or parks, and so on. In all scenarios, urban space management will demand formidable combined investments, in the north and even more in the south, both from municipal and local authorities and interested groups and from national public sources.

IV Protection of Mediterranean Environments
A Vital Need

16 Three Resources or One?

The prospective studies of sectoral activities stressed the chief impacts of these on the Mediterranean environment, such as accumulated fertilizer pollution stemming from agricultural development, the risk of pollution linked to industrial growth, atmospheric pollutant discharges from thermal power-stations or motorized traffic, tourist water requirements and their impact on coastal resources, the surface area covered by transport infrastructure, etc. When the basic data so permitted, an attempt was made to quantify a number of these emissions and/or impacts.

In an effort to advance further, a number of subsystems or 'environmental chains' were studied which link emissions or direct impacts to indirect effects through either causal relationships or feedback loops. Thus, environmental chains were formulated for domestic pollution, the forest, soil erosion and degradation, and agricultural pollutant discharges (fertilizers and pesticides). When chains are short and simple, they can furnish interesting and fairly cohesive findings, likely to provide indications on the scale of the Mediterranean basin or of a rather large region (the case of the domestic pollution chain, for example). The more complicated they are and the more factors are taken into account, the less these chains can finally be used at the global level. Aggregated data at the level of the basin or a large region have no real significance for a limited geographical area, and, conversely, local data are not available or usable for the national territory as a whole. Nevertheless, these chains are valuable tools for small areas, when the necessary data can be obtained and are moreover fairly uniform and consistent. This is the case, for example, with the chain developed for the Mediterranean forests.

But this approach is all the more difficult because, at the end of the chain, some environmental effects are themselves very poorly known, particularly in the marine environment (for pollution from heavy metals or the long-term effects of hydrocarbons, for instance). Moreover, it is not enough to add up the impacts deriving from different sectoral developments. On the one hand, some activities are mutually exclusive at the local level: it is unlikely that an aquaculture farm will adjoin a refinery. On the other, the various effects may create synergy, the final impact being greater than the sum of two independent effects (a well-known phenomenon for some pollutants). Even applied to a wide area, an 'addition' of this kind can only be an approximation. Nevertheless, it helps to form an initial idea of conflicts over the use of various elements, as will be seen for the Mediterranean coastline.

After a brief recall of the chief impacts, the focus here will be on the aspects which gradually appeared to be the most important, namely interactions, and the risk of major degradations, for which action is most urgently required.

1. About interactions

With regard to interactions among environments, or between environments and sectors, an initial observation is the existence of simple 'loops' between development and the environment, which can be described as the 'mining' type: the over-exploitation of a forest, artesian aquifer, or a tourist site destroys these resources to varying degrees until destruction becomes irreversible. In all cases, disappearance of the resource will curb, or even bring to a standstill, the development based upon it.

Quantitatively more difficult to grasp—and even more difficult to control because they are usually the responsibility of different institutions—are the relationships and/or loops among the main environments (soil, water, the forest) and the various sectors of activity.

Urbanization, energy, industry, tourism, or transport, for example, involve land use (some of which has been quantified in terms of the various kinds of scenario). Conflicts may arise on the use of space where it is limited, such as in the coastal regions or the Nile valley. This growing coverage of surface area, however, brings into play factors other than the mere 'gross' area used, expressed in hectares or square metres. The role of topography has been stressed in the case of cities. This coverage also prevents water infiltration in the soil, which leads

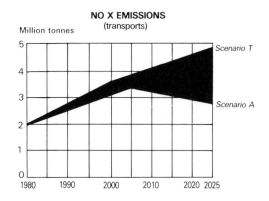

NO X EMISSIONS
(transports)

Million tonnes

Scenario T

Scenario A

1980 1990 2000 2010 2020 2025

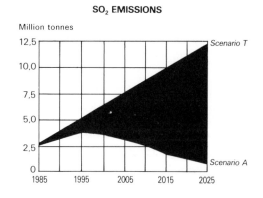

SO₂ EMISSIONS

Million tonnes

Scenario T

Scenario A

1985 1995 2005 2015 2025

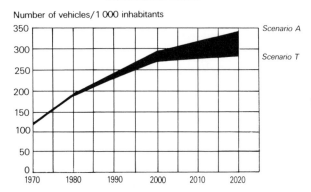

AUTOMOBILE STOCK

Number of vehicles/1 000 inhabitants

Scenario A

Scenario T

1970 1980 1990 2000 2010 2020

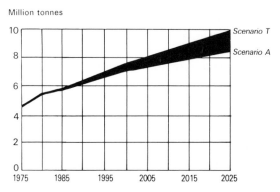

FERTILIZER CONSUMPTION

Million tonnes

Scenario T

Scenario A

1975 1985 1995 2005 2015 2025

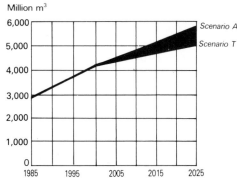

SEWAGE : COASTAL POPULATION

Million m³

Scenario A

Scenario T

1985 1995 2005 2015 2025

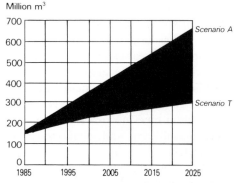

SEWAGE : COASTAL TOURISM

Million m³

Scenario A

Scenario T

1985 1995 2005 2015 2025

FIG. 16.1 Some results from the extreme scenarios for the Mediterranean countries as a whole. These diagrams, like the other prospective maps in the report, indicate in black the margin of uncertainty for the future between the two extreme scenarios on a given subject. The extent to which this margin opens up depends largely on the hypotheses chosen for the scenarios and on the efforts undertaken by countries to implement environmental policies. The figures which can be derived from these diagrams should therefore be taken only as indicative.

Source: Blue Plan.

to a considerable increase in run-off in the case of storms or heavy rain, characteristic of the Mediterranean climate. As a result, there is a growing risk of floods, landslides, or interference with water resources.

With regard to water, growing conflicts exist in a number of countries south and east of the

Mediterranean basin between the needs of industry and urbanization and those of irrigation and agriculture. The two chief sources for urban and industrial requirements are pumping from ground water and transfers from ever more distant sites. These transfers require growingly advanced techniques, rising energy consumption, and increasingly complex storage and distribution systems. However, sanitary installations advance far more slowly than connections to water systems. Hence the growing risk of polluting the ground water that provides part of the urban supply. An additional risk is linked to the rapid over-exploitation of the supply aquifer, which may entail subsidences (the case of Venice recently, or of Ravenna, Milan, etc.). One effect of these land subsidences is to damage the networks for the supply of water or the collection of waste water, whose leakage rates sometimes reach around 50 per cent and whose repair, when possible, is particularly difficult and arduous.

Over-exploitation of the forest is most often caused by either over-grazing (agriculture) or fuel-wood needs (energy). Aside from the gradual disappearance of the resource itself, one of the most serious effects is the loss of its regulating effect on the water regime: run-off increases, removes soil, and silts up dams. The disappearance of one resource (the forest) entails that of two others (soil and water), with negative reactions on the two economic sectors originally involved—agriculture (soil and irrigation dams) and energy (hydraulic dams)—without counting the fact that run-off increases the risk of landslides (threat to homes and infrastructure) and of flooding in valleys or plains.

These examples of interactions and more or less indirect loops, among all those explored during the studies, illustrate one essential point: the interdependence between resources or environments. The speed of interaction seems to increase with the intensity of human activities. In reality, the soil–water–forest 'system' should usually be considered as a single resource (as in fact illustrated in Fig. 5.1 above). Although the change or degradation of these resources has been tackled here from an 'individual' angle, it should be recalled that they must never be dissociated and that their evolution mechanisms are in fact closely related: the phenomenon of soil removal by run-off as a result of deforestation clearly illustrates this interdependence between three resources, which in fact are only one within what is known as the ecosystem.

2. About the scenarios

Although interrelationships between resources, or between resources and sectors can be rather easily examined, they are on the contrary extremely difficult to quantify in the future. So there is little justification for keeping a rigid distinction between the five different scenarios in this part of the report. In most cases reference will simply be made to the three main scenarios: the worst trend scenario T2, the moderate trend scenario T3, and an average alternative scenario. This gives the following general view:

● T2 worst trend scenarios envisage economic difficulties, absence of a long-term view, lack of resources, priority given to certain emergencies (socio-economic rather than environmental), all leading to a case-by-case approach to attend to the most serious and visible degradations. Development assistance projects themselves are poorly designed, dispersed, and often have an adverse effect on the environment or society.

● T3 moderate trend scenarios are characterized by strong economic growth, an incipient long-term view, larger resources, an understanding of the need to protect certain resources or environments and to curb, even prevent, serious degradation. These features lead to corrective and preventive action. Unfortunately, this is characterized by often belated decision-making and fairly slow implementation (which increases costs considerably) and a preference for sectoral intervention—lacking co-ordination, so ultimately less effective than anticipated.

● In contrast, the alternative scenarios feature the integrated approach, in other words the conviction that action must be taken on all resources simultaneously, starting with human resources: the centralized and 'technocratic' approach of the trend scenarios is replaced by a concern to involve populations in both decision-making mechanisms and their implementation. This concern was reflected from the economic viewpoint by the growing role of small and medium-sized enterprises, *inter alia* in the integration alternative scenario A2, or by the importance given to small-scale hydraulic installations, solar energy, etc. These alternative scenarios correspond to a real policy for physical planning and management of natural resources, incorporated from the outset in economic development strategies.

Without being able to enter into overall quantitative assessments—which, moreover, would scarcely have any spatial meaning in a given place in the region—an attempt is therefore made to provide a qualitative view of the future of the environmental components chosen and the issues involved, as well as a set of consistent deductions from the macro-economic and sectoral scenarios concerning the possible or predictable evolution of these components.

17 The Protective Forest

The evolution of Mediterranean economies leads to the gradual marginalization of so-called disadvantaged zones, under-populated north of the basin, over-populated in the south and east. In the north, in an industrialized economy, the forest is gaining ground on abandoned agricultural land, but it is no longer used and its management is neglected because of lack of labour and financial resources (in particular, forest income). In the south and east, where large areas still depend on gathering and subsistence farming to meet vital needs, over-exploitation by poor and growing populations, together with clearing—organized or otherwise—for the extension of agricultural land, is slowly destroying stands which cannot regenerate (because of the climate). In coastal areas the forest is losing ground because of urbanization, industrialization, tourism, fire, and too many visitors.

Generally speaking, forest ecosystems which played a major role in the evolution of the Mediterranean basin no longer have functions that are clearly defined, with an order of importance. The 'normal' Mediterranean forest, especially in the countries south and east of the basin, is a wooded area whose many functions often compete with one another and are occasionally incompatible. In addition, they are likely to vary in relative importance and priority during the same management plan, whose financial balance sheet is virtually always in deficit. Unlike the specific silviculture in temperate humid regions, forest management in Mediterranean areas is inseparable from the overall management of other neighbouring sectors and must include not only biological considerations, but also social and economic considerations external to the forest.

In what follows, the term 'forest' includes natural stands (trees over 6 m tall in 'closed' or 'open' forest), their various degraded forms (*maquis*, *matorral*, and *garrigue*, which often represent the largest part of wooded Mediterranean areas), afforestation, and wooded wild-land, characterized as a whole by its apparent heterogeneity. Ribbon plantings, village wood-lots (fuel-wood, fodder), urban plantings, and peri-urban parks, farm woodland, and oasis trees were not included, even though they play an ecological and often economical role (in Egypt, for instance).

There is a certain lack of definition with regard to categories, as well as the surface areas actually covered and the standing volumes, especially in some countries. Despite the advance of scientific studies over the past forty years and the availability of a considerable volume of selective or specific information, there are still many huge statistical gaps, especially concerning the Mediterranean regions *per se*. This prevents the effective assessment of changes in natural wooded cover. The concept of woody biomass would be better adapted to the economic and ecological realities of the region, but for the moment only theoretical and local figures exist.

1. Interactions between the forest and development activities

With regard to the development activities reviewed in the third part, Mediterranean forests fulfil a number of functions (the main ones being production and/or protection) and undergo a number of pressures. Concerning production functions, a . clear distinction has to be made between:

- commercial production—the only kind usually taken into account in official statistics—whose gross product is low;
- biomass production understood in a broader sense, i.e. related to the supply of all kinds of goods that can be used by man; in this respect the Mediterranean forest, including *maquis* and bushland, is highly productive (3–10 t/ha per annum for a healthy forest, 1–4 t/ha per annum for *garrigue* and coppices—figures which should be halved in semi-arid climates), and this overall production capacity is very valuable for a number of countries (e.g. in the Maghreb).

(a) The agro-food sector

Forest fodder production is an important source of indirect income, either at the end of the dry season for transhumant herds or for cattle feed in winter. A balance can be established between plant withdrawals and animal inputs; if this balance is temporarily disrupted, the resilience of the Mediterranean forest enables it to recover health and productivity following fairly long exclosure periods. If these pressures exceed thresholds, however, because of excessive herd density or because herds remain too long in the forest (virtually year-round grazing), stands are damaged and become degraded, and fodder capacity declines. Ultimately only a few trees are left in the midst of bare and stony expanses. This kind of over-grazing, unfortunately, is becoming increasingly prevalent in the countries south and east of the Mediterranean basin and is one of the basic factors of desertification starting from the arid and semi-arid desert.

Together with over-grazing, another pressure is the clearing of land to acquire new lots to cultivate. Ploughing is often temporary because of rapid soil degradation, which can also lead to the definitive stripping of the parent rock. Although it is not possible to provide accurate figures, it is estimated that several thousand hectares are stripped each year in the countries concerned.

(b) Industry

Average timber production of the Mediterranean forest is low (less than 1 m³/ha per annum for the basin as a whole) and considerably below industrial wood requirements. Plantations of fast-growing species (eucalyptus, acacia, poplar) or high-quality species (walnut, cherry, chestnut) form particularly fragile artificial ecosystems. In addition to wood, the forest provides various products which have considerable economic importance for some populations, such as cork, tanning products, resins, aromatic plants, etc., although their marketing is sometimes difficult.

(c) Energy

Very heavy pressure is exerted on the forest by energy requirements, still partly met in a number of southern countries (e.g. Morocco) and eastern countries (Turkey) by fuel-wood, because, among other things, it is free (see Chapter 12). Considerable volumes of wood are consumed, but these are not recorded, unlike charcoal, which is virtually always marketed. Over-exploitation of fuel-wood is the second chief cause, along with over-grazing, of the degradation and gradual disappearance of stands. The growing lack of fuel-wood induces rural populations to burn crop residues or dung, depriving cultivated land of the organic matter and mineral nutrients essential for its regeneration.

The fuel-wood productivity of natural Mediterranean forest ranges on average between 0.8 m³/ha per annum for closed broad-leaved stands and 0.1 m³/ha per annum for bushy woodland. Population requirements are estimated at approximately 0.5–1 m³ per capita per annum for rural population (and even more in some areas of the Maghreb or Turkey). Fuel-wood (or fodder-wood) plantations in soil-conservation districts would provide a good solution, but there are not enough of them so far.

Energy consumption, particularly the thermal production of electricity from fossil fuels, together with motorized transport, produces emissions (SO_2, NO_x, etc.) which may have considerable effects on the forest (thus the problem of acid rain, experienced mainly in central or northern Europe, although water acidification phenomena have been observed in Mediterranean Europe).

(d) Tourism

Silviculture and management must take into account the increasing number of tourists in the forest, and concern about the landscape is growing both south and north of the basin. Motor-car and motor-cycle traffic, the continuous trampling of fragile species, and increasing amounts of rubbish can cause significant damage. Negligence—rather than malicious intent—is a growing cause of fires, the number of which is rising rapidly in tourist areas.

(e) Transport

Aside from the possible effects of pollutants already mentioned, transport infrastructure sometimes requires cutting across stands, disturbing ecosystems and wild-life habits. On the other hand, specialized infrastructure (roads or hydroelectric dams, for instance) can be protected by forests managed for this purpose.

(f) Other pressures on the Mediterranean forest

Tourism is clearly not the only cause of fires, which each year affect, on average, about 200,000 ha of forest in the Mediterranean basin as a whole (about 90 per cent of these fires currently concern countries north of the basin, and their irregular pattern can involve a ratio of up to 1 : 100 depending on the year and climatic conditions). Repeated fires can have a cumulative sterilizing effect, to the point of mineralizing soils.

In addition, trees are normally host to parasites, fungi, or insects, but the traditional balance may be broken; in the Mediterranean this is the case with pine-, cedar-, and plane-trees. Trees' resistance to parasite attacks can be reduced by poisoning associated with pollutants, and trees thus attacked are also more prone to fire.

2. Ecological effects of deforestation

Of all the forest systems in the world, those around the Mediterranean (together with those of mainland China) have been the most degraded by human action. The combined action of clearing, over-grazing, and excessive use of wood as fuel and building material has caused incalculable damage. It is estimated that in Mediterranean Europe (including Turkey) the forest currently covers no more than 5 per cent of its original surface area. In the Maghreb and Near East deserts now exist in areas formerly covered with huge forests.

Regardless of the considerable loss of natural living resources, deforestation can be considered as a major ecological threat because it causes disturbances in the water-cycle and contributes to soil erosion. It leads to an increase in disasters that can no longer be described solely as 'natural', such as floods, landslides, the rapid silting up of river-beds (and dams), changes in deltas, etc. World-wide, deforestation is considered to be basically responsible for the increase in the frequency of disastrous floods occurring during past decades.

The most serious effect of deforestation is to upset the water-cycle, which is basically dependent on the nature of the soil and vegetation, and on the interplay of evapotranspiration and infiltration through the surface layer and parent rock, feeding ground water and subsequently watercourses. The foliage of trees reduces the kinetic energy of drops, and the depth of the humus and litter acts as a sponge (rapid absorption and slow restitution). Deforestation reduces evapotranspiration and infiltration, and above all it substantially increases run-off. According to FAO, nearly one-fifth of the world's arable land will be destroyed by the beginning of the next century solely by water erosion resulting from deforestation, if it continues at its present rate. In the Mediterranean catchment area, deforestation and subsequent soil removal are responsible for dams silting up much faster than expected: Serre-Ponçon in the Haute-Alpes (3m. m³

BOX 17A. **Two aspects of a Corsican inland county**

At the beginning of the nineteenth century the rural interior of Corsica was heavily populated and exploited. The richest crops, from the kitchen gardens and orchards (particularly chestnut), were grouped together on mountain shelves around villages, at an altitude of about 600 m. Beyond this first zone land was cultivated on the basis of a biennial cereal–fallow crop rotation. The villagers could also avail themselves of summer grazing in the mountains, and winter grazing on the eastern coast. Woods were exploited for fuel (in particular coppices of evergreen oak). Stock-farming, particularly of sheep, was very important and supplied—in adition to wool, meat, and milk—large quantities of manure from the night enclosures, which was spread on the rich kitchen garden and orchard plots.

This system ended fairly recently, following a severe and massive exodus. The cultivation of cereals, in competition with cereals imported from the Continent, was the first to be abandoned, followed, more slowly, by market gardening and orchard cultivation. Stock-farming, however, survived better. Fallow land, as it was no longer ploughed, was invaded by the woody plants which form the *maquis* (heather, arbustus, and cistus), little to the liking of sheep. To get rid of the *maquis* and allow grass to grow again, the simplest thing is to set it alight. This is how the cereals–fallow system was replaced by the burning–stock-farming–*maquis* system, which encourages the regrowth of non-edible woody plants. Since erosion caused soil fertility to fall, increasingly large areas had to be set alight, especially since the economic exploitation of the east coast had virtually done away with winter grazing. The former cereal–fallow rotation zone was finally covered by a *maquis* increasingly degraded by fire, until solutions were sought.

Source: after J. de Mongolfier.

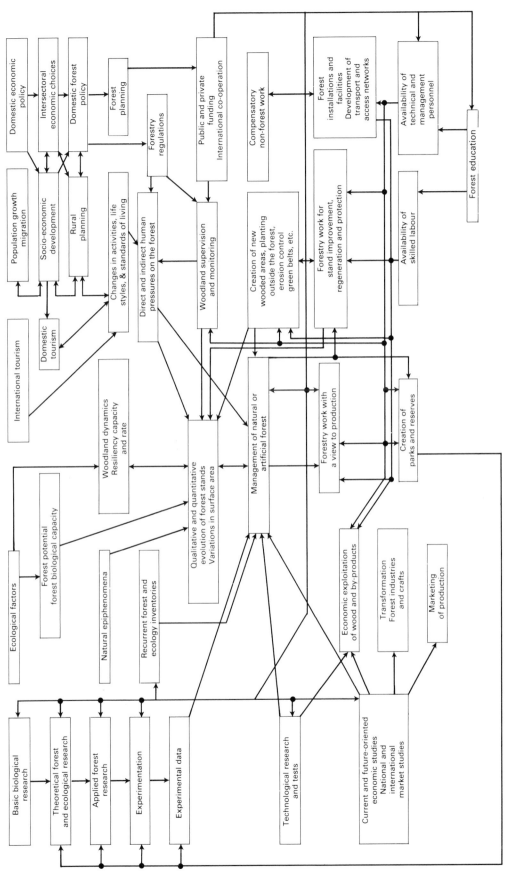

FIG. 17.1 Flowchart of Mediterranean forest interactions

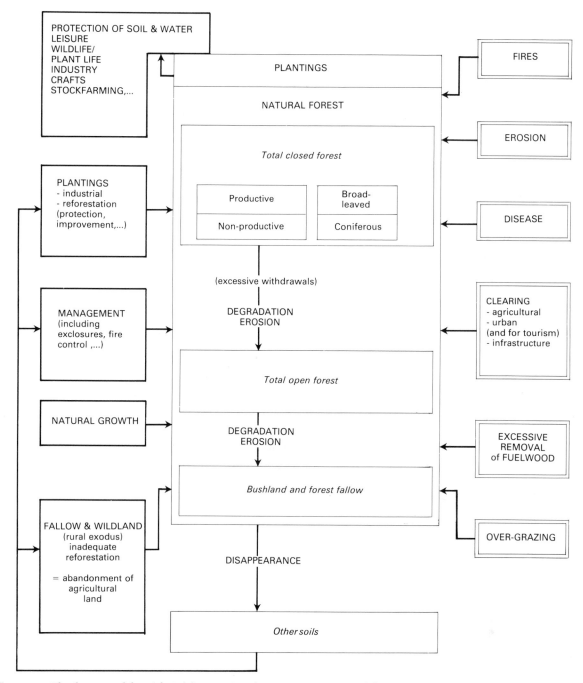

FIG. 17.2 The forest model or 'chain' (interactions between pressures and forestry systems)

per annum), dams at Hamiz and Cheurfa in Algeria, which had to be raised, and so on. On account of very irregular rains, steep slopes, and rapid silting up, the hill ponds in Algeria need walls over 15 m high, whereas 7 m is sufficient for the same type of construction in southern Italy. In areas where the forest has been destroyed, excessive precipitation often causes disastrous mud or landslides after soil erosion.

3. The Mediterranean forest in the scenarios

The complexity of forest issues in the Mediterranean is illustrated in Fig. 17.1. This complexity, and the statistical shortcomings and quantification diffi-culties already mentioned, make it clear that the prospective approach had to remain basically qual-itative with respect to the basin. The horizons of the

Blue Plan macro-economic scenarios seem fairly short with regard to the forest—if not for degradation phenomena, at least for the real effects that can be expected from protection and/or rehabilitation measures which may be decided upon and implemented in the light of the various scenarios.

A simplified environmental chain has been drawn up (Fig. 17.2) in an attempt to understand better the effects or pressures of the most significant factors in terms of the scenarios—notably fire, clearing, over-grazing, fuel-wood removal and plantings—in order to identify tentatively how much of the forest is disappearing, how much is gradually being degraded, and the counteraction taken through plantings and pressure control. Five natural kinds of stand have been considered for most of the Medittanean countries with forests: closed, managed forest; closed, non-managed forest; open forest; forest fallow; and bushy woodland. For some countries (such as Spain, Yugoslavia, or Turkey, where non-Mediterranean forests represent a considerable forest capital, less fragile than that located on the Mediterranean seaboard) lack of detailed data prevented the Mediterranean regions from being considered independently. In addition to indications supporting the prospective study, the model constructed can also provide interesting findings for forest areas where pressures are accurately known; however, it cannot be quantitatively applied to a very heterogeneous country, nor *a fortiori* to a region as huge and diversified as the Mediterranean basin.

(a) Trend scenarios

Applying this chain, in the worst trend scenario T2, characterized by slow and difficult economic growth, population problems will increase in the countries south and east of the Mediterranean basin (*a fortiori* in the hinterlands and arid zones, partly because of growing difficulties in international migration). The requirements of larger populations will rise sharply, leading to the increasing over-exploitation of fuel-wood, the clearing of marginal woodland (on slopes, unsuited to cultivation and very sensitive to erosion), and to a real devastation of range-lands, including forest ranges. Trends towards forest degradation (increase of open forest and bushy woodland) speed up disastrously, and by 2025 a large part of currently existing woodland would have disappeared, often irreversibly (a possible reduction of surface area by one quarter in 2000 and by a half in 2025), heightening the effect of desertification from the south. As a result, run-off will increase, removing

soil and silting up dam reservoirs, whose upkeep or replacement will be hampered by lack of financial resources (let alone the shortage of appropriate sites). In the worst cases of silting up, dams will be raised, not without increasing the risk of accidents.

In the countries north of the basin private forests in Mediterranean regions will be virtually abandoned, except those close to agglomerations, whereas public forests will be managed at 'minimum' expense, notably on the coast, where resources and personnel will be insufficient to combat forest fires, a situation aggravated by the poor maintenance of entry roads. Non-rehabilitated burnt areas and the encroachment of low-cost constructions on the coast will contribute to the degradation of natural areas and landscapes.

In the moderate trend scenario T3, characterized by vigorous economic growth and the consideration of environmental impacts (unfortunately often too late and too sectoral), considerable planning efforts will be made in countries south and east of the basin, and the improved availability of energy (replacement of fuel-wood by possibly subsidized fuels and subsequently by electricity) will tend to limit the increase of pressure on the forest. These pressures will nevertheless remain heavy (as on other natural resources) because of vigorous economic development and the needs of agricultural intensification, industrial growth, infrastructure, and urbanization, as well as the sharp rise in domestic and international tourism. The effect of rehabilitation or conservation measures, still too sectoral and centralized, will be delayed and the measures themselves will be more costly because they have been postponed. In fact, the forest situation will continue to evolve adversely, at least until the beginning of the next century, with the reduction of wooded areas, then possible stabilization due to multipurpose plantings. One of the risks of delayed reforestation is that trees planted in destroyed soil will not reconstitute a true forest, nor assume its many functions for all the resources.

In this scenario it will be easier for the countries on the northern shore to set up the legal, financial, and land-tenure measures required to resume gradually economic exploitation of abandoned land, and increase the number of protected zones. Forest-fire detection will be quicker and fires better cut off and controlled. Although the surface area of Mediterranean woodland will not increase, its quality will finally improve, and the extra financial cost will be borne by the taxpayer and user.

Depending on the kind of scenario, the findings of the environmental chain show that by 2025, for the Mediterranean countries as a whole, fires could have destroyed between 10m. and 12m. ha of forest, clearing between 5m. and 6m. ha, over-grazing between 2.5m. and 3m. ha, and fuel-wood removals between 0.5m. and 1m. ha (considering the substantial fuel-wood shortage, this means that all needs will be far from satisfied).

(b) The alternative scenarios

The alternative scenarios are characterized by an integrated approach, which is less centralized and involves greater participation on the part of local populations. Forest management and protection are considered as an inseparable element of other environmental components, starting with the soil and inland water, in the context of a long-term physical planning policy, an integral part of economic and social development.

In the reference alternative scenario A1, countries' efforts will be better co-ordinated and more consistent, with the European Community and specifically Mediterranean organizations (inspired by international organizations such as FAO, Unesco, etc.) playing an important role. The effectiveness of these efforts will be quickly felt as regards the gathering, processing, and dissemination of the data necessary for sound management, and with respect to research and training. Increased technical and financial co-operation among countries in the north

and those in the south and east of the basin will considerably increase the operational potential of southern and eastern countries, and the number of pilot projects in the field will rise, in the light of longer-term dynamic and sustained reafforestation policies and efficient protective management.

In the northern countries the general situation of woodland in the two kinds of alternative scenario will be fairly similar to that of moderate trend scenario T3, as policies inspired by the European Community would only produce effects gradually (rehabilitation of depressed areas would not start, for example, until after 2000 and would benefit from long-term and effective support). Since fires would not affect such large surface areas (because of the effectiveness of prevention, partitioning, and clearing of undergrowth), bushy woodland will recede towards the end of the period. Forest exploitation will, however, remain limited, without any noticeable development of wood products, aside from some regional lines. On the other hand, the network of parks and reserves (in particular 'biosphere reserves', which reconcile the objectives of conservation and development while ensuring the participation of the local population), will tend to expand, as well as rural forest tourism, both summer and winter.

In the integration alternative scenario A2 the country groups south and east of the Mediterranean

BOX 17B. **The true value of the forest**

Figures appearing in economic statistics converning the contribution of the forestry sector to the gross domestic product generally give a completely false view of the true value of the forest.

In the case of Tunisia, for example, annual income from the forest—in the form of cork, wood, fodder, hunting licences, and fines—amounted to 1.45m. dinars (about $2m.) in 1983. Add to this very modest figure the estimated annual value of direct income from hunting, produced by meat or exported animals (1.68m. dinars); from the alfa crop (2.34m. dinars), and, in particular, from firewood collected on the spot (38.6m. dinars) and the grazing of domestic animals (65m. dinars), and the total contribution of the forest to the Tunisian economy in 1983 amounted to 95m. dinars. This is more than 65 times the amount appearing in the statistics. To be fair, however, account should be taken of the fact that the excessive gathering of firewood and over-grazing exhaust the forest capital itself, and should not be limited only to the income obtained from it.

Consideration should also be given, however, to the fact that the some 760,000 people who live in the forest or around it depend on it to varying degrees—for work—(forestry and soil conservation required more than 10m. work-days in 1984), free fuel, and free or subsidized grazing, which contributes to the development of roads, transport services, and the supplying of rural zones which would otherwise have remained isolated.

This is without mentioning the ecological role of the forest, its role in the water-cycle: in conserving water—without the forest the water would run off uncontrolled, producing flash-floods—or in conserving the soil—(again, without the forest soil erodes quickly and soon silts up downstream dams or fills estuaries with sediment).

One should also remember the role of the forest in maintaining the beauty and balance of the landscape, and in serving as a place of rest and leisure.

In Tunisia, as in the other Maghreb countries and the east of the Mediterranean, the forest is the only defence against the desertification process which could start within the next twenty years.

Source: World Bank Country Studies.

basin, after an initial period, will experience more rapid and effective progress, with less duplication in what could be termed the 'preliminaries' for forest development (statistics, inventories, training, and research), and the harmonization of regulations will make a positive contribution. Pressure on forest areas would nevertheless persist at least until 2000, even 2010, with its consequences on water-cycles.

From this brief study it can be deduced that, regardless of the type of macro-economic scenario and environmental protection, the anticipated evolution of Mediterranean forests, which perform in particular an essential ecological role, is more than worrying—even in the absence of any unpleasant surprise—and that negative trends are speeding up. This kind of development could become truly disastrous for a number of countries. It could only be counteracted by considerable and prolonged efforts on their part, acting either individually or preferably in a co-ordinated and collective way, but absolutely as soon as possible if the increase of irreversible changes is to be avoided. Even if the shift from adverse trends is felt gradually, the true benefits of these possible efforts will not be evident in the best of cases until during the second period of the Blue Plan scenarios, i.e. between 2000 and 2025.

18 The Threatened Soil

Two very different kinds of pressure are exerted on Mediterranean soil:

● On the one hand, there is the land coverage of non-agricultural socio-economic activities, resulting in increasingly artificial soil used for these purposes only. This results in a change in soil-surface properties, often towards impermeability. When this involves farmland or land suitable for agriculture, it means a net loss in surface area for agriculture.

● On the other hand, changes occur in the properties of arable land under the direct or indirect effect of agricultural activities (e.g. loss of arable land removed by run-off following deforestation for energy needs, or the degradation of chemical and physical properties through the excessive intensification of agriculture). This evolution corresponds more often to degradation, which could lead to the definitive loss of agricultural potential (stripping of rock, desertification). As will be seen below, this kind of pressure is the most serious cause of concern in the Mediterranean.

1. Non-agricultural land coverage

In the third part of this report, devoted to the activities of the major economic sectors and their impacts on Mediterranean areas and the environment, a number of figures were given concerning land coverage related to prospects for these activities according to the various scenarios and in the light of a number of hypotheses. It should be noted that the starting values (1985 in general) are comparatively poorly known for most countries or do not always correspond to identical definitions.

In order to compare or incorporate the findings obtained, a few observations should be made about the hypotheses chosen. Findings generally stem from two factors, one obtained on the basis of the scenarios, the other being the 'unit value' deduced from knowledge of the current (or recent) situation and extrapolated to fifteen or forty years by experts in a rational but naturally arbitrary way. For example:

● urban population, multiplied by per capita unit coverage;
● accommodation capacity, multiplied by the bed unit coverage;
● road length, multiplied by the average width of roads, etc.

In the case of industry and energy, the diversity of plants and of their sizes prevented identification of unit or average values. In some cases only a few available figures for certain categories (power-plants, refineries, etc.) or for specific sites could be given, as will be seen especially where problems are most serious, i.e. in coastal regions and on the coast. When national inventories are available, it seems that in total this coverage is not very large (for example, industrial coverage represents about 0.25 per cent of the national territory of an industrialized country like France), and many other factors have to be taken into account for siting (populations and/or labour, water resources, waste disposal, transport networks, etc.). At the regional level, and *a fortiori* the local level, the problem is quite different.

Tourism essentially concerns the coastal regions and the coast, and will therefore be dealt in Chapter 20. This leaves two kinds of coverage, which are particularly important, distributed (sometimes very unevenly) over the whole of the national territory and usually involving agricultural land: urbanization and transport infrastructure (chiefly road).

At the horizon of 2025, the prospective scenarios for urban population and road and motorway development for all the countries of the Mediterranean basin gave similar coverages, in the region of 70,000 km². It is noteworthy that the ratio between the levels of urban population at the horizon of 2025 in the extreme case (1.17 for the worst trend scenario T2 and reference alternative scenario A1) is virtually the same as the ratio between the length of road and motorway networks in the extreme case (1.18 for the moderate trend scenario T3 and worst trend scenario T2). The final results concerning land coverage will therefore be especially sensitive to the choice of 'unit values'.

With regard to coverage per urban inhabitant,

the values chosen for 1985 vary according to the country between 40 and 250 m² (Mediterranean average 171 m²) and for 2025, between 75 and 250 m² (Mediterranean average 183 m²). A better knowledge of the starting situation could lead to changes in these figures as the 2025 values depend closely on conditions of socio-economic development and more especially on town-planning and housing strategies.

A final aspect that should be mentioned is loss of productive land to other uses. Clearly, different human activities are at odds over land use: among other things, urbanization and the need for land for communication routes compete with agriculture, sometimes on high-quality land, not to mention tourist and industrial developments (the problem being most acute in coastal areas). For northern countries however, farmland will generally continue to contract. This raises a management problem, namely how to prevent the spread of wild-land, unsuitable for leisure activities and prone to fire.

A few figures illustrate how acute the problem is on the southern and eastern shores of the Mediterranean:

● In Tunisia, between 1962 and 1974 land zoned for urbanization increased fivefold at Naboul, Hammamet, Sousse and Sfax. The annual urbanization rate for south Tunis in 1962 was 6 per cent; by 1984 it was 34 per cent.

● In Libya, urban areas covered 17.6 per cent of the best agricultural land in 1980, 6 per cent of good agricultural land, and 1.6 of land with average fertility.

● In Egypt, more than 15 per cent of farmland was lost to urbanization during early five-year plans, and the crop area per capita is shrinking annually by more than 2 per cent.

In the same way estimates for the road network were made with an 'average width' of 20 m (banks and shoulders included, significant in the Mediterranean region), with no change between 2000 and 2025 (although the 1985 value is more likely to be closer to 10 m). Real values will depend on spatial and transport management strategies (distribution among means of transport and respective shares of roads and motorways).

It seems clear, however, that even refining knowledge, hypotheses, and projections, urban growth and the development of road transport infrastructure will remain the two leading consumers of land (aside from agricultural activities), and that for some scenarios the area covered by roads could even exceed the urban area at the 2025 horizon for the

countries south and east of the Mediterranean basin as a whole, with a particularly bleak outlook in some individual instances. Even if the surface area involved is not always huge it is very often highly productive agricultural land that is effected.

2. The effects of agriculture

The transformation of agriculture in the Mediterranean basin is reflected by growing dependence on the industrial sector for the supply of inputs: agricultural equipment, fertilizers, pesticides, and herbicides. The emergence of new production objectives is changing the way land is used and the very conception of agrosystems. The soil reacts in different ways depending on whether it is well suited to increased production or is only marginal in terms of agriculture.

In non-irrigated areas north of the basin, cattle manure and the pace and diversity of crops help the soil to keep its regenerative capacity, provided human pressure on the environment maintains a certain balance. According to the scenarios, population growth and the compression of cultivated surface areas lead to the over-exploitation of some soils due to specialization and crop intensification, the exclusion of stock-farming from the tilled areas, and the mechanization of ploughing. If the return of organic material to the soil is reduced, it is likely to become impoverished and its structure will degrade more easily on account of new soil-preparation techniques. The continuous degradation of soil structure makes it increasingly vulnerable to erosion. Moreover, the modification of the calcium cycle due to the climate or to human action can reduce the availability of nutrients.

In the southern part of the basin the trend towards agircultural intensification could lead, in scenarios T2 and T3, to serious degradation of the physical and chemical properties of soil and to soil erosion as a result of mechanization unsuited to conditions: steep slopes, light soil with an unstable structure, unduly heavy machinery, and so forth. This is when wind erosion develops, which particularly affects marginal agricultural and range-land in the south and east of the basin. For example, the Maghreb steppe (375,000 km²) is naturally intended for pastoralism, but ranges are deteriorating because of over-grazing. Moreover, crop-land has been extended considerably over the past two decades, largely through mechanization. Soil systematically worked, with its structure destroyed, is now bare

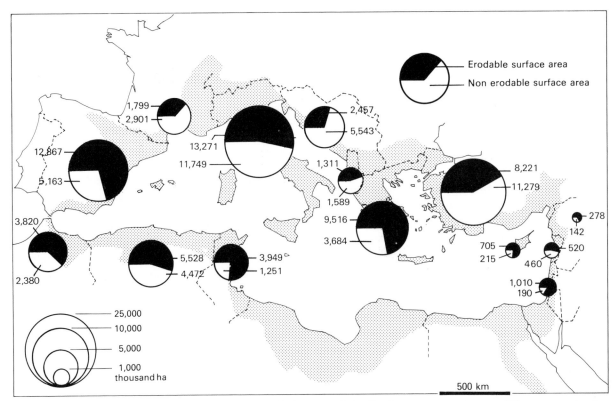

FIG. 18.1 Erodable land in the Mediterranean watershed (1,000 ha). The figures given relate to different years in the 1980s, depending on national sources. In Egypt and Libya water erosion is not a major source of soil degradation (compared with wind erosion, salinization, and waterlogging). Non-erodable land is land covered with forest, grass, or permanent crops as well as built-up areas.

Source: Blue Plan.

during most, if not all, the year. The effects of wind, hitherto limited, are becoming widespread and extensive. Only the protective measures envisaged in the alternative scenarios would make it possible to curb this phenomenon.

In the irrigated areas of the basin as a whole, waterlogging and the secondary salinization of poorly drained soil are common occurrences. Secondary salinization deserves very special attention, particularly in the countries south of the basin with heavy evapotranspiration and in all cases where irrigated districts are poorly developed or inadequately drained. According to FAO studies:

● Egypt has the highest risk in terms of surface area, i.e. 32 per cent of its Mediterranean part (coast and Nile delta up to Cairo); 30 per cent of soil in the Nile valley (80,000 ha of agricultural land) is already affected by salinization and waterlogging, and an additional 40 per cent shows signs of it.

● Syria comes second, with 12 per cent of its Mediterranean watershed threatened; it is estimated, however, that 50 per cent of irrigated land is affected

by salinization and waterlogging in the Euphrates valley.

● Of Mediterranean land, 5 per cent is undergoing salinization in Tunisia, 3 per cent in Algeria, 1 per cent in Morocco.

● In Greece 33 per cent of irrigated land is similarly affected.

At the world level, it is thought that salinization develops each year over surface areas equivalent to the new areas brought under irrigation.

In the Mediterranean basin salinization would be further aggravated by the conditions of economic and agricultural development characteristic of worst trend scenario T2. On the other hand, this trend would be reduced in moderate trend scenario T3, and in the alternative scenarios the phenomenon would be eliminated in some areas and reduced in others, following investment in drainage and the appropriate management of crop husbandry.

Lastly, it should be recalled that in the case of any soil under intensive non-irrigated cultivation, and even more in that of irrigated cultivation, the

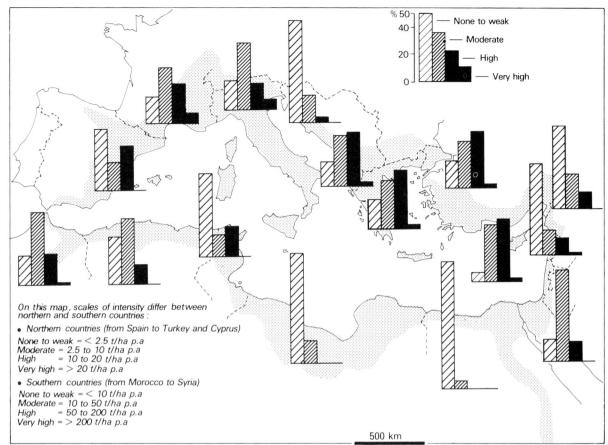

On this map, scales of intensity differ between
northern and southern countries :

● Northern countries (from Spain to Turkey and Cyprus)

None to weak = < 2.5 t/ha p.a
Moderate   = 2.5 to 10 t/ha p.a
High   = 10 to 20 t/ha p.a
Very high   = > 20 t/ha p.a

● Southern countries (from Morocco to Syria)

None to weak = < 10 t/ha p.a
Moderate   = 10 to 50 t/ha p.a
High   = 50 to 200 t/ha p.a
Very high   = > 200 t/ha p.a

500 km

FIG. 18.2 Intensity of water erosion in the Mediterranean watershed, 1980 (as a percentage of the total watershed
area). In most Mediterranean regions, more than half the land is prone to erosion because it lacks sufficient plant
cover or artificial protection. In the north, where rainfall is higher and more frequent than in the south—increasing
the amount and speed of run-off, hence the potential sediment load—water erosion occurs mainly on loose soils. In
the south, soil is very exposed to water erosion, chiefly because of the combination of intense rain and steep slopes,
and erosion rates are much higher than in the north.

Source: FAO/Blue Plan.

accumulation of fertilizer, pesticide, and herbicide
residues, together with the associated risk of
ground-water pollution, is a particularly serious
threat in the trend scenarios, even if all its long-term
consequences for the soil itself and for the environment cannot be assessed. Furthermore, the
dryer the climate the less these residues are carried
away or broken down. Finally, it should be noted
that a number of subsidizing practices for prices of
fertilizers and pesticides may result in excessive and
harmful use.

3. Water erosion

This is clearly the most serious threat to soil in
the Mediterranean countries, resulting from both
geological and human action. It particularly affects
bare soil and soil on slopes, either following de-

forestation or during the crop cycle. Only high-
density forest or grassland can moderate or eliminate
it. Arable land, on the other hand, can be fairly
well protected by fallowing, alternating crops (also
effective against physical and chemical degradation),
management, mixed tree crops, etc.

In Mediterranean regions, 31 per cent of land
suffers losses from erosion, amounting to over 15
t/ha per annum. Overall, more than half the land
in the watershed is prone to erosion because it is
not protected by a continuous plant cover, the risk
increasing with the slope of the ground, the nature
of the rock, and the distribution and intensity of
precipitation. The breadth of the northern watershed
explains why nearly two-thirds of removal and
sediment input into the sea occurs there, but the
consequences of erosion are much more serious for
the countries south and east of the basin. In some

catchment areas with fragile rock, such as flysch or marl in Italy, Morocco, Syria, etc., erosion rates may sporadically exceed 250 t/ha per annum. They can reach 200 t/ha per annum in some regions of Andalusia, and advancing erosion seems irreversible in parts of Mediterranean Spain. In Turkey, where 70 per cent of land is affected by erosion, it is estimated that 1,000m. t of fertile land is lost from run-off (and wind) each year.

It should be stressed that it is difficult to take stock of erosion: figures have been given to quantify sediment loss, either in centimetres removed per watershed or in millions of hectares lost each year by country. But these assessments are far from considering all the elements at play and remain approximate. The loss of 10 cm of soil has a different implication if it exposes the impermeable layer of a soil with calcareous crusts or if it represents one-tenth of the depth of a 'vertisol'. Nevertheless, it can be observed that the effects of erosion are increasing: accurate observations on watersheds, comparison between aerial photographs taken on successive dates, increasing speed of rising water during floods, all confirm that erosion phenomena are speeding up in the Mediterranean watershed.

Only the first of the three different phenomena related to water erosion—soil loss, carriage (and partial retention) of sediment in hydrographic networks, and discharge of sediment into the sea—will be considered here. In the same way as for Mediterranean forests, an 'environmental chain' was formulated to explore some of the important factors of soil evolution under the effect of water erosion in the light of the various socio-economic development scenarios. Confining observations to the catchment areas, the following surfaces were determined:

● For erodable surface area, calculations were made on the basis of FAO data and maps. This is non-forest land, not covered with grassland or built over, therefore largely cultivated arable land.

● For actual eroded surfaces, a coefficient was deduced on the basis of the situation observed in 1980, and applied to each country and scenario. Unfortunately, it was not possible with available data to adapt this coefficient in terms of time and/or other factors (an initial approach to the volumes of sediment actually discharged into the sea, taking into account time and transport conditions, was nevertheless developed with the help of another coefficient).

A distinction was made between two categories of eroded surfaces, depending on whether erosion can be considered as light (values never less than 5 t/ha per annum) or heavy (values never less than 10 t/ha per annum), the actual limits of these erosion rates varying with the country under consideration. The breakdown between slightly eroded and heavily eroded arable land was partly based on the amount of land on slopes, i.e. on the morphology of the watershed. Erosion rates were adapted in the light of the scenarios, increasing by 20–60 per cent, for instance, depending on the country, in worst trend scenario T2, and, on the contrary, falling by 10–30 per cent in the moderate trend scenario T3 (where some action is taken which helps to restrict sediment removal), and by 30–60 per cent in the alternative scenarios (more conservation action is taken and becomes increasingly effective). In fact, in a given watershed action to combat soil erosion can restrict sediment removal by as much as 50–80 per cent.

This model indicated that some Mediterranean regions would lose nearly 1 per cent of their 'agricultural land capital' each year. Worst trend scenario T2 would generally speed up losses considerably (except in Turkey and in France, the only countries with a strong agricultural potential), combining increases in agricultural surface areas involved and in losses per hectare. In order to stabilize, even reduce, major degradation related to moderate trend scenarios T3, huge biological and mechanical conservation and rehabilitation efforts should be made, at a very high cost (which would not prevent some irreversible trends), considering the growing agricultural pressure in countries south and east of the Mediterranean basin. In other words, and considering all the factors of degradation, the two trend scenarios would in fact spell doom for Mediterranean soils, the T2 because of real pressure on land, the T3 for economic reasons. And this, according to experts, would occur within ten to fifteen years—within the first period of the Blue Plan scenarios.

With the abandonment of agricultural land in the north, and lower growth of agricultural areas in the countries south and east of the basin through increased co-operation, the alternative scenarios give a slow-down in the loss of agricultural land compared with 1980, through effective biological soil-conservation efforts and reafforestation or forest-protection measures, whose implementation could require between ten and twenty five years.

It should be noted that even in the most propitious case the loss of agricultural land would remain a permanent problem, which could worsen at any time in the most threatened countries (Syria, Lebanon, the Maghreb, etc.) as a result of the lack of adequate management according to soil potentials. The inability to check soil-erosion and -degradation processes clearly seems to be one of the most serious threats.

All degradation processes, starting with wind and water erosion, in a climatic context in which dry periods are increasing, contribute to the advance of desertification both in the countries south and east of the Mediterranean basin (with an annual loss of about 20,000 ha per annum in Tunisia, for example) and in Spain, the most threatened country on the northern shore (nearly 10m. ha threatened in the medium or long term in its Mediterranean region).

19 The Water Constraint

The distinctive physical conditions obtaining in the Mediterranean environment and the inherent features of water use in the basin are such that they confer very specific shades of emphasis on the interactions between development activities and water. The marked relief of the greater part of the basin offers considerable scope for water-control schemes, especially storage reservoirs—although their useful life is liable to be curtailed in the long run by silt encroachment—but it has the effect of compartmentalizing the land areas into a very large number of independent basins differing widely in size, and it is not easy to transfer water from one basin to another in order to tailor resources more closely to demand. Even so, such transfers are possible in a number of cases, notably in the Mediterranean coastal plains of Spain, France, Italy, Greece, Cyprus, Tunisia, and Morocco, among other countries. The relative lack of major graded and converging water systems is a factor complicating the water-use conditions and makes local utilizations less interdependent.

Tourism generates a sharp seasonal peak demand (cf. Chapter 13), which is largely concomitant with the irrigation demand and adds to the drinking-water demand of local communities. As a result of the effect of its agricultural and tourist components, water demand is subject to a marked seasonal pattern, which runs counter to the surface run-off pattern. This exacerbates the tensions between requirements and resources in the summer season and justifies the extensive development of water-storage and -control schemes. However, the low inflows that are a fairly widespread feature of the dry season magnify the relative impact of the discharge of waste water into the surface water at the very time that demand is at its peak, on account of tourism, and this entails making a very special effort to provide sewerage and purification facilities. This problem is compounded in the semi-arid regions of the south, such as the Tunisian Sahel, which have no permanent watercourses, and in the offshore islands.

The concentration on the seaboard of growing urbanization, tourist activities, and a substantial proportion of the irrigated land is responsible for generating an aggregate water-supply demand in such areas that is much higher than the local resources available, and indeed these tend to be further reduced by the impact of that demand. In addition to the fact that conflicts over the use of the water sparked off by the build-up in demand become more widespread, the coastal regions exert a marked pull effect on inland water resources, and this may extend so far as to cover all the upstream watersheds, without being offset by the recovery of waste water in return, since this is largely discharged into the sea. The reduction in water resources, owing to urbanization and the growing density of coastal land occupation, is in fact the outcome of the artificial channelling of rivers and streams and of the depletion and contamination of the ground-water aquifers. In other words, the coastal regions tend to monopolize and consume a large proportion of the basin's water resources, while they lose part of their own resources. This pull effect may even extend beyond the basin, through transfers of water from outside sources, as is possible in a number of Mediterranean countries, such as Spain, Israel, and Libya. However, the urbanization of the coastline can also be said to generate a by-product in the form of the discharge of waste water collected. This represents a significant secondary water resource, whose reuse—although still very slight at the present time—could be developed in future. It would have a beneficial induced effect on the marine environment into which it is discharged, and could also contribute to reducing the conflicts over urban versus agricultural uses.

There are grounds for believing that the very large number of small and medium-sized Mediterranean islands which are the focal points of acute tension between local water demand and resources—and have little prospect of being able to draw on mainland resources—will prove to be eminently suitable testing-grounds for the development of non-conventional water resources, starting with the desalinization of sea water for domestic uses.

This is only one example pointing to the fact that, in future, the mobilization and use of water in many

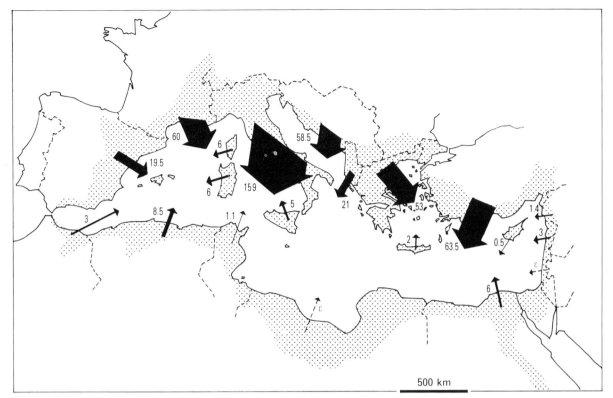

FIG. 19.1 Real average annual flows from each country to the Mediterranean, 1985 (1,000m. m³ p.a.). The stippled area represents the Mediterranean catchment area. Direct return of waste water to the sea is not included. The Nile has contributed very little to the flow of inland water into the Mediterranean since the building of the Aswan dam. Flows from Israel and Libya are very small (designated by ϵ).

Source: Blue Plan (J. Margat, 1988).

Mediterranean countries can be expected to entail sharply increasing costs in terms of funding and energy, owing to the need for transfer pumping, long-distance conveyance systems, deep boreholes, desalinization plants, and so on.

1. Irrigation

Irrigation is very widespread in the Mediterranean basin and it occupies a predominant place in the overall demand for water in almost all the countries, although there are significant differences depending on the parts of the basin concerned. In the north, for example, irrigation is more in the nature of an adjunct to rainfall than it is in the south. Two very different irrigation methods—the traditional and the modern—often exist side by side, and hence the water requirements per hectare are rather different. The considerable volume of water used for agricultural purposes boosts the final consumption figure

compared with the total draw-off, since the bulk of the withdrawal used for the other purposes is recovered.

A study has been carried out on a country-by-country basis in an attempt to set possible theoretical limits for the development of irrigation. In the north of the basin, from Spain to Greece, the water resources would make it possible—although the schemes required would be costly in some instances—to increase the irrigated areas by about 3.8m. to 4m. ha by the year 2025 (at an estimated cost of roughly US$70,000m. at 1985 prices). Turkey also offers very considerable potential for increasing the area under irrigation by about 2.5m. ha (at a cost which might amount to as much as US$30,000m.). Syria and Egypt have to contend with very special situations, and the cost of increasing the irrigated area would be very high (as much as US$30,000 per hectare in Syria compared with some US$12,000–13,000 in Turkey). In the Maghreb, by 2025 the increase in the irrigated area could amount to some 1.6m. ha, 60 per cent of the total being in Morocco. (The cost for the Maghreb as a whole could work out to as much as US$28,000m.–30,000m.) These limits could only be lowered by means of very substantial improvements in the specific water consumption per hectare, such as those obtained in Israel.

For historical and social reasons, the price of irrigation water is generally lower than its actual economic cost. But in any event, the progressive tapping of new water resources from the natural cycle will entail a considerable increase in the cost of the water available for irrigation, especially in the countries on the southern and eastern seaboards of the basin. So high a cost will influence the choice of crops grown, which will tend to go to high value-added produce, perhaps to the detriment of a cropping pattern that would ensure satisfactory soil conservation, with the added risk of salinization. All studies show that if high-yield intensive agriculture is introduced, water-saving techniques will have to become more widespread and drainage will have to be provided so as to enable part of the water to be recovered, among other things. Salt encroachment on the land would accordingly spread less quickly than expected, although this would not necessarily be true of the salinization of inland water and the subsequent pollution of sea water.

The intensive use of water from the natural cycle could cause a substantial decline in outflows to the sea. This is clearly illustrated by the example of the Nile: at the beginning of the century the volume of water emptying into the sea amounted to some 60,000m. m³ per annum, whereas now that the river flow is regulated it only discharges 5,000m. m³. This is the minimum volume of water needed to ensure flow conditions that are capable of 'sweeping' the river bed. (Indeed, those minimum flow conditions were dramatically threatened in 1988, following several years of drought, when the level of Lake Nasser fell very close to its critical elevation of 147 metres, below which electricity generation could no longer be possible.) Most of the rivers and streams will suffer a similar fate, in that the volumes discharged will decline and will at the same time be more heavily silt-laden. The role performed by the Atlantic (and the Black Sea) in compensating for evaporation in the Mediterranean will be enhanced.

The problem of treating urban and industrial

BOX 19A. **Statistics and forecasts for irrigation**

Some concepts relating to irrigated areas are unfortunately imprecise, and statistics fail to provide the necessary data. The form of irrigation is almost never stipulated. Depending on countries and circumstances, it may involve:

- *traditional random irrigation*, by submersion, spreading, or diversion of flood water or melted snow in mountain areas, along an irrigation furrow;
- *steady gravity irrigation*, along furrows or creeks, from obsolete structures, from reservoirs, canals, trenches, towers, etc.;
- *pressure irrigation* from a feeder network, spraying by means of sprinklers, canons, or trickle-drip, or any similar process from a closed feeder circuit with distribution through the soil near to the plant.

Similarly, the surface area stated in statistics is not defined with any precision. Depending on the methods of irrigation defined above, there are several possibilities:

- The area involved may be the *area equipped*, in other words with a water supply or intake that enables the user to water when he likes (for spraying, this is usually the only precise fact stated). For gravity irrigation, the same concept exists, the reference being to the surface area of plots where access to water is possible through the existing furrow network.
- Or the *area irrigated* each year may be meant, corresponding to the portion of the equipped area that can be watered each year, whether because of available water supplies or, more usually, because the farmer has been unable to sow irrigated crops over the whole of his land, for lack of labour. For sprinkler irrigation systems in French Provence, for instance, the irrigated area is only between 35 per cent and 60 per cent of the area equipped—whereas for gravity irrigation it is always above 70 per cent.
- Or the reference may be to the *area harvested*, when several crops are sown each year on the same plot. This area is usually defined by a cropping intensity coefficient, applied to the physical surface area actually irrigated. With crop rotation and fallowing, this coefficient is less than 1. When there is a multiple cropping, it is above 1 (it is usually taken to be 1.5 or 1.6 for Egypt, which offers a striking example of multiple harvesting).

Concerning the volumes used for irrigation, the concepts given above affect estimates. As can be imagined, they are very much influenced by the scarcity of rainfall and degree of evaporation (with consumption higher in the south and desert zones than in the north and coastal zones).

All these remarks explain the reticence concerning results, in view of the many imponderables in available data.

waste water has already become urgent in many countries. This problem is crucial for the Mediterranean countries, especially those in the south and east, and in fact water re-utilization plans already exist in several countries.

Depending on the scenarios, water will be used with varying degrees of efficiency in the year 2000, but the differences in its use for irrigation purposes will not be very significant (in the 10–15 per cent range) between the two most sharply contrasting scenarios, i.e. worst trend scenario T2 and integration alternative scenario A2. Moreover, the depletion of water resources and the increase in salinization hazards can plainly be seen from all the scenarios. Hence, efforts have to be focused on exploring the possibilities of cutting down on wastage, making use of technology in the most suitable and effective way possible, increasing retreatment capacities, etc.

In the alternative scenarios a positive answer to these points is expected to be provided through technological and financial co-operation. At the present time techniques for water saving, wastewater treatment, accurate fertilization, and drainage are known and are already operational. However,

their large-scale use calls for an effort to train skilled labour and for the availability of investment funds, in addition to very firm political determination, both nationally and internationally, based on a clearer perception of the issues involved.

On the subject of the types of irrigation used, mention has to be made of the questions that have recently come to be asked about projects connected with large dams. Since the end of the last war considerable sums have been invested in the construction of large hydraulic dams, and the results in terms of agricultural performance are regarded as not always having lived up to expectations (as in the cases of Algeria, Syria, Tunisia, and Egypt, among others). Apart from the ensuing salinization of the land (one of the secondary effects arising out of poorly managed irrigation), the main reasons for this lie in the fact that investments downstream of the dam were not as effective as they ought to have been, priority had to be given to providing drinking-water supplies, agricultural pricing policies were not suited to the purpose, or the population was not sufficiently involved in the project decisions or implementation and was not properly prepared for it. Districts scheduled to be irrigated were not

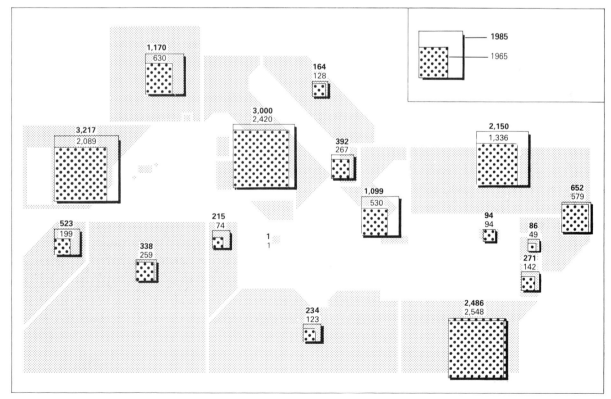

FIG. 19.2 Irrigated land: Trends 1965–1985 (1,000 ha)
Source: FAO/Blue Plan.

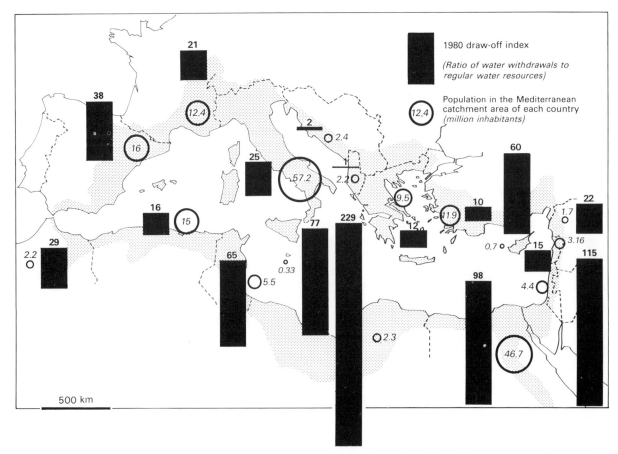

FIG. 19.3 Water draw-off in the Mediterranean catchment area, 1985 (annual withdrawal as percentage of resources). A high water draw-off index calls for utilization of non-conventional resources: non-renewable fossil aquifers, recycling of used water, multiple water uses, reduction of losses, desalination, etc.

Source: Blue Plan (J. Margat, 1988).

all equipped. The districts actually irrigated are often much smaller than foreseen, while water losses from the distribution systems tend, moreover, to increase with the course of time (to the extent that they account for 50 per cent of the inflow, or even more). By contrast, 'small-scale' irrigation has proved particularly dynamic in many countries and could be developed to a notable degree.

In addition to the role they play in irrigation and possibly in electricity generation, dams perform an important flood-control and prevention function. This need for protection will most probably grow sharply in many of the countries in the Mediterranean basin, where the flow patterns are extremely irregular (as in the case of the Maghreb). The bulk of the inflows occur at flood-time, sometimes in the space of only a few hours or a few days, and the morphology of the landscape changes at the same time. In the Maghreb, for example, some 15–20 per cent of the annual discharge of the Medjerda occurs in a single day, while the stream flow of the

Moulouya rises from one hundred to several hundred m³/sec in several hours. In October 1969 the flow in the Oued Zeroud, in central Tunisia, rose to 17,000 m³/sec, whereas its normal floods scarcely ever exceed 200–500 m³/sec.

Laden as they are with sediment and debris from upstream erosion, the swollen torrents cut into the banks and may carry down up to 15–20 per cent of solid matter, or indeed as much as 30 per cent (as in the case of the Medjerda in 1973). As a result, the dams are clogged with silt and, in other instances, there is catastrophic flooding. The Kairouan plain, for example, was covered by silt deposits more than a metre thick, which removed all trace of the crop layouts. In the city of Sfax, which is located in the middle of a large basin measuring 800 km², the lowest-lying districts were flooded in 1975. In Annaba, where the problem is a complex one, the districts situated on the plain were completely destroyed by the floods in November 1982. Unless extensive protection works are carried out, it will not be possible to integrate many low-lying flat areas into the future urban fabric.

In connection with the silting-up of dams, all the reservoirs in Algeria are estimated to be losing 2–3 per cent of their storage capacity, or some 90m. m³ of water each year. In other words, the 'siltation margin' entering into the calculation of the dead storage is in the range of 30–50 years. Owing to the scale of the floods on the Oued Zeroud and the susceptibility of its catchment area to erosion, the size of the reservoir was generously designed to provide for additional storage of 60m.–70m. m³, so as to allow for silting. The Chiba dam, also in Tunisia, which was brought into service in 1963, was silted at a level of 35 per cent some twelve years later, in 1975, and the level is now thought to be about 70 per cent.

2. Difficulties involved in the long-range forecasting of requirements

The growth in water requirements to keep pace with urbanization has already been mentioned, the capital cities being by far the most demanding (Algiers will need 540m. m³ in the year 2000 and Greater Tunis 235m.). Like land occupation, domestic water consumption is the product of two factors: the population, which can be estimated to within an accuracy of ±10 per cent by 2025, and unit consumption, which is currently difficult to calculate and much more difficult to evaluate for a horizon several decades ahead.

Demand for domestic uses has to compete with that from industry, to which it is even more difficult to put a figure for the medium or long run. In point of fact, while demand, which should not be confused with actual 'consumption', is fairly well known in the case of certain large consumer industries, such as steel, pulp for paper-making, and some branches of the agro-food sector, etc., the figures may vary significantly, depending on the features or the age of the plant being used. Some industrial sites are substantial consumers, like the Gabès area in Tunisia, which consumes more than 28.3m. m³ a year; the pulp mill at Mostaganem consumes a similar amount. However, the medium- or long-term demand is still very difficult to estimate for the country as a whole, since the consumer industries are becoming increasingly divided into those that are connected up—usually to the urban mains distribution system—and those that are not.

As a rule, a distinction also has to be made between two levels in respect of demand (and discharge): the level of consumer demand (and discharge) which the economic sectors require from the agencies responsible for water, such as distribution companies, and the level of demand (and discharge) required from the natural environment. Both these levels can, moreover, be expressed in terms of quantity and quality. Although the two last-mentioned aspects, quantity and quality, cannot be dissociated, it is usually difficult to gauge the impact which economic activities have on the quality of the water from the natural environment on a macroscopic scale. Almost the only measurements available are those made on a local scale, and it is virtually impossible to determine what relationship these bear, in quantitative terms, to action to combat pollution or attempts at purification.

The following considerations accordingly take only a globalizing approach, in an endeavour to estimate the water requirements of the different countries and to compare them with the resources available.

BOX 19B. **Water transfers between drainage basins: an example**

In Cyprus a project for transferring surface water from the drainage basin of the River Dhiarizos to that of the River Komis through a 15-km-long tunnel is the solution envisaged for the future water supply in the towns of Limassol, Larnaca, Famagusta, and Nicosia.

In the coastal area to the south-east of Mesaria, draw-offs from the aquifer amount to 25m.–27m. m³, whereas natural renewal amounts only to 14m. m³. This over-exploitation produced a drop in the water level and the seepage of sea water into the aquifer.

The only solution is therefore to import 'surplus' water from other regions. The solution will be complemented by measures to recycle water within the towns concerned, depending on its use (water for some household uses does not need to be potable).

In this region the demand for water is between 150 and 170 l per day for tourism and 130 l per day for households in rural areas.

3. Medium- and long-term outlook

In order to obtain an overall prospective view of the situation, it was considered useful to tackle the questions of future water requirements in the countries of the Mediterranean basin by means of a globalizing method, after having checked it for consistency against the straightforward summation of sectoral requirements. This method made it possible to propose a classification of countries into three groups, according to how acute their water-supply problems will be at horizon 2025.

The first assumption adopted was that the determining variable would be the size of the population. The second assumption was that the per capita requirements would remain constant to the year 2025, in other words that the growth in requirements would keep pace with population growth. Although this assumption may appear surprising, it was verified from a number of sectoral requirements furnished by the scenarios. For example, the irrigation-water requirements in Algeria were estimated as being likely to grow by a factor of 2.5 by 2025 while, according to the scenarios, the population is expected to grow by a factor of 2.5–3, virtually the same amount. Generally speaking, the variances proved to be in the 10–20 per cent range. This is not very significant, considering that the multiplier factors were in the region of 2–3.

It is possible, of course, to identify a number of factors which should give rise to an increase in per capita requirements (although these display some short-term inertia). These factors include:

- the growth in the drinking-water supply rate, especially for the rural population in the countries south and east of the basin;
- the growth in the population urbanization rate;
- the growth in the per capita drinking-water demand for the population being served, which is largely bound up with the growth in household incomes;
- the development of industrial output per capita;
- the growth in the share of agriculture in the total water requirements;
- the growth in the active population as a proportion of the population as a whole;
- the worsening of water-supply and -distribution loss-rates;
- the possible development of water exports.

There are, however, other factors also that could give rise to a decline in per capita water consumption or, more precisely, could prove to be an impediment to the above-mentioned growth factors. These include:

- advances in the introduction of water-saving techniques, especially in agriculture (through sprinkler systems and micro-irrigation) and in energy production (the progress made in using closed-circuit cooling systems as a substitute for open circuits);
- the extension of waste-water re-utilization methods;
- the development of 'non-conventional' water

BOX 19C. **The pollutant-receiving capacity of the Nile**

The River Nile is Egypt's main—and virtually only—source of fresh water. Apart from the Mediterranean Sea in the north, it is also the main outlet for the dumping of polluted effluents. Some of these effluents may be mixed with the topsoil and be absorbed by the subsoil, especially by the pervious sandy layers underlying the upper alluvial layers. However, some of the effluents will eventually be completely recycled if the economic and technical conditions permit. It is accordingly of the utmost importance to continue to monitor the Nile water, in order to ensure that it is still capable of absorbing, diluting, and precipitating all kinds of pollutants. The polluted water is used several times over for industrial purposes and for the country's irrigation needs before it is finally discharged into the sea.

Pollution-monitoring stations have been installed along the navigable waterway. Between Aswan and Cairo there are 22 collectors discharging more than 300m. m³ of industrial effluents into the Nile, while there are 45 other sewers discharging some 400m. m³ of waste water from agricultural uses. In addition, it is reckoned that there are 800 vessels plying the Nile, and these are required to be fitted with water-treatment equipment, while 6 land treatment plants have been built to take the effluents accumulated by vessels while they are at sea. Measures have been taken to clean up oil and grease spillage in localities that have been seriously affected by pollution.

It is important to engage in the periodic analysis of the water quality at different locations and times of the year. It should be possible to identify pollutants that are dangerous in terms of both quantity and quality and to draw up a reasonable effluent-treatment programme, so as to be able to deal with difficult cases, especially in instances where the river water is drawn off by pumping for domestic uses.

resources (such as the desalinition of brackish water or sea water);

● the reduction of water losses and leakage in supply and use;

● the cutting back of drinking-water supplies by means of rationing;

● the development of water imports, especially from outside the Mediterranean basin;

● changing attitudes and behaviour patterns particluarly as regards the true economic value of water.

An 'exploitation index' has been defined as being the ratio of the sum of all water draw-offs to the total volume of physical water resources. This index should only be regarded as being a macro-indicator of the 'pressure' which the demand exerts on the resources. It may exceed 100 per cent, which would mean the reuse of the water after it has been returned to the resource, or the tapping of non-renewable stocks (such as the depletion of the ground-water aquifers). In the event of the water being reused, an exploitation index of more than 100 per cent is significant in a further respect, in that it is bound up to some degree with the quality of the water, since it indicates that a growing proportion of the overall water flow is recovered after having been used. Lastly, the index has an economic significance, since water-production costs and consumer prices tend to increase in parallel with one another, and this could eventually have an effect on demand.

The findings (for the Mediterranean regions or for the whole country, depending on the case) show that there are no very significant variances in the different scenarios for a given country—this is the outcome of the method itself—but that, by contrast, the countries have to contend with very differing situations and can be roughly classified into three groups, as follows:

The first group consists of countries where water availability will remain adequate up to 2025 and beyond, and where there is even a fairly comfortable margin for increased per capita draw-offs. This group includes some with low population growth (France, Italy, Yugoslavia) and some with stronger population growth (Albania, Turkey, Lebanon). Maintaining this margin will require efforts to develop and manage water, and to preserve appropriate quality, which will be necessary in any event.

Secondly, there are countries where water availability, although still adequate at present, will drop considerably (Spain, Morocco, Algeria, Cyprus), but where the global demand for water could be met

up to 2025, chiefly with new water-resource development or through major interregional water transfers in countries where the resources are distributed very unevenly, provided that the per capita draw-off remains close to current levels. Any significant growth in the per capita draw-off would put these countries quite quickly in the critical situation being faced by the countries in the next group and would call for solutions other than conventional hydraulic works.

Finally, there are some countries where current water availability is already limited or negligible. As from the year 2000, the exploitation indexes will exceed, or will have already exceeded, 100 per cent. These include countries where population growth is low (Malta), average (Israel, Tunisia), or high (Egypt, Syria, Libya). In order to meet demand, per capita draw-offs on conventional resources will probably have to be reduced through various incentives, or else the country will have to resort either to the exploitation of non-conventional resources (such as fossil water or the desalination of sea water) or to importing water.

The above classification can be enlarged on by the following comments, which shed some light on the specific situations obtaining in various countries:

● In the north the exploitation indexes are rising in Spain and Cyprus, where they are already quite high (currently 40 per cent and 60 per cent). In both cases irrigation is a very dominant component of the water demand and is likely to remain so.

● Exploitation indexes are likewise growing in Turkey, although they started out from a moderate base, and will exceed 15 per cent only in the year 2000 and 20 per cent in 2025 in the worst trend scenario T2.

● Malta is a special case, in that the low rate of the per capita draw-off is already the outcome of the limited volume of resources. The index will level off in all cases at around 100 per cent, and it will only be possible to meet any further demand by means of non-conventional resources, such as desalination.

● In the Maghreb countries the index is increasing sharply, without any very appreciable variance between the scenarios, and it will increase twofold or more by 2025 (the maximum for T2). However, it reaches and exceeds 100 per cent only in Tunisia, from a current base value that is already high (more than 65 per cent). The index is liable to exceed 100 per cent by the year 2000, and could range as high as 130–155 per cent in 2025. Tunisia is the country where the re-utilization of water will be developed

BOX 19D. **Water in Algeria: the planning of a scarce resource**

In October 1980 the then current water uses were estimated to amount to 3,380 hm³ per annum, divided between domestic uses (700 hm³), industry (14 hm³), although the latter probably accounted for much more, and agriculture (2,540 hm³). This is by no means sufficient to meet the requirements, either in towns, where there are frequent interruptions in supply, or in agriculture, where the amounts applied are inadequate. At an approximation, out of the total of 3,380 hm³, the ground-water aquifers supplies 1,870 hm³ and dams 700 hm³, while the remainder is obtained from run-off.

The potential certainly exists and can be evaluated as follows:

● Available surface water amounts to 13,580 hm³, 4,900 hm³ of which could be mobilized by building dams at an acceptable cost. (This would represent seven times the current regulated volume of 700 hm³.)

● Total ground-water resources are estimated to amount to 3,300 hm³, out of which 1,870 hm³ are already used. However, these resources are chiefly located in the Sahara (estimated resources: 1,600 hm³, only 600 hm³ of which are already used), where the use of water, especially for the Albian, poses problems of distance and cost. In contrast, northern Algeria, whose ground-water resources are estimated to amount to 1,700 hm³, is already using 1,270 hm³, thereby leaving very little spare capacity (430 hm³).

Water requirements for the year 2000 have been the subject of projections worked out by the Ministries of Hydraulics and Planning on the basis of estimates for urban population growth, the average rate of satisfaction of the demand for drinking water, and the norms for the use of water in agriculture and industry:

● Drinking-water requirements will range between 2,000 hm³ (with the high assumption of 300 l per inhabitant per day) and 1,600 hm³ (with the low assumption of 200 l per inhabitant per day).

● Water supplies for industry account for 465 hm³, but industrial requirements generally are not well known.

● In the agricultural sector, 4,700 hm³ would be needed to irrigate 700,000 ha, with average applications ranging between 3,500 m³ and 8,000 m³ per hectare, depending on the region (excluding the Sahara).

This represents a total demand at the horizon 2000 of between 6,765 and 7,165 hm³, or double the amount used in 1980 (3,380 hm³).

Source: Maghreb-Machrek, 111 (1986).

to the greatest extent, in conjunction with water savings, irrespective of the scenario.

● In Israel, where the index has already topped 100 per cent, it could rise to 160 per cent in 2000 and to more than 200 per cent in 2025 (the maximum in scenario A2). It will obviously not be possible for the per capita draw-off to continue at the present level, even with the increased re-mobilization of water and the tapping of reserves. Even if the demand is held down by water savings, a growing proportion of the requirements will have to be met by turning to non-conventional resources and/or imports.

● In the Mediterranean part of Syria the same pattern is taking shape. Starting from a base value that is already high, it is unlikely that the per capita draw-off of 1,500 m³ per annum, which is caused by the large scale of irrigation compared with the small size of the population, can be maintained.

● Likewise, in Egypt, where the per capita draw-off is almost as high, the current exploitation index of almost 100 per cent would in all cases exceed 100 per cent in the year 2000, with wider variances in 2025, depending on the scenarios (the maximum being 200 per cent in scenario T2 and the minimum 175 per cent in scenario A2). Since the water

resources are virtually all imported (via the Nile), the growth in the index reflects the need to increase the inflow in the short or medium run—perhaps by means of development schemes in Sudan and Ethiopia—but it also suggests that there is a need to reduce the per capita demand in the long run, especially by stepping up the efficiency of irrigation.

● Libya records the highest growth in an index already far above 100 per cent (almost 250 per cent), in spite of a not unduly high per capita demand (similar to that of Tunisia and Israel). This growth is caused by the widespread use already being made of non-renewable resources, and indeed the theoretical index could exceed 500 per cent in 2000, and stand as high as 900 per cent or even 1,200 per cent in 2025. Even if this were to prove possible to some extent through the further drawing-down of reserves, as is actually planned, it will certainly be necessary to develop water-saving methods and non-conventional resources, such as desalination, in this country, whose renewable stocks of water are very limited.

To supplement these overall figures, the scenarios have made it possible to identify three possible types of evolution in the Mediterranean basin. These are as follows:

● The slow economic growth of the worst trend scenario T2, by adding to budgetary constraints and cutting back investments to a minimum, would make it difficult to meet the particularly marked growth in consumer demand for water, especially in the south, and in sewerage requirements, on account of: structural shortcomings due to the lack of amenities; reduction in the volume of water distributed per capita; the stagnating, and indeed declining, rate at which sewerage systems are being connected and purification plants are proving effective; and the slow pace at which the irrigated areas are being increased, coupled with the inadequacy of efforts being made to modernize irrigation methods that would be conducive to saving water. All this would tend to level out the pressure of demand for water in terms of quantity, but generally at the expense of efforts to provide sewerage facilities and protection both in the north and in the south and east. The outcome would be further and more widespread instances of local deteriorations in quality, and these would be above all numerous in the industrialized countries of the north.

● Stronger growth, but showing insufficient or belated concern for the environment (moderate trend scenario T3), would cater more readily for growing water-supply demands of consumers in the different economic sectors. The water supply would be increased primarily by stepping up the number of conventional water-management schemes—with a consequential escalation in mobilization costs—including provision for increasing the safety features in respect of sources of supply, flood protection, and so on, rather than by 'adjusting' demand through efforts that would fall on consumers to a much greater degree than they would on the community (as is the case with large-scale schemes). Since the only water savings would be those that would be of immediate advantage to consumers, wastage, in terms of both quantity and quality, would increase.

As a result, growing pressure would be exerted on the resources and the environment, and in particular the risk would be incurred, in the medium term, of depleting some of the non-renewable water resources of the countries in the south and east of the basin. Conflicts between users over control of the most accessible resources could become more widespread, especially in regions where water is scarce and, more generally, in coastal areas—above all between sectors whose economic and social impact is not the same (for example, as between the provision of a drinking-water supply for towns and the tourist industry as opposed to water for irrigation). Efforts to provide sewerage and water-protection facilities would not follow at the same pace, and the water quality, including that of the offshore sea water, would deteriorate in many sectors both in the north and in the south and east. Little allowance would be made for these external costs, except in cases where they would have feedback effects on drinking-water production costs, when

---

BOX 19E. **Use of low-quality water in Tunisia**

The state of the soil and the high degree of salinity of irrigation water make farming difficult in the lower part of the Medjerda valley in Tunisia. The Medjerda is a river which flows from west (in Algeria) to east, before emptying into the Mediterranean in the Gulf of Tunis. Some 40 km west of Tunis the river enters a broad coastal plain formed of heavy clay soil with a lime content ($CaCO_3$) of up to 35 per cent. The rate of seepage into this soil is very low, and the winter rainfall, of very low salinity, may remain on the surface for very long periods. During the growing season the soil dries out quickly and it shrinks and cracks (cracks of more than 5 cm wide in places). The water is quick to penetrate into the soil through these cracks, and the soil then swells and closes up again. The quality of the water from the Medjerda fluctuates to a considerable degree over the course of the year, ranging between 1.3 and 4.7 units of measurement (electrical conductivity). During the greater part of the year water from the Medjerda can be used for irrigating crops able to withstand a medium to high salt content, such as dates, sorghum, etc. The leaching of the soil in summer is not sufficient, owing to the large cracks that are formed, and the winter rains only partially wash out the salt in the topsoil. As a result, soil structure is poor and seepage rates are very low.

During the 1960s the Tunisian Government and Unesco carried out a major applied research and training programme on irrigation with saline water in this and other regions of Tunisia. The findings of this programme have proved very useful for both Tunisia and other Mediterranean countries which are obliged to use water containing several grams of salt per litre. The main proposal made in the study aimed at choosing the most appropriate period for leaching the soil, in order to save water, and the cultivation of certain types of crop, such as those capable of withstanding the expected salinity build-up.

Source: Bulletin de la qualité des eaux: l'eau et l'agriculture—Ire partie—(Mar. 1987).

they would be regarded more as a disamenity than as a shortcoming in environmental management. Levying a charge to remedy those disamenities, on the 'polluter pays' principle, might often degenerate into the acquisition of 'rights to pollute' in the settlement of conflicts over water uses, which would work to the detriment of the environment. As in the case of other environments, this scenario accordingly appears to be the 'best' from the development standpoint, but it would probably be the worst as far as the safeguarding of water resources is concerned.

● Thirdly, medium to strong economic growth, accompanied by a more action-orientated policy for safeguarding the environment and managing water resources, of the type depicted in the alternative scenarios, would enable a better balance to be struck between:

● water management and mobilization, though the institution of a system of 'earmarked' flows and quality goals, which would be monitored by resource-management authorities with the powers and the means to ensure compliance and a clearer understanding of those goals; and

● the adaptation or 'tailoring' of demand, in terms of usage, through water savings, tariff or other incentives, enhanced efficiency, recycling and reuse, all of which would make it easier for competing uses to exist side by side, and of the restoration of water to the environment through efforts to provide widespread sewerage and purification facilities, by improving the quality of the aquatic environment and thereby reducing drinking-water production costs.

Similarly, in the specific case of the mobilization of non-renewable water resources in the Saharan regions of the countries of the south, if these were managed as a 'heritage' it would lead to a more moderate rate of exploitation in favour of a longer time-scale and more effective economic use.

Whatever the outcome, it appears likely that the contrasts will become more marked between:

● those countries or regions where the overriding problem will be to reconcile the maintenance or moderate growth of the costs entailed in meeting consumers' demand for water—which is generally growing at a relatively slow pace—with the protection, and indeed restoration, of the natural environment; and

● those countries which are already engaging in—or will be compelled to engage in—'scarcity management', in which water saving will be progressively separated from the exclusive harnessing of water resources; 'primary' per capita draw-offs, which must of necessity be reduced, will have to go hand in hand with more efficient and sequential water uses—the same water having to be used several times—and with recourse to artificial resources.

20 The Coveted Coast

Social and economic development in the past few decades has wrought radical change in the Mediterraneean seaboard, and the foreseeable population trends and the development outlook for the different sectors of activity identified in the Blue Plan scenarios appear to presage even more far-reaching unheavals for the horizons 2000 and 2025. As a narrowly circumscribed dividing-line between land and sea, the Mediterranean coastline is a place where countless new development sites are being contemplated, whether it be for heavy or processing industries on the southern or eastern shores or 'high-tech' industries in the north, energy generation through the construction of power-stations, aquaculture, multimode transport, the creation of technology parks, and so on.

However, as the cradle of original civilizations, the Mediterranean seaboard is not merely a 'convenient location'. It also represents a cultural heritage common to all the coastal countries, on account of the prodigious wealth of its history and its incomparable and still more or less untouched landscapes; a fragile natural heritage, with intense exchanges taking place between land and sea; and a specific habitat for flora and fauna that are being increasingly threatened. It is therefore imperative that it be safeguarded.

The variety of the shorelines is so great and the contrasts in relief, geology, climate, population, activities, and other features are so marked that the exploration of their possible futures only becomes meaningful when it is narrowed down to a very local level. The Blue Plan scenarios accordingly have to be pursued on the coastal strip or belt proper, which may extend from a few hundred to several thousand metres on either side of the coastline, provided the necessary statistics become available. In the present future-orientated study, it has been necessary in most instances to limit the approach to much broader coastal regions, such as those defined on the basis of administrative units in the first part of this report (Fig. 2.3). In some of the areas studied, the scope has been extended to cover the watersheds (as in the case of water resources). However, wherever possible attention has been focused, if only in qualitative terms, on the coastal strip proper.

Failing the existence of 'coastal scenarios', an attempt was made to identify some specific features of the elements on which scenario definition was based, as follows:

● The coastal features of the 'environmental components' are of a physical and biological nature and include the saline and alkaline soils and river deltas; coastal or submarine aquifers, imported water and floods and flooding in coastal plains; the thermo-Mediterranean forest level and the reafforestation of coastal dunes; specific coastal ecosystems; structure of the offshore seabed; etc.

● The coastal features of the 'economic sectors' are of a spatial nature, on account of their location, which may be mandatory or a matter of choice, and include fishing and aquaculture; sea-water desalination; processing of imported raw materials; cooling of thermal power-stations; loading/unloading of oil products; seaside tourism and offshore yachting; land/sea transport interfaces; international transit, and so on.

The 'coastal system' operating pattern gives rise to particularly complex interactions and feedbacks, owing to the density of the activities involved. An attempt has been made to analyse the consequences of possible future trends in these activities, as outlined in the scenarios, for the specific environmental components of the coastal regions at the horizons 2000 and 2025. In the first instance these analyses focus on the population and its growth and distribution as between urban and rural areas, and on seasonal population migrations.

1. Population, urbanization and tourism

(a) Coastal concentration

In 1985 the population of the Mediterranean coastal regions was estimated at more than 133m. inhabitants. On average, some 37.5 per cent of the

BOX 20A. **Specific coastal features of the scenarios**

	Specific coastal features	Specific impacts	Corrective actions
International context	World strategic region Role of transnational corporations and of capital from outside the region	Conflicts—Region of competing great-power influences	International agreements
Development scenarios	Attempts to strike a balance between the interior and the coast National priorities	Setting-up of business activities	Interior/coastal balance
Population	Retired residents (in the north) Seasonal population Population growth as a result of the positive migratory balance History	Population and economic imbalances Clash of cultures Domestic waste	Staggering of leisure-time activities
Land use	Land status—Access—Competence Urban planning rules—Development and conservation legislation		Reforms
Environmental management	Rules and standards—Protected areas and sites Maritime pollution control laws Cross-frontier pollution: international agreements		Implementation Reinforcement
Soil formations	Land-sea interfaces Sedimentation in balance with watershed	Erosion Impact on upstream developments	Corrected watershed management
Water	Coastal or submarine aquifers Imported water Floods	Intrusion of seawater Imported pollution. Seasonal water deficit	Pricing policy, arbitration, rationing, re-use
Forests	Dune stabilization by reafforestation Endemic diseases The thermo-Mediterranean level (300–500 metres)	Forest fires Threats to species	Undergrowth clearing Protection education
Coastline	Lagoons—Cliffs Dunes—Deltas Islands—Insalubrious coastal plains	Landscape and wetlands destruction	Integrated management Landscape protection
Sea	Structure of the offshore seabed World strategic region	Cross-frontier pollution	International norms
Food and agriculture˙	Fisheries Aquaculture	Over-fishing Competition	Quotas, agreements Wetland protection
Industry	Desalination Processing of imported raw materials	Coastal location Toxic wastes	Clean technology Depollution
Energy	Power station cooling systems Loading/unloading of petroleum products	Disturbance of coastal water temperatures Oil pollution	Oil-spill contingency plans Reception facilities
Tourism	Seaside resorts Yachting	Tourist amenities: excess capacity and use of concrete Marinas	Spreading vacations Boat hire Land parking
Transport	Load transfer zone: land/sea transport interface International transit region	Restructuring. Interruption of physical land/sea exchanges if facilities are on coast	Management of facilities

Source: Blue Plan.

Table 20.1 Mediterranean population and population density, 1985

	Area (1,000 km²)			Population (1,000 inhabitants)			Density (inhabitants/km²)		
	Total	Mediter-ranean	Mediter-ranean/total (%)	Total	Mediter-ranean	Mediter-ranean/total (%)	Total	Mediter-ranean	Mediter-ranean/total (index)
Region A									
Spain	504,800	95,504	18.92	38,500	13,860	36.00	76	145	1.9
France	547,000	46,248	8.45	54,600	5,496	10.07	100	119	1.2
Italy	301,200	226,685	75.26	57,300	41,829	73.00	190	185	1.0
Greece	131,900	100,278	76.03	9,880	8,862	89.70	75	88	1.2
Yugoslavia	255,800	42,448	16.59	23,200	2,582	11.13	91	61	0.7
TOTAL	1,740,700	511,163	29.37	183,480	76,629	39.58	105	142	1.3
Region C									
Monaco	0.002	0.002	100.00	27	27	100.00	13,500	13,500	1.0
Malta	0.316	0.316	100.00	383	383	100.00	1,212	1,212	1.0
Albania	28,748	28,748	100.00	3,050	3,050	100.00	106	106	1.0
Cyprus	9,251	9,251	100.00	669	669	100.00	72	72	1.0
Lebanon	10,400	18,400	100.00	2,670	2,670	100.00	257	257	1.0
Israel	20,770	20,770	100.00	4,250	4,250	100.00	205	205	1.0
TOTAL	69,487	69,487	100.00	11,049	11,049	100.00	159	159	1.0
Region B									
Turkey	780,600	122,612	15.71	49,300	10,000	20.28	63	82	1.3
Syria	185,200	4,190	2.26	10,500	1,155	11.00	57	276	4.9
Egypt	1,001,400	103,894	10.37	46,900	16,511	35.20	47	159	3.4
Libya	1,759,500	313,500	17.82	3,610	2,284	63.27	2	7	3.6
Tunisia	163,600	45,712	27.94	7,080	4,965	70.13	43	109	2.5
Algeria	2,381,700	68,294	2.87	21,700	11,500	53.00	9	168	18.5
Morocco	446,600	41,950	9.39	21,900	3,390	15.48	49	81	1.6
TOTAL	6,718,600	700,152	10.42	160,990	49,805	30.94	24	71	3.0
TOTAL MEDITERRANEAN BASIN	8,528,787	1,280,802	15.02	355,519	133,483	37.55	42	104	2.5

Note: For Regions A and B the Mediterranean density ratio is higher than 1 (except for Italy and Yugoslavia as a result of the choice of administrative units of Fig. 2.3). For Region C the total population has been considered as Mediterranean.

total population of the coastal countries inhabited 15 per cent of the land surface (Table 20.1). The spatial distribution of the population differs widely from country to country. In general, for Region A as well as for Region B the density of population is higher in coastal regions than at the country level, except for Italy and Yugoslavia. In Yugoslavia, for instance, the coastal regions account for 17 per cent of the country's total land area, but have only 11 per cent of the population, and the population density (61 inhabitants/km² against 91 inhabitants/km²) is lower than in other parts. These figures are a clear reflection of the importance of the development axis represented by the valley of the River Danube, which comes outside the scope of the Mediterranean region. By contrast, in Algeria, 53 per cent of the population live in the coastal regions, which accounts for barely 3 per cent of the country's total land area, and the population density is 18.5 times higher than in the rest of the country. Almost 20 per cent of the population lives in the Algiers region, which covers only 17 per cent of the national territory, and the population density there is close on 700 inhabitants/km². These striking percentages are obviously bound up with the overwhelming presence of the Sahara desert, but they nevertheless point to the very heavy concentration of population on the coast.

Generally speaking, the rise in the population in the Mediterranean regions is bound up with their economic development: the persistence of marked disparities between the hinterland and the coastal fringe in the densely populated and highly urbanized north-west countries illustrates the fact that the Mediterranean regions form a specific zone which will continue to exert considerable attraction owing to the amenities of climate and the economic opportunities that it offers (Alpes Maritimes, Liguria, etc.). The redistribution of the population there in the past twenty years, through economic and social development, has mainly benefited the attractive urban areas (especially the coastal areas sufficiently dynamic to counteract the influences of the inland cities). In the countries north-west of the Mediterranean (Spain, France, and Italy) the growth of the population of the coastal regions remains slightly higher than the national average, migration balances being distinctly positive, although these figures conceal the demographic decline and, in particular, the ageing of the populations.

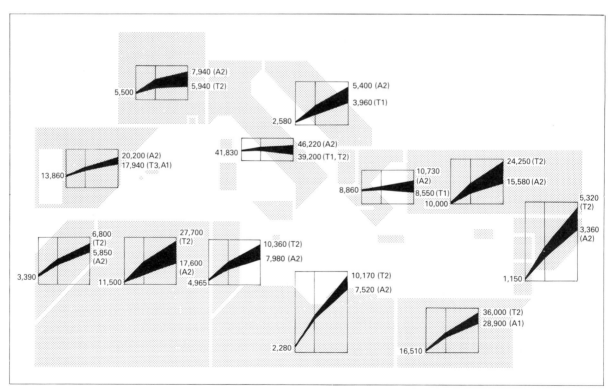

FIG. 20.1 Coastal population in the Mediterranean countries (000s): Extreme scenarios 1985–2025. The coastal areas considered here correspond to the coastal administrative regions illustrated in Fig. 2.3.
Source: Blue Plan.

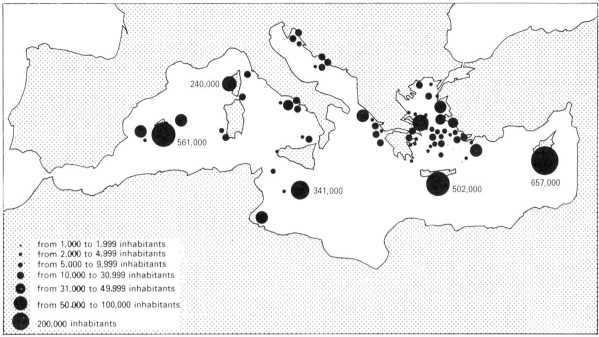

FIG. 20.2 Population of the Mediterranean islands with over 1,000 inhabitants. Length of island coasts (km): Spain 910; France 802 (Corsica); Italy 3,766 (including Sardinia and Sicily); Malta 180; Yugoslavia 4,024; Greece 7,700; Turkey 809; Cyprus 782; Tunisia 210.

South and east of the Mediterranean, the poor areas, often situated in the hinterland, have often functioned as reservoirs of people destined to swell out population numbers in the cities. It is these rural areas which, through the flow of their emigrants abroad, partly account for the relative decrease in the population of certain Mediterranean administrative regions. Looking at the matter in more detail, the level of development in these countries varies a great deal from one coastal area to another: the decrease in areas under cultivation (under the effect of the population explosion, the growth needs of cities, tourism, and industry), the resulting drop in agricultural production, and the siting of industries capable of providing work for those who have abandoned the agricultural sector have left a not inconsiderable proportion of the labour force without employment, who have therefore gone off to the cities and to foreign countries. But the excess of births over deaths makes up for the generally negative migration balances.

Depending on the scenarios, the population of the coastal regions of the Mediterranean is expected to stand at between 195m. and 217m. inhabitants in 2025, representing an increase of between 45 and 62 per cent. The most marked growth is liable to occur in the case of the worst trend scenario T2,

according to which there would be 83m. additional inhabitants compared with 1985, some 85 per cent of whom would be living in the coastal regions of the countries of Region B, where the population is expected to have increased 2.5 times. In reference alternative scenario A1 the population would still increase by 60m. inhabitants, notwithstanding a lower growth-rate. This increment would admittedly be more evenly distributed, since only 72 per cent of the new inhabitants would belong to the coastal regions of the Region B countries.

Apart from Monaco and Malta, which are special cases, the population density in coastal regions would be highest in Syria, with an increase from 272 inhabitants/km² in 1985 to 1,271 inhabitants/km² in 2025 in the case of scenario T2. It would be followed by Lebanon, Algeria, Israel, and Egypt, and to a lesser extent by Tunisia.

The concentration of the population on the coast, or 'littoralization', defined as the percentage of the total population living in the coastal regions, would record a slight increase in the regions of the countries of Region A (from 39 per cent in 1985 to 40–41 per cent in 2025). This is particularly true of Yugoslavia, where the Mediterranean population would rise from 11 per cent in 1985 to 17–18 per cent in 2025. In the coastal regions of the countries

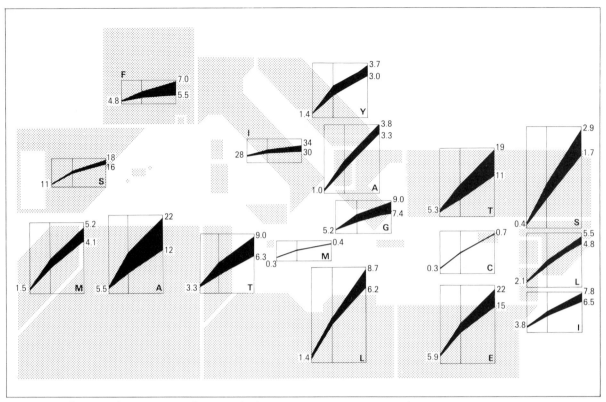

FIG. 20.3 Urban population in coastal regions (m.): Extreme scenarios 1985, 2000, and 2025
Source: Blue Plan.

of Region B this phenomenon is magnified in the trend scenarios, but levels out or even declines, compared with 1985, in the alternative scenarios, except in the case of Libya. Algeria is an exception, since in 2025 the coastal population concentration will be much lower than in 1985 in all cases, and especially in scenario A2 while of course the coastal density will increase considerably.

(b) Urbanization

Although no attempt has been made here to undertake a systematic retrospective study of the coastal regions and the littoral proper, it may be noted, to exemplify the development, that the urban population of those regions rose between 1962 and 1968 from 2,745,000 to 3,329,000 for France, from 824,000 to 1,357,000 for Morocco, and from 2,532,000 to 4,262,000 for Algeria. The attraction of the coast, also a factor in tourist development, is thus clearly seen.

This population growth in the coastal regions is accompanied by the growth of the urban population. In 1985 this stood at 82m. urban dwellers. It is expected to rise in the year 2000 to 113m. in the

case of the worst trend scenario T2 and to 105m. in the case of the reference alternative scenario A1, while in 2025 the corresponding figures would be 170m. for scenario T2 and 144m. for scenario A1.

The current urbanization rate is slighly more than 61 per cent for the coastal regions as a whole, but it is expected to range between 74 and 78 per cent and upwards at the horizon 2025. The worst trend scenario T2 is that in which urban growth is at its highest:

• In the coastal regions of the countries of Regions A and C more than 85 per cent of the population would be urbanized, with maximum values topping 96 per cent in Spain and Israel.
• In the countries of Region B, 74 per cent of the coastal population would be living in urban areas, with rates of 87 per cent in Tunisia and 85 per cent in Libya.

In other words, there would be more than 88m. additional urban dwellers compared with 1985, i.e. more than the total population growth of the coastal areas. Three-quarters of these new urban inhabitants would be in the countries of Region B.

Table 20.2 illustrates this true explosion of the

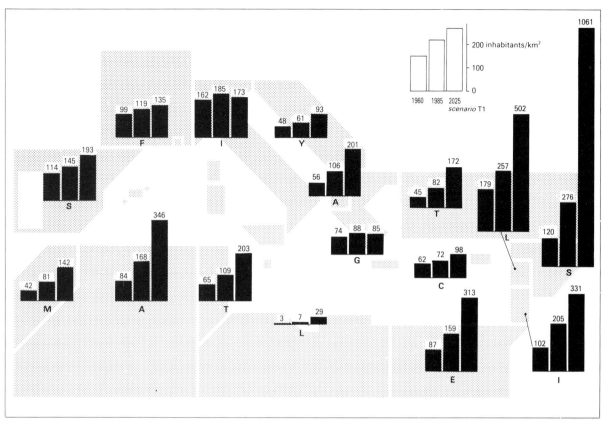

FIG. 20.4 Population density in coastal regions, 1960, 1985, and 2025. Densities shown on this map relate to coastal regions as defined in Fig. 2.3. In all countries these densities tend to increase more rapidly than average national density. Where the coastal region considered is narrow, as in Syria, the increase is emphasized, whereas it is blurred for Italy and Greece, where large coastal provinces have been used, thus reflecting more national density trends.
Source: Blue Plan.

Table 20.2 Growth in the coastal population and the coastal urban population, 1985–2025 (m.)

Region	Coastal population						Urban Coastal population					
	1985	Growth 1985–2025 (scenarios)					1985	Growth 1985–2025 (scenarios)				
		T1	T2	T3	A1	A2		T1	T2	T3	A1	A2
A	72.6	3.7	4.1	8.7	8.7	17.9	50.6	12.7	14.9	15.3	15.3	21.2
C	11.0	8.2	8.2	8.2	8.2	10.9	7.7	8.1	8.7	8.1	8.1	10.4
B	49.8	56.1	70.8	53.1	43.6	37.8	23.4	51.9	65.3	45.7	38.7	35.0
TOTAL	133.4	68.0	83.1	70.1	60.5	66.6	81.7	72.8	88.9	69.2	62.2	66.7

urban population. It shows, alongside the figures for 1985, the net growth of the coastal population and the coastal urban population for each scenario at horizon 2025. Urban growth will clearly be a major phenomenon in the coastal regions of the Mediterranean in the coming decades. From the standpoint of jobs, housing, education, health, transport, and other facilities, this phenomenon will generate considerable requirements in terms of amenities and infrastructure, and these will present a formidable challenge for land-use planning.

Under the trend scenarios, the added urban burden would be a significant contributory factor in the deterioration of the coastal environment, and indeed in its destruction, through growing urban sprawl into the surrounding countryside in the north and virtually uncontrollable growth of outlying suburbs in the south and east. In all cases, regardless of whether the pace of economic growth is fast or slow, the lack of a proper long-term view of the situation and the failure to engage in long-range thinking would lead to the limited and fragile natural resources of the coastal strip proper being improperly used, unless adequate precautions are taken.

Under the alternative scenarios, urban growth would cause less damage. On account of population pressure, land-use policies would have to be highly goal-orientated and a very considerable volume of funds would have to be mobilized, among other purposes for ensuring that the concepts of the optimum use of coastal space and rational management of its natural resources are built into projects right from the outset.

(c) Tourism

It will be recalled that there were some 51m. international tourists in the coastal regions of the Mediterranean in 1984, in addition to which there were 45m. domestic tourists or holiday-makers. There is likely to be a considerable increase in this figure of some 100m., and it could double or even triple. Table 20.3 sets out the estimates for tourism in the coastal regions in the light of the different scenarios at horizons 2000 and 2025.

The effects of tourism on the coastal strip will largely depend on the measures taken to foster the staggering of holidays and leisure-time activities. It is assumed that if the peak-period pattern, whereby some 20 per cent of the tourists all congregate on the coast in the space of 4–5 weeks each year—and that pattern seems likely to become even more marked—were to continue in the case of the trend scenarios, there would be between 35m. and 52m. visitors at the height of the tourist season in 2025. This figure would be equivalent to the present population of countries like Spain, France, Italy, Turkey, or Egypt. The requirements in terms of amenities and infrastructure would be considerable and, if they were to be met, would entail providing systematically for extra spare capacity in respect of water supply, sewerage, transport facilities, and so on. This seasonal population overflow would also be instrumental in causing pollution and congestion, by affecting standards of hygiene on beaches, traffic flows, visits to certain natural or historical sites, etc. All this could engender negative attitudes among the host population. These disamenities would be made even worse by the fact that, during such peak periods, the vast majority of the tourists are concentrated on the coastline itself.

Table 20.3 Number of tourists in coastal regions, 2000 and 2025 (m.)

Scenario	2000		2025	
	International tourism	Domestic tourism	International tourism	Domestic tourism
T1	85.4	53.9	147	72
T2	76.4	45.0	125	48
T3	94.0	64.1	162	98
A1	97.7	71.4	168	130
A2	107.0	77.3	193	148

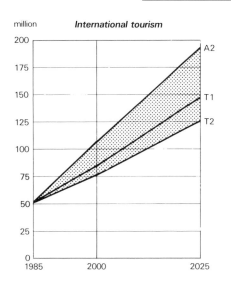

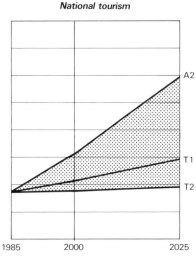

FIG. 20.5 National and international tourists in the coastal regions, 1985–2025: Scenarios T1, T2, and A2

Source: Blue Plan.

Although this would not necessarily lead to extremes of anti-social behaviour, the social and cultural impact is by no means the least important factor entering into the phenomena of acculturation and disparagement of cultural identity caused by an excessively wide gap separating the tourists' life-style from that of the local population, especially in some of the trend scenarios.

Space-use strategy would accordingly not be the only consideration in contending with the growth of the tourist population: the construction of unobtrusive amenities that would at the same time be available to the local population and the promotion of 'soft' tourism and new forms of leisure could prevent too great a strain being placed on societies and environments alike (as in the case of the alternative scenarios).

2. Impact of the population and economic activities on the environment

Population growth and the development of sectors of economic activity in the coastal regions are instrumental in drawing down natural resources, generating pollutant discharges, and in launching new developments and furthering uses of the environment that are bound to have some destructive effect.

(a) Site coverage

In 1985 the land area covered by urbanization in the coastal regions of the Mediterranean was estimated at 14,000 km². Almost 90 per cent of this urbanized land area is located in the coastal zones of the countries of Region A.

At horizon 2025 the urbanized land area is expected to cover between 28,000 and 31,000 km², depending on the scenario, and some 27–33 per cent of this would be in the coastal regions of the countries of Region B. These findings do not, at first sight, suggest a very significant difference from one scenario to another. This stems from the fact that the highest urban growth scenario assumes that there would be fewer amenities, infrastructural facilities, and green spaces than in the scenario where growth is lower but economic wealth is greater. The overall land area consumed by urbanization thus appears to be relatively slight. For the coastal regions as a whole, it accounted for little

more than 1 per cent in 1985 and would represent almost 2.5 per cent in 2025. It has to be borne in mind, however, that this land area is primarily taken from the coastal strip.

With the exception of Monaco, the two countries occupying proportionally most space would be Malta and Syria, with 10 per cent and 9 per cent respectively in 2025 (scenario T2). In other countries, where the percentages are lower (especially in those of Region B), it should be stressed, however, that the urbanized areas would grow very steeply: by 2025 they would increase 20 times in Libya, 9.5 times in Egypt, 8 times in Algeria, and 6 times in Morocco, Tunisia, and Turkey (trend scenarios).

These gross figures give only a partial picture of the qualitative impact of the extension of the urbanized land area, such as the gradual whittling away of the most productive agricultural land; the transformation of the traditional landscape as a result of growing encroachment; the spoiling of sites by construction of buildings out of all proportion to their surroundings and by proliferation of advertising panels; the use which some countries are making of standardized materials and of plans that were designed for other climates and other cultures, the destruction of wetlands vitally important for the conservation of birdlife, etc.

In 1984 the land area occupied by tourist amenities, which can be likened to a specific form of urbanization, was estimated to cover 2,000 km² in the coastal regions of the Mediterranean and could rise to 4,000 km² in 2025 according to the alternative scenarios and the moderate trend scenario T3. Although this is a negligible figure compared with the overall land area of the Mediterranean regions, the space taken up by tourism chiefly affects the narrow coastal strip, which is the prime attraction for the regular inflow of tourists.

As already noted, the siting of industrial activities will follow two patterns:

● In the north, the basic industries will go into decline or will be phased out, as a result of which a large number of shut-down industrial facilities could be rehabilitated, while new 'high-tech' industries will be developed and will give rise to new sites taking the form of technology parks or 'science cities', as in the case of Sophia-Antipolis in France.

● In the south and east there will be a sharp growth in basic industries, through either the extension of existing production capacities or the setting-up of new industrial zones.

In recent years the areas made available for new

industrial zones have been quite large and have included, for example, 7,000 ha at Fos near Marseilles, 3,500 ha at Arzew, and 2,000 ha at Skikda, both in Algeria. In the above cases, however, the sites were completely new and were located outside the urban area proper, whereas a very large number of industrial establishments are closely interwoven with the urban fabric. This is why there are no reference documents giving an inventory of the industrial use of the land area, although this can be said to be smaller than the urbanized land area in the industrialized countries (in France, for example, industry occupies 1,300 km², or about 0.23 per cent of the country's total land area). In the industrializing countries new sites have primarily affected productive agricultural land, since it has presented fewer drawbacks in that it is flat and well drained, and is often even equipped with a water supply. The eastern Mitidja valley, in Algeria, is estimated to have lost some 10–12 per cent of its cultivated area for that purpose in the space of twelve years. This trend would only really change in the case of alternative scenarios.

A fairly comprehensive estimation in respect of 1987 is available for 157 major industrial facilities (cf. Table 20.4) located on the Mediterranean seaboard from Turkey to Morocco, as well as for 67 facilities at the project stage.* The commissioning of these facilities would be consistent with a moderate scenario (T3) in 2000 and the production capacities should increase even further at the horizon 2025. The number of coastal power-plants in the same regions is currently estimated at 170 plants already in service and 43 at the project stage (Table 20.5).

In the case of industry, and to an even greater extent in the case of energy production, these facilities located in the coastal regions cater not only

* In the case of some countries, notably Turkey, the figures obtained from other sources are different from those of the Blue Plan study, used in compiling Tables 20.4–5. These differences may be due to the way in which the industrial facilities were counted—i.e. by the number of sites or by the number of major units.

for the needs of those regions, but often for those of the countries as a whole. The coast is obviously bound to be the location for oil and mineral ports, besides being an eminently suitable location for thermal power-stations and refineries. The question is how many of the extensions or new plants in the energy sector provided for in the scenarios will be located in the coastal regions. This all depends on the policy decisions, the technical courses adopted (i.e. whether they are water-cooled or air-cooled), the funds available, etc. According to the findings of the energy scenarios, the situation would be as follows:

● There would be 90–120 offshore drilling operations a year, together with considerable shore-based installations for logistical back-up purposes.

● There would be from 150–250 thermal power-stations on the southern and eastern shores alone, depending on the electricity growth-rates and the unit size of the power-stations, some of which could be nuclear-powered.

● There would not be any great change in the volume of oil traffic, but more products would be carried by smaller vessels unloading at a larger number of ports.

● The oil-refining capacities on the southern and eastern shores and the number of dispatching and landing areas for gas pipelines crossing the Mediterranean might be doubled.

● Coal imports would amount to 200–500m. t per annum, depending on the type of development.

Road transport networks take up a great deal of space, and can be almost compared with urbanization. In 2025 the total length of these networks may have increased 3.2 times and even by a maximum of 4.3 times in scenario T3. In the coastal regions they would cover a land area ranging between 10,000 and 20,000 km², part of which is already on the coastal strip.

All in all, to simplify matters somewhat, in 2025 between 3.5 and 4.6 per cent of the land area of the coastal regions would be taken up by urbanization,

Table 20.4 Number of coastal sites for some industrial activities in the southern and eastern Mediterranean, 1987

	Petrochemicals		Steel		Chemicals		Total	
	Existing	Projected	Existing	Projected	Existing	Projected	Existing	Projected
Turkey	17	2	10	1	13	7	40	10
South and east coast	56	29	18	7	43	21	117	57
TOTAL	73	31	28	8	56	28	157	67

Table 20.5 Energy installations on the Mediterranean coast, 1987

	Oil terminals	Refineries		Thermal power-stations		Total	
		Existing	Projected	Existing	Projected	Existing	Projected
North	31	33	0	30	4	94	4
Turkey	5	3	1	11	5	19	6
South	22	15	10	23	23	60	33
TOTAL	58	51	11	64	32	173	43

tourism, industry, and transport, as illustrated in Table 20.6. Here again the percentages at the scale of the coastal regions of the Mediterranean may seem small, but it has to be emphasized that perhaps half of the land occupied will be on the coastal strip. If this 46,000-km-long strip is arbitrarily considered as being 1 km wide, then half of the strip's area itself would be occupied in the case of the low assumption and two-thirds in the case of the high assumption. Added to this, there would be 68 refineries, some 50–75 nuclear units, 100–150 thermal power-stations, and so on.

(b) Impact on water

The consumption of water by the urban and rural populations of the coastal regions has been calculated in respect of Regions A and B for the different scenarios at the horizons 2000 and 2025 (Table 20.7). When these figures are compared with the estimates for 1985, it will be seen that the total consumption would not greatly increase in the coastal areas of Region A; the multipliers over the period 1985–2025 vary from 1.36 (scenarios T1 and T2) to 1.43 (scenarios T3 and A1) and 1.58 (scenario A2).

The situation would be very different in the coastal areas of Region B. At horizon 2025 the lowest consumption figures would still be three times higher than those in 1985 in the cases of scenarios T2 and A2. It is interesting to note that these very similar

Table 20.6 Land area of coastal regions taken up by urbanization, tourism, industry, and transport, 2025 (km²)

	Low assumption	High assumption
Urbanized land area	28,000	31,000
Tourist amenities	4,000	4,000
Industry	3,000	4,000
Transport	10,000	20,000
TOTAL	45,000	59,000

BOX 20B. **Protection of the Spanish coastline**

The tourist and population boom that has affected the Mediterranean coast in recent years has made it necessary to adopt protective policies and sanitation schemes to reduce the amount of pollution discharged into the sea.
Such measures include:

● the Costa Brava Sanitation Infrastructure Plan, which is now fully operational;
the Costa del Sol Comprehensive Sanitation Plan, which is now being implemented;
the Barcelona, Valencia, and Benidorm Eastern Coastal main sewer systems (the largest).

All in all, 77 of the 190 local authorities on the Spanish Mediterranean seaboard have water purification plants, with 36 more under construction, and immediate action is being considered in 96 other cases. Accordingly, in the very near future 60 per cent of the municipal authorities will have sewage plants capable of treating 90 per cent of all urban pollution.

Approved sanitation plans on the Mediterranean coast represent an investment of 48,000m. pesetas, 80 per cent of which had already been invested by the end of 1984.

There are also sea-pollution monitoring and control programmes, which are co-ordinated by the 'Autonomous Communities' (the regions) and the central government.

Source: Spanish national scenarios for the Blue Plan.

Table 20.7 Annual consumption of domestic water in Mediterranean coastal regions, 1985, 2000, and 2025 (1,000m. m^3 p.a.)

	1985	T1 2000	T1 2025	T2 2000	T2 2025	T3 2000	T3 2025	A1 2000	A1 2025	A2 2000	A2 2025
Region A											
Urban	4.60	6.30	6.9	6.40	7.10	6.40	7.2	6.4	7.2	6.60	7.80
Rural	1.20	1.20	1.0	1.20	0.80	1.30	1.1	1.3	1.1	1.30	1.40
TOTAL	*5.80*	*7.50*	*7.9*	*7.60*	*7.90*	*7.70*	*8.3*	*7.7*	*8.3*	*7.90*	*9.20*
Region B											
Urban	0.84	1.60	3.4	1.60	3.20	1.57	3.7	1.5	3.4	1.42	3.15
Rural	0.47	0.61	0.7	0.56	0.57	0.63	0.9	0.6	0.8	0.59	0.79
TOTAL	*1.31*	*2.21*	*4.1*	*2.16*	*3.77*	*2.20*	*4.6*	*2.1*	*4.2*	*2.01*	*3.94*
GRAND TOTAL	7.11	9.71	12.0	9.76	11.67	9.90	12.9	9.8	12.5	9.91	13.14

Source: Blue Plan (Margat, 1988).

findings have been arrived at from a set of assumptions that are diametrically opposite to one another, namely those in scenario T2, in which the population and urbanization growth-rates are very high and the specific consumption remains stable; and those in scenario A2, in which population growth is more moderate but is more evenly distributed between urban and rural areas and between the interior and the coast, with the specific consumption on the increase. The scenario showing the highest water consumption would be T3, in which it would be 3.5 times higher in 2025 than in 1985, while population growth would continue to be high and the specific consumption would still be increasing. However, these findings do not make it possible to conclude on the draw-off of resources, since no data forecasts are available for the efficiency of the networks.

The consumption of water for domestic uses, especially in urban areas, would compete with its use for other purposes, above all for agriculture, and could give rise to a difficult problem in respect of priorities and funding. Indeed, the provision of a water supply for large coastal connurbations may mobilize a substantial proportion of a region's water resources and financing capacity, as in the case of Athens, Algiers, and other cities (cf. Chapter 19).

The volume of water consumed by tourism has been calculated from the number of overnight stays. The results show that at the horizon 2025 the consumption of water for tourist purposes is expected to rise by between 100 and 350 per cent compared with 1985.

The one important factor that has to be stressed in this connection is not so much the amount of water consumed by tourists (since it is, in fact, relatively small and accounts for only 6–9 per cent of both urban and rural consumption) as the seasonal nature of the consumption, which usually occurs in summer—the dry season in the Mediterranean—when the demand for irrigation water is at its highest. In many locations along the coastal strip and in the offshore islands, such as along the Tunisian coast, on Malta, and in the Almeria region, this situation currently makes it necessary to impose restrictions, and agriculture is the first to be affected. Moreover—and this is even more serious, since the deterioration of a resource is involved—excessive pumping may lower the level of the ground-water table, causing contamination by the infiltration of sea-water, as has happened in the Balearic Islands and along the coast of Catalonia. Since the question of the improved staggering of holidays is considered only in the alternative scenarios, the water situation in the coastal strip during the summer is bound to grow worse in the trend scenarios, and especially in scenario T3.

The prospective study of water consumption for industrial uses and energy production does not make it possible to produce precise figures with respect to the findings. It can be said, however, that the consumption of water for industrial uses, compared with that for agriculture and domestic purposes (the population and tourism), is expected to decline, although not so much in volume terms as in its relative share, owing to improvement in manufacturing methods and the progress made in developing recycling techniques.

(c) Impact on forests

It is worth while to stress some of the specific aspects bound up with the pressures to which forests in the coastal strip proper are subject. Those pressures are chiefly exerted by the urban explosion and by the development of tourism and transport. The corollary of urbanization can be said to be as follows:

● There is a demand for building land, which has the effect of progressively encroaching on the neighbouring forest stands. While that demand is not very significant in terms of area, it may have catastrophic consequences in the event of fires. Since the fire-fighting facilities are used, as a matter of priority, for protecting people and property, the more buildings there are to be protected, the larger the area of forest that is liable to be burnt down.

● The use of forests as recreational areas for the urban population causes the land to be heavily trodden down, and this jeopardizes the conservation of plant species, while significantly increasing the risk of fire, all the more so where grazing and undergrowth clearing are abandoned.

Tourism has broadly the same effects, although these are exacerbated because they chiefly occur in summer, when forests are more vulnerable to fire. For example, during the summer holiday period the tendency is for people camping outside authorized sites to prefer the wooded areas immediately behind the coastline, with the many adverse environmental effects that this implies as a result of the lack of hygiene, the trampling down of the undergrowth, and the risks of fire. On the northern seaboard the construction of holiday homes in the wooded areas on the coast has been very widespread and, although that trend now seems to have levelled out, it has to be strictly controlled.

The road and rail networks on the coast itself have far-reaching effects on the forest ecosystems as they skirt the wooded areas and prevent natural exchanges taking place between the different parts of the forest stands through which they have been driven. The forests on the coastal strip may also be damaged or even destroyed by chemical pollution from the sea, which attacks them in the form of air-borne matter in suspension. This phenomenon is widespread on the western coast of Italy.

(d) Impact on the coastal strip

The land area considered in this chapter generally covers the whole of the Mediterranean 'coastal regions', and therefore embraces the coastal strip proper, the only part discussed in this section. More precisely, this strip consists of the area formed by the coastal communities, which extends inland for a distance ranging between several hundred and several thousand metres, and the offshore sea area (whose limits are much less precise and which includes in particular the near-shore sea-bed and lagoon areas). The difficulty stems both from the complexity of the environment and from the many and varied pressures exerted on it by human beings and their activities, and their interactions and feedbacks. This restricted area, combining both land and sea, is made up of virtually all the environmental components and all human activities.

Before an attempt is made to embark on a qualitative evaluation of the different possible futures of this coastal strip in the light of the different scenarios, it is important to recall the nature of the main factors having an adverse effect on it. On the marine side they include the following forms of pollution:

● Bacterial pollution is caused by the domestic waste water discharged by urban areas along the coast, which contains particles of mainly organic matter in suspension. The self-purifying properties of the sea water and the choice of appropriate locations for the discharge-points make it possible to reduce the pollution reaching the shoreline to a minimum and to protect people using the bathing resorts. However, this form of pollution may affect the food chain, contaminating fish and shellfish, and then having very serious consequences for the human population.

● Pollution as a result of the dumping of solid urban waste in the sea (plastic packaging in particular) may be significant in certain specific areas, owing to the influence of the sea currents. Non-biodegradable plastics and tar balls accumulate on the beaches and in creeks all along the Mediterranean coast.

● Chemical pollution is caused by industrial waste, such as toxic chemicals, detergents, petroleum products, used lubricating oils, pesticides, and heavy metals. These forms of waste are a serious source of pollution of the sea and of marine products, even though the amounts discharged may be slight. Some of this waste, such as detergents, has adverse effects on both land and sea. The most disquieting effect of chemical pollution probably lies in the contamination of the food chain and the build-up of the most toxic substances in marine organisms.

● Secondary organic pollution, caused by the discharge of substantial amounts of organic matter,

BOX 20C. *Posidonia*

Posidonia oceanica is a marine phanerogam that is a relic of the Mesogean flora. It usually covers broad expanses of the inshore sea-bed, at depths ranging between 2–3 m and 30–40 m, and it is prevalent along the northern coastline in the western part of the Mediterranean. In addition to the important function they perform in the primary production and supply of oxygen to the shallow neritic zone close inshore, Posidonia meadows form one of the richest biocenotic communities in the demersal zone from the biological, ecological, and economic standpoints. In particular, they are feeding-grounds for many demersal fish species.

Urban and industrial pollution has plainly had an adverse effect on these plant colonies. In the Gulf of Marseilles, for instance, where they extended from depths of 4–35 m in 1947, they are now only found at depths of between 10 and 25 m, and the few remaining colonies are in a very poor state. The fact that their lower growing limits are now closer to the surface is clearly due to the decline in luminosity, as a result of the widespread increase in turbidity caused by the higher suspended-matter content and periodic bursts in plankton reproduction. Their disappearance from the upper 10 m or so is the direct outcome of their having been poisoned by pollutants, which are highly concentrated at that level. The pollution-induced effects, such as the increased turbidity, are accompanied by those created by the following factors:

● the construction of infrastructural facilities, whether linear, as in the case of roads and embankments, or non-linear, like airports, both of which may encroach on the inshore sea-bed to varying degrees;
● the anchoring of many yachts at uncontrolled moorings along the coast and in creeks;
● dredging for the installation of beaches or the extraction of sand and gravel.

Source: A. Augier, Council of Europe.

such as urban waste water, agricultural waste, and factory effluents, gives rise to far-reaching ecological changes. In some rather enclosed sea and lagoon areas like the Gulf of Tunis this affects all the local natural species and always results in a decline of their numbers. In 1988 the eutrophication of the Adriatic, due to land-based pollution, proved to be a major economic and ecological phenomenon (the flight away of tourists).

● Temperature pollution is caused by the warm water discharged by thermal power-stations of large industrial complexes and can give rise to far-reaching ecological changes, which affect the marine flora and fauna and alter the sea's productivity.

With regard to the land, in addition to urbanization, industrial plants, and energy installations mentioned above, consideration should be given to the following:

● The road and rail transport infrastructure located in the vicinity of the coast inhibits the natural processes of shore formation and development and can cause significant coastal erosion, one of the feedback effects of which may be the destruction of the infrastructure itself, as has been the case with many railway lines in Italy. In this connection, it should be noted that public works on rivers, although located far upstream, may have similar effects. This is what is now happening in Egypt, where the Aswan Dam holds back the alluvial silt that used to be carried down the Nile delta, so that, as a result, the shore is exposed to intense marine erosion.

● The reshaping of the shoreline, through the construction of sailing harbours, back-filling, coastal-defence works, and artificial beaches, has an irreversible destructive effect on the inshore sea-bed (down to a depth of 40 m), which is the habitat of the Posidonia sea-grass meadows that are literally the 'nurseries' of the Mediterranean marine species. These construction works completely alter the flow pattern of the sea currents and the coastal dynamics, and can be instrumental in the disappearance of beaches and the silting up of harbour sites.

● The gradual drainage of wetlands—vital for nature conservation, including bird life—for the extension of urban areas, the establishment of port complexes, or the construction of airports has a very negative effect on the natural environment.

A long-range study of the pollution of coastal water by domestic waste has been carried out for the coastal regions, on the basis of the population figures and of assumptions in respect of water consumption and sewer connections for urban or rural habitats for the different scenarios at the horizons 2000 and 2025. The results, which provide a pointer to the treatment capacities that will be required, are set out in Tables 20.8 and 20.9 for the main countries of both the northern shore and the southern and eastern shores. They show that in the most unfavourable cases, the amount of waste would double on the northern shore and would increase four times on the southern and eastern shores. These results are consistent with the more general findings presented in the following chapter,

Table 20.8 Assessment of domestic pollution on the northern coasts,[a] 1985, 2000, and 2025

| | | Scenarios | | | | | | | | | |
| | | T1 | | T2 | | T3 | | A1 | | A2 | |
	1985	2000	2025	2000	2025	2000	2025	2000	2025	2000	2025
Hypotheses											
Population (000s)	72,629	76,414	76,336	76,775	76,703	77,913	81,348	77,913	88,348	80,615	90,492
Urbanization rate (%)	69	75	82	76	85	75	81	75	81	74	79
Water consumption (m³ per capita):											
Urban	91	109	109	109	109	109	109	109	109	109	109
Rural	54	65	73	65	73	65	73	65	73	65	73
Sewage connection (%):											
Urban	70	78	80	78	80	78	80	78	80	78	80
Rural	15	18	20	18	20	18	20	18	20	18	20
Results											
Waste vol. (m. m³)	2,294.7	3,281.6	3,583.3	3,310.3	3,678.4	3,324.4	3,760.3	3,324.4	3,760.3	3,415.4	4,118.4
BOD (1,000 t)	996.7	1,140.3	1,199.2	1,148.3	1,220.9	1,158.4	1,266.4	1,158.4	1,266.4	1,193.8	1,395.7
COD (1,000 t)	2,246.0	2,563.7	2,692.3	2,581.5	2,740.2	2,604.6	2,843.9	2,604.6	2,843.9	2,684.4	3,135.1
SS (1,000 t)	1,316.9	1,414.2	1,431.0	1,412.7	1,443.4	1,440.6	1,521.9	1,440.6	1,521.9	1,489.1	1,688.9
TDS (1,000 t)	1,413.0	1,748.2	1,918.2	1,763.8	1,972.2	1,770.3	2,010.6	1,770.3	2,010.6	1,818.0	2,199.5
N (1,000 t)	127.8	158.1	173.4	159.5	178.3	160.1	181.8	160.1	181.8	164.4	198.9
P (1,000 t)	15.5	19.2	21.0	19.3	21.6	19.4	22.0	19.4	22.0	19.9	24.1

[a] Spain, France, Italy, Yugoslavia, and Greece.

Table 20.9 Assessment of domestic pollution on the southern and eastern coasts,[a] 1985, 2000, and 2025

Scenarios	T1			T2		T3		A1		A2	
	1985	2000	2025	2000	2025	2000	2025	2000	2025	2000	2025
Hypotheses											
Population (000s)	49,805	70,514	105,914	75,229	120,604	69,753	102,931	66,710	93,403	64,502	87,641
Urbanization rate (%)	47	56	71	58	73	54	67	54	66	53	66
Water consumption (m³ per capita):											
Urban	36	39	45	36	36	41	54	41	54	41	54
Rural	18	20	23	18	18	20	27	20	27	20	27
Sewage connection (%):											
Urban	50	55	65	50	45	55	70	55	70	55	70
Rural	10	12	13	10	10	12	20	12	20	12	20
Results											
Waste vol. (m. m³)	544.2	887.8	1,777.9	881.7	1,474.8	900.0	2,018.8	857.6	1,820.8	827.4	1,711.2
BOD (1,000 t)	527.3	806.4	1,397.0	840.6	1,383.9	790.7	1,373.0	754.2	1,240.8	728.1	1,165.5
COD (1,000 t)	1,198.6	1,827.9	3,152.0	1,907.0	3,136.5	1,792.8	3,096.6	1,710.3	2,799.0	1,651.3	2,629.0
SS (1,000 t)	854.3	1,228.2	1,902.8	1,304.1	2,102.1	1,212.7	1,854.0	1,159.2	1,680.8	1,120.5	1,577.5
TDS (1,000 t)	523.7	912.1	1,899.8	916.8	1,573.2	882.2	1,889.8	838.1	1,700.6	807.2	1,599.1
N (1,000 t)	47.3	82.5	171.8	82.9	142.2	79.8	170.9	75.8	153.8	73.0	144.6
P (1,000 t)	5.7	10.0	20.8	10.0	17.2	9.7	20.7	9.2	18.6	8.8	17.5

[a] Turkey, Syria, Egypt, Libya, Tunisia, Algeria, and Morocco.

dealing with the sea. It should be noted here that disposal of liquid sewage at sea (as long as it does not contain contaminated indiustrial waste) through sufficiently long submarine outfalls presents less risk than disposal after treatment in poorly functioning plants.

In a bid to safeguard a small portion of the Mediterranean seaboard from all these adverse effects, a hundred or so specially protected areas have been singled out by the coastal countries. They cover an extremely wide variety of ecosystems, including lagoons and humid coastal land, dune bars, rocky coasts, coastal forest formations, the inshore sea-bed, etc. There is a growing tendency also to step up the regulatory protective measures, to monitor the catches taken in hunting and fishing (particularly underwater fishing) and the gathering of rare endemic plants, and to increase the number and coverage of the protected areas.

One specific threat to the coastline is the gradual rise in sea-level as a result of the 'greenhouse effect' caused by the increased concentration of combustion and industrial gases released into the atmosphere. The heating up of the climate would in general cause the oceans to swell, which, in the Mediterranean, could produce a rise of at least 20 cm by 2025. A rise of this nature would not have very significant effects, except for the balance of some lagoons. Combined with soil subsidence, however, it could lead in some areas to a far greater 'sinking'. The widely-held expert view is that, in the event of any rise above 50 cm, the cost of taking protective measures would be considerable and that a policy choice would have to be made between protecting some areas and leaving others to their fate. The areas most threatened naturally include deltas and low-lying coastal plains, which, although few in number in the Mediterranean, are the centres of population concentrations and of a large number of economic activities that are vital to some of the countries. Among the examples that can be cited are notably the mouths or deltas of the Rivers Ebro, Rhone, and Po, the Venezia and Romagna regions of Italy, the Ceyhan delta in south-eastern Turkey, and the Nile delta. Within the next century the combined effects of the quickening coastal erosion caused by the interruption of the supply of silt retained behind the Aswan dam, the rising level of the Mediterranean, and the sinking of the geological formations by about 50 cm every hundred years, could cause the Nile delta to recede by about 30 kilometres. Moreover, in a number of spots on the Mediterranean coast the rise in the sea-level is likely to hasten the salinization of coastal aquifers—essential for human activity as a whole—through the infiltration of sea water. Although any attempt to quantify the phenomenon would be risky at this stage, the threat of the sea-level rising within the span of the next generation is a factor that can no longer be discounted in any long-range study of the Mediterranean seaboard. Consequently, the initial work carried out on this matter within the Mediterranean Action Plan must be actively continued.

In conclusion, a few ideas for engaging in a more detailed study of the possible futures of the coastal strip, in the light of the Blue Plan scenarios or types of development, are suggested in Table 20.10.

3. Conclusions concerning the coast

Some of the areas of the Mediterranean coast are under serious threat. The Mediterranean cannot be effectively protected on a lasting basis unless a start is made by protecting and safeguarding its coastline on both the land and the marine side.

All the work performed in connection with the Blue Plan shows that the long-range studies and thinking about the future relationship between development and the environment have to be pursued more thoroughly by means of a regional approach. The coastline calls for discriminating land-use planning, and this has to be prepared with the medium- and long-term outlook in mind.

On the basis of the study of the global scenarios for the Mediterranean, which was the main purpose of the Blue Plan, it is possible to 'zoom in' on the local level by scanning each of the following areas in turn:

- the area represented by all the countries of the Mediterranean basin, at a scale of about 1 : 1,250,000, by means of the global scenarios;
- the area occupied by the individual countries, at a scale of about 1 : 500,000, by means of the national scenarios;
- the 'Mediterranean coastal area', at a scale of 1 : 100,000 to 1 : 200,000, by considering the coastal regions;
- the local land area, at a scale of 1 : 2,000 to 1 : 25,000, through a closer view of the coastal strip.

The first three levels have already been analysed to some extent, but the fourth is still relatively unexplored and calls for a different approach. An

Table 20.10 Factors in the evolution of the coastal strip (three scenarios)

Scenario	Population urbanization	Fisheries, agriculture, aquaculture	Industry	Energy	Tourism	Transport
T2	Uncontrolled restructuring of the coastline due to the urban explosion Discharge into the sea of untreated domestic waste	Loss of agricultural land through urbanization, industry, energy, and transport Food-supply problems Contamination of living marine resources	Pollutant waste Short-sighted view of industrial siting	Hot-water outflows	Formation of tourist 'ghettos' Financial circuits outside local control Takeover of coastal sites by affluent elites	Congestion and pollution due to network overloading Marine pollution by petroleum products
T3	Deterioration of the coastal landscape by land encroachment and the use of standardized materials	Water shortages and the decline in water quality Loss of marine productivity through over-fishing and destruction of the inshore sea-bed Destruction of potential aquaculture sites	Low-efficiency depollution Creation of 'high-tech' industrial zones Land wastage due to inadequate control over industrial sites	Hot-water outflows with outfalls Pollution of coastal areas by petroleum products	Excessive water consumption at peak periods Intensive occupation of coastal sites at peak periods Restructuring of the coast through duplication of amenities such as ports, artificial beaches, and islands	Widespread construction of coastal roads for serving seaboard sites Encroachment on the sea and coast for airport and motorway accesses
A1	Controlled restructuring of coasts Treatment of domestic waste	Fisheries: rational stock management Effective protection of productive land and aquaculture sites	Depollution of waste Rational siting of industries	Marked reduction in hot-water outflows	Voluntary limitation on coastal developments Over frequentation of areas of natural beauty along the coast	Deballasting stations Access to the sea by slip-roads Parking areas well away from the sea

Rational water management

exclusively global approach will be of little value for the studies conducted at this level, even if they are bound to make use of the findings obtained for the other levels. It is true that those findings will influence the main guidelines and major trends (in terms of population, economic activities, co-operation, environmental policies, etc.), which will affect balanced land use and the rational use of resources in the coastal strip. However, for a variety of reasons—the physical features represented by climate, relief, and vegetation; the existing human activities, geared to industry, urban growth, tourism, and agriculture; the social problems connected with health, education, and employment; the financial, scientific and technical, and institutional resources that are available and can be mobilized—each community along the coastal strip has to contend with problems which differ from those faced by its neighbours and which cannot be solved in identical ways. Consequently, 'scenarios' for the coastal strip can only be envisaged at the local level, although it must always be borne in mind that they have to be integrated into the much broader contexts represented by the parent coastal region, the country concerned, and the Mediterranean basin as a whole. The extremely complex problem of how the local, national, and supranational levels tie in together will be a key factor in the process involved in planning, developing, and managing the seaboard regions and their coastal strips.

21 The Common Sea

The task of the Blue Plan was not to analyse the situation and evolution of the marine environment as such, since this is studied in detail under the MEDPOL programme. But the prospective studies described above lead, nevertheless, to the sea itself, in two different ways.

In the first place, during the previous chapters and the study of possible trends of the economic sectors and environmental components, interactions with the marine environment were indicated, such as fertilizer input into the sea, marine pollution due to offshore oil operations, hydrocarbon transport, or domestic pollution in coastal regions. Although unsuited to integration, these data facilitate useful cross-checks or throw light on some specific aspects. The chief sources of pollution in the high seas, in particular the transport of pollutant goods and offshore oil operations, will be briefly recalled here.

In this chapter, however, an attempt will be made to assess globally the possible trends of land-based pollution in terms of the different kinds of development or scenario.

Transport of pollutant substances

Aside from hydrocarbons, which constitute a major cause of pollution in the Mediterranean, the most dangerous substances for the marine environment are certain chemicals, which, if accidentally spilt, either sink or, depending on the case, form sheets or clouds of gas or vapour, part of which is dissolved or dispersed in water. The products that are transported in bulk, such as phosphoric acid, nitric acid, benzene, methanol, phenol, trichlorethane, are carried in special tankers, suitably equipped with closed compartments and a double hull to reduce spills in case of accident. Products transported either packed or in drums, loaded like general goods on cargo boats, particularly ro-ros, are not the least harmful because they include hydrazine, sodium hydrosulphite, and arsenic anhydride. Some industrial or nuclear waste also travels in drums or armoured casks, but their loading on non-specialized vessels should be totally prohibited.

Clearly any prospective study of the subject brings into play assessments of the hazards involved in the combination of ship, load, and navigating conditions, along with the formulation of appropriate precautionary or emergency measures. The increased risk stemming from expected growth in the traffic of hazardous materials should be partially offset by technological progress in maritime safety and increasing automation on ships. The coming into force of Annex II of the MARPOL 73/78 Convention should also have a positive effect.

The risk of marine pollution is likely during the following operations:

● *Exploration.* Drillings are made from installations (self-elevating, semi-submersible) or drilling ships which use mud during operations. Drilling muds are combinations of inert substances and chemicals such as corrosion inhibitors, biocides, etc. dispersed in water, oil, or refined mineral oils, and handled in such a way as to cause no environmental damage under normal conditions. Excavated material can amount to 300 t a day: discharged into the sea beneath the drilling rig, it usually suffocates the demersal organisms living there, and toxic effects are detectable to a distance ranging from 500 m (water muds) to 3,000 m (oil muds), depending on the degree of treatment prior to discharge. The most serious risks arise from blow-out, estimated at one blow-out every 500 exploratory wells drilled. The consequences can vary considerably, from slight and brief to very serious.

● *Production.* The difference between production and prospection operations is that production installations remain in position (for twenty to thirty years or more), and there is no drilling mud. One problem arises from the water accompanying the oil, extracted at the same time and reinjected to maintain oilfield pressure, or discharged into the sea after treatment on the platform (reduction of oil content to a monthly average of 40 p.p.m.), or conveyed by pipeline to the coast. In addition to oil contamination, this water may contain chemical additives to increase production performances, some of which (biocides, corrosion or oxidation inhibitors) are quite toxic. The risk of blow-out still exists, but

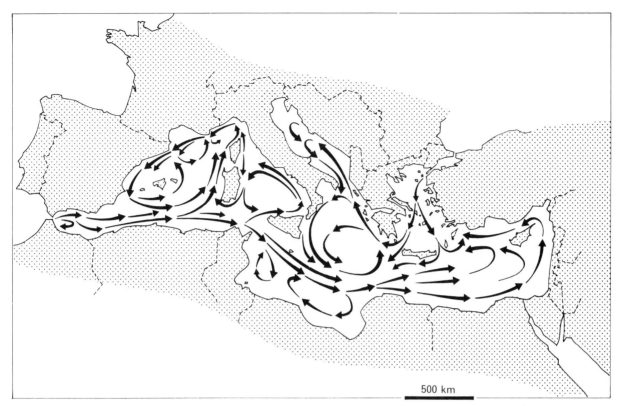

FIG. 21.1 General trends of surface currents in summer. The flow of water in and out through the Strait of Gibraltar is highly complex. Water of lower salinity from the Atlantic enters on the surface, while an almost equivalent amount of Mediterranean water leaves at depth. It is, however, the relatively small difference between the two amounts which provides the major contribution for balancing evaporation and maintaining the level of the Mediterranean.

Source: adapted from H. Lacombe and P. Tchernia (1974).

less than during exploration, estimated at one blow-out (with widely varying consequences) per 3,200 well-years of operation. Risk is greatest during maintenance or repairs, after temporary shut-down of production. According to some experts, a well delivering 1,000 t per day produces, under normal conditions, seepage of approximately 100 p.p.m., i.e. 100 kg of oil per day.

● *Removal.* This is usually done by pipes to the mainland or by tanker, depending on the size and conditions of the field. The most serious environmental pollution risk arises from the possibility of a small leak which may remain undetected for a long time because of safety-device tolerance margins, or of pipe breakage caused, for instance, by a ship's anchor in cases when the originally buried pipe has been uncovered by the erosive action of currents. Risk of accidental leakage is slightly higher during transfer operation when tankers are used for oil removal.

Once production is over, installations have to be removed under the 1958 Convention on the continental shelf, and the United Nations Convention on the Law of the Sea, the clauses of which have been adopted by all Mediterranean countries. Once they are abandoned, however, no one retains any responsibility for proper maintenance of a pipeline (although the absence of tides and associated currents in the Mediterranean reduces the risk of it being uncovered).

These operations, and similar operations relating to minerals are being considered in a draft protocol to the Barcelona Convention on 'the exploration and exploitation of the continental shelf, the seabed, and its subsoil'.

In principle, the scenarios concerning the Mediterranean Sea itself should not be as 'open' as for the other sectors or environmental components, considering the restraining effect of the Barcelona Convention and its protocols, as well as other international agreements on the sea, notably the MARPOL Convention. In fact, very open scenarios could be formulated to compare two extreme trends, namely what would happen if no action were taken, or conversely, the result if all the protocols and conventions were applied to the letter, 'immediately and without delay'. Reality will no doubt lie some-where between the two. Experience has shown, in a number of industrialized countries, that it has sometimes taken a decade for anti-pollution stand-ards to be effectively applied at a rate of 30–50 per cent. Moreover, it is not enough to build powerful treatment plants: they also have to be maintained and operated, which has not always been the case during recent years. It could therefore be assumed for a prospective approach that in the case of the most adverse kind of economic development there would be little change in the number of treatment plants compared with the present situation and that, conversely, in the most propitious case, most of the installations needed would be built, would use increasingly efficient depollution processes, and would operate properly.

The task of formulating scenarios for trends in pollutant discharges into the Mediterranean is especially difficult for several reasons:

● It would have been worth while to pursue this approach on the basis of an updating of the MEDPOL X project up to 1985 (direct and indirect assessment of pollutant inputs into the Mediterranean carried out in 1976; although incomplete it still remains the only global study on the subject).

● Because there has been no systematic as-sessment over a long period, information was lacking on a 'zero state' of pollution in the Mediterranean. For example, a comparison could have been made between the situation during the 1950–70 period, one of rapid economic development with little con-cern about the environment, and that of the fol-lowing period—with weaker economic growth but which witnessed the incipient use of anti-pollution techniques. Although more data are available for this last contemporary period, they do not yet allow for an overall and reliable view of the real state of the Mediterranean because of their dispersion in both time and space.

● Consideration would also have to be given to pollution of atmospheric origin which might contribute as much as land-based sources to pol-lution of the Mediterranean Sea. Unfortunately, available data are very difficult to interpret and circulation models do not allow for a rigorous

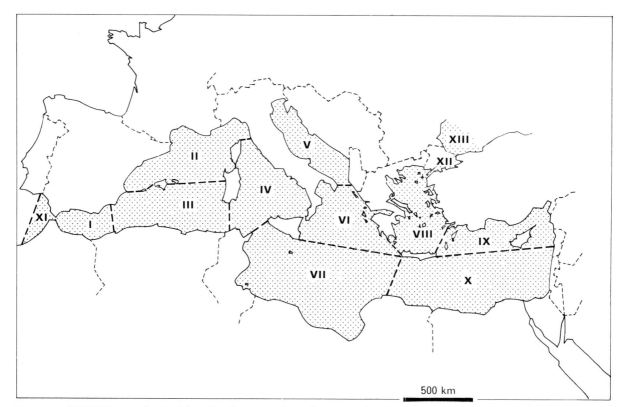

FIG. 21.2 MEDPOL zones for land-based pollution studies. This zoning has been used for studies of land-based pollution under the MEDPOL component of the Mediterranean Action Plan, and was used by the Blue Plan for tentative sea-pollution scenarios. Small islands have not been indicated.
Source: MAP.

quantification of pollutant inputs, the sources of which may be very distant.

The overall method finally used by the Blue Plan consisted of adapting the MEDPOL X values for the ten reference zones covering the whole of the Mediterranean Sea (Fig. 21.2) to the 1985 situation (because of population figures) and to validate the overall findings obtained by comparison with experimental values concerning mercury, lead, and bacteria. Projections for various discharges in 2000 and 2025 were then obtained:

- through the population effect;
- by attributing different reduction coefficients (possibly related to the spatial distribution of populations and industries, the development of manufacturing processes, changes in materials, etc.) and depollution coefficients depending on the scenarios (Table 21.1): clearly, depollution processes will make significant progress in the coming decades, and this expected technical progress can be used to distinguish between the scenarios.

The findings of this prospective study according to the scenarios are described briefly below:

- *T1 scenario* (reference trend). The increase in land-based pollution as a result of population increase in southern and eastern countries would in general be more or less offset by depollution techniques under way (especially in the European Community countries on the northern shore and gradually in the countries on the southern and eastern shores). A slight improvement would be observed for the BOD, COD, nutrients, and detergents, pollutants for which depolluting techniques are the most effective.
- *T2 Scenario* (worst trend). Gradual industrialization in the basin, without the spread of depollution techniques to the southern and eastern countries, would offset the reduction of pollution in the northern countries due to the decline of heavy industry, even for pollutants which showed a slight improvement in the T1 scenario.
- *T3 scenario* (moderate trend). Increased pollution stemming from rapidly growing economic activity

Table 21.1 Depollution coefficients according to treatment used in pollution scenarios

Bacterial levels		
raw sewage:		3m. bacteria/ml
sewage after conventional treatment:		30% drop
sewage after new treatment:		90% drop
Organic matter COD[a]		
raw sewage:		COD 500 mg/ml
sewage after conventional treatment:		60% COD drop
sewage after new treatment:		90% COD drop
Particle load		
raw sewage:		280 mg/ml
sewage after conventional treatment:		85% drop
sewage after new treatment:		90% drop
Metals		
Mercury	without treatment:[b]	600 mg/ml
	after treatment:	75% drop
Lead	without treatment:[b]	70 g/l
	after treatment:	65% drop
Copper	without treatment:[b]	70 g/l
	after treatment:	75% drop

Spatial distribution of population and pollution sources[c]
50% decrease in industrial use of the coastline
75% decrease in the pollutant load through natural purification and sedimentation for bacteria, detergents, hydrocarbons, biodegradable pesticides, and organic matter during their river transit

Air pollution
Smoke filtration:	75% drop

[a] COD/BOD = 2.5 in sewage.
[b] i.e. recycling and administrative measures.
[c] Decrease through hinterland use of space and discharges into rivers.

and the demography of southern and eastern countries would be partly offset by an attempt to achieve a better distribution of activities tending to protect the coast, as well as by the spread of depollution techniques (resort to the 'polluter pays' principle). This would lead to less land-based pollution than in 1985, but at a fairly high economic cost and without being able to avoid a number of (more or less localized) accidents.

- *A1 scenario* (reference alternative). A similar situation to that of T3, but with reduced pollution through the spread of depollution techniques to all the zones as a result of increased international co-operation, supplemented by increasing use of less polluting techniques (in the industry and energy sectors, as well as for agricultural development through better mastery of inputs).

- *A2 scenario* (integration alternative). A situation likewise improved throughout, due also to a better spatial distribution of economic activities, the result of regional integration.

In the case of the trend scenarios, and chiefly the T1 and T2 scenarios, estimates show that the levels of polluting products coming from urban waste water, such as bacteria, viruses, organic matter, detergents, and products from hydrocarbon combustion, are likely to rise, following population growth-rate fairly closely. This overall finding is obtained by considering the fact that improvements in zones with declining populations and growing use of depollution techniques (and whose pollutant discharges will diminish) are offset by the situation in zones with high population growth, which encounter the greatest difficulty in devoting the necessary investment to depollution plants (and whose pollutant discharges will increase).

BOX 21A. **Eutrophication in the Mediterranean**

Eutrophication is a process whereby the aquatic environment becomes richer in nutrients, particularly phosphorus and nitrogen compounds. It is a natural phenomenon in freshwater lakes, considerably aggravated at present by the massive use of fertilizers and detergents, whose action and effects are familiar (lack of oxygen, death of fish, proliferation of algae, and so on).

Eutrophication in a marine or lagoon environment is a more complex phenomenon and less well known. In recent years it has made a spectacular appearance in the Mediterranean—in coastal waters and lagoons—as a result of the excessive discharge of eutrophicating substances from agriculture, industry, and urban centres. Each case found in the Mediterranean had different characteristics and requires specific measures.

The Saronic Gulf and the Elevsis region in Greece, for example, are naturally unproductive, with no inflow of fresh water. However, they receive massive discharges from the Athens sewers and nearby industry, causing anoxic conditions at depth in summer, which can only be remedied by the appropriate treatment of effluent. The Lake of Tunis is eutrophicated by growing sewage discharges, causing the proliferation of large algae in summer. The decomposition of the algae in autumn leads to anaerobic conditions, causing the water to turn milky and red, and the large-scale destruction of fish. The only solution is the removal of excess biomass or an improvement of the water exchange with the sea.

In the northern Adriatic the sudden appearance of 'red tides' due to the accumulation of plant plankton organisms—Diatoma or dinoflagellates—was an occasional phenomenon up to 1969. Since then it has occurred more frequently. The dinoflagellates that proliferate in summer can be harmful to humans and have serious toxic effects on the marine ecosystems and fishery resources.

It is known that algal blooms and the odour of decomposition led many tourists to abandon the coasts of Emilia Romagna, Venezia and Friuli during the summer of 1988. In this case phosphorous inputs were the chief cause and the Italian authorities have taken measures to reduce the amount of phosphorus in detergents.

In 1988 there was also a proliferation of algae due to the eutrophication of the Venice lagoon, with extremely disagreeable consequences for the population and tourists, including an invasion of insects and the release of hydrogen sulphide. An attempt was made to 'gather' the floating biomass by improvised mechanical means, since it could possibly be used as a fertilizer or for industry. All the lagoons and deep bays in the Mediterranean, areas of major interest for aquaculture, shellfish-breeding, and the reproduction of marine species, may be affected by various forms of eutrophication (the lagoons in the Gulf of Lions, the Bay of İzmir, Lake Maryut near Alexandria, etc.).

In general terms the recent worsening of eutrophication in various places around the Mediterranean calls for mobilization of the scientific and technical means available and the application of preventive measures by all the countries concerned. Continuous surveillance and assessment of eutrophication must be carried out and research encouraged, *inter alia* in areas such as the modelling of phenomena, receiving capacities, and long-term effects.

Source: Unesco Reports in Marine Science, 49 (1988).

No doubt technological progress in industrial processes could be the most striking as regards pollutant emissions, and new plants in industrializing countries on the southern and eastern shores would in addition benefit from these advances more quickly in the alternative scenarios. In fact these alternative scenarios assumed both the use of less polluting processes and the installation of urban sewage-treatment plants (following the objectives of the Genoa Ministerial Declaration; see Box 24A below) and deballasting stations. While this latter issue will arise differently in so far as crude oil will be replaced by petroleum products, it can be noted that a MAP study estimates that as many as 58 Mediterranean harbours in 15 countries should be equipped to face current needs for treatment of ballast- and bilge-water: (only about thirty of these harbours are equipped with reception facilities, often only partly adequate). A crucial factor for the success of these scenarios is clearly the speed and the schedule with which these measures will effectively be applied. In this respect the alternative scenarios stand out, not only because of the special use of 'clean technologies', but also because of a much faster application of marine protection measures, compared with the T3 trend scenarios with strong economic growth but insufficient—and often belated—concern about the environment. In other words, the 'findings' of the alternative scenarios, especially as regards the sea, provide an idea of the efforts required (both in time and space) if certain depollution and environmental quality objectives are to be achieved (reduction factors in the region of 3–5).

Table 21.2, established in the framework of the Mediterranean Action Plan, provides an estimate of current construction costs of treatment plants and submarine outfalls for all Mediterranean coastal cities with more than 10,000 inhabitants, one of the targets of the Genoa Declaration. Estimated costs are given for each country and for various population ranges.

With regard to the impact of pollution on Mediterranean marine life, bacterial and viral pollution, which is an obstacle to tourist development or a hazard when it reaches shellfish-breeding grounds, seems in fact to be gradually coming under control. It is less worrying than chemical pollution, whose harmful effects can be divided into three groups:

- those which have a direct toxic action on wild life and plant life, reflected by a loss in the nutritional capital;
- those which disturb interspecies relations and

which will produce an 'ecological drift' of the marine environment;

- those which, through the fixation and concentration of residual pollution along the various links of biological chains, will be at the origin of pathogenic disorders for seafood consumers.

Once in the marine environment, chemical products are subject to a dual process:

- attack by bacteria which withdraw the substances needed by their metabolisms; the product then disappears through 'biodegradation'

Table 21.2 Estimated construction costs (1987) of treatment plants and submarine outfalls for Mediterranean coastal towns with population over 10,000

(a) By country

Country	No. of coastal towns	Population (000s)	Treatment plant construction cost (US$000)
Albania	4	146	24,820
Algeria	35	3,561	356,640
Cyprus	4	255	39,200
Egypt	11	3,637	238,710
France	36	2,798	328,620
Greece	27	4,568	369,780
Israel	15	1,454	193,820
Italy	254	15,471	1,790,240
Lebanon	7	1,910	185,900
Libya	16	2,036	243,590
Malta	11	155	26,500
Monaco	1	27	3,860
Morocco	3	519	64,170
Spain	62	5,767	621,180
Syria	4	394	50,020
Tunisia	20	2,963	399,380
Turkey	19	2,021	221,150
Yugoslavia	10	585	82,210
TOTAL	539	48,267	5,139,790

(b) By population range

Population range	No. of coastal cities	Treatment plant construction costs (US$000)
10,000–20,000	215	513,470
20,001–50,000	171	732,430
50,001–100,000	74	819,640
100,001–1,000,000	70	2,039,420
1,000,001–3,000,000	9	1,034,830

Note: The total cost—including construction of sewage treatment plants for cities over 100,000 inhabitants and construction of appropriate outfalls and or/treatment plants for towns over 10,000 inhabitants—comes to about US$5m.

Source: Mediterranean Action Plan, Technical Reports Series No. 28.

(this is the case with hydrocarbons or bio-degradable detergents among other things);
● concentration in biological chains, which counteracts this biodegradability.

One of the most irritating signs of Mediterranean pollution is the continuing presence on the beaches of tar balls coming from degassing at sea or oil leaks. It is estimated that about 600,000 t of oil are spilt this way each year by ships in the Mediterranean and that 30 per cent of this oil reaches the coast in the form of the tar balls so disliked by bathers. Combatting this kind of pollution, which is still important, particularly in the Eastern basin, clearly depends directly on the effective application of the conventions mentioned above.

In the open sea, the Mediterranean, more than any other water body, is also polluted by floating debris that is not (or barely) biodegradable, plastics in particular. Clearly this involves packaging and wrapping, dispersed by waves and currents, discharged from merchant or naval vessels, yachts, or the coastal regions themselves. It also includes certain raw materials such as plastic pellets used in the manufacture of plastic products, which may be ingested by turtles or sea birds. This problem has become increasingly serious over the past years, particularly for fishing nets, and cannot be solved without the close surveillance of the coastal countries, such as that envisaged in the alternative scenarios. The mandatory use of biodegradable packaging, as will be the case in Italy in 1991, will help to reduce this nuisance in the Mediterranean.

Organic pollution caused by spills of large quantities of nutrients (phosphorus, nitrogen, sediments, etc.), agricultural run-off, and waste water from cities and industrial plants can cause the chaotic proliferation of some species through eutrophication concerning not only the coastal strip but the sea itself. An ecosystem modified in this way is invaded by a very small number of extremely resistant, proliferating species, especially in summer when the temperature is a contributing factor. In 1988 a phenomenon of this kind covered a large part of the Adriatic, a true ecological 'alarm bell', the cause of which will take about a decade to eliminate: pollution discharged by the Po and other northern Adriatic rivers (see Box 21A). The insidious nature of this kind of pollution, its threshold phenomena, the length and cost of rehabilitation or elimination of causes, underscore the need for the urgent application of protection and conservation measures, as is in fact assumed in the alternative scenarios.

V Synopsis and Suggestions for Action

22 Choosing a Sustainable Form of Development

Slow growth of the world economy would be reflected by equally slow economic growth at the Mediterranean level because of the interdependence between this area and other regions. These development conditions would affect virtually all sectors (worst trend scenario T2, with low economic growth). Economic stagnation in the countries north of the basin would produce tremendous development difficulties in the southern and eastern countries to the extent that some countries would experience decreasing levels of production and/or per capita consumption in some sectors as vital as agricultural production or energy consumption, which means a gradual erosion of their socio-economic situation rather than an improvement. The financing of industrial growth would be curbed by the lack of resources and the burden of persisting debt. International tourism would be neither beneficial nor 'healthy', involving both low-cost mass tourism and an 'élitist' tourism, object of fierce competition among the different countries.

Environmental protection would have few resources for intervention or prevention, reflected by delayed and inadequate case-by-case measures adopted to meet the most urgent needs, within the context of poorly applied regulations and reticence at all levels. One of the most worrying environmental trends would be the gradual disappearance of many forests (used for fuel-wood and grazing), causing accelerated (and sometimes irreversible) soil degradation and disrupting run-off patterns and water regulation. Marginal land in the southern and eastern countries would be subject to heavy pressure leading to their degradation (erosion), and water resources in the major agricultural regions of the northern countries would be threatened by growing pollution (nitrogen from fertilizers). In contrast, some pressures, as well as most kinds of pollution, would be lower than for other development patterns because of the stagnation or weak growth of economic activities. The Mediterranean population would reach its maximum level, and the very large population groups of working age would be faced with insurmountable underemployment. Urbanization would also be at its highest level (in absolute terms) and virtually uncontrollable, and a minimum of services and sanitary conditions would be a cause of concern in the cities.

Following the rules of the game for the scenarios, this kind of growth (T2 scenario) was continued up to the end of the period, i.e. 2025. It is likely, if not certain, that social or geopolitical disruptions would occur well before the end of the period—since the situation would deteriorate faster after the turn of the century—and would impose a change of policy and behaviour, i.e. a 'change of scenario'.

The recovery of economic growth at the world level in the 1990s and better co-ordination among the major economic partners would have a definite spill-over effect on the economies of the Mediterranean basin countries (moderate trend scenario T3, with strong economic growth). The countries of the European Community, for instance, would gain on average about half a point in growth—significant over a long period of four decades—which would have a positive effect on the development of the other basin countries. In the southern and eastern countries the overall rise in production levels would be strengthened by less dynamic population growth (total and urban), leading to a noticeable improvement of per capita socio-economic indicators, i.e. of economic and social well-being. Agricultural productivity and yields would virtually double by 2025, and part of the output of highly intensified agriculture would be directed towards the major European and international markets, in a general atmosphere of trade growth. Industries in the countries north of the basin would increase their specialization in high-technology sectors (special materials, fine chemicals, information technology, and process control, etc.). The basic industries in the southern and eastern countries—primary processing of raw materials, manufactured goods, and agro-food—would undergo spectacular development, to the point of exceeding production levels of the countries north of the basin after 2000.

Agricultural intensification itself would produce strong industrial demands in these countries: fertilizer, tractors, machinery, etc. Industrial growth, agricultural intensification, the ensuing development of transport—requirements for the population's well-being—would all lead to the vigorous growth of energy consumption (about 70 per cent higher than in the previous scenario), particularly for electricity. All sources of energy should be mobilized (coal, oil, natural gas, uranium, and, to a lesser extent, renewable energies).

Although the legislative and financial resources and technical means to undertake environmental protection are easily available, this kind of scenario paradoxically proves to be the most harmful for the Mediterranean environment and the one which creates the most pollution, because of the high level of all economic activities and delays in the application of measures which, in any event, aim at combating the effects of pollution a posteriori rather than preventing them. Although this is not a case of 'uncontrolled growth' as in the past— which populations and governments would no longer tolerate—this kind of growth is insufficiently concerned about the environment. Many effects will no doubt be felt after the end of the period (such as the greenhouse effect), but some trends could evolve rather quickly (forests, soil, water resources, coast and near-shore sea-bed) and would be virtually irreversible. Pressures on the coast would be particularly heavy and virtually impossible to control since most activities would be concentrated there and would provoke bitter conflict about resource uses (some of which are mutually exclusive). Economic disruptions—starting perhaps with hydrocarbon supplies—and even irreversible ecological degradation would be the inevitable alarm signals of later, but even more serious, dangers.

These two extreme kinds of scenario demonstrate the difficulties of development, especially in the countries south and east of the Mediterranean basin, in an international climate of fierce competition, whether economic growth is weak or strong (with its adverse effects), resulting in little or inadequate attention being paid to the environment. By contributing to a better distribution of effort, to a sharing of knowledge, experience, and practice, and to market organization, international co-operation in a multipolar and better-balanced world (and more specifically north–south or south–south Mediterranean co-operation) could provide a fresh impulse to economies and to societies (alternative scenarios).

This desire for co-operation, based on the solidarity of coastal countries, would promote strong agricultural growth (tripling of production) through the increase of irrigated land (doubling), fertilizer use, and mechanization (tripling for the basin as a whole), as the output of the southern and eastern countries would be directed either towards outside markets (European in the case of reference alternative scenario A1 with strong north–south co-operation) or towards regional self-sufficiency (the case of the A2 alternative scenario with south–south regional integration). Industrial growth in the countries south and east of the basin would be strong and well balanced for the main branches (except perhaps for the capital goods industry, which may present problems) and would include the export of manufactured goods towards the countries north of the basin, substantial in the case of strong north–south co-operation, or based more on regional complementarity in the case of predominant south–south co-operation. As with the previous scenarios (type T3), strong industrial, agricultural, transport, and other growth would entail high energy consumption, but with two main differences: greater attention (even a priority) would be given to energy saving and there would be a clear preference for some sources (very vigorous development of natural gas, clean fuel, and expansion of renewable energies, especially at the end of the period). North–south or south–south relations, together with rising incomes and living standards, would further tourism, whose development would be at its highest level (about 700m. tourists in all), with the vigorous growth of domestic tourism.

In addition to north–south or south–south international co-operation, promoting the exchange of experience and knowledge, the alternative scenarios are also characterized by a completely different approach to environmental problems: incorporation of protection costs in budgets, consideration of environmental factors in decision-making processes, less centralization but better co-ordination, involvement of local populations in decisions and management, and so on. The forest, soil, and water would no longer be considered as three different environments, the subject of more or less independent action, but as ecosystems forming a single resource, protected and managed as such. Similarly, the coast would be the subject of integrated planning, linking the three levels of decision-making and development: local, regional, and national.

Since agricultural intensification would be carried out while seeking the most efficient use of inputs, industrialization would resort to less polluting processes, energy use would be orientated towards cleaner sources, tourism would be better distributed in time and space, urbanization would be based on a well-balanced network of small and medium-sized towns, employment would gain from the (encouraged) dynamism of small and medium-sized enterprises, impacts on the environment and resources would be minimized (although they would not entirely disappear, of course). Land-based pollution and the physical and biological degradation of the Mediterranean coast would also be minimized, even halted.

The trend scenarios therefore proved to be unstable, either because of the growing deterioration of socio-economic conditions in a number of countries (exacerbating the geopolitical instability of the Mediterranean basin), or because of the accelerated degradation of environments and resources, leading to 'natural' disasters—floods, landslides, the irreversible loss of soil, desertification, and so forth—in fact largely aggravated by human action.

Only the alternative scenarios seem able to reconcile economic growth and protection of the Mediterranean environment in the long term (even the very long term), i.e. ensure 'sustainable development'. This is understood as a form of development that strives to meet the basic needs of current generations as a whole while ensuring that its impact on the environment and natural resources will not compromise the capacity of future generations to meet their own needs. The key to these scenarios lies, rather than in growth-rates, in greater Mediterranean co-operation and the integrated management of environments in the development process. The A1 scenario, with strong north–south co-operation, would no doubt contribute to faster economic development in the countries south and east of the Mediterranean basin; the A2 scenario, with predominant south–south co-operation, could lead to a better balance. A combination of the two over a period of time would probably be the most propitious.

The Blue Plan horizons 2000 and 2025 may seem remote to experts in economic forecasting. In fact 'economic time-spans' are rather short compared to the 'ecological time-spans' of forests, soil, or water, although a distinction should be made between the long time-spans for genesis and/or rehabilitation of environments and the increasingly short time-spans associated with degradation: by 2000 the loss of soil and decimation of forests could reach disastrous levels.

The conclusions of the scenarios must be somewhat nuanced depending on whether consideration is given to a country as a whole, or only its Mediterranean coastal region, or the sea itself. At the level of countries and coastal regions, the most worrying medium-term threat seems to be the inability to check advancing soil erosion and degradation; soil protection requires protection of the forest upstream. At the level of coastal regions and the sea, priority should be given to protection of the coast, defined as the narrow strip where land and sea meet, in which direct action can only be local and/or national, but where threats to the environment are the worst, even in the most favourable scenarios. Rather than the sea in general, the coastal strip is where the future of the Mediterranean environment hangs in the balance.

Finally, it seems that beyond 2000 foreseeable population growth will change even the very dimension of problems for most countries south and east of the Mediterranean basin. Whatever the scenario, production will necessarily have to be increased through greater technification based on better scientific and sociological knowledge, closely involving local populations in these efforts; or population growth will have to be decisively reduced. Most probably both will be needed.

In addition to raising the awareness of all Mediterranean people about the issues of their environment, the challenge of the development/environment alternative scenarios is not so much to establish a 'new' economy but a new rationality for decision-making, where space, time, and system interactions would be fully integrated.

23 Acting on Economic Sectors and the Environment

The sectoral analyses sometimes raised major issues concerning the possible futures of economic activities. Reflection on environmental components stressed predictable trends, stemming from sectoral developments, and the risk of short- or medium-term degradation of the most essential environments— the soil, inland water, the forest and the coast— where effects accumulate. Everyone, and this includes decision-makers in particular, now has to draw conclusions and take the necessary measures to foster a desirable form of development, or to counteract a specific adverse trend. This chapter groups together some possible suggestions for action. Most of them will not seem too original to the specialist, but they have been targeted either on various specific interactions between economic sectors and the environment, or even more on the protection of the most endangered Mediterranean environments. These suggestions are directed especially at the national, even local, level, as those for Mediterranean co-operation are presented in the following chapter.

1. Urbanization

Whatever kind of development is pursued, urbanization will continue at a rapid pace in the Mediterranean basin, reaching rates in the region of 70–80 per cent around 2025 (this is already the case in some countries north of the basin). Requirements in terms of equipment, services, and infrastructure stemming from this growth probably present the biggest challenge to officials and managers. Environmental protection in the Mediterranean coastal strip will depend more on the way urbanization is handled than on any other activity.

The quality of life in Mediterranean towns and agglomerations in the next forty years will depend largely on physical planning policies in the coming years, firmly implemented or on the contrary neglected. Main efforts should focus on:

- *water* supplies, sanitation, combating the wast-
age of this precious resource for which various uses compete (agriculture, industry): savings could be effected by recycling water and making a distinction between uses;
- the *elimination of toxic waste* and its possible reuse: there should not be the least temptation to export urban waste, as is done, for instance, by some American cities;
- the *creation of green spaces*, essential in Mediterranean towns which already have less (on average four times less) than north European towns; green spaces must be supplemented by the maintenance or creation of pedestrian precincts (medinas, roads closed to traffic, etc.);
- the *saving of energy* by developing *solar technologies* for domestic use and space-heating, and by supervising the use of coal and fuel (as in Ankara) in towns already severely affected by air pollution;
- the strengthening of efforts to *reduce motor-vehicle pollution* at the origin (clean cars, vehicles designed especially for urban traffic, etc.) as air pollution, already severe in some towns, may become unbearable with the growth of motorized traffic; efforts made to restrict the source (new cars) must be quickly extended;
- the *reduction of pressure*, sometimes considerable, on peri-urban *agricultural land* in countries where it is scarce and in most coastal regions; in this respect some successful experiments demonstrate that land-control legislation and practice can provide lasting protection for agricultural areas near towns and avoid uncontrolled urbanization;
- the maintenance or development of *types of architecture, urbanism, and housing* adapted to spatial constraints and the ecological and cultural conditions of the country.
- the protection and rehabilitation of *historic urban centres*, associated with strict regulation for new construction activity, advertising, and motor-vehicle circulation.

2. Agriculture

Rising population levels and living standards in the countries south and east of the Mediterranean basin will considerably increase agro-food needs, and only vigorous intensification will help to reduce food dependency, which has become more pronounced in recent years. This intensification should not be carried out in a haphazard or poorly controlled way, but on the contrary should be well targeted and properly guided, by co-ordinating the technological mastery of industrial inputs (fertilizers, pesticides, machinery, etc.) and by integrating the production of these inputs into the industrial and agricultural development process. This will contribute to reducing as much as possible the damaging effect of the large expected increase of these inputs.

In the north, attempts should be made to stabilize the amounts of industrial inputs used in order to master their application thoroughly. In addition, improved knowledge of the evolution of pollutants (fertilizers and pesticides) in the environment would help to combat their impact more effectively.

The following measures should also help to improve agricultural production while paying more attention to the Mediterranean environment:

● Soil salinization (one of the biggest threats to agricultural land) and waterlogging could be avoided to a large extent by improving and maintaining the drainage networks in existing irrigation districts and by taking care to install them correctly in new districts.

● Investments in major irrigation dams should always be preceded by thorough and systematic action to combat upstream erosion and followed by investment and necessary measures to equip irrigation districts appropriately, in close co-operation with local populations (duly trained and informed).

● The development and application of bio-technologies likely to increase or improve agricultural production (nitrogen fixation, crop protection, animal feed, etc.), a prime area for international co-operation, should be more strongly encouraged in the region.

● The conservation of cultivated plant varieties and domestic animal breeds is essential for the development of future production in the Mediterranean region.

● Means of tackling the very uneven production from one year to another, caused by the vagaries of the Mediterranean climate, could be bolstered through technical and institutional mechanisms which would contribute to reducing pressure on soil and water.

● Lastly, special attention should focus on the ways in which agro-food industries develop in Mediterranean coastal areas, as to both site coverage and the risk of pollution and of discharges into the sea.

3. Fisheries and aquaculture

Fisheries and aquaculture are a specific sector which could contribute more to meeting food requirements in the Mediterranean basin. First of all, statistical data should be co-ordinated and standardized, as well as the various systems for assessing stocks, in order to increase the accuracy and reliability of results.

With regard to fisheries, concerted action among states should be pursued, and optimal use of the coastal strip should be ensured, particularly in view of small-scale fisheries and the installation of artificial reefs and aquaculture facilities in the open sea.

Concerning aquaculture, it would be useful:

● to identify and protect potential aquaculture zones in each country, notably lagoons;
● to carry out necessary experiments to develop various new products;
● to give more systematic attention, from the viewpoint of aquaculture potential, to the location of marinas.

4. Industry

The impact of industrial growth on the Mediterranean environment will be considerable during the next forty years, especially in the countries south and east of the basin. Trends or transformations both in the north and in the south and east, which will gradually alter the industrial landscape, will be equally important. But this impact will change completely depending on the policies followed or measures undertaken by states, industrialists, or local authorities.

Impact related to the heavy pressure of new activities, many of which would be concentrated on the coast, will largely depend on land-use policies decided upon and implemented at the national, regional, or local levels. The prior development of 'industrial zones', duly drained and equipped with installations for the evacuation or reprocessing of waste, or for water recycling, will produce savings in resources, such as space and water (which are bottlenecks in development).

The various Mediterranean countries, either alone or jointly (following the example of practice within the European Communities), could be stricter about waste; but relevant regulations are insufficient, and all will depend on the quality of the inspectors for industrial plants, and on their capacity for dialogue with those responsible for production in the enterprise.

With respect to the existing industrial stock, identification and supervision of 'hazardous industries' is a priority (one which some Mediterranean countries have in fact already considered). State action should also focus on the evacuation of toxic wastes: an organized system for evacuation and treatment, which scarcely exists at present even in the most advanced countries, is essential in the Mediterranean.

Lastly, the role of the enterprise is at least as vital as that of the state. Improvements as regards industrial pollution depend on the enterprise. De-pollution installations are sometimes expensive (as in steel works), but the introduction of depollution techniques, and above all processes, can also be profitable (reuse of 'waste' or 'by-products', recycling, etc.). In this respect the development of information exchanges on 'clean technologies' would be very useful both internally and between countries. In any event national and regional incentives for the application of existing industrial anti-pollution techniques (which are not always used) should be improved and training stepped up in this area.

5. Energy

Future demand can be anticipated fairly accurately in the Mediterranean energy sector: resources are subject to heavy constraints related to the international context. The coastal countries do, however, have some options open to them. Exchange of information and practices, and the establishment of suitable policies geared as a priority to energy conservation and environmental protection, would be useful.

Electricity and gas networks in Mediterranean countries of the European Community are already interconnected to a large extent. It would be appropriate to extend this kind of interconnection to the other Mediterranean countries. Electricity

development prospects should be closely followed, with a view to the exchange of information and experience (for pollution control, among other things).

In the southern and eastern countries, the search for a solution to the fuel-wood problem in rural areas (distribution of LPG, followed by decentralized rural electrification) is urgent in order to spare the often over-exploited forests.

Even with a high rate of growth and penetration, the contribution of solar energy would not be significant in the Mediterranean countries in the short or medium term. In the long term, however, it should become more important. Through more systematic targeting, solar energy could already make a useful contribution, particularly for scattered dwellings and irrigation in the rural world.

Lastly, the consequences of the trend towards a heating up of the climate due to the greenhouse effect should be closely followed by all the coastal countries, which should play an active role in international co-operation on the energy policies related to this problem.

6. Tourism

Tourism is destined to be one of the major resources of the future for many Mediterranean countries. In principle it would be possible to receive four times more tourists in the Mediterranean (a level intimated by some scenarios), but countries, local authorities, and those working in the tourist sector, who in addition are competing with each other almost everywhere in the basin, will not be able to handle this kind of growth without an effort to improve information, analysis, and co-operation.

Each country, as far as it is concerned, should aim at improving distribution spatially (distribution of flows to avoid saturation) and especially throughout the year (partial staggering of holidays, short stays, winter tourism) to spread the load, increasingly concentrated on the narrow coastal strip. Collaboration with local populations at the decision-making level and more careful integration into the physical and cultural environment are essential to avoid the risk of rejection. The joint use of installations by the local population and by domestic and foreign tourists is one of the ways of achieving this objective.

The rapid development of different kinds of tourism must be closely followed by each country, as the trend towards more active tourism (sport, culture, conferences) has become more important. Lastly, systematically raising the awareness of tourists as regards protection of the environment they have come to enjoy is essential in the countries as a whole. The protection of some prestigious and over-visited natural or cultural sites could be promoted by this awareness-heightening, but it may also require new solutions (recreational areas).

7. Transport

In the maritime area, crude-oil transport should drop, while the transport of products refined by the producer countries should rise, which changes somewhat the transport profile in favour of smaller ships with specialized cargoes (some of which, more polluting or more toxic, would increase risks during major accidents). Renewal of the tanker fleet should take at least twenty years. Hence, in order to reduce discharges at sea by ships, the need to speed up the installation of land facilities with a view to complying with the Barcelona Convention and the MARPOL 1973/8 stipulations concerning the dumping of oil.

With respect to other products transported by sea, as industrialization proceeds in the countries south and east of the basin, and trade grows, there will be an increase in the transport of chemical products, either in bulk, in drums, or packed, and a parallel rise in the risk of accidental pollution (some of these products are highly toxic). An entirely new approach should be developed, by seeking in particular better safety conditions for this kind of transport.

Roll-on, roll-off cargo ships would be increasingly used on intra-Mediterranean links and their number would increase. Care should be taken to ensure that the loading of merchandise hazardous for the marine environment is authorized only on those 'ro-ro' vessels which will meet the new, much stricter, international safety regulations currently being drafted.

At the national level priority could be given to:

- the installation of facilities in port complexes to reduce maritime transport nuisances as far as possible;
- greater efforts to speed up the installation of deballasting facilities (about twenty are needed).

With regard to infrastructure for rapidly expanding road transport, considerations such as incorporation into the landscape or protection of potential agricultural areas should encourage the careful choice of routes and avoidance of inhabited areas (to cut down noise).

To be effective, efforts to reduce emissions at the source should be vigorous and quick because the renewal of the Mediterranean motor-vehicle stock, particularly in the south and east, is fairly slow (about fifteen years). Greater attention should focus on diesel vehicles and those with small cubic capacity (more numerous in the Mediterranean than in northern Europe), the supervision of used vehicles (also more numerous in the basin countries), and the harmonization of speed limits. The wider use of gas engines (LPG) would be an interesting contribution to the reduction of pollution. Specific regulations on automobile traffic set at the national level are essential in congested agglomerations. Collaboration on trucks would be useful.

Lastly, the problem of air corridors and the risk of congestion over airports (stemming from the explosive growth of tourism) must be carefully examined by the national civil and military authorities. This also requires Mediterranean collaboration, especially because the air network will be decisive in the creation of a new Mediterranean geography and the process of bringing Mediterranean countries, regions, and cities closer together.

8. The forest

The production role of the Mediterranean forest remains important for some countries (Maghreb and Turkey particularly) where management will be orientated towards improving wood and grass production and ensuring regeneration. The Blue Plan scenarios highlighted, however, the fundamental protective role of the forest and also demonstrated that the problems presented by Mediterranean woodland cannot be solved, even if no unpleasant surprise occurs, without a considerable and prolonged effort on the part of the various countries concerned. If the first positive results of this effort are to be obtained before 2025, with an effect on adverse trends, and if an increase in irreversible situations is to be avoided locally, this action will have to be taken immediately, as time is short and negative trends are gaining ground. It has to be based on the rational management of the forest wherever this is still possible and on reforestation with the species best suited to the ecological and economic objectives pursued.

Forest research will have to be better integrated into regional planning processes (with an improvement, among other things, of the links between research and applications), with a view to strengthening the role of the forest in rural development. It is no less urgent—and no doubt more difficult—to change attitudes radically through information, extension services, or persuasion (political decision-makers, forest officials, coastal populations, the media, etc.).

Despite a time-lag between the northern countries and those south and east of the basin, the very existence of woodland in coastal regions and areas with a strong human concentration is threatened by trampling, degradation, fire, pollution, and disease, and by abuse of man-made creations (artificial plantings, dune stabilization, green spaces, urban parks, etc. that are generally replacing areas once naturally wooded). One of the few effective and lasting means of defending areas to be preserved regardless would be to turn them into national estates managed by specialized bodies. In these regions, the setting up of partially or totally artificial plantations, sufficiently resistant to the needs and constraints of human occupation, could prove necessary.

In the hinterlands of the countries south and east of the basin management conditions are far from optimal and need to be improved. The biomass balance of the forest could be improved by reducing the removal of fuel-wood (improved efficiency of cooking and heating utensils, supply of substitute fuels, planting of fast-growing fuel-wood trees near villages) and by improving the fodder 'system' (fodder trees, improved grazing supplemented by artificial feed, etc.). Jobs could be created in this sector—even a civil service—linked to work beneficial to ecosystems, and local communities could be reimbursed for some of the direct or indirect benefits obtained from the forest in downstream areas, or even far away. In these hinterlands the stakes in the forest are considerable, for their future depends to a large extent on forest evolution. Responsible authorities would gain in encouraging new forms of co-operation with local people to protect endemic forests from over-grazing. The setting up of biosphere reserves (MAB) could further this action.

In the countries north of the basin, lasting protection of the forest, beyond fire control, would be achieved by way of the study of diseases and of the prospects for autochthonous species. Care must also be taken over the way in which production, leisure, and landscape-protection functions will be incorporated.

Lastly, forest protection can facilitate conservation of the genetic heritage of the particularly rich Mediterranean flora. In this vein, the over-systematic planting of foreign species where endemic ones are economically viable should be avoided. In both the north and the south, action could focus on the establishment of protected areas for endemic species and of appropriately managed and protected conservation areas (species banks, conservatories, etc.).

9. The soil

Whatever the scenario, the erosion of Mediterranean soil and inability to check its processes clearly seem to be one of the most worrying threats. Soil policy implies both rapid and very long-term action, along with the mobilization of considerable resources. Experiences are very different. An initial prerequisite would be to prepare an inventory for all those concerned and analyse the reasons for success or failure, related either to the characteristics of the soil itself or to neglect of the socio-cultural aspects of the problem, which may have been tackled from a purely technical viewpoint.

Necessary agricultural intensification should take into account, from the outset, control techniques for combating potential erosion in the case of dry farming in the Mediterranean climate (cereal/alfalfa rotation patterns, replacing deep mechanical ploughing with surface ploughing), and the risk of salinization in the case of irrigated farming (with improvement and maintenance of adequate drainage networks). The water-retention capacity of some soils with a calcareous crust could be improved by encouraging deep scarification and the introduction of species with deep roots to break up the soil below surface ploughing.

For mountainous regions, countries could give higher priority to soil maintenance by adopting measures to combat over-grazing and deforestation. On the slopes, they could foster the maintenance or repair of the traditional steps and terraces, which are stabilizing elements. Abandoned and eroded agricultural land on steep slopes could be gradually converted into fuel-wood forests. In the northern hinterlands local authorities and forest officials could join forces to ensure suitable management of abandoned rural areas, *inter alia* through preventive afforestation and the timbering of agricultural wasteland.

10. Inland water

Water resources in many Mediterranean countries are naturally restricted by the climate. But for most of them this constraint could be overcome by rational and skilful management. Solutions are rather well known and can simplify difficult choices between several competing uses. But adaptations will in any event be necessary sooner or later: the sooner they are introduced the less often will economic growth occur to the detriment—partly irreversible—of the environment in both the north and the south and east (with, naturally, varying degrees of intensity). As in the case of soil or forest resources, rapid economic development, neglectful of the environment and resources, may seem less expensive, but only to the extent that these adaptations would be postponed (with increasing costs).

The hierarchy of water problems, motivations for conserving water in the environment, and the choice of components to be preserved will depend on the countries, on whether their water is plentiful or scarce, or on their state of economic development. These choices would have to be based on:

- less global and more regional analyses and prospective studies, extending those of the Blue Plan and drawing from them as regards development prospects;
- processes of consensus for adopting qualitative and quantitative objectives concerning the conservation levels for aquatic areas to be protected, and the regime and quality of water to be conserved, particularly in coastal regions.

Options chosen should fit into water management and protection schemes incorporated into development plans.

Effective achievement of objectives would imply:

- the setting up of mechanisms to incorporate various external effects of water use in the economic decision-making process;
- the establishment of integrated water management authorities (basin agencies or commissions), endowed with appropriate legal and financial resources and empowered both to guide and co-ordinate water management and conservation and to intervene as regards uses and tariffs in general;
- the development of information systems—assessment networks, regular census-taking operations, data-banks—working as an 'observatory of water resources and uses' for management authorities and the general public.

There is also a need for improving the technical aspects of water uses (especially for irrigation) by encouraging water saving, particularly in countries where resources are scarce, and developing the treatment and recycling of urban and industrial effluent for agricultural use.

Lastly, as pointed out for the forest and soil, social inertia adds to that of nature, and for results to be significant and lasting efforts would have to be made, in this case also, to change attitudes and behaviour and to develop a better appreciation of the true value of water.

11. The coast

Particularly vigorous policies are required from states, regions, and local authorities in order to achieve effective protection and avoid destructive coastal concentration; integrated planning, which could be based on the scenario method at the local level, seems essential for short-term, or (to an even greater extent) long-term planning.

This kind of integrated planning requires the co-operation of specialists in very different disciplines related to both economics and ecology, as well as the land and the sea. Examples of this kind of co-operation are few and it is the task of national or local authorities to organize it. At the level of action and management, the situation is even more difficult because of the dispersion, overlapping, or lack of administrative responsibility on the land and sea sections of the coastal strip in virtually all countries. New administrative bodies could be set up, as in the case of water-resource management: physical-planning agencies, coastal committees, and so on.

Among the actions which seem to be the most urgent or necessary are:

- exchange of experiences (and possibly of projects) for the more effective use of the specific features of different coastal regions and their complementary aspects;
- the use of modern computerized geographical information techniques, especially geared to processing environmental data;
- a deliberate option, when making choices, for flexibility in a number of installations, facilitating subsequent adaptation to changing situations and prospective management;
- an inventory of the areas of the coastal strip most threatened by future development, and the

preparation of physical plans for development zones, while identifying as from now areas to be protected at all cost and potential aquaculture zones;

● the systematic consideration of the effects on soil and land areas by means of impact studies on the environment in coastal regions;

● bringing under protection, as quickly as possible in each country, a significant part of the land and marine coastal strip—about a third of its total length—through legislation, purchase (coastal conservatories), agreement with local populations or private owners, etc.;

● efforts, in the implementation of projects to be established on the coastal strip, to reduce to a minimum impingement on the near-shore sea-bed and to protect marine species in their larval and young stage by prohibiting certain kinds of fishing in defined zones;

● establishment of a better linkage or co-ordination between coastal development and that of the hinterland, in order to achieve a certain degree of decongestion on the coast.

It should be recognized that regulatory and legal action alone is likely to be ineffective in the longer term and that it should be accompanied by deliberate intervention in economic mechanisms (price formation), notably in those of the property market. This implies setting up agencies able to define the development objectives of specific zones within the context of regional and national development scenarios, duly endowed with the necessary means of implementation.

12. The sea

Clearly threats are most serious on the marine coastal strip which falls under the jurisdiction of each country. However there is a continuity between the coastal sea and the high seas. Pollution does not recognize the limits of territorial waters. This is why the findings of the various Blue Plan scenarios must be observed on the sea itself, common property of all the coastal countries. Clearly there is no question here of adding to the guide-lines for action concerning protection of the Mediterranean Sea which, over almost fifteen years, have been formulated, discussed, and decided upon by the various organs of the Mediterranean Action Plan. From the Blue Plan work, however, it seems that the studies, and the decisions stemming from them, would benefit from being set squarely in the more general context of the economic and social development of the coastal countries and of the environmental policies they incorporated in their national plans. Protection of the sea starts with protection of the coast; as has been repeatedly stressed, all the environments are found on the coast and all the economic activities are carried out there. But environmental trends on the coast depend on environmental trends in the hinterland (forest, watersheds, etc.), and sectoral activities depend on the strategy and economic level of the entire country. Although it is true that land-based pollution is the biggest threat to the Mediterranean Sea, the complex application of the relevant protocol and the time-spans involved for its effective implementation by all countries in all its aspects suggest that application should be closely correlated with the overall prospects for economic development and environment in the coastal states, either at the level of the basin as a whole, or at the level of particular areas concerning one or several countries.

It is clear that the state of sea pollution will depend on the effective application of all the international conventions and protocols intended to avoid or reduce pollution, whether from land-based inputs, transport of hydrocarbons, discharges from ships and yachts, or the maritime transport of hazardous substances. International monitoring of maritime 'corridors' is in particular essential to avoid clandestine degassing operations and ensure safety. However, it is clearly at the national level that habits and practices will be formed and installations set up for the more or less effective application of international agreements. It is at this level, or at the local level, that it was decided that in the past (and could still be decided in the future, under more or less difficult economic or other circumstances), the voluntary clandestine disposal of industrial waste too cumbersome on land. Thus, the fate of the sea is determined on land in minds and by the human will.

Many local or lesser measures can also be taken at the national level. These will initially affect the coastal environment, but ultimately the state of the whole sea. Control of any form of pollution which destroys the marine biomass and of any excessive aggression against the marine environment by the dumping of toxic or non-biodegradable substances or by the destruction of the sea-bed should, in the Mediterranean even more than anywhere else, form part of an ethical attitude concerning the marine environment which still runs counter to age-old habits.

24 From the National Level to the Mediterranean Level: Suggestions for Co-operation

The struggle for the environment will take place primarily at the national level . . .

The hypotheses of the Blue Plan studies took into account, for the 'alternative' scenarios, a consolidated policy of environmental protection and, especially, an improvement in its incorporation into development or physical planning policies. However, the work also highlighted the fact that, even in the case of the 'trend' scenarios, reference to policies followed over the years did not reflect reality in many respects, because the effective application of government decisions was far removed from the intentions expressed or laws passed.

In this respect the biggest discrepancies lie in the following areas:

● *Control of urbanization.* The will to direct or curb urbanization through urban planning, land-use planning, or guide-lines on coastal development is sometimes thwarted or deflected by decentralization of the competent authorities. Lack of supervision and numerous 'dispensations' have been observed as regards housing or tourism. Reality scarcely corresponds to the expressed intention to create protected areas or to shield some zones from urban encroachment. The coast in particular is increasingly subject to the pressure of vested interests. The coast, rather than the sea itself, is where the future of the Mediterranean environment is unfolding. And yet in two decades nearly 2000 kilometres of coastline have been sacrificed through haphazard urbanization and buildings that disfigure the landscape, even though this was not the intention at the national level.

● *Supervision of productive or transport activities.* Monitoring of industrial plants and discipline as regards maritime transport do not comply with the relevant requirements. Plans and strategies concerning industrial waste are clearly inadequate, and its destruction, storage, or transport are often a hazard. There is also a discrepancy between stipulations and practice with respect to the monitoring of degassing operations on ships in transit.

● *Waste-water treatment plants.* The level of land-based pollution requires adequate measures. And yet, aside from the major rivers, there is little evidence of real progress. On the coast, waste-water depollution rates are rarely available, but do not exceed 15 per cent on average. Many treatment plants are not in a suitablle operating condition.

Nevertheless, despite the discrepancy between intentions expressed or programmes adopted and the reality of environmental practices, the Blue Plan studies show that decisions on the bulk of environmental protection will be made (or not) largely at the level of the state. Essential legislation and standards will have to be established at this level, as well as the necessary mechanisms and institutions with the financing and competence to apply them (based, for example, on the 'polluter pays' principle). The heterogeneity of geographical, socio-economic, or cultural situations leads in the same direction: only states can stipulate and implement a suitable policy within their borders.

The intensification of efforts currently under way (trend scenarios), and even more the strengthening of environmental policy (alternative scenarios), imply a change of direction and more goal-orientated action, focusing in particular on:

● the strengthening of institutions and mechanisms for planning, managing, and regulating the environment at national and regional levels, with a view to ensuring rational management and conservation of natural resources;

● the adoption of physical planning and, if necessary, the formulation and publication of national and regional environmental protection plans with deadlines set for objectives;

- the application of an approach by scenario for the establishment of coastal 'charters', including the active participation of local institutions, socio-professional organizations, and the population;
- the study of employment policies for young people and the contribution that could be made in this respect by taking into account the objectives of environmental protection and the more effective economic use of natural resources;
- the training of environmental experts able to ensure the link between scientific research, control of regulations, and the implementation of new development activities;
- the sensitizing to environmental challenges of elected representatives and the officials of local authorities and national agencies working in the area of development or physical planning, as well as the establishment, if need be, of appropriate environmental institutions.

Without greater awareness on the part of the public about the interactions between, on the one hand, the environment and natural resources and, on the other, individual and collective activity, it will be futile to expect a rapid and smooth evolution towards satisfactory forms of sustainable development in the Mediterranean basin as a whole. More systematic and consistent efforts would therefore have to be undertaken to:

- develop general education concerning the Mediterranean environment with the help of teaching materials focusing on the realities and problems of the region;
- disseminate objective and serious information to the public about the possibilities and constraints of the local and regional environment in which they live, directed at various age-groups and stressing the fact that one generation takes over from another;
- encourage national and local associations for environmental protection and landscape conservation, underscoring in particular tangible action and demonstration of results.

. . . but broad fields are open to Mediterranean co-operation

The prospective study of the Mediterranean basin could only be initiated with the agreement of all the coastal states concerned, anxious not to be overtaken by their fate and the passing years with respect to development and the environment, and no doubt also to the role of their region in the world. Accordingly, this last part of the report is devoted to co-operation between coastal countries, starting with issues likely to emerge, or become more pronounced, in the near future. In accordance with the original intentions of the Blue Plan, some suggestions for intra-Mediterranean action, identified in the light of the scenarios and the accompanying studies, are therefore submitted to decision-makers, so that they may assess their suitability for implementation. This could be based on multilateral or bilateral co-operation, on the establishment of exchange networks, on joint projects, or on the development of solidarity.

1. The progress of knowledge

Concerning data and statistics, it must be recognized that in the Mediterranean collecting and measuring mechanisms still provide a very inadequate basis for projections, analyses, and choices. The statistics supplied by international organizations, which divide up this part of the world somewhat artificially into Africa, Western Asia, and Europe, are limited. Entire areas elude analysis, or are documented by unreliable data. This is the case, to take just a few examples, with data on relationships between air and sea pollution, endangered species, the quality of surface water and ground water, domestic and even international tourism by coastal region, and so on.

The establishment of some fifty series of comparable socio-economic statistics and a number of key indicators on the quality of the environment would be useful. The places where environmental data are gathered and processed should be better identified and their efficiency and accessibility improved. Networks accessible to each coastal country could also be established, based on specialized, but well-interconnected, data-banks.

Moreover, experience has shown how difficult it was for a number of countries to obtain data concerning the Mediterranean regions as such and the coastline. The harmonization of statistical data-gathering according to administrative districts of comparable level, or appropriate spatial divisions (e.g. by watershed), could be the subject of collaboration between countries and would be of great help for future work.

The development of new techniques could facilitate or partly modify the measuring, gathering, and processing of data and their presentation (automatic cartography, for instance). Remote sensing will contribute significantly to renewing monitoring techniques for plant life, the soil, the climate, the coastal strip, and urbanization. Intra-Mediterranean co-operation for monitoring by 'ecozones', with the setting up of multi-disciplinary teams, would make it possible to develop links, as yet very inadequate, between the production of basic images and the users, on the basis, for example, of the joint interpretation of some illustrative coastal sites, especially where monitoring networks have already been established.

With regard to basic and applied research, the countries could identify existing gaps between scientific knowledge and decision-making or practical application. Thus, environmental meteorology, the study of complex, multi-purpose ecological systems, the clinical study of plant diseases, the rehabilitation of degraded ecological systems, the recycling of water resources, the application to agriculture of genetic discoveries concerning conservation or selection, and so on, could be useful to all Mediterranean people. Without an active policy for the intra-Mediterranean dissemination of knowledge, gaps are likely to widen between countries in, for example, the application of bio-technology to agriculture.

Generally speaking, the Blue Plan would like to have been able to give more consideration to the question of new technologies and their future role in the search for patterns of development that are more mindful of the environment. With regard to technological innovation, efforts had to be confined to an appraisal of the most likely developments of special interest to the region.

Similarly, the Blue Plan work also lacked a study of social perception and behaviour, especially trends in demands and needs. Some existing social prospective studies (use of leisure time, food consumption, environmental awareness, etc.) showed that the forecasting exercises needed a social prospective, closely linked to the different cultures of the region. The establishment of a network, notably in the academic context, enabling the exploitation throughout the Mediterranean of studies and research undertaken, could improve the situation.

2. Co-operation on management and the environment

Concerted action among Mediterranean states could, in this case, speed up the strengthening of environmental policies and especially their incorporation into development policies. Some forms of co-operation could be based on existing structures: this is the case, for instance, with the General Fisheries Council of the Mediterranean, for fisheries, or of 'Silva Mediterranea' for the forest; other structures remain to be established in areas where exchanges are still at a very low level. In this respect the formation, on a formal or informal basis, of exchange and co-operation networks is quicker and more effective than establishing new institutions.

BOX 24A. **The ten priorities of the Genoa Ministerial Declaration (1985)**

The bordering States will attach priority to:

1. establishment of reception facilities for dirty ballast waters and other oily residues in ports of the Mediterranean;
2. establishment as a matter of priority of sewage treatment plants in all cities around the Mediterranean with more than 100,000 inhabitants and appropriate outfalls and/or appropriate treatment plants for all towns with more than 10,000 inhabitants;
3. applying environmental impact assessment as an important tool to ensure proper development activities;
4. co-operation to improve the safety of maritime navigation and to reduce substantially the risk of transport of dangerous toxic substances likely to affect the coastal areas or induce marine pollution;
5. protection of the endangered marine species (e.g. the monk seal and Mediterranean turtle);
6. concrete measures to achieve substantial reduction in industrial pollution and disposal of solid waste in the Mediterranean;
7. identification and protection of at least 100 historic sites of common interest;
8. identification and protection of at least 50 new marine and coastal sites or reserves of Mediterranean interest;
9. intensification of effective measures to prevent and combat forest fires, soil loss, and desertification;
10. substantial reduction in air pollution, which adversely affects coastal areas and the marine environment, with the potential danger of acid rains.

The Genoa Declaration (1985) foreshadowed this kind of linkage by proposing, for example, to identify a hundred historic sites of Mediterranean interest, which were adopted in 1987, or fifty new protected natural sites on the coast. Those responsible for the sites are expected to exchange experiences within the context of the Mediterranean Action Plan. (Those responsible for historic sites have recently met in Marseilles.) Similarly, managers of the 'biosphere reserves' meet within the framework of Unesco's Man and the Biosphere (MAB) Programme. The MEDPOL programme, which links about a hundred research and analysis laboratories, and PAP, which gathers together specialists on specific subjects, operate in the same way.

A better idea of requirements can be obtained by specifically reviewing the main potential areas of Mediterranean co-operation.

(a) Co-operation on spatial management

● *Coastal management*. For reasons that were clearly stressed by the Blue Plan, development of the Mediterranean coast—including the islands—calls for an exchange of experience on national policies and development practices likely to reduce pressure on the coast and encourage development of the hinterland. Co-operation, particularly through comparative studies, could start with planning and development methods, conservation regulations, legal and financial protection mechanisms (e.g. coastal conservatories), promotion of awareness among tourists of environments to be protected, conservation of the near-shore sea-bed, the use of remote sensing, and so forth. Meetings between officials responsible for coastal regions would be very fruitful in this respect. The necessary information, exchange, and training activities would be facilitated by the establishment of a 'Mediterranean Coastal Observatory', focusing its attention on the changes taking place in the coastal strip.

The current inadequate rate of installation of sewage-treatment stations in coastal regions implies that the objectives of the Genoa Declaration may not be met. Even though measures are the responsibility of each state, at least a MAP questionnaire could be drawn up at the Mediterranean level, enabling preparation of a public overview of the situation and prospects for the next five years. Plastic packaging distributed in coastal regions should be replaced by biodegradable packaging. Lastly, an efficient co-operation network among port authorities could be useful for identifying problems

and bottlenecks. The co-operation already under way between the European Community and the Mediterranean countries could help to complete port installations where they are needed for the application of the MARPOL Convention on degassing.

● *Urban management*. In 2025 more than 150m. people will be living in the towns of the Mediterranean regions (82m. in 1985). Collaboration among specialists could, in this case, focus mainly on the creation of new towns, control of the use of peri-urban areas where agricultural land is destabilized, economical urban transport, paraseismic engineering, the protection and restoration of historical centres, the reduction of air pollution, the design of low-cost housing and public areas, small-scale urban systems in harmony with rural areas, and so on. Urban management as such (waste, sanitation, water, traffic, plantings, etc.) could give rise to exchanges through direct 'technical twinning' between Mediterranean towns.

● *Water resources management*. The uncertainty and irregularity of water resources constitute a real bottleneck for Mediterranean development, particularly for the southern and eastern countries. Collaboration could focus on several aspects: resource-management institutions, distribution of drinking water, introduction of tariffs, sanitation techniques, water-saving irrigation techniques, reuse of waste water for agriculture, solar pumps, desalination of sea water, supply of water to small islands. The organization of internships and regional training courses for water-resource management (domestic, agricultural, and industrial uses, integrated planning and management) is a prime area for intra-Mediterranean co-operation.

● *Forest management*. Co-operation could be very beneficial in the following areas: upkeep and testing of stable, multipurpose farm–forest-cum-grazing systems, management and protection of watersheds, multipurpose forest management (including management for hunting), the succession process of different kinds of vegetation, diseases specific to Mediterranean trees, procedures for timbering by stages (choice of trees for retimbering), combating of forest fires, techniques and equipment for clearing undergrowth, exploitation of by-products, alternatives to fuel-wood. Here again the organization of specialized regional internships and training courses could be encouraged.

● *Management of protected areas*. The rich genetic heritage of the Mediterranean region, as regards both wild species and cultivated or domestic varieties, is seriously threatened. The application of the Barcelona Convention protocol on 'specially protected areas' and the work of the Salambo (Tunisia) Regional Activity Centre should help to develop the protection of coastal and marine regions and particularly wetlands of international importance for bird migration that may come under the Ramsar Convention. In co-operation with the World Conservation Union (IUCN), it is essential to extend action to all the Mediterranean-climate land ecosystems in the region, particularly through the expansion and improvement of the terrestrial and coastal biosphere reserve network (MAB), the creation of biotope reserves, and the adoption of a regional conservation strategy. The conservation of outstanding sites and Mediterranean landscapes should bolster this effort to conserve ecosystems, and could also be an area of co-operation. The participation of local populations in the management of protected areas and in the protection of coastal landscapes is indispensable, and could also offer an opportunity for an exchange of experience.

● *Management of marine living resources.* Although they are not abundant, Mediterranean living resources could contribute to reducing the food dependency of some coastal countries if exploitation were carried out in a rational way so as to be sustainable. This kind of objective requires effective international co-operation, for which the General Fisheries Council for the Mediterranean provides a sound framework, but which should be stepped up and suitably co-ordinated with the action of other sectors, such as pollution control. Information about existing fish stocks (demersal and pelagic species), and their migration and reproduction cycle (especially in the less studied eastern basin) is a prerequisite for developing, and thus optimizing, fisheries. A joint assessment of species should be encouraged for this purpose. In addition, broader use should be made of under-exploited species such as small pelagics. Above all, priority should be given to concerted action between countries exploiting the same resource, the formulation, if necessary, of measures to limit fishing activity and ensure distribution of this resource, and supervision of their effective application. Legislation on use of the coastal strip by means of artificial reefs and, in general, national management and development plans for fisheries, should be harmonized as far as possible.

(b) Co-operation on appropriate technology

The establishment of new industries in the south and east of the basin in particular will create an urgent need for information on precautions to be taken concerning installation, recycling, and depollution devices. It will be equally useful, however, to exchange the mechanisms and processes of 'clean technologies' introduced into industrial processes, which make it possible—and often profitable—to reduce waste, save materials and energy, and reuse by-products. This could offer a broad area for exchange and co-operation between specialists from the north and south, in fields such as energy, water, biotechnologies, or waste, which may possibly receive support from the European Community.

(c) Co-operation on major hazards

● *Erosion of the genetic heritage.* The Mediterranean bovine, ovine, and caprine domestic species amount to only 10 per cent of what they were a century ago; populations of shrub species and plants that are part of the traditional diet are rapidly disappearing. Only the urgent establishment of biological conservatories, gene-banks, botanical gardens, and biosphere reserves, covering the land ecosystems of the Mediterranean region, can contribute to conserving ex situ and in situ the components of the wild or domestic genetic heritage of the region. In this way the domestic species and wild fellow creatures essential for the genetic selection of varieties needed for agriculture and stock-farming in the future will be maintained. A Mediterranean network of botanical conservatories and arboretums could be established. A Mediterranean association for the protection of nature could prove useful.

● *Natural hazards.* Natural telluric hazards have always existed in the Mediterranean, whether earthquakes, volcanic eruptions, or landslides. Moreover, the irregularity of the climate causes floods and recurring disastrous droughts. Solidarity is all the more effective in these spheres as it concerns neighbouring countries likely to be affected, in turn, by the same calamity. Studies on seismic hazards and promotion of seismic engineering, undertaken in the region under the auspices of UNDP, Unesco, and PAP could be fruitfully extended to the Mediterranean basin as a whole. Work carried out on drought and agro-climatology is also an important area for regional co-operation.

● *Maritime hazards.* Concerted effort among coastal

states to deal with maritime hazards must advance rapidly in order to tackle this growing problem. Concerted oil-spill contingency plans should be developed. It is worth noting in this respect the decision taken in 1988 by these states to enlarge existing co-operation on hydrocarbon transport carried out in the Malta Centre to include the prevention of accidents at sea involving the transport of chemicals. Nevertheless, it is clear that in this new area, much more difficult to delimit than that of oil, increased co-operation among maritime and port authorities will be needed in order to improve identification of loads and their destinations.

● *Technological hazards.* Technological hazards are becoming increasingly serious in the Mediterranean basin, with the development of industrialization, the manufacture and transport by land and sea of new chemical products, the increase in toxic waste, the production of nuclear energy, and so forth. Co-operation could focus on prevention techniques and practices, identification and marketing of new products (pesticides in particular), adoption of suitable legislation, measures to be taken in case of accidents, or trans-border co-operation between local authorities. All coastal states could take advantage of the progress made by some industrialized countries, and of European collaboration, already under way. Broadening the fields of competence of the Malta Centre coincides with this recognition of new risks concerning maritime accidents.

Among the top priorities is co-operation on industrial waste, particularly toxic waste (destruction, transport, storage, reprocessing, etc.). The organization of regular contacts among industrialists, in co-operation with public authorities, would be a positive step.

3. From collaboration to Mediterranean solidarity

The work of the Blue Plan has often highlighted the need for collaboration much further upstream in a number of major sectors of economic activity, as a prerequisite for true Mediterranean solidarity. In this respect it was observed that bilateral relations between states only marginally covers environmental problems. These issues should be given more importance in bilateral scientific, technical, or commercial agreements between Mediterranean countries.

Relations between neighbouring countries have

to be facilitated to achieve better international balance: improved maritime, air, and road transport, electrical interconnections, communications, and so on. A network of exchanges should link up the Mediterranean basin, where currently preference is given to links along certain main lines whose lesser ramifications tend to stagnate. The situation can be improved by strengthening short-distance links, still too limited, particularly among southern countries.

At the regional or international level, increasingly numerous forms of collaboration are pursued within organizations in which the Mediterranean states find themselves involved in decision-making processes that do not pay sufficient attention to the Mediterranean identity, especially the distinctive features of the Mediterranean environment. Very different kinds of international agencies, such as FAO, WHO, Unesco, or development organizations (IBRD, UNDP), represent collaboration or decision-making levels in which the Mediterranean countries participate, but are a minority and never create a group. It would be appropriate for these bodies to take the special nature of the Mediterranean into account as far upstream as possible, on the basis of prior consultations within MAP, for instance. The concerns of the Mediterranean countries would benefit from being better known before the adoption of environmental policies by these institutions. The same holds true for regional organizations, such as the European Community or the League of Arab States, in which some countries of the region participate. Three major areas of economic activity— food and agriculture (resources and consumption), energy, and tourism—seem in this respect suited to a more advanced form of collaboration.

● *Food and food resources* should be given special consideration. In forty years self-sufficiency levels in the Mediterranean regions have fallen from 60 per cent to 40 or even 30 per cent. In order to halt or reverse this trend, a stronger kind of solidarity, which would avoid a rupture with its many repercussions (including effects on the environment), should be the subject of intra-Mediterranean collaboration and co-operation with other regions (of Europe in particular).

The drop in self-sufficiency in many Mediterranean countries, which appears unavoidable in the short and medium term, raises the issue of food security. Suitable financial or commercial co-operation would facilitate orderly specialization in production and would justify an intensification which, properly managed, would exert less pressure on the environment. Closer co-operation in agronomic and agro-ecological research would be useful (soil fertility, efficient use of irrigation water, pesticide utilization, creation of varieties and conservation of species, etc.). A priority research and development programme on products subject to shortage (cereals, oil-seed, etc.) or to strong demand (fruit and vegetables) would be welcome. The same kind of approach is valid for stock-farming. Co-operation on fisheries and aquaculture, to the point of controlling regulations to be observed, is essential.

● *Energy* is another sector where effective collaboration could start up rather quickly. The differences between oil-consumer and -producer countries will tend to dwindle with time, and all countries have experienced or will experience the vigorous development of electricity. Electrical energy is therefore a special area for the exchange of experience and know-how, particularly on supply and on clean combustion techniques. The use of natural gas, already significant and a link between various Mediterranean countries, could increase considerably. Co-operation could focus on exploitation (deep drilling), production (small deposits), and utilization techniques (efficient industrial uses, chemicals such as methanol, combined electricity production, fuel-gas, etc.).

Knowledge acquired on solar energy and other renewable sources of energy could, in the end, create a true technological bridge between north and south and strengthen south–south co-operation, particularly on equipment for water (irrigation pumps), dispersed dwellings, the production of baked-clay materials, the drying of agricultural products, etc. An exchange of technical and administrative experience in energy saving would be desirable.

● *Tourism*, finally, rapidly developing in a somewhat haphazard way, in which all Mediterranean countries compete, could be the subject of collaboration initially concerned with information about demand and occupancy rates in the region (where the margin of error for figures exceeds 30 per cent). Concentration could also be focused on the improved management of intra-Mediterranean tourism, which currently accounts for 25 per cent of international tourism (tariffs and air services, and especially the staggering of peak periods through 'time-planning'). This could involve the concerted appeal to tourism outside the Mediterranean. Lastly, if it were recognized that foreign tourists are willing to contribute to protection of the Mediterranean, and that $5 per one-week stay would bring in more than $250m., the establishment of a voluntary

contribution, which could only be set up at the Mediterranean level, could have a considerable impact, especially if it were supplemented by a parallel contribution from the countries involved. Generally speaking, tourists, who benefit greatly from the quality of life, the coastline, and the Mediterranean landscape, must be invited to make a tangible contribution to their protection.

4. A programme for the young generations

The future of the Mediterranean may be seriously affected or modified by the implementation of policies for the education, information, and awareness-heightening of the young public—tomorrow's generations. Young people are not always aware of the time needed for a tree to grow, to manage a forest, or make the soil fertile and save it from desertification. They are not always aware of the fragility of the world they have inherited. This area could be the subject of fruitful exchange between coastal countries: handbooks for young people, teaching experiences in the field, or television programmes. It would be useful to take stock of public action taken and show that its effect may be decisive (e.g. to increase waste-water treatment from 20 per cent to 30 per cent in ten years).

State policy and its implementation, together with policies of local authorities, are too little known and publicized. It would therefore be useful to disseminate information among Mediterranean people about efforts undertaken in countries other than their own. Incentives among countries, cities, and associations could mobilize some people or bolster the efforts of those who, in the sphere of the environment, occasionally feel isolated. The launching, in 1988, of the 'International Week for the Mediterranean' is a step in this direction, but its scope is still too reduced.

Raising the awareness of young people about the fragility of the environment is one aspect: entry into working life is another. Joint efforts will therefore have to be made for training in environmental professions, and even more in the professions which must take into account basic concepts about the environment. In this respect the training of town planners, engineers, and technicians is one of the most fruitful means of north–south co-operation, one of the easiest to implement, and the one whose results will prove to be the most useful. This kind of co-operation for training, already under way among Mediterranean countries in some areas, could be developed for all areas of environmental protection, resource management, or any other field identified above.

Sombre employment prospects raise the increasingly difficult problem of the incorporation of the young people into working life. Communal work schemes mobilizing youth are being tried out in various places. Environmental protection can and must be given an important part in these initiatives, with the organization of exchanges and internships among countries, facilitating effective participation in tangible action.

It is not easy to grasp the extent of the changes which will take place in the Mediterranean basin during the next forty years. Perhaps it can be better understood if one considers that 60 per cent of the people who will be living in the Mediterranean in 2025 are not yet born. These 325m. or so Mediterranean people of the future will perhaps not have the same cultural and material references as the present generations, but their basic needs will not be very different from ours. It is the present generations whom they will hold accountable for the environment they find. It is for the Mediterranean people of today to take immediate action to counter adverse trends and to prepare an acceptable future for themselves and their descendants.

INDEX